International Series on Computer Entertainment and Media Technology

Series Editor
Newton Lee
Institute for Education, Research, and Scholarships
Los Angeles, CA, USA

The International Series on Computer Entertainment and Media Technology presents forward-looking ideas, cutting-edge research, and in-depth case studies across a wide spectrum of entertainment and media technology. The series covers a range of content from professional to academic. Entertainment Technology includes computer games, electronic toys, scenery fabrication, theatrical property, costume, lighting, sound, video, music, show control, animation, animatronics, interactive environments, computer simulation, visual effects, augmented reality, and virtual reality. Media Technology includes art media, print media, digital media, electronic media, big data, asset management, signal processing, data recording, data storage, data transmission, media psychology, wearable devices, robotics, and physical computing.

More information about this series at http://www.springer.com/series/13820

Barbaros Bostan

Editor

Games and Narrative: Theory and Practice

 Springer

Editor
Barbaros Bostan
Fac of Communication, Mueyyedzade Mah
Bahcesehir University
Beyoğlu, Istanbul, Turkey

ISSN 2364-947X   ISSN 2364-9488   (electronic)
International Series on Computer Entertainment and Media Technology
ISBN 978-3-030-81540-0   ISBN 978-3-030-81538-7   (eBook)
https://doi.org/10.1007/978-3-030-81538-7

This Springer imprint is published by the registered company Springer Nature Switzerland AG
The registered company address is: Gewerbestrasse 11, 6330 Cham, Switzerland

Foreword

Video Game Narrative: A Vibrant Topic for Research and Practice

The chapters in this collection are testimony to a thriving research field and growing practice of video game narrative. That video game narrative both as an academic topic and as a practice clearly is 'alive and kicking' today is testimony to the importance of the topic despite the catastrophic impact of the so-called 'ludology vs narratology debate' in which Jesper Juul infamously declared that games are not a narrative medium (Juul 1999). While Juul later modified that particular pronunciation, his and other's subsequent writing (Aarseth 2001, 2004; Eskelinen 2001; Juul 2001, 2005) further cemented the supposed dichotomy between games and narrative. This foundational positioning exerted a considerable influence on games studies and had a long-lasting impact on the development of the topic of game narrative. With narrative conceptualized as 'the other', as the topic of an imaginary enemy, there was little to encourage theoretical development or research into specific aspects of video game narrative. Important earlier work on the topic by scholars like Mary-Anne Buckles (Buckles 1985), Brenda Laurel (Laurel 1986, 1991), Gloriana Davenport (Davenport 1987), Joseph Bates (Bates 1992, 1994), Pamela Jennings (Jennings 1996) and most importantly Janet Murray (Murray 1997) was misconstrued and ignored. Murray never was an enemy of games or games studies, the role she was framed in, as the original creator of the term ludology—Gonzala Frasca (who completed his masters' thesis with Murray as the main advisor)—explained in a 2003 paper (Frasca 2003), yet his clarification had little impact.

In fact, research and theoretical development on interactive narrative—of which video game narrative is an important subgroup—never stopped, but it happened slowly and mostly outside of games studies at places like the MIT Media Lab's Interactive Cinema Group, at conferences like ICIDS (International conference on interactive digital storytelling), AIIDE (Conference on Artificial Intelligence and Interactive Digital Entertainment), the AAAI (The conference of the Association for the Advancement of Artificial Intelligence), ACMTVX (The ACM conference on Interactive Experiences for Television & Online Video, now ACMIMX) and the INT (Intelligent Narrative Technologies) workshop, but also at the Electronic Literature Organization (ELO), and in work concerned with interactive TV (Ursu et al. 2008), film (Hales 2005) and interactive documentary (Gaudenzi 2013). Additionally, monographs like Nick Montfort's Twisty Little Passages (Montfort 2003) or Weimin Toh's multimodal approach (Toh 2018), edited collections such as Mateas and Senger's *Narrative Intelligence* (Mateas and Sengers 2003) and *Interactive Digital Narrative* (Koenitz et al. 2015) (in which the present author is a co-editor), work on virtual reality (Aylett and Louchart 2003), emergent narrative (Louchart and Aylett 2004) and indexical storytelling (Fernández-Vara 2011), as well as on a purpose-made evaluation framework (Roth et al. 2010; Roth 2016)— to name but a few examples—carried research and practical insight on interactive forms of narration further.

However, without a disciplinary framework for research on interactive digital narratives, it is difficult to keep track of developments in the field, as individual contributions are marginalized in their respective home disciplines (e.g. Computer Science, Communications, Games Studies, Literary Studies, Film Studies) and their visibility is reduced. This situation was one of the reasons for the founding in 2018 of the Association for Research in Digital Interactive Narratives (ARDIN, https://ardin.online), which provides a home for the vibrant community of researchers and practitioners as the field is getting closer to being a recognized discipline (Koenitz 2018). Together with Mirjam Palosaari Eladhari, I have described some additional challenges, in particular the dependency on legacy analytical frameworks (Groundhog Day), the lack of a shared vocabulary (Babylonian Confusion), the missing institutional memory of the field (Amnesia), the absence of established benchmarks (No Yardstick) and the overproduction of uncoordinated and quickly abandoned tools (Sisyphus) (Koenitz and Eladhari 2019).

My own contribution to this volume (co-authored with Mirjam Palosaari Eladhari, Sandy Louchart, Frank Nack, Christian Roth, Elisa Meckler, and Péter Kristóf Makai) describes an effort to solve one of these issues, namely the lack of a shared vocabulary, with a community-authored Encyclopedia of Interactive Narrative as a product of the EU COST action INDCOR (Interactive Narrative Design for Complexity Representations).

The other challenges still need to be addressed and the contributions in this volume bring us closer to solving them, too. In this collection of essays, many aspects are considered, including classification systems (for the interaction of gameplay and narrative by Sercan Sengun) and practice-oriented insights (on systemic branching by Leanne C. Taylor-Giles; low-fidelity narrative generation by Henrik Warpefelt; the use of quantum computing for narrative game design by Natasha Skult and Jouni Smed). There is also the much-needed clarifications of a particular concept (the fourth wall by Öznur Özdal and Güven Çatak), proposals for novel approaches (Kindness as the aim of emergent narrative by Demi Schänzel, Leanne C. Taylor-Giles and Jane Turner, the concept of allegation in game analysis by Aleksandra Mochocka) as well as reflections on the societal impact and relevance (on gender bias in virtual worlds by Sercan Sengun, Jennifer Price, Lyndsie Schlink and Kristin Walker; a consideration of video games as contemporary art by Tolga Hepdinçler; the ethics of interactive storytelling by Sami Hyrynsalmi, Kai K. Kimppa and Jouni Smed; and the application of an interactive storytelling game to increase moral reasoning by Katelyn M. Grasse, Edward F. Melcer, Max Kreminski, Nick Junius, James Ryan and Noah Wardrip-Fruin).

Furthermore, historical perspectives help the reader to understand the lineage of game narrative (analysing interactive fiction by Kirsty Michelle McGill, tracing the history of game narrative in Turkish video games by Ertuğrul Süngü and Esin Selin Güregen) and approaches to evaluation with the aim to improve the reflection on the experience and professionalize criticism (Narrative as game user experience by Seray Şenyer and Barbaros, the use of retellings as an instrument of narrative design analysis and criticism by Tonguc Ibrahim Sezen and Digdem Sezen, the use of heuristics in player evaluation by Çakır Aker and Barbaros Bostan). Finally, academic and industry-focused case studies round up this rich collection in the form of investigating the use of religious elements in Assassin's Creed Origins by Özge Mirza and Sercan Sengun; reflecting on aspects of history and the non-fiction/fiction dualism in Attentat 1942 by Michał Mochocki. Further studies consider the transmedial interplay between Marvel's Avengers and Marvel Cinematic Universe by Hasan Kemal Suher and Tuna Tetik as well as the lessons learned during the development of Frostpunk Narrative by Wojciech Setlak and the reflection on Wordless Storytelling by Radim Jurda.

It is an exciting time for researchers and practitioners to work on interactive forms of narrative and especially on game narratives—there is still much unchartered territory and ample creative opportunity.

Amsterdam, The Netherlands   Hartmut Koenitz

References

E.J. Aarseth, Genre trouble, in *First Person: New Media as Story, Performance, and Game*, ed. by N. Wardrip-Fruin, P. Harrigan, (MIT Press, Cambridge, MA, 2004) Retrieved from www.electronicbookreview.com/thread/firstperson/vigilant

E.J. Aarseth, Computer game studies, year one. Game Stud. 1(1)

R. Aylett, S. Louchart, Towards a narrative theory of virtual reality. Virtual Reality **2003**, 1–27 (2003). https://doi.org/10.1007/s10055-003-0114-9

J. Bates, *The Nature of Characters in Interactive Worlds and the Oz Project* (1992)

J. Bates, The role of emotion in believable agents. Commun. ACM **37**(7), 122–125 (1994)

Buckles, M. A. (1985). *Interactive Fiction: The Computer Storygame "Adventure."* University of California, San Diego. Retrieved from https://search.proquest.com/docview/303372594/

G. Davenport, New Orleans in transition, 1983–1986: The interactive delivery of a cinematic case study, in *Presented at the the International Congress for Design Planning and Theory, Education Group Conference*, (Boston, MA, 1987)

M. Eskelinen, The gaming situation. *Game Studies 1*(1) (2001) Retrieved from http://www.gamestudies. org/0101/eskelinen/

C. Fernández-Vara, Game spaces speak volumes – indexical storytelling. Presented at the Digra 2005. (2011)

G. Frasca, *Ludologists Love Stories, Too: Notes from a Debate that Never Took Place* (2003). DIGRA Conf

S. Gaudenzi, *The Living Documentary: From Representing Reality to Co-Creating Reality in Digital Interactive Documentary* (2013, January 22)

C. Hales, Cinematic interaction - from kinoautomat to cause and effect. Digital Creativity **16**(1), 54–64 (2005). https://doi.org/10.1080/14626260500147777

P. Jennings, Narrative structures for new media. Leonardo **29**(5), 345–350 (1996)

J. Juul, *A Clash between Game and Narrative* (1999). Danish Literature

J. Juul, Games telling stories. Game Studies **1**(1) (2001)

J. Juul, *Half-Real* (MIT Press, 2005)

H. Koenitz, Thoughts on a discipline for the study of interactive digital narratives, in *Interactive Storytelling: 11th International Conference for Interactive Digital Storytelling, ICIDS 2018*, ed. by R. Rouse, H. Koenitz, M. Haahr, (The 3rd International Conference for Interactive Digital Storytelling. Retrieved from, Cham, 2018), pp. 36–49. https://doi.org/10.1007/978-3-030-04028-4_3

H. Koenitz, M.P. Eladhari, Challenges of IDN research and teaching, in *Technologies for Interactive Digital Storytelling and Entertainment*, vol. 11869, (Springer International Publishing, Cham, 2019), pp. 26–39. https://doi.org/10.1007/978-3-030-33894-7_4

H. Koenitz, G. Ferri, M. Haahr, D. Sezen, T.I. Sezen, Interactive digital narrative : history, theory, and practice, in *Routledge Studies in European Communication Research and Education*, (Routledge, New York, 2015)

B. Laurel, *Toward the Design of a Computer-Based Interactive Fantasy System* (Ohio State University, 1986)

B. Laurel, *Computers as Theatre* (Addison-Wesley, Boston, MA, 1991)

S. Louchart, R. Aylett, Narrative theory and emergent interactive narrative. Int. J. Continuing Eng. Edu. Life Long Learn. **14**(6) (2004)

M. Mateas, P. Sengers, *Narrative Intelligence* (John Benjamins Publishing, Amsterdam/Philadelphia, 2003)

N. Montfort, *Twisty Little Passages: An Approach to Interactive Fiction* (The MIT Press, 2003)

J.H. Murray, *Hamlet on the Holodeck: The Future of Narrative in Cyberspace* (Free Press, New York, 1997)

C. Roth, *Experiencing Interactive Storytelling* (Vrije Universiteit Amsterdam, 2016) Retrieved from https://research.vu.nl/en/publications/experiencing-interactive-storytelling

C. Roth, P. Vorderer, C. Klimmt, I. Vermeulen, *Measuring the User Experience in Narrative-Rich Games: Towards a Concept-Based Assessment for Interactive Stories* (2010). Entertainment Interfaces

W. Toh, *A Multimodal Approach to Video Games and the Player Experience* (Taylor & Francis, 2018)

M.F. Ursu, M. Thomas, I. Kegel, D. Williams, M. Tuomola, I. Lindstedt, et al., Interactive TV narratives: Opportunities, progress, and challenges. ACM Trans. Multimedia Comput. Commun. Appl. **4**(4), 25–39 (2008). https://doi.org/10.1145/1412196.1412198

Contents

Part I
Narrative Design and Theory

Chapter 1
Six Degrees of Videogame Narrative

Sercan Sengun

1.1 Introduction

At the beginning of the 2000s, narrative and gameplay were proposed as an oxymoron duo (Aarseth 1997; Frasca 2003). The action of gameplay in videogames was a new discourse and its relations (or distinctions) with previous media and cultural forms, especially the potential of gameplay for narrative, were undefined. The narrative segments (e.g., cutscenes) and the gameplay segments typically stayed as detached entities and interrupted each others' flow. Various scholars (Laurel 1991; Murray 1997; Plowman 1996 among others) explored the applicability of familiar narrative theoretical frameworks from previous media to videogames and reported similarities between those models and gameplay processes (such as Genette's 1983 construct of *histoire*, *récit*, and *narration* offered to being applicable to the branching structures of video game narratives by Şengün 2013a).

   In this chapter, I explore the usage of narrative and narrative elements in videogames through the lens of the theoretical distance between gameplay and storytelling segments, as well as the temporal timeframes that those segments offer or exist on, by asking "what are the different ways that gameplay and narrative sequences interact and intersect in videogames?" One of the prominent critics of the vagueness of the term narrative in videogame studies is Frasca (2003) with their assertion that "[researchers] seem to systematically fail to provide clear, specific definitions of what they mean by narrative" (p. 96). As a result, I begin my exploration by looking at different definitions of narrative in the medium and through my formal analysis I keep an open mind about what can or cannot be

S. Sengun (✉)
Wonsook Kim School of Art, Creative Technologies Program, Illinois State University, Normal, IL, USA
e-mail: ssengun@ilstu.edu

© The Author(s), under exclusive license to Springer Nature Switzerland AG 2022
B. Bostan (ed.), *Games and Narrative: Theory and Practice*, International Series on Computer Entertainment and Media Technology,
https://doi.org/10.1007/978-3-030-81538-7_1

3

considered as a narrative intervention to the gameplay. My aim in this exploration is to offer a tiered framework to help talk about and define the different ways that videogames employ storytelling outside or within their rules, mechanics, and gameplay sequences. Through my analysis, I discover, define, and discuss six distinct forms that gameplay and narrative can intersect and call them the six degrees of video game narrative.

1.2   Background

The meaning of the concept of narrative is conflicted inside the medium of videogames, etymologically stuck between the story and discourse. As much as new terminology arises to compensate for how the narrative is understood, an expressive and interdisciplinary distinction between a story and its telling still seems amiss. Academicians like Koenitz (2014, 2015, 2016) avoid terms like storytelling and prefer conceptual framings like IDNs (Interactive Digital Narratives) to avoid further confusion.

Juul (2011) describes games as a resultant of rules and fiction—two directions that are in cooperation and competition. This outlook defines the fictional universe of the game as means (but not an end) for implementing rulesets; the inclusion of a fictional universe is first and foremost about creating a spatial interface for the player to experience and experiment with whatever rulesets are behind the software code. The participation of the audience has been an issue in many media prior to videogames, especially the way the producers textually encode media products and the ways audiences decode them (Hall 1980). Videogames seemingly need to at least employ a textual activity—one which Aarseth (1997) calls 'extranoematic,' a non-trivial effort that manifests outside the subconscious. To be more precise "[videogames] have varying levels of interactivity, which demands that players make choices, choices which can then alter (sometimes very distinctly) the story or experience of a particular game" (Consalvo 2005).

In terms of videogame narratives, the definition problem centers around the issues of encoding and decoding. Since videogames allow their audience to be hyper-active inside the medium, the players have the ability to completely deny the textual information or content confined within the game's code and use the software as a tool for their own ends of meaning-making. Jenkins (2004) differentiates between these domains as embedded and emergent narratives. Embedded narratives are encoded content such as the snippets of text, visual, video, and storytelling embedded within the fictional space by the developers, in the purpose of allowing the players to find and experience them, resulting in the construction of a story more or less intended by the encoder. Emergent narratives, in contrast, are decoded narratives, those that arise during the playtime by the participation of the player. They may or may not include the embedded components, be intentional or unintentional, foreseen or unforeseen. Calleja (2009) offers the concepts of scripted narratives and alterbiographies, as a similar duo. While scripted narratives match more or less with the concept of embedded narratives, alterbiography practices are associated with player personalities and point to personal narratives built around game experiences that fundamentally retain its language over different games, since it coalesces with a personae rather than a game. This coincides with Ryan's (2004) implication of destiny-ruled autotelic game worlds, wherein the player is self-motivated to interact, solve, and progress, while creating a personalized textual setting. Deriving from Fludernik's (1996) natural narratology, Ensslin (2014) describes videogames as 'unnatural narratology' with a distinction that operates on two different layers: the story level and the discourse level. On the story level, unnatural narratives may include "multiple contradictory endings of a story, or two parallel timelines that unfold at different speeds" (Ensslin 2014, p. 47). On the discourse level, however, they are anti-mimetic, deviating in narrative design and sequentiality.

Bailey (1999) describes three main approaches in interactive story generation: author model, story model, and world model. In the author model, the generative software tries to emulate an author in writing a narrative. In the story model, the narrative is generated with the structural approaches to storytelling as abstract formulations. In the world model, the generation focuses on creating a coherent story-world with rules and motivated characters who struggle to achieve their goals, thus creating the narrative. Bailey's trihedral model has been utilized in explaining interactive drama generation (Mateas 2002; Szilas et al. 2003), character-driven story generation (Riedl and Young 2003, 2004), and virtual intelligent narrators (Szilas 2001). Later studies propose an addition to these approaches: user-centric (Bostan and Marsh 2010) or the player model in which "the members of the audience become themselves characters in the story, so the role of authorship is progressively becoming distributed between the interactors and the designers" (Gervás et al. 2006, p. 49).

When translated into videogames, certain traditional narrative elements have different representations of conveying meaning (Cameron 1995). For example, the mysteries might be presented in the form of real puzzles that players have to overcome. The synchronous or asynchronous use of interactive segments and puzzle-solving might signify pacing. Similar to problems in the pacing of a film or novel, there may be problems in the balance of interactive and passive segments of videogames that affect its pacing. As traditional narratives are offered to have story time and discourse time (Chatman 1990), videogames also have their own temporal frames. Narrative games will typically employ a story time (the period of time that the story's events take place), but they will also have gameplay times (the expected total time that a game might be finished) that becomes very important in players' perception of the game (Jenkins 2004). A discourse time on the other hand infers the emphasis given inside the narrative in dwelling on certain content. In this light, session times (an average time of play between two meaningful gameplay points, such as puzzles, battles, scenes, etc.) might be offered as a parallel to discourse time. The closure of a videogame is based on its consumption—a narrative game with a beginning and an end might present closure by reaching the ending, while a videogame with no predetermined ending might supply closure by (sometimes player devised) achievements, such as getting all upgrades, beating a certain score, etc. Theoretically, the games that do not provide closure have the potential to be played indefinitely. As Brooks' (1977) adaptation of Freud's Masterplot, the player creates episodic sessions of play during which they become more skillful and better at the game. However narrative games will rarely offer the motivation for replays.

Carr's (1997) approach of the first order and the second order narratives have interesting significations inside the videogame medium. While the first order narratives signify stories that individuals create about themselves and their experiences, the second order narratives are individuals telling stories of other people's experiences. Inside videogames first and second order narratives are fused together to create a meta-narrative. From the viewpoint of the player, there is a double-layered first order narrative: as much as the player embodies a character and acts the events that happen to that character, they also create a personal narrative of themselves living that experience. From the viewpoint of the developer of the game, there is also a double-layered second order narrative: the developer designs the limits of the narrative that the agents of the game can go through, yet they also try to design the narrative of the player experiencing the game (e.g., the developer aiming to frighten the player at a certain point in the game). This distinction is also similar to Somers and Gibson's (1994) representational vs. ontological narratives. While the narrative content embedded inside the games creates representational experiences, the gameplay of the game itself creates an ontological narrative. In the age of YouTube playthroughs and Twitch streaming, the process of playing is not an ontological experience for the self alone but becomes a social projection. This projection becomes a discursive play/show that fuses representation, self, and the public together.

1.3 Methodology

First, to investigate my research question, I gather a set of videogames that can be mobilized for analysis. Media studies research has been offered to support sample sets of products gathered from thematic theory-based areas (Gunter 2012). I use the distribution platform Steam to select my sample of videogames as the platform was reported to account for 75% of all digital games sold for personal computers (Tyson 2015). Previous studies have also used data from Steam (Sifa et al. 2015; Lin et al. 2019; Coutu et al. 2020; Harrell et al. 2021) for various analyses purposes. Starting from 2014, the Steam platform allows users to associate the games with user-generated tags (Te 2014). I use two tags offered in a previous study (Şengün 2016) as the best ones to discover narrative videogames ("narrative" and "story rich") to identify an arbitrary selection of 15 videogames[1] during the first quarter of

---

[1]These games are *Celeste, Epistory, Florence, Gone Home, Hades, Half-Life: Alyx, Journey, Kentucky Route Zero, Max Payne 2: The Fall of Max Payne, Neo Cab, Oxenfree, Pendragon, Portal 2, Resident Evil 2*, and *The Witcher 3: Wild Hunt*.

2021 from the "Top Sellers" and "Top Rated" lists of both individual and combined tags.

Second, I perform a combination of formal (Fernandez-Vara 2014; Bizzocchi and Tanenbaum 2011) and temporal (Tychsen and Hitchens 2009; Wei et al. 2010) analysis on the selected videogames. Both methods have been formalized and deeply discussed in Lankoski and Björk (2015). As a formal analysis, I perform a close reading on the theoretical distance between gameplay and narrative sequences, as well as interactivity and autonomy of game elements as related to their narrative potential, by systematically capturing the role of each component that results in the game being tagged "narrative" and/or "story rich." As a temporal analysis, I investigate the role of actual and metaphorical temporal concepts in the game (e.g., duration, action, reaction, timeline, turn, calendar, etc.) in progressing the game's narrative flow. I do this within the framework of socio-cultural references in the game-world that can also create temporal fictions that may or may not correspond to real-world counterparts. Many games use multiple temporal frames that overlap or occur one after the other. Some of these temporal frames might be informed by previous media (e.g., flashbacks as used in movies, novels, etc.) or might be specific to the medium (e.g., taking turns, taking the time to solve a puzzle, or selecting a dialogue option, etc.).

Finally, I extrapolate my findings to develop six distinct narrative forms that might manifest exclusively or in combination in videogames. I discuss these forms in relation to the videogames from my sample set, as well as others from my personal, anecdotal, or secondary experiences.

1.4 Results

In this section, I define and compare the six distinct forms (or degrees) of mobilizing narrative elements inside the videogames medium ordered by ascending intensity. To create and order these degrees, I use: (1) the theoretical distance between gameplay and narrative elements (from undemanding, crude storytelling occasions to traditional forms and other emerging, experimental forms) as determined qualitatively by a close reading of the game texts; (2) narrative interactivity as relating to temporal frames that the game presents (meaning whether the player is only exposed to the narrative elements versus becomes an interactive agent in its presentation); and (3) narrative autonomy (meaning if the player choices can orient the narrative flow). I present how these resulting forms relate to my selection of games in Table 1.1. However, as I discuss them in more detail, I tried to use examples from games (modern or classic) that are outside my selection to showcase that the framework can be applied to the wider medium and not confined to the selection-at-hand.

Table 1.1 How the selection of games relates to the six degrees of videogame narrative presented in this study

	First degree:[a] Narrative elements as tools for internalization	Second degree: narrative and gameplay sections swap	Third degree: narration blurs into gameplay sequences	Fourth degree: universe at pause	Fifth degree: non-sequential autonomy	Sixth degree: experimental storytelling
Celeste	■		■			
Epistory			■	■	■	
Florence			■			■ (narrative through game mechanics)
Gone Home	■		■	■		
Hades		■	■		■	■ (roguelike narrative elements)
Half-Life: Alyx		■	■	■		
Journey	■	■				■ (uncontrollable multiplayer)
Kentucky Route Zero	■	■	■	■		
Max Payne 2: The Fall of Max Payne		■	■			
Neo Cab			■		■	
Oxenfree		■	■	■		
Pendragon	■	■	■		■	■ (roguelike narrative elements)
Portal 2	■					
Resident Evil 2		■	■	■		
The Witcher 3: Wild Hunt		■	■		■	

[a]Although it could be argued that all videogames employ these types of elements, I wanted to point out those that heavily rely on this method

1.4.1   First Degree: Narrative as an Internalization Tool

In this form, I use the term internalization as a combination of performing conceptualization, recognizing conventions, inferring patterns, and creating expectations
through personal or social values. The conscious or subconscious experiences
gained from the rules and mechanics of a videogame can result in invoking
expectations and conventions without constructing or needing a narrative structure
or a collection of story elements. If players find a key in a game, they would
assume that there would be something locked somewhere in the game where the
key would be useful through a mental process of expectations and patterns, as
well as expectations from game genres (Breault 2020). This process might be
sparked through common knowledge about what a key is and does, as well as the
literacy around the medium (Squire 2008). The story behind why the key is there
and who locked the object with this key is less relevant and might be incoherent
in a traditional storytelling setting. These kinds of non-abstract setups can spark
internalized behaviors. For example, if players see a door and a key in a single-
screen, they might be more likely to interact with the key first before going to the
door due to assuming that the door would be locked. In Nintendo's 1981 game
Donkey Kong, the game's antagonist (a gorilla) throws circular objects recognized
as barrels to the path of the game's protagonist (Jumpman, who will later become
the gaming icon Mario). It is relatively easier for a first-time player (a first-timer
for this specific game or for videogames in general) to instinctively resolve what
their action should be against the barrels rolling toward them. Since, it could be
seen that the barrels are thrown by *Donkey Kong*, the antagonist, they are bound
to be detrimental to the player's progression. Since the player knows the character
they are controlling is a person and what is rolling toward that character is a barrel,
without being instructed, the player could conclude that the barrel should be avoided
and within the two-dimensional game world, the most logical course of action to
achieve that would be to climb a ladder or jump over the barrel. This is not a
storytelling structure that we understand in the traditional sense, but it constructs
a narrative *occasion*—an enactment of conventional behavior or a repetition of an
acceptable reaction pattern against stimuli ("a barrel was rolling toward me, so, I
jumped over it").

Bruner (1991) asserts that a narrative is already "a version of reality whose
acceptability is governed by convention" (p. 4). Then, when a videogame borrows
conventions and patterns from physical reality and adorns or transforms them
with consistent game-world logic and rules, it can create narrative *occasions* that
can exist both as metaphorically connected as well as unattached from reality—
a state of existing as half-real (Juul 2011). In this way, the process works toward
helping the player internalize what is taking place on the screen and quickly
determine the appropriate courses of action without really relating to the motivations
or characterizations of agents or the progression of a plot. The game does not
continuously try to tell a story but instead uses story elements to render its rules
and mechanics approachable and adaptable.

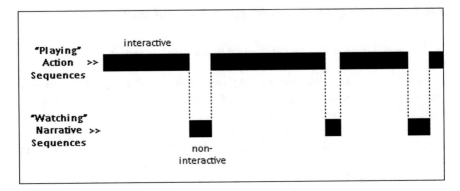

Fig. 1.1 A typical progression for second degree videogame narration

1.4.2   Second Degree: Swapping Gameplay and Narration

In this form, videogames rely on methods that fall outside the temporal confinements of gameplay to tell a story, and, typically, oscillate between gameplay sessions
and non-interactive narrative sequences that run in parallel to each other (see Fig.
1.1). The most common forms of these narrative sequences are pre-rendered or
scripted cutscenes that interrupt the gameplay in a "characteristic rhythm" (Klevjer
2002) that come as awards for finishing certain portions of the game or the game
itself. Players are usually cued to "remove their hands from the controls and simply
watch the information that advances the game's narrative" (Rehak 2003, p. 127). In
this aspect, storytelling happens outside the gameplay but still within the boundaries
of the videogame as a media artifact. King and Krzywinska (2006) assert that
"narrative reliance on cut-scenes and other 'out-of-game' devices [...] is one of the
main reasons why the narrative dimension is often seen as essentially opposed to that
of gameplay" (p. 44). In some cases, the context of gameplay and cutscenes match
coherently, thus creating an effective convergence of action/narration oscillation.
For example, in Brøderbund's 1993 release *Prince of Persia 2*, at the end of the first
cutscene, the protagonist is seen jumping out of a window. So, when the gameplay
sequence starts, the protagonist begins the level on a balcony under a broken
window. Advancing in the level by fighting and moving through the platforms, the
protagonist ends up on the docks and jumps into a ship. The next cutscene shows
the ship sinking and the next gameplay sequence starts on a beach, and so on.

However, there might also be stark disconnects between the story told in the
narrative sequences and the actions taken in the gameplay sequences. In casual
mobile games like *Small Town Murders* or *Lily's Garden,* the games' narratives
progress by playing match-3 puzzle levels, collecting virtual currency, and using
this currency to advance the games' narrative cutscenes. The narrative elements have
only superficial connections to the rules and mechanics (but mostly to the milieu) of
the games.

On one hand, since the narrative is constructed outside of gameplay and without input from the player, they might be treated as non-essential to the game, resulting in players choosing to *skip* them and ignore the storytelling aspects of the videogame. In fact, the decision to make unskippable cutscenes has resulted in criticism in the past (e.g., see the discussions of Rosenberg 2010, and McShea 2010, on *Metroid: Other M*). This approach may indicate an attempt at establishing authorship by adjusting the exposure to cutscenes (narrative) at the expense of the player's dominance over the gameplay flow. In return, it may become an issue of grievance on the part of the player and may be perceived as an invasive attempt. On the other hand, gameplay sequences can act as gatekeepers for players who are interested in seeing the narrative advance. YouTube channels (such as Gamer's Little Playground[2]) emerge that create and publish *game movies*—a post-produced combination of all cut-scenes and other kinds of storytelling sequences in a game— for players who do not want to go through the gameplay or who do not have the necessary gameplay skills to advance in or finish the game but just want to watch what happens in the story. While game developers have reasons to make narrative sequences skippable, the opposite does not seem to be applicable[3] as it might push the resulting experience outside the boundaries of a videogame. Other interesting concepts to note at this point are walkthroughs, playthroughs, and solution guides. Consalvo (2003) describes walkthroughs as "detailed descriptions of where to go and what to do—in sequential order—to get through a game successfully." In this aspect, this kind of content can become instruments to easily *skip* the gameplay sequences and to reach narrative sequences. However, if the game depends heavily on physical skills, even a walkthrough may not help a player pass the action sequences so easily.

1.4.3 Third Degree: Narration Blurring into Gameplay

In this form, the narration sequences are constructed inside the gameplay segments using the game's rules, mechanics, agents, environments, etc., while the gameplay continues. Some very common methods are distributing discoverable items in the game world such as (1) readable items (e.g., notes, pages, journals, etc.); (2) visual items (e.g., photos, posters, maps with notes, etc.); as well as scripted events that happen in the game world, triggered as a result of reaching a specific location or performing specific actions, such as (3) virtual screens that show pre-rendered

---

[2]https://www.youtube.com/c/gLPLayground/featured

[3]I want to underline two instances that can present alternatives to this issue. First, Nintendo has devised a feature in their 2009 release *New Super Mario Bros Wii*, called the Super Guide. In this feature, if a player loses eight lives in a level, they can choose to have the computer play and finish the level for them. Second, emergent videogame genres such as *walking simulators* can construct experiences wherein gameplay aspects are very minimal, and storytelling is on the focus. See Şengün 2017, for a detailed discussion of this genre.

videos[4]; (4) audio broadcasts, recordings, radio transmissions, player character's monologues, or non-playable character (NPC) conversations; (5) NPC movements; and, finally, (6) scripted events happening in the game world such as objects moving in the back- or foreground. Similar to the option of skipping the cutscenes, the players may choose not to interact with these narrative tools (for example, not picking up a journal entry, or picking it up but not reading it; looking at another direction as an NPC performs a scripted action, etc.). They may also miss these narrative tools, by not discovering them at all or by failing to see or hear them completely as they pass by. Additionally, there is the possibility of accessing the narrative tools out of the intended order, also called *sequence breaking* (Shelley et al. 2013) (for example, finding a journal entry before finding and reading its predecessor).

All these possibilities encourage constructing personalized narrative experiences for different players even though the overall narrative itself is designed as sequential. Consider Tecmo's 2003 game *Fatal Frame II: Crimson Butterfly*. In this survival horror action game, the protagonist Mio is searching for her lost sister Mayu in a haunted village while using the camera obscura she carries to shoot photos of ghosts and exorcise them. Each time she enters a haunted building, she finds bits and clues about the story of the ghost who haunts the location. Among these narrative props are journals, photos, items belonging to the deceased, etc. Frequently ghosts themselves appear and deliver cryptic messages about their personal stories in scripted events. Eventually, when the final room of the location is accessed, the ghost manifests itself in this predetermined area and a fight is initiated. Although finding the clues about ghosts is non-sequential, the dominant progression of the location is not. The sequence of the locations the player has to enter and the ghosts they have to exorcise to finish the game is also predetermined, however, the game offers a total of six different endings within different releases of the game. All endings except one are achieved through gameplay, such as finishing the game in normal mode or finishing the game in hard mode; they are not associated with narrative choices made throughout the gameplay. As discussed before, there may be players who choose to pass all narrative content of these games and prefer to focus on enjoying the gameplay mechanics. These players would most likely skip all cut-scenes, not search for and read journal entries, or stop to listen or watch background events. Yet by doing these things they are likely to miss important clues for the progression of the game and may get stuck on where to go or what to do next in some parts of the game. Some games may merge narrative clues and gameplay sequences so well that avoiding narrative may become impractical. At the beginning of Square Enix's 2013 game *Tomb Raider*, Lara Croft tries to escape from a cave that she is imprisoned in while constantly talking to herself, assessing the situation she is in, and deciding on

---

[4]In Microsoft's 2010 game *Alan Wake,* among other discoverable items in the game world, there were also TV sets that broadcast a fictional show called *Night Springs*, and radios that broadcast local talk shows that the player can choose to stop and listen or watch.

what to do as her next action. If the players fail to listen to the monologue, they may have trouble finding the right things to do to progress in the game.

1.4.4 Fourth Degree: Universe at Pause

In this form, I would like to introduce the concept of *the universe at pause*. This phenomenon occurs mostly in adventure games and their subgenres, as well as some genres of role-playing games as well. Although these games strive to build their virtual world consistent within itself, a common deviation occurs in the usage of temporal frames wherein until the players find the correct action to perform, the whole progression, narrative, and the game world will pause or get stuck in short loops. An NPC may keep repeating the same lines over and over; an animate object may be looping an action, etc. until the player finds the correct action that will progress the game. Even traveling long distances will not help; the players will find a location that they have left for a long time, exactly the same as they have left it when they return. Hanson (2018) likens this phenomenon to Huizinga's (1949) concept of the magic circle which offers that a game has its own boundaries of time and space. Pedersen (2009) defines it as when "usually all gameplay, storytelling, or advancement [. . .] is paused until the puzzle is solved" (p. 37). In this aspect, these games may offered to be oscillating between narration and puzzle-solving sequences (see Fig. 1.2).

Here, I use the term puzzle in Montfort's (2004) appropriation of a riddle wherein the player tries to determine the best course of action that will change the state of the world not through management, fighting an opponent, strategy, or tactics (Rollings and Adams 2003) but through a similitude with fiction (e.g., whom should the character speak to, what should they say, which item should they use and where, which location should they go next, etc.). In this aspect, the videogame becomes a sequence of riddles that the game's flow explicitly or vaguely eludes to.

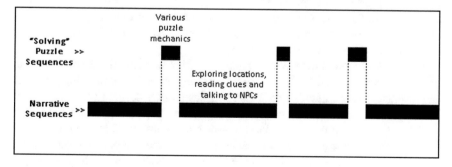

Fig. 1.2 A typical progression for fourth degree videogame narration

It must be highlighted that temporal vacuums might also be observed when some games are left alone without human interaction and the game achieves a state that is similar to a software pause. For example, if a player leaves a real-time game like *StarCraft* without any input, the AI-controlled enemy would eventually attack and beat them. In contrast, when a player stops playing a game like *God of War* as they are transitioning between locations when there are no enemies around, the game state can safely stay there until when the player picks up the controller again. This kind of temporal vacuums does not match with the phenomenon of the universe at pause. In fact, the universe at pause typically works well with the approach of eliminating the feelings of urgency or being in constant danger during gameplay. Consider Revolution Software's 1996 adventure game *Broken Sword: The Shadow of the Templars*. Toward the end of the game, as the protagonist George Stobbart and his partner Nico is traveling by train to the final location of the game, Nico gets kidnapped and George has to save her. This kidnapping creates no urgency in the game. The player can walk around the train and spend time talking to NPCs or examining locations as much as they like because it is apparent by the gameplay so far that there is no countdown. The events will not progress until George finds a way to reach the front of the train.

1.4.5 *Fifth Degree: Non-sequential Autonomy*

This form of narrative manifests itself in role-playing, open-world (sandbox), open-world role-playing, and massively multiplayer role-playing genres wherein the players can (and even encouraged to) stray away from the main storyline (if any) and venture into exploration, questing, and discovery. Although, in some cases, a main narrative storyline determines where the actual game begins or ends, parallel or side stories, locations, and narratives can keep the player off this main story line for an important portion of gameplay time. By contrast, massively multiplayer online role-playing games do not have traditional storylines where the game has an ending; instead, they get regular updates that keep expanding on the stories, locations, and quests. The majority of such engineered worlds are meant to be experienced non-sequentially, although many offer a character-level system to decide where would be safe or dangerous for the players to explore.

In Blizzard Entertainment's iconic game *World of Warcraft*, the characters begin in a small town dictated by their race and by doing quests move onto bigger towns and eventually into capital cities. However, players may decide not to follow this flow, they may choose to move to other race's cities and starting zones—although the journeys could prove to be perilous—or move between cities earlier or later than expected. As the game progresses, the player has more options on where to go, which quests to do, where to explore, and where to hunt. It is easily possible for a *World of Warcraft* player to have no knowledge of several locations, towns, and quests available in the world. A player can easily bypass all narratives portions of the game, by not reading quest texts or dialogues of the non-playable characters as well as skipping all available cutscenes or walking away from scripted in-game story events. Instead, the player might focus on other dynamics of the game like player vs player combat, strengthening a character to beat game-end enemies and encounters or additional mechanics such as collecting and battling pets. Yet, there is no denying that the narrative portions of the game invade a large part of its production and presentation value and even if the player specifically focuses on bypassing them, to some degree, they are extremely hard to avoid completely. The player would eventually need to do a quest, follow a scripted event, or listen to what an NPC says to progress in whatever gameplay goal they are after.

In the fifth degree narrative form, the overall narrative is constructed through the actions of the player and the narrative flow has autonomy and is non-sequential. Offline role-playing games may employ the universe at pause principle described previously: a town, a city, or a narrative hub may remain the same till the player performs an action. Some role-playing games employ the concepts of day and night or seasons to invoke the feeling of passing time. The non-playable characters change places according to the time of the day or the year, or extra narrative elements may emerge in different temporal frames.[5] This can also be true for online games—through periodic upgrades the world can expand and reshape, breaking the convention of the universe at pause.

1.4.6 Sixth Degree: Experimental Temporality and Autonomy

It must be underlined that studies that seek categorization of certain phenomena, such as this one, are always in danger of staying as snapshots of the current state of things and failing to capture future innovations and developments. Videogames are a dynamic medium that transforms and expands with technology and producers constantly seek and frequently discover new forms of interactions and storytelling. Although the previous five degrees capture the majority of the videogames in their use of narrative elements and storytelling mechanics, there are some instances in games or a few stand-alone experimental products that cannot fit into narrative definitions as effortlessly as others. As a result, I want to propose the sixth degree as an easy way to mention these instances of experimental temporality and autonomy. For example, Westwood Studios' 1997 game *Blade Runner* heavily mobilizes the third and fourth degree storytelling techniques, however, completely ignores the universe at pause. The game was marketed as a "real-time adventure game" wherein the game time will not wait for the actions of the player; if the player loses time in

---

[5] Such as *Guild Wars 2*'s pop-up events. These are scripted events that begin and end randomly around the game world. The players can only experience them, if they are there at that specific time or if they camp (waiting at the place where the event is supposed to randomly pop) for it. This creates an even more chaotic narrative autonomy as a result since a player who experiences an event in a certain place may visit that place with another character and may not be able to find that event happening there and then.

solving a puzzle on a screen, they will arrive at the next screen late and the AI characters that are trying to complete their own objectives would be ahead of them. The various endings of the game are not only determined by the choices made by the player but also the time they take in the progression of the story. In Konami's 2001 game *Silent Hill 2,* interesting actions can affect the ending of the story such as some actions taken in the inventory (e.g., examining an item repeatedly) or the physical distance the player keeps between the protagonist and a side-character (Şengün 2013b). *Metal Gear Solid* series employ many fourth-wall breaking elements such as the in-game characters asking the player to turn off the game console in *Metal Gear Solid 2: Sons of Liberty.*

1.5   Discussion

In this study, I tried to categorize the different ways that gameplay and narration sequences can intersect and interact in videogames. These sequences have been offered as being diametrical for the medium and as interrupting each other frequently. To explore this question, I made the formal and temporal analyses of multiple games by playing them and performed close readings on their gameplay and storytelling structures. I created my sample set from games that are offered to have high levels of narrative potential by the gamer communities.

The results highlighted several strategies and videogame narrative forms that I grouped into six categories. By applying a theoretical ordering of the categories through the intensity of narrative context, I ended up with six degrees of video game narrative. These degrees can be mobilized separately or in conjunction. In the first degree, the narrative elements are mobilized as tools for internalization of gameplay by employing tropes, conventions, and patterns onto gaming actions. In the second degree, the narrative and gameplay sections swap to construct a narrative arc wherein the game mechanics and game story exist in separate but overlapping and frequently abstract dimensions. In the third degree, narration blurs into gameplay sequences and emerges at the same temporal frame and spatial existence. In the fourth degree, the gameplay sequence is in service of storytelling and the world adheres to a phenomenon called the universe at pause wherein the game world waits for players to solve riddles and advance its state. In the fifth degree, a non-sequential autonomy emerges that allows players to explore the world in order to find narrative setups that are designed to be experienced non-sequentially. Finally, in the sixth degree, experimental storytelling techniques that defy the rules of temporality and autonomy are employed.

The results have implications for further research. Although the categorization is informed by a sample set of contemporary and classic games, the discourse of videogames is progressing on a fast track as new technologies, target segments, and creative approaches emerge. This constant change is bound to generate products that will not abide by and transform current paradigms.

A.1 Ludography

Alan Wake (Microsoft, 2010)
Blade Runner (Westwood Studios, 1997)
Broken Sword: The Shadow of the Templars (Revolution Software, 1996)
Celeste (Matt Makes Games, 2018)
Donkey Kong (Nintendo, 1981)
Epistory (Fishing Cactus, 2016)
Fatal Frame II: Crimson Butterfly (Tecmo, 2003)
Florence (Annapurna Interactive, 2020)
God of War (Sony Computer Entertainment, 2005)
Gone Home (Fullbright, 2013)
Guild Wars 2 (ArenaNet, 2012)
Hades (Supergiant Games, 2020)
Half-Life: Alyx (Valve, 2020)
Journey (Annapurna Interactive, 2020)
Kentucky Route Zero (Cardboard Computer, 2013)
Lily's Garden (Tactile Games, 2020)
Max Payne 2: The Fall of Max Payne (Rockstar Games, 2003)
Metal Gear Solid 2: Sons of Liberty (Konami, 2001)
Neo Cab (Fellow Traveller, 2019)
New Super Mario Bros Wii (Nintendo, 2009)
Oxenfree (Night School Studio, 2016)
Pendragon (Inkle, 2020)
Portal 2 (Valve, 2011)
Prince of Persia 2 (Brøderbund, 1993)
Resident Evil 2 (Capcom, 2019)
Silent Hill 2 (Konami, 2001)
Small Town Murders (Rovio, 2020)
StarCraft (Blizzard Entertainment, 1998)
The Witcher 3: Wild Hunt (CD Projeckt Red, 2015)
Tomb Raider (Square Enix, 2003)
World of Wacraft (Blizzard Entertainment, 2004)

References

E.J. Aarseth, *Cybertext: Perspectives on Ergodic Literature* (Johns Hopkins University Press, Baltimore, 1997)

P. Bailey, Searching for storiness: story-generation from a reader's perspective, in *Technical Report FS-99-01 from Working Notes of the Narrative Intelligence Symposium*, (AAAI Press, Menlo Park, 1999), pp. 157–164

J. Bizzocchi, J. Tanenbaum, Well read: applying close reading techniques to gameplay experiences, in *Well Played 3.0: Video Games, Value, and Meaning*, (ETC Press, Pittsburgh, 2011)

B. Bostan, T. Marsh, The interactive of interactive storytelling: customizing the gaming experience. Lect. Notes Comput. Sci. **1**(6243), 472–475 (2010)

M. Breault, *Narrative Design: The Craft of Writing for Games* (CRC Press, Boca Raton, 2020)

P. Brooks, Freud's masterplot, in *Literature and Psychoanalysis*, vol. 55/56, (Yale University Press, New Heaven, 1977), pp. 280–300

J. Bruner, The narrative construction of reality. Crit. Inq. **18**(1), 1–21 (1991)

G. Calleja, Experimental narrative in game environments, in *Proceedings of 2009 DIGRA International Conference*, vol. 5 (2009)

A. Cameron, Dissimulations: the illusions of interactivity. Millenium Film J. **28**, 32–47 (1995)

D. Carr, Narrative and the real world: an argument for continuity, in *Memory, Identity, and Community: The Idea of Narrative in Human Sciences*, (State University of New York Press, New York, 1997), pp. 7–25

S. Chatman, *Coming to Terms: the Rhetoric of Narrative in Fiction and Film* (Cornell University Press, Ithaca, 1990)

M. Consalvo, Rule sets, cheating, and magic circles: studying games and ethics. Int. Rev. Inform. Ethics.**4** (2005)

Y. Coutu, Y. Chang, W. Zhang, S. Sengun, The relationship between cohesive game design and player immersion: a case study of original versus reboot thief, in *Game User Experience and Player-Centered Design*, (Springer, Berlin, 2020)

A. Ensslin, *Literary Gaming* (The MIT Press, Cambridge, 2014)

C. Fernandez-Vara, *Introduction to Game Analysis* (Routledge, New York, 2014)

M. Fludernik, *Towards a 'Natural' Narratology* (Routledge, London, 1996)

G. Frasca, Ludologists love stories, too: notes from a debate that never took place, in *Proceedings of Level Up—1st International Digital Games Research Conference 2003*, (University of Utrecht Press, Utrecht, 2003), pp. 92–99

G. Genette, *Narrative Discourse: an Essay in Method* (Cornell University Press, New York, 1983)

P. Gervás, B. Lönneker-Rodman, J.C. Meister, F. Peinado, Narrative models: narratology meets artificial intelligence, in *Workshop Toward Computational Models of Literary Analysis* (2006), pp. 44–51

B. Gunter, The quantitative research process, in *A Handbook of Media and Communication Research: Qualitative and Quantitative Methodologies*, (Routledge, London, 2012)

S. Hall, Encoding/decoding, in *Culture, Media, Language*, (Routledge, London, 1980), pp. 128–138

C. Hanson, *Game Time: Understanding Temporality in Video Games* (Indiana University Press, Bloomington, 2018)

D.F. Harrell, S. Şengün, D. Olson, Africa and the avatar dream: mapping the impacts of videogame representations of Africa, in *The Digital Black Atlantic*, (University of Minnesota Press, Minneapolis, 2021)

J. Huizinga, *Homo Ludens: A Study of the Play-Element in Culture* (Routledge, London, 1949)

H. Jenkins, Game design as narrative architecture, in *First Person*, (The MIT Press, Cambridge, 2004)

J. Juul, *Half-Real: Video Games between Real Rules and Fictional Worlds* (The MIT Press, Cambridge, 2011)

G. King, T. Krzywinska, *Tomb Raiders and Space Invaders: Videogame Forms and Contexts* (Palgrave Macmillan, New York, 2006)

R. Klevjer, In defense of cutscenes, in *Proceedings of Computer Games and Digital Cultures Conference*, (Tampere University Press, Tampere, 2002)

H. Koenitz, Five theses for interactive digital narrative, in *Interactive Storytelling*, (Springer, Basel, 2014), pp. 134–139

H. Koenitz, Towards a specific theory of interactive digital narraitve, in *Interactive Digital Narrative*, (Routledge, New York, 2015), pp. 91–105

H. Koenitz, Interactive storytelling paradigms and representations: a humanities-based pespective, in *Handbook of Digital Games and Entertainment Technologies*, (Springer, Sigapore, 2016), pp. 1–15

P. Lankoski, S. Björk, *Game Research Methods: An Overview* (ETC Press, Halifax, 2015)

B. Laurel, *Computers as Theatre* (Addison-Wesley Longman Publishing, Boston, 1991)

D. Lin, C. Bezemer, Y. Zou, A.E. Hassan, An empirical study of game reviews on the steam platform. Empir. Softw. Eng. **24**(3), 170–207 (2019)

M. Mateas, *Interactive Drama, Art and Artificial Intelligence*, Unpublished Doctoral Thesis, Carnegie Mellon University (2002)

McShea, T, *Metroid: Other M Review*, Gamespot.com (2010, August 27). Available from https://www.gamespot.com/reviews/metroid-other-m-review/1900-6274531/. Accessed 1 Mar 2021

N. Montfort, *Twisty Little Passages: An Approach to Interactive Fiction* (The MIT Press, Cambridge, 2004)

J.H. Murray, *Hamlet on the Holodeck* (Free Press, New York, 1997)

R.E. Pedersen, *Game Design Foundations* (Jones and Bartlett Publishers, Burlington, 2009)

L. Plowman, Narrative, linearity and interactivity: making sense of interactive multimedia. Br. J. Educ. Technol. **27**(2), 92–105 (1996)

B. Rehak, Playing at being: psychoanalysis and the avatar, in *The Video Game Theory Reader*, (Routledge, New York, 2003)

M.O. Riedl, R.M. Young, Character-focused narrative generation for execution in virtual worlds, in *Virtual Storytelling: Using Virtual Reality Technologies for Storytelling*, (Springer, Berlin, 2003), pp. 47–56

A. Rollings, E. Adams, *Andrew Rollings and Ernest Adams on Game Design* (New Riders, San Francisco, 2003)

A. Rosenberg, *Metroid: Other M Review-In Space, Everyone Can Hear You Monologue*, MTV.com (2010, August 27). Available from http://www.mtv.com/news/2461752/metroid-other-m-review-in-space-everyone-can-hear-you-monologue/. Accessed 1 Mar 2021

M. Ryan, *Narrative across Media* (University of Nebraska Press, Lincoln, 2004)

S. Şengün, Cybertexts, hypertexts and interactive fiction: why shan't the prodigal children overthrow their forefathers, in *Innovation, Difference, Irregularity, LIT FICTION'13 Conference Proceedings*, (Mimar Sinan University Press, Istanbul, 2013a), pp. 58–66

S. Şengün, Silent Hill 2 and the curious case of invisible agency, in *Proceedings of International Conference on Interactive Digital Storytelling*, (Springer, Cham, 2013b), pp. 180–185

S. Şengün, *Narra Ludens: Explaining Video Game Narrative Engagement through Player Types and Motivations*. Unpublished Doctoral Thesis, Istanbul Bilgi University (2016)

S. Şengün, Ludic voyeurism and passive spectatorship in Gone Home and other walking simulators. VGA Reader **1** (2017)

M. Shelley, W. Shi, J.P. Corriveau, On preventing sequence breaking in video games, in *Proceedings of 2013 12th Annual Workshop on Network and Systems Support for Games (NetGames)*, (IEEE, Piscataway, 2013), pp. 1–2

R. Sifa, A. Drachen, C. Bauckhage, Large-scale cross-game player behavior analysis on Steam, in *Proceedings of the AAAI Conference on Artificial Intelligence and Interactive Digital Entertainment*, vol. 11, no. 1 (2015)

M.R. Somers, G.D. Gibson, Reclaiming the epistemological other: narrative and the social constitution of identity, in *Social Theory and the Politics of Identity*, (Blackwell Publishing, Cambridge, 1994), pp. 37–99

K. Squire, Video-game literacy: a literacy of expertise, in *Handbook of Research on New Literacies*, (Erlbaum, Mahwah, 2008)

N. Szilas, A new approach to interactive drama: from intelligent characters to an intelligent virtual narrator, in *Proceedings of the AAAI Spring Symposium on AI and Interactive Entertainment* (2001), pp. 72–76

N. Szilas, O. Marty, J. Réty, Authoring highly generative interactive drama, in *Virtual Storytelling: Using Virtual Reality Technologies for Storytelling*, (Springer, Berlin, 2003), pp. 37–46

Z. Te, *Steam Introduces Tagging System for Games and Software*, Gamespot.com (2014, February 12). Available from https://www.gamespot.com/articles/steam-introduces-tagging-system-for-games-and-software/1100-6417705/. Accessed 1 Mar 2021

A. Tychsen, M. Hitchens, Game time: modeling and analyzing time in multiplayer and massively multiplayer games. Games Cult. **4**(2), 170–201 (2009). https://doi.org/10.1177/1555412008325479

M. Tyson, *PC Game Sales to Eclipse Value of Console Games Sales in 2016*, Hexus.net (2015, June 15). Available from http://hexus.net/gaming/news/industry/83972-pc-games-sales-eclipse-value-console-games-sales-2016/. Accessed 1 Mar 2021

H. Wei, T. Bizzocchi, T. Calvert, Time and space in digital game storytelling. Int. J. Comp. Games Technol. **2010**, 897217 (2010). https://doi.org/10.1155/2010/897217

Chapter 2
Systemic NPC-Side Branching in Linear AAA Video Game Stories

Leanne C. Taylor-Giles

2.1 Introduction

Games have been described as "a series of interesting choices" and while there is debate about meaning and non-trivial choices in games (Sicart 2013), and degrees of player agency in their choice-making (Murray 2017), player choice opportunities and scope have grown considerably (Consalvo et al. 2019). For games scholars, a focus of discussions in this area is how the expanding sophistication of choice-making opportunity engages moral and ethical questions on the part of the player and more recently, whether there is a feedback loop as a result of choice-making behaviour (Bostan et al. 2020; Katsarov et al. 2019). However, beyond developments in AI (Fraser et al. 2018), there is less discussion about the intricacies of the design of such choice opportunities despite the recognition that they are becoming increasingly sophisticated.

Choice-based dialogue interfaces have been common since the first Computer Role-Playing Games (CRPGs) but their inclusion—if not carefully managed and curated—results in complex web of checks and balances that requires exponential amounts of quality assurance testing before the product can be brought to market (Taylor-Giles 2014). Recent CRPGs such as *Torment: Tides of Numenera* (2017) and *Disco Elysium* (2019) contain labyrinthine branching conversations, but similar moments of agency can also be experienced in linear stories by having non-player characters (NPCs) refer to the player's in-game actions within choice-less dialogues.

This reference to player activity within the game represents a distinct form of agency where, following from Murray's definition of "making something happen in a dynamically responsive world", agency is evident in the (apparent) memories

L. C. Taylor-Giles (✉)
Drop Bear Bytes, Torquay, VIC, Australia
e-mail: writer@leannectaylor.com

© The Author(s), under exclusive license to Springer Nature Switzerland AG 2022
B. Bostan (ed.), *Games and Narrative: Theory and Practice*, International Series on Computer Entertainment and Media Technology,
https://doi.org/10.1007/978-3-030-81538-7_2

of player activity that each NPC holds. The following three case studies provide examples of elegantly-structured conversation design that result in comments from the NPCs which feel like agency on the part of the player, even though she might not have been specifically thinking about making meaningful choices during the gameplay or decision-making processes that resulted in those comments (Murray 2017). The case studies are then used to support a discussion of best practices in systemic NPC-side branching design approaches, as well as their implications for player agency.

2.2   Case Studies

Disco Elysium (ZA/UM 2019), *Hades* (Supergiant Games 2020), and *The Signifier* (Playmestudio 2020) are three recent games that apply the principle of responding to the player's in-game actions in dialogue, expanding the player's sense of meaning-making beyond the bounds of typical one-to-one NPC conversations. Each game was selected not only for the presence of NPC-side branching, but because of the complexity presented to the player by reasonably simple behind-the-scenes checks. Choice-based gameplay moments were identified, retraced to their inciting action, then tested against other, similar moments within each game to identify both the temporal distance between a player's choice and an NPC commenting on it, and the complexity of the check required to arrive at that specific comment.

  This analysis will begin with *Disco Elysium*, as it follows more current CRPG dialogue conventions than *Hades* or *The Signifier* do, including a listed and numbered choice-based dialogue interface.

2.2.1   Case Study #1: Disco Elysium

Disco Elysium is characterised by an encyclopedic series of skill checks that result in a unique gameplay experience for each player. All of the 24 player character skills can be called upon in dialogue either passively (by the game) or actively (by the player); further, some of these skills unlock checks of other skills, resulting in chains of pass/failure skill-checking that either add or obscure additional information (Fig. 2.1).

  For a system such as this one to function elegantly and with few errors requires two aspects: phenomenal compartmentalisation, and, to a certain extent, the attribution of triviality. Every element of every skill check must be complete and discrete, referring only to themselves except in specific cases; and every skill check (especially if instigated by the game) must have minimal bearing on the overarching flow of the conversation and the game.

  The central conceit that makes this system possible in *Disco Elysium* is an exaggeration of two video game tropes: that of the amnesiac hero, who can act

Fig. 2.1 A screenshot from Disco Elysium (2019), showing two chained skill checks, one of which was a prerequisite for the other. The second line—"You." would not have appeared if the player did not pass the Empathy skill check, and neither line would have appeared if the player did not pass the Conceptualization skill check

as the player's proxy in asking questions that would otherwise be perceived as inane or self-evident to anyone already residing in the game's world, and that of the troubled detective (from film noir) which comes with an internal monologue of various moral bents (Abrams 2006). Combining these two archetypes allows for a dialogue system in which sudden revelations about and moral ruminations on the game's events become natural and acceptable. The in-built "learning caps" for each type of skill also make it impossible for any one player character to excel in every category, lending a sense of inevitability to certain skill checks or actions that primes the player to be more accepting of failure.

It's in this context that the game also refers to the player's in-game actions with alternate lines or additions from NPCs. For the purposes of this chapter, the focus will be on only the player's actions and not her previous dialogue choices, which fall into the already well-documented strictures of a standard choice-based dialogue system (Taylor-Giles 2014, 2020).

2.2.1.1 Lieutenant Kitsuragi and Ludic Recognition

Temporality: Immediate
Complexity: Minimal
Effect: Moderate (Fig. 2.2).

Fig. 2.2 A screenshot from Disco Elysium (2019), showing Lt. Kitsuragi's dialogue if the player has the Yellow Plastic Bag equipped when discovering a corpse on the boardwalk

One example of the game recognising the player's in-world actions comes when she discovers the piteous corpse of a drunk at the end of a pier. The player has an ongoing task to pay for the destruction of the player character's hotel room, which occurred before she started the game. One method of acquiring money is to equip a specific yellow plastic bag and collect "tare"—discarded plastic and glass bottles that the player can exchange for a little cash. This behaviour is not required at any point, which strengthens the moment when, confronted by the body of the dead drunk, Lieutenant Kitsuragi asks the player not to collect the tare around the unfortunate corpse, as doing so would be disrespectful. The game enforces this moral value by making the tare inside the nearby wastebin examinable but not collectable.

As visible (or, rather, invisible) in Fig. 2.3, when the player does not have the Yellow Plastic Bag equipped, Lt. Kitsuragi makes no mention of tare.

This kind of branching will only be made apparent to players repeating the game, or accessing the same situations under different circumstances/with different tools equipped. While this may encourage some players to purposefully seek these moments of ludic recognition, for the majority of players they will serve the important function of making the player feel as though the game world is paying attention to her, a critical component of agency (Murray 2017; Taylor-Giles 2014). This imparts a sense of gravitas to the player's actions that may otherwise have been missing, and reinforces Lt. Kitsuragi's character and personal morals at the same time.

Fig. 2.3 A screenshot from Disco Elysium (2019), showing Lt. Kitsuragi's dialogue in the absence of the Yellow Plastic Bag

2.2.1.2   Illusory Listening

However, as with all player-based systems, it is best to be rigorous and avoid making assumptions. A less rigorous example than the previous one is an instance during Lt. Kitsuragi's evening debrief, where he comments on the player's actions during the first day of the investigation.

Temporality: Distant
Complexity: None
Effect: Minor (Fig. 2.4).

Unfortunately, the dialogue line saying that the player runs a lot is present in the conversation regardless of whether the player chose to walk or run for the entire day (Bell 2019). There are a couple of reasons why this might be the case: (1) Since traversal in video games often serves the function of "time" within video game worlds (Wei et al. 2010), many players will choose to run in order to compress the time between narrative beats. This is further supported by the in-game navigation which transitions from walk to run depending on how far away the player clicks; (2) It's not worth the amount of tracking that would be necessary to plot the player's trajectory for the entire course of the day in order to have an accurate record at the end.

In either case, the likelihood that Lt. Kitsuragi's line will correctly give the *illusion* that the game is listening to the player's actions is greater than the likelihood that his comment will be incorrect, at which point it becomes a question of realism versus replayability (Taylor-Giles 2020, pp. 299–300), and which only a dedicated replay of the entire first day would reveal to be a lie. This is therefore an example of

Fig. 2.4 A screenshot from Disco Elysium (2019), showing Lt. Kitsuragi's dialogue during the end of Day 1 debrief, which says: "What's with all the *running*? You run a lot."

non-systemic dialogue that feels as though it is systemic, which can be a solution to tracking certain complicated player behaviours as outlined above.

2.2.1.3   Complementarity and Modularity

Ultimately, in both of the previous examples, the situations described come with low stakes. The game does not hinge on how often the player walks or runs, nor on how much tare she collects. Therefore, any discrepancies are forgivable and even forgettable—because information is added in layers, any passed checks feel like additional insight (a bonus) rather than part of the core game flow.

A more complex check, and one which relies on the culmination of the player's choices up to this point, comes during a standoff with some mercenaries.

Temporality: Distant
Complexity: Complex
Effect: Profound.

The chained skill checks in Fig. 2.5 are those my character received. However, in order to uncover skill checks that I didn't successfully pass—or invisibly fail—would require returning with a different version of the player character, who had a different set of skills (otherwise known as a "build"). With 24 skills whose various levels determine success or failure, and the values of those skills incremented or decremented throughout the game up to this point, it would be possible, but incredibly time-consuming, to arrive at the same situation with unique builds in order to determine which lines were missed in each individual playthrough.

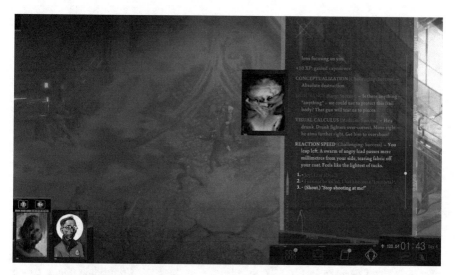

Fig. 2.5 A screenshot from Disco Elysium (2019), showing a series of chained successful skill checks

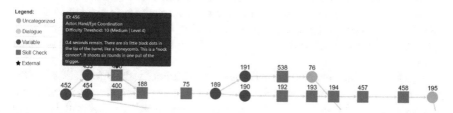

Fig. 2.6 A screenshot from Disco Reader (Eow 2020), showing a failed Hand/Eye Coordination check that did not appear in Fig. 2.5

Fortunately, Eow, a fan of the game, created a tool called the Disco Reader (2020) which allows anyone to search for certain phrases or actors and examine all of the possible dialogue choices and outcomes independent of the game.

Using this tool, it's possible to see what would have happened if my character's Hand/Eye Coordination skill had been lower (Fig. 2.6), or to see that the game elected to show a successful Visual Calculus check of Medium difficulty over an Endurance check of Easy difficulty (Fig. 2.7).

The benefit of this system—showing the player only the skill checks she passed (except in certain circumstances), and showing only the more difficult successes— leads to the sense that every additional fragment of dialogue has been earned by the player's choices, making them feel like rewards. Repeated successes—as in Fig. 2.5—coming as they do from the different "points of view" of the different skills, rarely overlap, yet when they do it is with complementary information. Given that no player character can excel in every skill during a single playthrough, this resolves into the possibility of a holistic view of each scenario, predicated upon replaying the

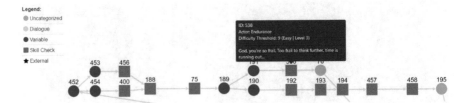

Fig. 2.7 A screenshot from Disco Reader (Eow 2020), showing an Easy Endurance check that was superseded by my success at a Medium Visual Calculus check in Fig. 2.5

game with many different builds, which is not necessary in any way to comprehend the scene as it plays out. These chained checks invite repetition without demanding it, a necessary element of player-centred branching conversation design (Taylor-Giles 2020).

Interestingly, succeeding at some checks also blocks the player from accessing others. As can be seen in Fig. 2.7, succeeding at the Easy Endurance check (node 191) but not the Medium Visual Calculus check (node 190) passes the player back to the previous choice hub (node 76), whereas succeeding at the Visual Calculus check opens up the possibility of further passive checks (readable in the Disco Reader interface) using Savoir Faire (Medium—node 193), Suggestion (Formidable—node 194), Esprit de Corps (Formidable—node 457), and Half Light (Legendary—node 458).

By chaining these checks in ascending order of difficulty, the information that the player receives gains in importance, making it feel as though the player character is synthesising information into increasingly relevant insights that will help him in the coming crisis. It also fulfils the illusion of stretching time, giving a sense of frenzy to the rapid-fire thoughts (successful passive checks) flooding the player with information, replicating a situation some people find themselves in when faced with unexpected or high-affect situations (e.g., an impending disaster) (Özoğlu and Thomaschke 2020, p. 301).

Once again, however, these additional insights are just that—additional. Since the player is unaware of the majority of the skill checks she fails, unless the failure is included to give the player insight into just how badly her character failed to read a situation and which provides its own kind of information, modularity in these information snippets is key. It is to *Disco Elysium*'s credit that each possible combination of successful skill checks flows seamlessly, both appearing to be the only possible course of events at any given moment <u>and</u> opening the player's mind to the possibility of different outcomes if she had specialised in different skills.

2.2.1.4 Conclusions

Disco Elysium uses NPC-side and skill-based branching to customize the player's experience of the game based on her playstyle. Driven by the player's actions either during the game or when choosing which skills to focus on, both types of branching feel like natural extensions of a world that observes as much as it is observed. This feeling of mutual regard encourages identification and investment on the part of the player, more so than in a situation where only dialogue choices result in consequences, and grounds the player character as an active inhabitant of the game's world instead of simply existing as a player-driven vehicle for accessing said world.

2.2.2   Case Study #2: Hades

Hades (2020) is an isometric roguelike brawler with a subtle integration of NPC-side branching. The most evident is when the player gets killed by a new type of enemy for the first time and winds up back in Hades—Hypnos, the underworld's clerk of sorts, welcomes the player's return with a comment about what killed her (Fig. 2.8).

There are, however, nuances to this system that are not immediately apparent unless looking at the game's code.

2.2.2.1   Granularity and Generality

Temporality: Immediate
Complexity: Minor
Effect: Moderate.

Fig. 2.8 A screenshot from Hades (2020), showing Hypnos' dialogue if the player is killed by a Wretched Lout-type enemy

The key to Hypnos' prescience lies in tracking which enemy caused the player's health to drop to, or below, zero. However, all lines of dialogue in Hades are voice-acted, meaning that care had to be taken to constrain the possible number of permutations that Hypnos could be called upon to respond to. It would also be necessary for him to be able to react to any enemies that were added after the game's release (or during its long Early Access period) without needing to go back to record additional voice lines for each iteration.[1]

Looking in the game files, then, it's possible to see that the Wretched Lout referenced in Fig 2.8 applies to two enemy types: "PunchingBagUnit" and "PunchingBagUnitElite". Some lines reference more than two enemy types; some are specific to only one. Since each line only plays once for each save file—the player is expected to die and return many times, but each instance does not result in a separate playthrough, merely the end of that particular "run"—it's unlikely someone simply playing the game would notice that specific lines apply to more than one type of enemy. Coupled with the fact that the player is more likely to die to an enemy the first time she encounters it, before she's figured out its pattern of attacks, it becomes vanishingly unlikely that any given player will encounter a variant on the base enemy type—as signified by appending "Elite" to the enemy's in-code name—before she has been killed by the basic version of that enemy. This results in what feels like a natural dialogue with Hypnos, where—in the case of more than one line for an enemy type—it appears as though he remembers the player's previous failures and comments on them accordingly.

2.2.2.2 Watching, but Not Stalking; a Guide to Recognizing Player Behaviour

Temporality: Distant
Complexity: Minor
Effect: Moderate.

These specific instances where Hypnos comments on the player being killed by the same enemy type for a second or third time—likely dictated by the frequency with which certain enemies occur—build the sense of a persistent and reactive world. They also act as a reward mechanism to alleviate player frustration, by providing a moment of humour or commiseration to soften the blow of having died yet again (Fig. 2.9).

The key to the efficacy of Hypnos' responses is two-fold: first, he expresses sympathy for the player and, while generally providing spurious advice on how to avoid dying next time, doing so at least makes it feel as though he is on the

---

[1]Although Supergiant Games has already released a substantial voice-over-related update to address a lack of variety in some character lines, this may not always be an option and certainly requires additional planning to ensure the most efficient use of resources, i.e., a large content update, as opposed to adding a line or two of additional VO.

Fig. 2.9 A screenshot from Hades (2020), showing Hypnos' dialogue if the player is killed by a Wretched Lout-type enemy for a second time

player's side; second, he rarely comments more than twice, to avoid cementing the player's failure and the risk of activating her shame reflex—the "specific discomfort produced by the sense of being looked at" (Cavell 2015, p. 278). As of this writing, the only instances for which Hypnos has more than two death reaction lines are mini-bosses, the ultimate boss, and the after-ultimate-boss (without going into spoilers).

There is another in-game event that Hypnos comments on which is worth mentioning here: how many times the player has died (Fig. 2.10).

Once again, the key to this feature being encouraging rather than frustrating is Hypnos' positive view of what would otherwise be regarded by the player as a failure. It also occurs relatively infrequently—the current code includes instances for 5, 50, 100, 300, and 500 deaths. These lines are probably queued to play—and are certainly written to play—any time there isn't a more specific line for Hypnos, for example dying to a new enemy type, or reaching a new area of the map.

To keep these comments relevant, they are also constrained to the player's progression: for example, the five deaths line in Fig. 2.10 will only trigger between four and ten completed runs (deaths). This avoids the case where Hypnos will be too far off from the player's actual number of deaths, and keeps his death-count-related remarks spaced reasonably far apart. If this were not the case, it would be possible to have Hypnos comment on the player's "at least five" deaths immediately before him commenting on her having died "fifty times *at least*!". The close occurrence of these comments would reveal a lack of granularity within the game's tracking systems and remind the player that she is interacting with lines of code instead of a character who is interested in and supportive of her progress throughout the game.

Fig. 2.10 A screenshot from Hades (2020), showing Hypnos' dialogue if the player has died five (or more) times, up to ten times

2.2.2.3   Interplay of Gods

Temporality: Distant
Complexity: Minor
Effect: Profound.

The final type of NPC-side branching to be discussed in *Hades*, though it is by no means the last of note within the game, is the dialogue triggered when the player accepts a boon (skill) from one god after having previously accepted a boon from a different god. Occasionally, the second god will comment on their relationship with the first, be it amity or rivalry (Fig. 2.11).

This builds upon the narrative illusion that the gods of Olympus are following the actions of the player character, Zagreus, which remains a key plot point throughout the game. It also identifies to the player, in very few words, the kind of political infighting of which she may not be aware if she has never studied Greek mythology. For example, Ares' other lines include one for Dionysus: "*That drunkard Dionysus cannot help you near as much as I, my hell-born kin. Compare the gift he gave to what I offer you.*" whereas his line about Zeus is far more respectful: "*Lord Zeus has gotten to you first, I see? My father's gifts are generous, indeed, though... I think I can help in my own way.*"

There are also instances where the player is offered the choice between the boons of two gods—in such a case, the spurned god will try to kill the player. This becomes understandably strange if they have previously granted the player the use of their power in the form of an activatable skill that the player can now use against them. In narrative terms, it means the player is asking the gods to help her defeat themselves,

Fig. 2.11 A screenshot from Hades (2020), showing Ares' dialogue if the player has previously accepted a skill from Aphrodite during the same run

which Zagreus responds to by saying *"Sorry!"* or *"This is awkward!"* among other lines.

Both types of dialogue—comments from gods about other gods, and Zagreus' reactions to using a god's own power against them—support the conception of the world as a persistent space in which the player's actions have both consequence and meaning. By implicating the player in existing interpersonal relationships, and through the narrative device that the gods can speak to Zagreus but not hear him, the game builds a world in which the player has a place where she can belong, if only she's able to reach it.

2.2.2.4   Conclusions

Hades makes use of NPC-side branching in incredibly specific ways. While there are some dialogue sequences that only play after certain other dialogue sequences have been heard, or other gameplay-specific conditions have been met, the majority of the lines that the player will hear were written to play only once, in one particular situation. This specificity supports the notion that the characters the player is interacting with are aware of their previous statements, as well as the player's actions, rendering both meaningful through their transience. The game also includes multiple variations for those lines which the player is guaranteed to hear repeatedly, such as when Zagreus accepts a boon from a god or when he dies and returns to Tartarus, continuing the illusion of a persistent and reactive world. Thus, with specificity and multiplicity, *Hades* constructs a world that has been praised for its depth (Park 2020), all while staying below the budget of lines usually allocated to the main characters of a AAA game of similar length.

2.2.3 Case Study #3: The Signifier

The final case study in this chapter is a game constructed around the concept of objectivity and subjectivity. In *The Signifier* (2020), the player must attempt to sort through the stored memories of a dead woman to determine her cause of death. While *The Signifier* does include a choice-based dialogue interface and a largely linear story, at the end of the game its attention to the player's actions and attitude becomes resoundingly evident.

2.2.3.1 This Marriage Between Complexity and Time

Temporality: Distant
Complexity: Accumulative
Effect: Profound.

Throughout *The Signifier*, the player is constantly required to view scenes from multiple levels of abstraction, interpreting subjective data based on known facts and examining why events or people take the shapes that they do within the deceased woman's memories (Fig. 2.12). This investigation is at the core of what *The Signifier*

Fig. 2.12 A screenshot from The Signifier (2020), showing a key scene from the end of the game

accomplishes with its ending, in embracing multiplicity in a way that is convincingly tailored to the expressed opinions of the player.

There are several perfect listening devices built into the story in service of the abstraction that reflects the player's decisions at the end. First, there is Evee, the artificial intelligence operated by voice command who manages the loading and parsing of the dead woman's memories. Since a lot of the game takes place in the player character's laboratory, it's reasonable to assume that Evee is aware of all of the player's decisions within that space. The second listening device is the player character's daughter, who has a connection to the deceased woman that can only be discovered by confronting her with evidence from within the reconstructed memories. And the third, though not final, listening device is the player character's own psyche. There are comments and notes about keeping the subjective state of the recorded memories separate from the subjective interpretations of the observer that come into startling focus during the game's climax.

It's through these channels that the game has a visible pathway to connect the player's actions with the eventual outcome of her investigation. Its abstraction of the player's choices is both complex and removed in time, so that the ending the player sees feels like the only natural outcome of her actions. Inevitability is a core theme of the game's story, yet the different ways it can be expressed or fought against form the basis for the variations that lend the ending such pathos.

2.2.3.2 Why Would I Mind to Be Two Again?

Spoilers for *The Signifier* follow.

At the end of the game, the player is trapped inside the simulation, along with an amalgamation of the dead woman's memories and the player's artificial intelligence, Evee. That entity speaks with and over itself, different voices layering meaning in response to the same questions. For example, the voice of Evee will often cover simple concepts, such as a mug or a tree, while the voice of Johanna, the dead woman, will cover more abstract (human) concepts, such as a window or a horizon.

In one of the rooms in the ending sequence, the player will always hear the following poem, spoken by Johanna and Evee both together and separately.

(Lines spoken by both are in **bold**, lines spoken by Evee are <u>underlined</u>, and lines spoken by Johanna are *italicised*.)**After all, I'm all that stays/** <u>Behind the curtains,</u> *beneath the waves . . . /***And I may be frightened**, *born* <u>unsaid</u>/**But after all**, <u>I'm all that's there</u>/*So who are we* (Who are we?), **in this shell of tales/***That will be gossip*, and empty games/**After all, we're all that's there/Beneath the surface**, *behind the veil*.

The intertwining of the voices further serves to emphasise those moments when they deviate, either from one another, in conflict, or in different endings that the player can witness depending on her choices, each of which constitutes "an irreversible act in which uncertainty collapses to certainty" (Wheeler 1998, p. 337, as cited in Cobley 2018). For example, in choosing to tell the amalgamation that another character is dead, the player will hear either "I used him. I feel so sad for

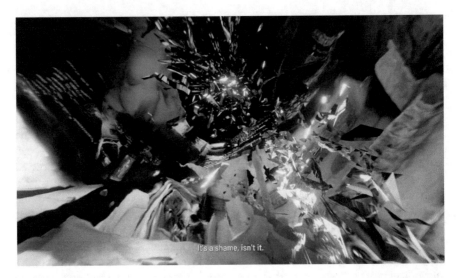

Fig. 2.13 A screenshot from The Signifier (2020), showing a key scene from the end of the game with the subtitle "It's a shame, isn't it."

him." or "She used him. She's so sorry for him." indicating the degree to which Evee has identified with and taken on the characteristics of Johanna, a decision which is influenced by the player's choices at key moments.

These touches, while subtle, provide insight into the different facets of the personalities of both Johanna and Evee, in direct response to the player's previously-expressed opinions of those facets. For example, if the player sided with the mask representing Johanna's father during the night club sequence, she cannot speak to her in the ending as that facet of Johanna's personality has been consumed by shame. If the player restores the relationship between the player character and the player character's daughter, Laura, by expressing acceptance and tolerance, yet still forces Johanna's psyche to collapse under the burden of shame, Laura's parting words ("You seem like a different person.") will end up in Evee's vocabulary when asked what she wants. And, as a final example, how the player treated the people she encountered during the game—including Johanna, the dead woman—will determine her own fate at the end (Fig. 2.13).

2.2.3.3 Conclusions

The Signifier is a masterclass in organic NPC-side branching. Its ending both employs inevitability and irony and reinforces the player's own notions of who Johanna is, based on decisions made during her investigation. Although the calculations behind the scenes may be relatively simple, the end result establishes the player as an integral and irremovable link in the chain of cause and consequence that suffuses the game's parallel stories. Not knowing which moments contribute to which parts of the ending leads a curious player to tease apart every possible decision point in search of the complete truth about Johanna, mimicking and mirroring the core conceit by inducing real-world behaviours and reinforcing the title of the game: the search for the Master Signifier.

Ultimately, the player can only arrive at her own interpretation of Johanna and the events that led to her death, as would be the case in real life. It remains to be seen whether the upcoming Director's Cut of the game provides more information, and therefore a more authored experience. However, in the spirit of semiotics it seems likely that these events will nonetheless remain open to interpretation, retaining the game's collaborative storytelling approach that places the player simultaneously in the role of both the observer and the observed (Cobley 2018) while ensuring her presence remains integral to the story.

2.3 Best Practices for NPC-Side Branching

While each of the case studies detailed above differs in their methods of implementing NPC-side branching, there are certain easily replicable components that can be used in any game, and specifically in games which have a limited localisation or recording budget. These best practices combine reactivity with precision to encourage the player to believe that the game world is watching her actions, that she is an embedded and remarkable inhabitant with interpersonal importance to the NPCs around her, thereby increasing her sense of agency.

2.3.1 Additive Dialogue

This type of dialogue includes the option to add an additional line along the critical path for players who meet certain conditions. For example, if the player arrived more quickly than the NPC expected, or if she has developed a reputation as a certain kind of person that the NPC might have heard of, the NPC can comment on it before continuing with the rest of the conversation (Fig. 2.14).

Additive dialogue is best implemented during low-stress situations, where conversational digressions or asides wouldn't seem out of place or forced.

2.3.2 Alternate Dialogue

This type of dialogue includes the option for mutually-exclusive responses to player behaviour. For example, if the player killed a lot of enemies on her way to the NPC, or if she avoided all of them through stealth gameplay (and the NPC is in a position to be aware of the player's actions) the NPC can comment on it. It can also be

Fig. 2.14 A graph showing
additive dialogue

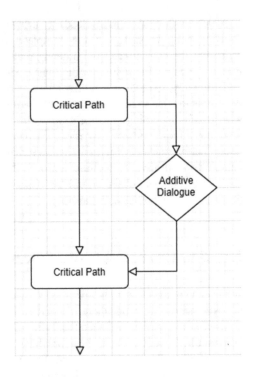

easily applied to other areas of the game, such as quest outcomes, player character
equipment, or time spent performing certain tasks (Fig. 2.15).

For a more robust system, it's also possible to include a link directly between the
two Critical Path lines, in case the player mixed several playstyles or didn't reach
the threshold for either dialogue line. In that case, the diagram would look like this
Fig. 2.16.

It's important to remember that *not* commenting on player behaviour if it doesn't
reach specific, pre-determined thresholds is also its own kind of reactivity. Better
to not react to player behaviour than to incorrectly react to player behaviour, as the
latter foregrounds the constraints of the game's design and dismantles the player's
sense of agency.

Alternate dialogue can be used in high-stress or emotional conversations, due to
the fact that its inclusion is part of the dialogue's core flow, i.e., the content of the
alternate nodes follows the critical path discussion in both tone and subject.

Alternate dialogue is not suitable when the NPC that the player is speaking with
has no strong opinion on the subject at hand, because that indifference will render
the alternate dialogue lines meaningless (and make them difficult to write).

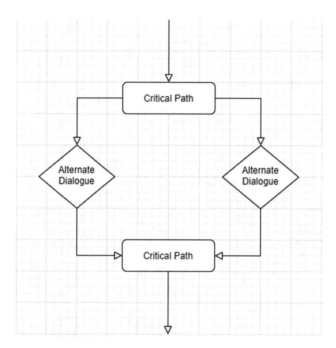

Fig. 2.15   A graph showing alternate dialogue lines

2.3.3   Building on Expectations

In order to have appropriate granularity and generality, as discussed in the cases of both *Disco Elysium* and *Hades*, it's necessary to assign ranges to player behaviour, rather than specific numbers. For example, a best-guess scenario for a given CRPG which has been separated into gameplay segments may have cumulative totals that look something like Table 2.1.

It is key, however, that these guesses are supported by or updated using playtest data. For example, players may be far more or far less likely to die than Table 2.1 indicates; similarly, they may kill more or fewer enemies than the averages listed.

If the system is set up correctly—as discussed in the next section—changing these numbers will require minimal effort for an enhanced player experience. Ensuring that dialogue responds appropriately to the player's level and type of engagement with the game world is crucial to selling NPCs as real characters and not merely people-shaped objects accessing lookup tables.

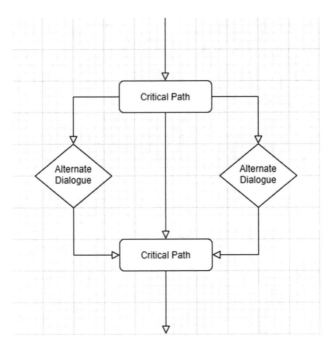

Fig. 2.16 A graph showing alternate dialogue lines with a direct link to the next conversation node, in case the player did not meet the conditions for either path

Table 2.1 Example variables that could be tracked as the player progresses through 4 segments of gameplay

Variable	Expected segment 1	Expected segment 2	Expected segment 3	Expected segment 4
TreasureFound	3	7	12	21
QuestsCompleted	1	3	5	7
RiddlesSolved	0	0	1	2
PCDeaths	1	8	16	32
NPCsSaved	3	3	9	12
EnemiesKilled	5	15	30	50
AlliesKilled	1	1	2	3

2.3.4 Anonymizing Player Data

The way to keep NPCs sounding human is to obfuscate the direct line between a variable and the NPC's reaction to it. Part of that is ensuring that every character doesn't care about every single event in the world. For example, as in Fig. 2.17 a Quest NPC who the player speaks with once or twice will generally only have one interest—themselves. A Secondary NPC, who the player may interact with several times, may have two interests—the political and the social structures of the

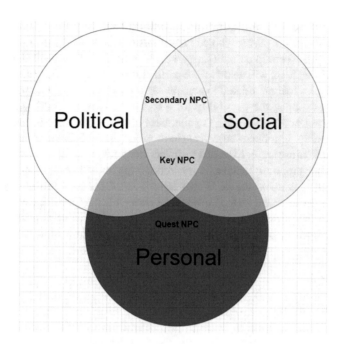

Fig. 2.17 A Venn diagram showing the topics of interest to different classes of NPCs

Table 2.2 Example adjectives that could be applied to variable-derived player data

Variable	Low number	High number
TreasureFound	Straight-forward	Detail-oriented
QuestsCompleted	Focussed	Capable
RiddlesSolved	No-nonsense	Thoughtful
PCDeaths	Careful	Impulsive
NPCsSaved	Expedient	Altruistic
EnemiesKilled	Restrained	Aggressive
AlliesKilled	Loyal	Determined

world they live in. And a Key NPC, who the player speaks with frequently, or who accompanies the player on her journey, can care about all aspects of life, because their ongoing relationship with the player affords them the space to discuss more than one topic of importance.

Keeping in mind, then, that NPCs should only ever react to variables that they a) could reasonably have access to in a game-world context and b) only relate to those issues that are of interest to or directly affect them, it will be necessary to develop a table of reactions similar to Table 2.2.

When writing, it's important to understand how gameplay-related traits would be expressed by the player in visible ways. For example, a player who has found a lot of treasure may have equipped more expensive or magical items, allowing an NPC to comment on her general appearance. She may also have taken longer to arrive at a location where the NPC was expecting her, adding another dimension on which the NPC can comment. A player who has few allies (because she killed more of them) yet has arrived at a certain point in the game, meaning she accomplished great things with little evident help, will also evoke a particular response from an interested NPC. Finally, variables that are related to general word-of-mouth—i.e., QuestsCompleted or NPCsSaved—open the possibility for a socially-connected NPC (e.g., one in a city, not one out in the wilderness) to comment on the player's reputation.

When developing a list of adjectives to describe player behaviour, however, it is vital to **ensure those adjectives are positive**. Remember that the player is playing the game in her preferred manner; if the actions she undertakes are undesirable for the developer, it is up to the developer to stop her from performing them, rather than chastise her after the fact. This does not mean that NPCs must always respond favourably to the player, but *developers* need to keep a positive mindset regarding different methods of play, and provide in-game rewards (i.e., additional dialogue) accordingly.

2.4 Conclusions

Questions to ask when writing NPC-side branching dialogues.

Including NPC-side branching within linear games provides the player with both an increased sense of agency and ownership over the game's storyline. Establishing her as a critical component of the game's world and the player character as an active inhabitant of that world, instead of merely an empty vessel which the player must pilot to interact with the game's systems, grounds her in a sense of time and place that is conducive to immersion and emotional attachment.

In the interests of creating a cohesive yet responsive world, the following questions are aimed at helping to situate possible branching NPC dialogue moments within the game's context, and at keeping the dialogue constrained where possible so as not to add unnecessarily to the game's writing, recording, and localization budgets.

1. Does the NPC have access to this data through in-world channels?
2. Is the topic something the NPC cares about or which affects them directly?
3. Is the NPC willing to risk angering the player, e.g., by calling them aggressive or war-mongering, if they know that the player has a habit of killing people who displease them?
4. Will the NPC's reaction to the player break the critical path by creating a situation in which the NPC would no longer be willing to speak to or work with the player? If so, what are the alternative methods by which the player can continue the game?
5. Are the default values for each variable (and therefore their High/Low thresholds) based on replicable playtest data?

6. Is the NPC commenting on something which the player had no control over, e.g., gender or race when the player character is pre-defined; combat propensity if no equally-accessible stealth mechanic exists, etc.?
7. Does this additional dialogue add to the player's understanding of the NPC or of the world in which the game takes place?
8. Does it feel natural for the NPC to insert an additional line of dialogue between two others, or does the momentum of the conversation prohibit linguistic asides?
9. Has another NPC referenced the same variable in recent memory (to be defined according to play session length or other factors)?
10. Are the additive or alternate lines written in such a way as to convey that they are based on the player's actions but that they don't necessarily define or constrain the player's options in the future?
11. If providing negative feedback on the player's playstyle, will the opportunity to prove the NPC wrong be available in the immediate future?

Following these guidelines will provide increased reactivity in direct response to player agency. Making the player feel both seen and heard will enable her to reflect on her gameplay choices within a linear narrative in the same way she might reflect on moral quandaries introduced within branching dialogues in other games, contributing to her self-understanding and encouraging more mindful play.

References

J.J. Abrams, From Sherlock Holmes to the hard-boiled detective in Film Noir, in *The Philosophy of Film Noir*, ed. by M. T. Conard, R. Porfirio, (University Press of Kentucky, Lexington, KY, 2006), pp. 69–88

Bell, *Wot I Think: Disco Elysium* (2019). https://www.rockpapershotgun.com/2019/10/15/disco-elysium-review

Bethesda Game Studios, *The Elder Scrolls V: Skyrim [Computer Software]* (Bethesda Softworks, LLC, Rockville, MD, 2011)

BioWare, *Mass Effect [Computer Software]* (Electronic Arts, Redwood City, CA, 2007)

BioWare, *Dragon Age: Origins [Computer Software]* (Electronic Arts, Redwood City, CA, 2009)

B. Bostan, Ö. Yönet, V. Sevdimaliyev, Empathy and choice in story driven Games: a case study of telltale Games, in *Game User Experience and Player-Centered Design*, (Springer, Berlin, 2020), pp. 361–378

S. Cavell, The avoidance of love: a reading of king Lear, in *Must We Mean What We Say?: A Book of Essays. Cambridge Philosophy Classics*, (Cambridge University Press, Cambridge, 2015), pp. 246–325. https://doi.org/10.1017/CBO9781316286616.014

P. Cobley, Observership, knowing, and semiosis. Cybern. Hum. Know. **25**(1), 23–47 (2018)

M. Consalvo, T. Busch, C. Jong, Playing a better me: how players rehearse their ethos via moral choices. Games Cult. **14**(3), 216–235 (2019)

Eidos Montreal, *Deus ex: Human Revolution [Computer Software]* (Square Enix, El Segundo, CA, 2011)

D.N. Eow, *Disco Reader* (2020). https://disco-reader.gitlab.io/disco-reader/#/. For the graph of Lt. Kitsuragi asking the player not to collect tare around the dead body on the boardwalk, search for "tare" with Actor Kim Kitsuragi. For the graph of the interaction with the stained glass window (chained Conceptualization & Empathy checks) search for Actor Stained Glass Window. For the graph of the interaction with the gun (Visual Calculus check) search for "lightest"

J. Fraser, I. Papaioannou, O. Lemon, Spoken conversational AI in video games: emotional dialogue management increases user engagement, in *Proceedings of the 18th International Conference on Intelligent Virtual Agents* (2018), pp. 179–184

inXile Entertainment, *Torment: Tides of Numenera [Computer Software]* (Techland Publishing, Wrocław, 2017)

J. Katsarov, M. Christen, R. Mauerhofer, D. Schmocker, C. Tanner, Training moral sensitivity through video games: a review of suitable game mechanisms. Games Cult. **14**(4), 344–366 (2019)

J.H. Murray, *Hamlet on the Holodeck: The Future of Narrative in Cyberspace* (MIT Press, Cambridge, MA, 2017)

E. Özoğlu, R. Thomaschke, Knowing your heart reduces emotion-induced time dilation. Timing Time Percept. **8**, 299–315 (2020)

Park, G, *Here's How 'Hades' Makes Going Back to Hell Feel Fresh* (2020). https://www.washingtonpost.com/video-games/2020/10/13/hades-game-origins

Playmestudio, *The Signifier [Computer Software]* (Raw Fury, Stockholm, 2020)

M. Sicart, *Beyond Choices: The Design of Ethical Gameplay* (MIT Press, Cambridge, MA, 2013)

Supergiant Games, *Hades [computer software]* (Supergiant Games, San Francisco, CA, 2020) Early access release date: 2018, December 6

L. C. Taylor-Giles, *Toward a Deeper Understanding of Branching Dialogue Systems*. Masters Dissertation, Queensland University of Technology, (2014)

L. Taylor-Giles, Player-centred design in role-playing game branching dialogue systems, in *Game User Experience and Player-Centered Design*, (Springer, Cham, 2020), pp. 295–325

H. Wei, J. Bizzocchi, T. Calvert, Time and space in digital game storytelling. Int. J. Comput. Games Technol. **2010**, 1–23 (2010)

J.A. Wheeler, (with Ford, K.) *Geons, Black Holes and Quantum Foam: A Life in Physics* (Norton, New York, 1998)

ZA/UM, *Disco Elysium [Computer Software]* (ZA/UM, London, 2019)

Chapter 3
Breaking the Fourth Wall in Video Games: A New Terminology and Methodology

Öznur Özdal and Güven Çatak

3.1 Introduction

Videogame culture is not a foreigner to the narrative concepts and terms recruited from other mediums, such as plot, theme, setting, and many others. Furthermore, various visual and auditory techniques conventional in videogame design had already existed for several years in visual and performance arts. Due to having such a vast amount of aspects in common, the fourth wall break concept has also found its route to the existing videogame design terminology.

The emerging issue with this conception is that the interactive nature of the videogame medium does not offer the grounds on which the term aforementioned nestles without doubt. Even though there are various examples of traditional fourth wall breaks in video games, with a medium that is dependent on the input of the player, it is nonsensical to imagine a transparent wall that separates the player and the medium.

A qualitative study conducted on experienced and inexperienced players to test the idea of expanding and contracting magic circle by Conway, resulted that the non-traditional fourth wall breaks in video games can be applied as tools to immerse the player further in the gameplay instead of just being humorous encounters (Jesper 2016).

Though there are various design techniques of breaking the fourth wall for other mediums, fourth wall break techniques for videogames, do not have a proper

Ö. Özdal (✉)
BoomHits, Gdańsk, Poland
e-mail: oznur.ozdal@boombit.com

G. Çatak
Department of Digital Game Design, Bahçeşehir University, Istanbul, Turkey
e-mail: guven.catak@comm.bau.edu.tr

© The Author(s), under exclusive license to Springer Nature Switzerland AG 2022
B. Bostan (ed.), *Games and Narrative: Theory and Practice*, International Series on
Computer Entertainment and Media Technology,
https://doi.org/10.1007/978-3-030-81538-7_3

framework. Given the interactive nature of the medium, even though there are many ways to make use of this technique, there is no collective study with different examples of how to implement them into the videogame experience, enhancing the experience further without disrupting the immersion of the player.

This study provides a concise definition of the fourth wall in accordance with the videogame medium, the classification of various techniques that have already been applied and an implementation guideline for the designers to utilize. Various examples of the technique from different games are offered classifying the type of the technique used, allowing the designers to have an understanding of the state of the final products featuring the techniques. The chosen examples not only feature the fine usage of the methods, but also the misuse or overuse of the technique leading to player frustration.

3.2 Literature Review

When you write or act, think no more of the audience than if it had never existed. Imagine a huge wall across the front of the stage, separating you from the audience, and behave exactly as if the curtain had never risen (Diderot 1758)

'Breaking the fourth wall' relates to any practice which seeks to dispel the illusion that the audience is watching a slice of 'real-life'. Coleridge (1817) first coined the term "suspension of disbelief" and described it as the cessation of judgement towards the questionable nature of the narrative, given the writer could infuse a "human interest and a semblance of truth" into a marvellous tale (Coleridge 2014). Therefore, breaking the fourth wall is essentially breaking the suspension of disbelief. The same expression is also used in relation to film and fiction to describe a text's acknowledgement of its artifice, which is usually achieved by a direct address to the audience.

Originally, the fourth wall is a theatrical term used by seventeenth-century French dramatist Molière, but the idea of such a division is attributed to French philosopher Denis Diderot. The term signifies the invisible 'wall' dividing the theatre audience from performance, especially that taking place in a three-walled box set of a proscenium theatre. Diderot believed that establishing such separation between the performance and the audience would assure faithful enaction of everyday reality. Therefore, the term is firmly associated with nineteenth-century realism in the European theatre (Cuddon et al. 2013).

The concept of a fourth transparent wall was widely criticized in the twentieth century due to its disruptiveness towards dramatic literary devices such as soliloquy, chorus, aside, etc. These devices would unify the audience and the performers in the same theatrical space. Correspondingly appeared the dramatic device "Breaking the fourth wall", a special technique of modernist theatre. Even though the method was used in theatre since antiquity, the appearance of the term would standardize the use of the device and the variety of the techniques to apply it (Davis 2015).

Bertolt Brecht is the playwright to attribute the development of the technique, even though he was not the first modernist to use it. Until his approach, the device had appeared to achieve a comedic effect in early twentieth century films of Chaplin and Keaton. Brecht was the first to seriously consider the social, political, and philosophical implications of the technique and made use of the device to transmit direct messages to the audience (Davis 2015). His technique Verfremdungseffekt – loosely translated as Alienation Effect – was deployed to disrupt the impulse towards realism. The effect was achieved through captions, songs, role reversals and artificial narrative interventions to maintain a critical detachment from the play rather than submitting to the staged illusion or easy emotional identification with character or situation. The purpose of the effect was to change the perception of the work as a dramatic illusion and construct. Via this distancing or estrangement, the work creates resistance to passive escapism and compels reflection on the characters as participants in broader historical, social and political processes (Cuddon et al. 2013).

As a trademark of post-modernist literature, the technique manifests itself as metafiction, a term coined in 1970 by William H. Gass to define the so-called anti-novels. In the opening chapter of her book Metafiction, Patricia Waugh explains the term 'metalanguage' developed by linguist L. Hjelmslev in 1961 as the root of the term metafiction. According to Hjelmslev "a metalanguage is a language which, instead of referring to non-linguistic events, situations or objects in the world, refers to another language: it is a language which takes another language as its object". Waugh also quotes from Goffman "in novelistic practice, this results in writing which consistently displays its conventionality, which explicitly and overtly lays bare its condition of artifice, and which thereby explores the problematic relationship between life and fiction – both the fact that 'all the world is not, of course, a stage' and 'the crucial ways in which it isn't" (Jefferson and Waugh 1984).

Throughout the history of the video game medium, about the instances in which the medium consciously oversteps the boundaries between the game world and the real world, the terms that have been applied to the technique are breaking the fourth wall or metafiction, the literary devices that are primarily defined for theatre or literature. The metafiction may be regarded as more of an umbrella term; still, the videogame medium has its unique status as an interactive medium; therefore, it requires its own terminology. Videogames do not automatically provide the player a new fictional and immersive world where he/she may enter and experience. Instead, it requires the active participation of the player (Keogh 2014). In her book Hamlet on the Holodeck, Janet Murray (1997) notes:

> When we enter a fictional world, we do not merely "suspend" a critical faculty; we also exercise a creative faculty. We do not suspend disbelief so much as we actively create belief. Because of our desire to experience immersion, we focus our attention on the enveloping world, and we use our intelligence to reinforce rather than to question the reality of the experience. (Murray 1997, p. 121)

Attempting a new conception of the fourth wall in game terminology, Steven Conway revisits the magic circle concept attributed to Huizinga and defines the technique according to the videogame medium as expansions and contractions of the magic circle. According to Conway, when the make-believe world of videogames expands to the real world surrounding the technological apparatus of the medium or paratexts packaged with the game, the expansion of the magic circle occurs. The contractions, however, happen when the magic circle excludes the player by shrinking behind the display, e.g. Sonic tapping his foot on the floor, annoyedly looking at the screen or the game crashing.

In his study, Conway also affirms the convenience of using the traditional fourth wall break concept in the following cases:

- A character directly talking to the player,
- A display of self-awareness by the product to its status as a videogame,
- Referring to an artefact, event or person that is obviously outside the fictional world of the game.

As put forward by Conway (2010), instead of labelling these instances as fourth wall breaks, we need a new terminology that is applicable to the videogame medium.

3.3   Towards a Conclusive Terminology and Framework

> All play moves and has its being within a playground marked off beforehand either materially or ideally, deliberately or as a matter of course. Just as there is no formal difference between play and ritual, so the "consecrated spot" cannot be formally distinguished from the playground. The arena, the card-table, the magic circle, the temple, the stage, the screen, the tennis court, the court of justice, etc., are all in form and function playgrounds, i.e. forbidden spots, isolated, hedged round, hallowed, within which special rules obtain. All are temporary worlds within the ordinary world, dedicated to the performance of an act apart (Huizinga 1949)

Attributed to Dutch historian Johan Huizinga (1949), the magic circle is a term condemned continuously by academics for defining game worlds as formal structures that precisely separates the game experience from the ordinary life. Ongoing debates feature various definitions that limit or delimit, open or close, shape-shift the concept that it is impossible to use the term without choosing from one of the definitions and adjusting it according to the context of the study subject.

In his study, Jaakko Stenros (2014) interprets various definitions of the concept magic circle and argues that the reason for the term to be debated as such, the implications of a border that delimits an instance of playing resonates as if it creates an enclosed and separate space for the play to happen. Furthermore, the description of the magic circle by Salen and Zimmerman (2003) happens to coincide with this type of definition of the concept, even though it was a tool for the designers that should be evaluated based on its utility. Providing a collection of descriptions that classifies the boundaries of the magic circle as social, mental and cultural, Stenros creates a pathway for the academics to use the term according to the context of their study.

In this study, the magic circle is treated as a playground defined by Huizinga, a temporary world with permeable boundaries within the ordinary world, dedicated to the performance of an act apart dependent on rules, where the player finds himself/herself in an Apterian psychological bubble in a paratelic state. Paratelic is a playful mindset characterized by freedom and is voluntary. Apter describes this space as a small and manageable private realm that may be shared, and temporarily the outside world problems cannot intrude. Even if the real world permeates this virtual world, it would be transformed in the process, not being able to harm (Kerr and Apter 1990).

This psychological bubble encompasses all aspects of videogames from the virtual game world to its paratexts. In videogames, the player enters the magic circle by "plugging himself into a cybernetic circuit" (Giddings 2005). During videogame play, the body of the player becomes hybridized, incorporating body, hardware and virtual aspect of the game world. This circuit requires the player to become cyborgian, that cannot be separated from the videogame play (Hayles 1999).

3.4 Magic Circle Manipulation as an Umbrella Term

As formerly stated, to create a framework for the so-called fourth wall breaks in digital games, this study will utilize Conway's idea of referring to the fourth wall as the magic circle since it is a fictional world that the player enters while playing a game. It is a temporary world with permeable boundaries, dependent on rules, dedicated to an act apart and the player enters this world voluntarily with a paratelic state of mind. Conway's study (2010) on magic circle's expansions and contractions refers to the player as if he/she was a passive observer that could be included in or excluded from the magic circle when the design decisions reach out to the non-diegetic elements of the game or when the game decides to shut the player out for misbehaving. This approach disregards the player's condition in the circuit, where both the player and the game share an active agency when they each provide, decipher and resolve the actions of the other, and this creates a hybrid of the player and the game (Keogh 2014). Activity and passivity are fluctuations in videogame play, not complete opposites (Kennedy and Giddings 2008, p. 30). Therefore, it is impossible to consider the player as a separate part of the videogame, that is continuously in or out of the magic circle.

When the designer decides that the game AI will be able to alter the rules, include the paratexts, or reach out to the non-diegetic elements, the aim is not to pacify the player or to contract the magic circle. One of the goals is to create a power battle between the player and the game, which forces them to be creative to overcome the challenges presented. Not only this creativity may manifest itself as the player opening the console in *Max Payne* (Remedy Entertainment 2001) and writing GetAllWeapons to obtain all the weapons not deserved, but also Monica erasing all the other club members from the game files to make the player fall in love with her in *Doki Doki Literature Club* (Team Salvato 2017). This power battle makes the player feel more challenged since the characters they come across behaves as if they were humans and just like the player, they also try to beat the game to go on with the next challenge. Indeed, creating a power battle is not the only aim to manipulate the magic circle. Also, utilizing the techniques, the designer may aim to navigate the player or evoke certain feelings. When Psycho Mantis in *Metal Gear Solid* (Konami Computer Entertainment Japan 1998) activates the in-built rumble function of the controller of PSX to move it sideways, the goal is to intimidate the player and inform him/her that the villain he/she came across is not an ordinary character. When Sam in *Death Stranding* (Kojima Productions 2019) winks at the player, he intends to create a solidarity and encourages the player to bear with him the exhausting missions that the game offers. When he shouts "I'm Sam" towards the wilderness and receives an unexpected answer; "Hey, my name is Sam, too!", it gives the player an escape from the loneliness of the post-apocalyptic world and a feeling of hope and joy.

The next part of this study will provide magic circle manipulation techniques classifying manifestations from various video games. The umbrella term that will encapsulate all the methods is Magic Circle Manipulation, and it encompasses two subgroups as magic circle deformation and magic circle perforation. While magic circle deformation consists of techniques that previously referred to as expansions and contractions, magic circle perforation will classify the traditional fourth wall break techniques according to the videogame terminology. Also, the implementation methods to the dramatic elements of the game will be introduced with examples. Conclusively, the aims of the methods will be covered from the player experience perspective.

3.4.1   Magic Circle Deformation

When the synthetic game world expands beyond the screen and invites the technological apparatus or the paratexts packaged with the game into the gameplay experience, the magic circle expands to immerse the player further. The contractions occur when the magic circle shrinks behind the display (Conway 2010). The definition provided by Conway falls short of mentioning the simultaneous shape-shifting phenomena that may occur with the combined use of the techniques. While this deformation occurs, the player is an element of the game that is continuously allowed or denied the control. While the immersive nature of the game stays intact, the challenge for the player is to keep up with the game's new dynamics that emerge with the use of the methods. Even though the player becomes a passive onlooker, his immersed state continues, and the player looks for alternative solutions to gain power to advance in the game. Therefore, he/she is still a part of the magic circle, but the circle commences to behave unconventionally, shattering player expectations. The reason for renaming it as deformation, the playground that the player is a part of is now a twisted place, deforming its previous state as a rulebound and separate place for the videogame experience.

3.4.1.1 Non-diegetic Play

When the non-diegetic elements of the videogame such as the user interface, HUD, character subtitles, loading screens, game menu or on-screen buttons are accessed by the game's characters or the game itself and used unconventionally, the magic circle deforms, and this leads to an alteration in player's expectations of the game. This type of deformation is prevalent; thus, there are many examples throughout videogame history.

Undertale (2015) Created by indie developer Toby Fox (2015), *Undertale* is a game that uses various techniques to manipulate the magic circle. Normally, the game offers a pacifist mode, where the player can use the mercy button to continue without killing. When the boss Asgore appears, he destroys the mercy button, leaving the player no choice but to fight him until the end. The accessibility of a UI element by a game character is an evident deformation that delimits the player's options creating a power battle.

3.4.1.2 Medium Play

When the game commences behaving unexpectedly, accessing and altering the platform-specific hardware or software of the videogame, the deformation occurs. The method may incorporate various elements of the system, such as console buttons, controllers, memory card, game code, online gaming platforms, and others. The effect may manifest itself as glitches, errors, unconventional use of the system elements, etc.

Pony Island (2016) Asmodeus, one of the boss demons of the arcade hell *Pony Island* (Daniel Mullins Games 2016) asks the player basic questions, and his primary demand is not to lose focus. First, he asks the player his own name, since it is written directly under his avatar, he lowers the player's expectations towards difficulty. And then he asks the player to write down something disgusting. After the player writes whatever comes to his mind, Steam messages start to appear on their usual place on the screen. Distracted by the ongoing messages that appear to be coming from player's friend including the disgusting word previously entered, the player loses focus and cannot catch the next thing Asmodeus asks him/her to write. Only after being defeated, the player realizes that the game has been creating the messages through Steam interface.

3.4.1.3 Real-World Play

When the game includes paratexts, internet searches or use of information or objects specific to the real world, the magic circle deforms. The game's manual, its website, real-world objects may be incorporated into the gameplay to achieve the deformation and change the player's preconception of the game.

StarTropics (1990) Soaking the game's paratexts – a letter in this case - in water may sound extreme, but this is precisely what the player must do to advance in *Startropics* (Nintendo R&D3 and Locomotive Corporation 1990). Mike, the main protagonist of the game, needs to use his uncle's submarine, and it does not operate without two codes. He learns the first code from his uncle's assistant, but the second one is nowhere to be found. When the assistant reveals the first code appearing to be possessed, he also tells Mike to dip the letter in water. The player may search all the depths of the game world; it does not exist in the game. It may be evil or genius, dipping the letter that comes with the packaging of the game in water reveals the code to operate the submarine.

3.4.2   Magic Circle Perforation

Perforating the magic circle is the equivalent of traditional fourth wall breaks in other mediums. When the game addresses the player directly using his/her identity in the real world or as the player; when the game openly lays bare its artifice admitting to being a game; when it displays awareness of anything or anyone that does not belong to its fictional world (Conway 2010), the game perforates the magic circle, as if it creates a window to the real world.

3.4.2.1   Direct Address

This method refers to the instances when the game-world characters, the narrator or any element of the game-world acknowledges the existence of the player, referring to him/her as the player or 'you', or looking at the screen of the medium gesturing to the player. As a result, the game perforates the magic circle creating a window to the real-world.

Stanley Parable (2013) The game was released as a free mod for *Half-Life 2* and re-released as a standalone remake under the Galactic Cafe studio (2013). *Stanley Parable* is another metagame that continuously plays with the magic circle. The game has multiple endings, and direct address technique is especially outstanding in one of them. This ending is assumed to be the real ending to the Stanley Parable since it is the only one in which the player sees the credits roll. Also, it is the most complex of all endings.

The game features a Narrator that pre-narrates all the decisions that the player character Stanley should make. If the player continuously chooses not to, he/she prompts the Narrator to realize that he is not actually Stanley. After understanding that a real person is controlling Stanley, the Narrator perforates the magic circle to blame the player for being so insensitive with Stanley's fate, and for failing to respect the narrative of the game. As the game world continues to fall apart, the connection of the player to Stanley becomes more and more fragile until the player floats away from him, forced to watch his frozen body stand helpless in the empty office.

This ending is reached through a mistake that the Narrator made designing the game. There is a voice-controlled device, but Stanley does not have a voice. Forgetting the inability of his creation, the Narrator rants to the player for ruining his work. Even at this point, all the problem is caused by the mistake of the Narrator; therefore, the imperfection of the story causes the mission to fail. The entire story is useless and irrelevant if there is no player that can make decisions. The player and the creator need a symbiotic relationship for the game to exist. The completeness or perfection of a story does not make any difference if there is no player input that carries the story further. The protagonist, Stanley, was created to be controlled by an active consciousness; without it, Stanley is just an empty shell of a character. As a result, both the player and the Narrator are left with no game to play. It is possible for the player to move around, but there is nothing to be done. Also, the Narrator is left with no story to narrate. In the end, they both are aimless, and all the Narrator has the regret of not letting the player explore different options in his story. At that point, he is ready to cooperate and let the player explore, but it is too late.

Since the commentary on the symbiotic relationship of the player and the player character is parallel with the topic of this study, it is appropriate to include an extended reading of *Stanley Parable*; also, it is an excellent example of the usage of the technique where it is not used solely for its comedic effect.

3.4.2.2 Self-Awareness

When the videogame becomes aware of its artifice and admits being a game, whether mentioning the production process or complaining about the designers, etc., the magic circle perforates.

Max Payne (2001) An example from Conway's study, *Max Payne* (Remedy Entertainment 2001) has a demonstration of this method. The game is a third-person shooter which features comic-book cutscenes. After being drugged with Valkyr, Max enters a nightmare level where his family home from the first level appears to be ruined by drug addicts that murdered his daughter and wife. Looking for a way out, he comes across a letter from his late wife that ruptures the magic circle. The note reveals in a comic book style cutscene that Max is in a computer game. This leads to Max's memorable monologue:

> The truth was a burning green crack through my brain. Weapon statistics hanging in the air, glimpsed out of the corner of my eye. Endless repetition of the act of shooting, time slowing down to show off my moves. The paranoid feeling of someone controlling my every step. I was in a computer game. Funny as hell, it was the most horrible thing I could think of. *Max Payne* (Remedy Entertainment 2001)

3.4.2.3 ⸱Awareness of the Real-World

This method is realized when any instance that refers to a realm other than the game world happens in the game world. This technique may manifest as easter eggs, in-jokes & references about the real world, other videogames, real people or objects, and many others.

Watch Dogs II (2016) Recent developments in the game industry made many companies multibillion-dollar enterprises that are subject to constant examination of weak points. Therefore, appeared the leaks - screenshots, builds, plot details of games that are under development unveil before the critical eyes of the players. Ubisoft was one of those companies that suffered from leaks that even led them to publish a buggy release of *Assassin's Creed: Unity*. Since it would become a horrendous and futile pursuit to find the suspects and sue them, Ubisoft chose a different approach, to embrace the fault and make fun of it.

Watch Dogs II is an action-adventure game published by Ubisoft for PS4, Xbox One and PC (2016). The player takes role of the free-running hacker Marcus Holloway and teams up with DeadSec – Anonymous inspired community – to attack a massive corporation that controls the city.

The mission "Ubistolen" features the company's headquarters in which the player is supposed to intercept the communication between game developers. The conversations cover everything from the *Assassin's Creed* leaks to prevention of the upcoming leaks. While this is what the company is busy with, Marcus hacks a trailer of an upcoming game and his team makes fun of the fact that the players will comment on viciously, even if it was just an unfinished trailer. This is a fine manifestation of the technique, allowing the designers to comment on the real-world issues that the company is facing.

3.5 Magic Circle Manipulation: Player Experience

The three engage-ability pillars for game user experience is presented as motivation, emotion and game flow in the book The Gamer's Brain (Hodent 2017). Player inputs in the cybernetic circuit are results of a combination of emotion and motivation. While the game flow offers the player a dynamic experience, the feelings evoked by the gameplay and the resulting motivated state are processes that are resulted from the human brain. Since the designer should aim the player to have an engaging videogame experience, he/she should provide the player reasons to be motivated and should evoke emotional responses.

Defining emotion is an arduous task. The two-factor theory of emotion explains that two elements of emotion are physical arousal and a cognitive label (Schachter and Singer 1962). This means that the emotional experience starts with a physiolog-ical response to the stimulus leading to the cognition of the mind. For example, when Psycho Mantis reveals his knowledge of the player's taste in games (the stimulus), it is followed by the physical arousal (eyebrows raised, pupil dilation, dropped jaw, increase in heartbeat, startle response). The process continues with the cognitive labelling (association of physical reactions to surprise and fear) followed by the cognitive experience of the emotion (surprise, fear). The surprise factor, combined with fear, will alter the preconceptions of the player about the game world, motivating him/her to be more alert towards the boss he/she came across. It is impossible to generalize the emotional state of all players since many factors would affect the emotional responses of individuals. Still, when the designer desires to affect a portion of his/her audience's emotional state, he/she should investigate the psychological predisposition of the target audience.

3.5.1 Implementation of Magic Circle Manipulation

Being highly subjective, the quantification of emotions may be impossible, but the stimulation of a wide array of emotions through design is the most deliverable requirement. In their study on emotional requirements in video games, Callele et al. (2006) explain that the emotional requirements can be expressed in two segments: emotional outcome intent of the designer and the process of inducing the target emotional state utilizing spatial and temporal qualifiers when necessary. The following analysis of three video games reveals that using the study mentioned above, it is possible to include magic circle manipulation in the game design document for further explaining the purpose of applying it.

Doki Doki Literature Club! (2017) Disguised as a cute dating simulator, *Doki Doki Literature Club* (Team Salvato 2017) is an example that becomes a metagame that interferes with the players' decisions to make them fall in love with Monica, the club president. She takes over the game and forces the player to select her through a series of tricks that deforms and perforates the magic circle towards the game files. Simultaneously it deauthorizes the player and allows the game to recognize that it is a game: the mouse moves in the direction of Monika's name, her image locks on the screen and prevents the other characters from interacting with the player, she conspires against other characters and reveals that she wants to get rid of them to be with the player. At some point, the game becomes a power battle through continuous deformations and perforations of the magic circle. She even deletes the character files resulting in the on-screen suicide of them. The technique appears to such extent that the game becomes an interactive psychological horror experience.

The intuitive implementation of the techniques would only include the technical details of the UI manipulation and the character description sheet for Monica. Utilizing the following method, the designer may benefit from communicating his/her ideas better towards the expected emotional and motivational outcomes.

Example Case

After the player character decides to join the *Doki Doki Literature Club*, Monika starts giving writing tips. One of the tips goes "Sometimes you'll find yourself facing a difficult decision… When that happens, don't forget to save your game!". This is the first magic circle manipulation to appear in the game, and it directly indicates that something is going to change. There is a compilation video that shows the player reactions to Monica asking the player to save the game. Almost all the players respond by pausing and immediately saving their games (ReadyPlayerReact 2017).

Since this is part of a dialogue, the narrative designer's implementation according to the technique of Callele et al. would be as follows:

The intent of the designer:

I want the player to feel a combination of confusion and anxiety when he/she reads Monica telling the player to save the game. As a result, the player will immediately pause the game and save it.

The means by which the designer expects to induce the target emotional state, the narrative context:

The player will feel confused and anxious since until this point in the game there has not been any perforation of the magic circle.

Nier (2010) Published by Square Enix, *Nier* (Cavia 2010) is an action role-playing video game that is a spin-off from the Drakengard series and follows the fifth ending of the first game. The player controls Nier through third-person perspective. The following deformation is a significant example of effectively inducing a vast range of intense emotions leading to a feeling of completion.

Example Case

There are four different endings to Nier and to be able to experience all the story, all endings should be completed. If the player reaches to endings C&D, an option to sacrifice himself/herself to save his/her friend Kaine appears. In case the player sacrifices himself/herself, Nier disappears along with all the save files and stored data. All items, quest information, exploration data disappears in front of the player's eyes.

The game designer would implement this deformation as follows:

The intent of the designer:

I want the player to feel emphatic pain, anger and sadness but also a sense of relief and satisfaction when he/she loses all the saved data due to sacrificing his existence.

(continued)

The means by which the designer expects to induce the target emotional state, the narrative context.

The player will feel emphatic pain, anger and sadness but also a sense of relief and satisfaction because ordinarily, the choice of sacrificing himself/herself in a video game would not have any ramifications, but sacrificing 50+ hours of gameplay data will make the player feel as if he really is sacrificing his existence in the game world.

3.6 Conclusion and Future Research

Since videogames appeared much later than the other mediums, the predominant tendency is to use the preestablished concepts that appeared a long time ago. Instead of recruiting the terms explicitly defined for other mediums, it is essential to produce new concepts on which the appropriate terminology may continue to be applicable for the latest advancements.

This study presented a new terminology for fourth wall breaks utilizing magic circle concept of Huizinga. Inspired by the ideas of Conway, the name proposed for the fourth wall breaks is magic circle manipulation and it is divided into two subcategories: magic circle deformation and magic circle perforation. While magic circle manipulation refers to all instances where the game world reaches out to anywhere other than the diegetic, magic circle deformation presents three subcategories according to the deformation scope, non-diegetic play, medium play and real-world play. Moreover, the proposed term for the traditional fourth wall breaks in game terminology is magic circle perforation, revealing three subcategories; direct address, self-awareness and awareness of the real-world.

Furthermore, this study provides a method for implementing the magic circle manipulation techniques through affective design and requirements engineering technique, without overlooking the shared agency of the player and the game, contributing to design studies of video games. Various examples of the technique from different games are offered classifying the type of the technique used, allowing the designers to have an understanding of the state of the final products featuring the techniques. The chosen examples not only feature the fine usage of the methods, but also the misuse or overuse of the technique leading to player frustration.

Since this study overlooks the immersive technologies, such as augmented reality (AR), virtual reality (VR), mixed reality (MR), so on, the applicability of the magic circle manipulation techniques should also be assessed accordingly.

References

D. Callele, E. Neufeld, K. Schneider, Emotional requirements in video games, in *Proceedings of the IEEE International Conference on Requirements Engineering*, (IEEE, Minneapolis/St. Paul, MN, 2006), pp. 292–295. https://doi.org/10.1109/RE.2006.19

Cavia, *Nier. [Video game]* (Square Enix, Tokyo, 2010)

S. T. Coleridge, in *Biographia Literaria*, ed. by A. Roberts (Edinburgh University Press, Edinburgh, 2014). http://www.jstor.org/stable/10.3366/j.ctt14brwk4

S. Conway, A circular wall? Reformulating the fourth wall for videogames. J. Gaming Virtual Worlds **2**(2), 145–155 (2010). https://doi.org/10.1386/jgvw.2.2.145_1

J.A. Cuddon, R. Habib, M. Birchwood, Alienation effect / fourth wall, in *A Dictionary of Literary Terms and Literary Theory*, (John Wiley & Sons Ltd, Hoboken, 2013). https://doi.org/10.1002/9781118325988.ch6

Daniel Mullins Games, *Pony Island*. [Video game]. Daniel Mullins Games (2016)

N. Davis, "Not a soul in sight!": Beckett's fourth wall. J. Mod. Lit. **38**(2), 86–102 (2015). https://doi.org/10.2979/jmodelite.38.2.86. Indiana University Press

Galactic Cafe, *The Stanley Parable*. [video game]. Galactic Cafe (2013)

S. Giddings, Playing with non-humans: digital games as technocultural form, in *DiGRA '05 - Proceedings of the 2005 DiGRA International Conference: Changing Views: Worlds in Play* (2005)

N.K. Hayles, How we became Posthuman: virtual bodies in cybernetics, literature, and informatics. J. Artif. Soc. Soc. Simul. vol. 4 (1999). University of Chicago Press. http://www.amazon.com/dp/0226321460. Accessed 9 Mar 2020

C. Hodent, Engage-ability, in *The Gamer's Brain: How Neuroscience and UX Can Impact Video Game Design*, (CRC Press, Baco Raton, 2017), pp. 135–172. https://doi.org/10.1201/9781315154725-15

J. Huizinga, *Homo Ludens: A Study of Play-Element in Culture*. Routledge & Kegan Paul Ltd, London (1949). http://art.yale.edu/file_columns/0000/1474/homo_ludens_johan_huizinga_routledge_1949_.pdf. Accessed 9 Mar 2020

A. Jefferson, P. Waugh, Metafiction: the theory and practice of self-conscious fiction. Poetics Today **7**, 574–576 (1984). https://doi.org/10.2307/1772516

O. Jesper, *Breaking Fiction: How Fiction Breaks Can Be Used to Enhance a Player's Immersion in Video Games*. School of Informatics, University of Skövde (2016). Retrieved from http://his.diva-portal.org/smash/get/diva2:932514/FULLTEXT01.pdf

H.W. Kennedy, S. Giddings, Little jesuses and fuck- off robots: on aesthetics, cybernetics, and not being very good at Lego star wars, in *Computer Gaming: Essays on Cultural History, Theory and Aesthetics*, (McFarland & Co, Jefferson, NC, 2008), pp. 13–32

B. Keogh, Across worlds and bodies: criticism in the age of video games. J. Games Crit. **1**(1), 1–35 (2014). http://gamescriticism.org/articles/keogh-1-1

J.H. Kerr, M.J. Apter, *Adult Play: A Reversal Theory Approach* (Swets & Zeitlinger, Amsterdam, 1990)

Kojima Productions, *Death Stranding. [Video Game]* (Sony Interactive Entertainment, Tokyo, 2019)

Konami Computer Entertainment Japan, *Metal Gear Solid. [Video Game]* (Konami, Tokyo, 1998)

J. Murray, *Hamlet on the Holodeck the Future of Narrative in Cyberspace* (The Free Press, New York, NY, 1997)

Nintendo R&D3, & Locomotive Corporation, *StarTropics. [Video Game]* (Nintendo, Kyoto, 1990)

ReadyPlayerReact, *Let's Players Reaction To Monika Breaking the 4th Wall | Doki Doki Literature Club – YouTube* (2017). https://www.youtube.com/watch?v=ek7-4XktKW8&t=6s. Accessed 9 Mar 2020

Remedy Entertainment, *Max Payne. [Video Game]* (Gathering of Developers, New York, 2001)

K. Salen, E. Zimmerman, *Rules of Play: Game Design Fundamentals* (The MIT Press, Cambridge, MA, 2003)

S. Schachter, J. Singer, Cognitive, social, and physiological determinants of emotional state. Psychol. Rev. **69**(5), 379–399 (1962). https://doi.org/10.1037/h0046234

J. Stenros, In Defence of a magic circle: the social, mental and cultural boundaries of play. Trans. Dig. Games Res. Assoc. **1**(2), 147–185 (2014). https://doi.org/10.26503/todigra.v1i2.10

Team Salvato, *Doki Doki Literature Club!* [Video Game]. Team Salvato (2017)

Toby Fox, *Undertale*. [Video Game]. Toby Fox (2015)

Ubisoft Montreal, *Watch Dogs II* (Ubisoft, Montreal, 2016)

Chapter 4
Gamifying Kindness: Toward a Praxis of the Ephemeral

Demi Schänzel, Leanne C. Taylor-Giles, and Jane Turner

> *There is a nimbus of kindness around the kind person that*
> *equally radiates a world of kindness . . . kindness can*
> *aestheticize the environment.*
>
> *(Hamrick 2002, p. 246)*

4.1 Introduction

Since their infancy, video games have remained largely reliant on binary states to quantifiably track players' progress, such as *Spacewar!* (Russell et al., 1962), *Pong* (Atari, 1972), and *Wizardry: Proving Grounds of the Mad Overlord* (Sir-Tech, 1981), which all involved competition between the player and another player (PvP), or between the player and the game's environment/foes (PvE). This constraint initially pushed games toward a central conceit grounded on resolving conflict through abstract acts of combat, and gave rise to a milieu in which violence and the most easily quantifiable goals remained those offered most frequently within the medium.

Much has been written about the nature of games as systems which scaffold play through their mechanics (Salen and Zimmerman 2004, 2005), with the weight of such meaning-making oft delegated to the term aesthetics (Hunicke et al. 2004) – an accumulative portmanteau of the subjective qualities of a game (player engagement, narrative or emotional connection, etc.) which often focuses on the competitive elements of games over any inherent self-expression. However, this aesthetic framework for understanding games merely situates mechanics as an abstraction

D. Schänzel
Auckland University of Technology, Auckland, New Zealand

L. C. Taylor-Giles · J. Turner (✉)
Queensland University of Technology, Brisbane, QLD, Australia
e-mail: writer@leannectaylor.com; j.turner@qut.edu.au

© The Author(s), under exclusive license to Springer Nature Switzerland AG 2022
B. Bostan (ed.), *Games and Narrative: Theory and Practice*, International Series on
Computer Entertainment and Media Technology,
https://doi.org/10.1007/978-3-030-81538-7_4

of the wider game experience, without parallel to any real-world circumstances and innocent of any inherent meaning-making in their own right.

As a result of such design assumptions, players are often relegated to reiterating the same stories of heroism that such competition has always lent itself to. Within this traditional framework for understanding video games, the player is always considered the hero of the embedded narrative and the central performer of any potential emergent stories. Embedded and emergent narratives may be mapped out as a directional pathway of staged accomplishment, or they may be left as a smorgasbord so the player can pick and choose, but the outcome remains the same. By the nature of the material space of the game, someone has thought through all the available possibilities, listed them, and committed them to a design sprint. This somewhat pragmatic state of design has meant that the art of the narrative designer, the one whose concern is the facilitation of the player's emotional engagement with the game, is often only concerned with the potential of the narrative, both embedded and emergent, rather than the distinct and separate opportunity for a meaningfully unique player experience.

As the medium of video games has matured, however, and theories of player psychology have progressed, emergent storytelling (that is, the player's personal experience, dialogue, and connection with the game) and our assumptions of player motivation have slowly received wider critique and attention. By drawing on theories of self-determination (Deci and Ryan 2011), designers can ascertain that players are no longer considered to be extrinsically motivated purely by reasons endogenous to the game world, but also by their own intrinsic needs and desires, which are radically more complex than the binary conditions (dead/alive, weak/powerful) of games past. Under this new model, it's theorized that games also remain captivating in how they inherently open players up to examining alternative characteristics of themselves (Przybylski et al. 2012) – allowing for the exploration of intrinsic motivations, within fictitious or otherwise imagined settings, that can be utilized by designers to guide the player toward a meaningful sense of self-fulfilment through any number of diverse behavioural systems.

With this critical shift toward emergent player meaning-making and open-ended agency over singular mediated experiences (such as vast open worlds which remain largely founded upon motivations supplied by the designers), many games now feature a wide collection of softer mechanical systems used to inform the player's time within the game space; centralizing the player's motivations around their own intrinsic needs rather than the wider game aesthetic. Players and game designers have thus moved away from rationalist design derived from theories that stipulate the form of games as essentially competitive but separate from everyday life, such as those of Huizinga (1949), and towards more intuitive design approaches which aim for more evocative, emotionally-endearing outcomes. This in turn has led to increasing discussion of game mechanics as both meaning-making and a means to their own ends. That is, mechanics are no longer merely used as an abstracted tool to progress between levels, but rather as tools to engage with the player's own sense of self-fulfilment, with ample opportunity for reflection and a tighter focus on the implicit values these mechanics impose.

By more closely examining video games through the systemic design of their central mechanics and their implied values, rather than purely through their accumulative aesthetic qualities, it's possible to analyze how alternative methods of game design may lead to formative and otherwise undiscovered modes of play which inspire more ethically-conscious behaviours within their players. Rather than simply observing mechanics as abstracted systems divorced of any real-world parallel, designers have begun considering how certain mechanics situate the player within the accumulative worldness of their virtual setting (otherwise understood as the collective atmosphere of a virtual world: Klastrup 2003, 2008), where players derive intrinsic meaning from their personal connection to a virtual space, alongside the stories and characters that may reside there.

Shifting our discussions on video games toward how they conform to the wider socio-political settings they reside in enables designers to dissect how these virtual experiences can more closely reflect the values and behaviours they most wish to encourage or discourage within their player base, including those behaviours which may inadvertently possess certain inharmonious or harmful qualities. An early example comes from Sicart's (2003, 2005) critique of the original *Sims*, wherein Sicart suggests that through the very behaviours that players are constrained by and emboldened to perform, the game forwards a highly ideological vision of a Western post-capitalist society that fundamentally undermines its own central conceit of being a neutral or default social simulation. As such, it has become critical to note how even those games which aesthetically draw on principles of compassion may at times fall prey to certain dissonant values represented by their own mechanics, potentially undermining their central message or even imbuing the central play experience with inconsistent ideological principles (Nay and Zagal 2017). As addressed by Barr et al. (2006), this focus on value (within the broader hemisphere of games) may be defined as the understanding that since video games mediate all participatory behaviour within their digital ecosystem, certain behaviours are naturally enforced or normalized over others by the game designer, instilling in players a (sub)conscious understanding of the values they should adhere to whilst within the game space.

This distinction becomes deeply necessary when reflecting on video games such as the acclaimed Animal Crossing series, which initially began as a game embodying the ideals of a creator trying to reconcile with their country after a decade of deep-set sociocultural crisis (Gordon, cited in Cesar 2020). Behind the game's otherwise charmingly-kindred atmosphere, lingers a deeply-embedded critique against the established neolibral-capitalist ideologies and fluid re-negotiations of Japan's fading cultural boundaries of the time (Cesar 2020). Although these aesthetics were originally presented in a relatively dystopian light, designed to push players toward critically reflecting on their own experiences with socio-cultural structures of authority and guide them toward alternative methods of social connectivity, following games in the series have seen these values progressively watered down. Recent entries – *Animal Crossing: New Horizons* (Nintendo, 2020), for example – encourage players to perform behaviours that resemble the same socio-cultural structures the game once critiqued, undermining the very pastoral, rural existence the series was originally created to convey and which drew players to its world in the first place.

This conscious reflection on how games possess the ability to reflect genuine socio-cultural ideologies, and thereby normalize behaviours which might otherwise be considered antithetical to their vision, has parallels with compassionate design. This theory builds on notions of user-centred design, empathetic design, and those design approaches which focus on the user's experience but, according to Seshadri and Reid (2015), adds an emotional response to the specific user on the part of the designer. Within the context of video games, compassionate design might then be usefully defined as an approach that recognises that video games do not exist in isolation, but rather as inherently socio-political products imbued with their own (sub)conscious ideologies and value systems. Recognising that we share a world, and our collective experience of that world, with others encourages a more nuanced ludonarrative experience beyond the standard competitive milieu of games past.

4.2 The Nature of Kindness

Kindness as a concept is somewhat vague and elusive. As commentators note, we all recognize kindness when we see it, and feel its absence quite keenly (Brownlie and Anderson 2017). For a description of its qualities, we return to Hamrick:

> *[Kindness] considers the kind of practical wisdom required to hold together in inevitable tension apparently contradictory qualities in the practice of critical kindness: trust with suspicion, openness with closedness, generosity with discipline, activity with passivity. In other words, the life of kindness must nurture cautious trust, hesitant openness, a checked readiness, controlled activity, or restrained vitality. There are, indeed, times when one should not be kind . . . when, say, there are high stakes in terms of possible direct and indirect exploitation and/or coercion, and a substantial risk of playing into evil hands (2002, pp. 240-1).*

However, a pure definition of kindness proves somewhat fluid and evasive. A kind act should not occur as part of a formal structure, nor should it be undertaken for any recompense other than a sense of satisfaction, although acts of kindness do happen within formal organisations and structures. However, they are notable as being kind in and of themselves and not dictated by the organisation (Clegg and Rowland 2010).

Kindness should be thoughtful and considerate. It is often opportunistic and random rather than planned. Brownlie and Anderson (2017) point out that kindness is 'porous' and 'unstable'. Its meaning shifts quickly into obligations, civility, duty, reciprocity, and, as Hamrick observes (1985), is often mistakenly conflated with "benevolence, beneficence, or even love" (p. 204). It is associated with moral and ethical behaviour and 'acts' of kindness. More profoundly, however, the essence of its meaning is also imbricated in emergent conditions for humanity (Nietzsche 1996) and is related to the old English 'kin' (meaning family, race, sort) and so connected to older meanings of kindred, family, and tribe. The generally small and elusive nature of kindness as a phenomenon is thus both socially embedded and sociologically important as an indicator of the health of a society.

More recently, conceptualizations of kindness have been eroded by its uncomfortable tension with the individualistic, neo-liberal, competitive cultures of the western world (Campling et al. 2020). Competition has an antagonistic aspect which creates context that is at odds with kindness and which is displaced and disparaged as "sentimental and un-rigorous" (Phillips and Taylor 2009, p. 722). As a result, kindness has become associated with overtly Christian values of self-sacrifice which can, in their own framework, be misconstrued as self-serving acts (Brownlie and Anderson 2017). Kindness has been denigrated as contrary to rigour and inappropriate in institutional contexts (Clegg and Rowland 2010), and has become eroded in the public imagination even though the same small expressions of humanitarian kinship might not themselves have disappeared (McDermott 2013).

Hamrick (2002) notes that, compared to the urgency of the injustices and traumas in the world, kindness seems like an unaffordable luxury: too soft an idea for the harshness of the real world; too much at odds with the emphasis on free competition and getting ahead under your own steam (often by treading on those below who now must also be responsible for their own follies). The positioning of kindness as superficial or weak is at odds with its function as a social glue – in Hamrick's own words, (p. 3): "Kindness emerges in our relationships with others and their reciprocal relationships with us. Kindness is, therefore, one modality of our primordial situation, I-in-the-world with-others."

The kinship and 'within kind' aspect is also emphasized in Brownlie and Anderson's work on community (2017). Kindness, they argue, has an 'infrastructural quality' which has atmospheric potential. What they mean is that kindness on the micro-scale is unrecognized essential social glue - contributing to what Edith Turner (2012) refers to as *communitas*, or unstructured community spirit. Kindness is not about the specific acts of generosity but it is about "recognizing our shared humanity and interdependency" (p. 1224). This wider aura of kindness is very much about accumulated experiences.

Brownlie and Anderson propose four key features for what they call 'ordinary' (everyday) kindness. This low-level kindness has an infrastructural quality. It is manifest in small acts which effectively keep things going and facilitate a person's membership of the infrastructure, e.g., practical help and support, such as putting the bins out for someone. Infrastructures, systems that support both material and conceptual systems, are vital in the formation of resilient communities (Star 1999). Ordinary kindness has an unobligated character. The act must be a voluntary response to a perceived need e.g., loaning someone money for a cup of coffee. Such voluntariness is not exactly random, but it is also not 'expected'. In this, Brownlie and Anderson distinguish kindness from civility where certain types of kindly acts are expected of the civilized person.

These two features of kindness are especially relevant as a result of what Brownlie and Anderson refer to as the micro- or inter-personal focus. Ordinary kindness is performed in small detail: the picking up of a dropped item, the handing over of a still valid parking permit. Together, these three features add up to the fourth feature of kindness, which is how it becomes a web that supports social capital and one's sense of being comfortable in a place, or its atmospheric potential. As Brownlie and Anderson say (p. 1228):

> Kindness encourages a focus on the nature of the relationships which take place within broader dimensions of belonging and allegiance and which are shaped, but also act back upon, these dimensions.

The situating of kindness within broader dimensions is what leads Hamrick (2002) to point out that kindness differs from empathy precisely because it is not an easy option, but takes place within the tensions of relationships. In this sense, kindness is indeed what Star would refer to as an invisible infrastructure. A single act of kindness might be rewarded with a sense of pleasure, but it is being a contributor to the atmospheric potential that creates Hamrick's 'nimbus of joy' around a kind person.

4.3   Kindness and Caring in Game Worlds

Yet when it comes to designing systems that prioritise kindness, we run into an ideological disconnect. Kindness as a mechanic or narrative trope is rarely the sort of kindness Hamrick considers as genuine but, because the apparent act of kindness or caring is part of the player's toolkit to achieve success, invariably becomes the kind of non-altruistic act that Nietzsche (2013) directs so much anger towards.

Nevertheless, the use of (superficial) acts of caring and kindness as a way to accumulate points and experience is a long-standing tradition in video games. Ever since early simlife games such as Activision's 1985 *Little Computer People*, where the essential purpose of the game is to be kind to digital creatures in order to win, game designers have used kindness and caring as shorthand to obscure a core mechanic which is simply to gain points and in-game rewards. Being 'kind' to non-player characters (NPCs) by choosing between certain predetermined options in order to gain advantage later in the game might constitute a risky act, as Hamrick would argue (2002, pp. 240–1), but it is clearly an expected condition of gameplay. While such tropes are therefore convincingly presented as opportunities for kindness, the fact remains that failing to act in the appropriate way – failing to be kind – will prevent the player from progressing in the game. These examples of player actions that they can choose to perform, but which are essentially programmed and which are part of player pathways to a final win condition, are, for many commentators, the essence of what games are about (Salen and Zimmerman 2004, 2005). Yet constructing kindness in this manner transmutes it into obligation, a different beast entirely.

There do exist, however, games in which unrequired (and occasionally unre-quited) kindness forms the bedrock that supports the player's interactions with the game world. These games usually exist as consciously anti/non-combative, mindful, or otherwise relaxing experiences where failure is improbable, mitigated through gentler learning-curves, or only possible through goals the player has set for themselves. In these instances, the collective experience and its respective mechanics, its accumulative worldness (Klastrup 2003), nourish a kindred relationship to the game (one which is respectful of the player, as a form of self-care and personal fulfilment) and inspire the player to engage with more compassionate modes of play. Indeed, emerging research suggests that video games with an explicit focus on kindness-orientated mechanics (often referred to as "persuasive", "prosocial" or "wellbeing" games) may even inspire a more open-minded willingness toward acts of compassion within their players, nourish a deeper sense of humanity within oneself (Greitemeyer 2013), increase acts of prosocial behaviour after the play-session has finished (Whitaker and Bushman 2012), and collectively elevate the positive language being used within a game's respective online community (Seamus and McDonnell 2020).

Recent releases such as *A Short Hike* (Adamgryu 2019), *Far from Noise* (Batchelor 2017), and *Depanneur Nocturne* (KO_OP 2020) each focus on evoking kindness and a kindred understanding of others by encouraging players to consciously reflect on their own experiences as part of the larger world in which their actions take place. These games (and others) acutely demonstrate how mechanics consciously imbued with a kinder perspective may lead to more compassionate spaces and player behaviours; respectful of the player, the virtual setting, and the simulated denizens with whom they coexist. These experiences indicate that it's possible to imbue a game with an intrinsic sense of kindness through careful selection of game mechanics, and the accumulative atmosphere of a game's space; where what is grown is a deeply reciprocal relationship between the player and the virtual setting they've come to inhabit, where respect and gentleness with one another result in new forms of player expression.

4.3.1 Case Study #1: A Short Hike (2019)

A Short Hike places the player in the role of Claire, a young bird awaiting a phone call in Hawk Peak Provincial Park. To receive the call, she must climb the highest mountain to get cellphone reception. In the end, the call turns out to be a heartwarming exchange between Claire and her mother, expressing mutual concern and fondness, and promising to speak again soon. However, other aspects of the route to the summit support the core message of the game, such as:

One activity the player can take part in is called "beachstickball", which is essentially beach volleyball, except the participants hit the beachball with sticks instead of their hands (or wings). In contrast to other games and perhaps the player's expectations, the NPC who invented the game reveals that the score is reached cooperatively, rather than competitively. Further, if the player starts a game of beachstickball, the NPC will never fail to hit the ball back to them, giving the impression that the player is good at the game (i.e., their delivery of the ball is always correct), even if it is inevitably the player's failure to hit the ball that will result in the end of a session.

Another example is a character who has lost their lucky headband and feels unable to take part in a race without it. Normally, in these situations, the player would expect to find the lost headband after solving a puzzle, or for another character to have found and taken it. However, the actual resolution of this quest couples an expected action (asking another character with a red headband if it's theirs) with an unexpected one – learning that the red headband belongs to the person who is wearing it, but that they're willing to give it away if it will help a stranger get up the courage to join the race.

Likewise, the player needs Golden Feathers to progress and finds out another character has hoarded them all and is selling them for 1000% markup; if the player asks, they will discover it's because that NPC lacks college tuition for the next semester, and will still be 400 coins short after selling the remaining feathers. The player can then choose to collect and provide the missing amount if they so desire. Another character lost their camping permit when a fish ate it; the player can catch fish until they recover the permit, for no reward except the relief of the person who lost it.

Finally, the player is forced to adhere to the "kindness level" of the game world by Claire's inhabitance of it. After collecting a large number of shells for another character, they then turn the shells into a necklace and ask you to deliver it to Claire's aunt. When Aunt May expresses admiration for the other character at having spent so much time collecting shells to make the gift, Claire herself chooses to omit that it was, in fact, her work, in favour of Aunt May thinking fondly of the gift-giver. This is an act of kindness the player may not have chosen to perform, yet which is in line with the actions of other characters toward Claire throughout the game.

4.3.2   Case Study #2: Far from Noise (2017)

George Batchelor's *Far from Noise* is a narrative told entirely in dialogue fragments as the player character sits inside a car teetering on the edge of a cliff. Although fraught with moments of anxiety as the car appears to topple toward certain destruction, the ending of the game ultimately proposes no resolution except a black screen and then a view of the empty cliffside. There are no sound effects to indicate whether the car fell or was able to reverse, leaving the result of the player's decisions to their imagination and/or preference.

Throughout the narrative, the player is offered moments in which to panic, and moments in which they are required to sit still and examine the world around them. The game recognises and plays with several events that could have ended badly for the player, such as a heavy owl landing on the hood of the car, a sudden tempest, and other interactions with nature, maintaining a sense of tension broken by moments of reverie and humour. While the threat of a fatal outcome looms on the horizon, the game is nevertheless aimed at providing the player with a gentle experience.

There are no timed interactions, and no wrong answers. Regardless of the player's dialogue choices, the conversation flows smoothly, even occasionally referring to previous choices for comedy, or reframing them based on new information. The soundtrack is likewise relaxing, composed primarily of the sounds of nature and little else. It could be called a guided meditation, but for the inherent tension of the player character's context and the necessity of interaction to continue, yet even this is folded into the narrative in a meaningful way.

4.3.3 Case Study #3: Depanneur Nocturne (2020)

In *Depanneur Nocturne*, the player is tasked with visiting a local depanneur (convenience store) to find a gift for their partner ("bichette"/doe) because she's been working late nights and could use a pick-me-up. The game is kind to the player in several key ways:

- While items cost money, the player has an unlimited budget;
- While the player can irritate the shopkeeper by throwing items (accidentally or on purpose) there are no real consequences for this, and none of the items break;
- If the player insists on using the bathroom, there turns out to have been a good reason for the shopkeeper to refuse, but the player isn't penalized for it;
- No matter which or how many items the player chooses, their girlfriend will be happy to see them, and thank them for the gift(s).

Similarly, the shopkeeper is also positively disposed toward the player, and will accommodate their actions and requests with good humour. She even goes so far as to offer a selection of special gifts, free of charge, if the player is having trouble deciding what to buy.

In essence, by removing the possibility of disapproval/disappointment from the game – there are no stakes, because it's not bichette's birthday, anniversary, or other celebration, and because the player character is doing something nice but unexpected – *Depanneur Nocturne* creates a space in which the player is free to be generous and is socially rewarded, regardless of their choices, by the provision of a robust pre-existing relationship and the context established at the beginning of the game.

4.3.4 Conclusions

A Short Hike, Far from Noise, and Depanneur Nocturne thus fit, and even exceed, Brownlie and Anderson's (2017) definition of atmospheric kindness. The acts of kindness that are available to the player are small and made casually. Playing through the game doesn't particularly create a need for altruistic behaviour, nor is progression blocked by not performing it. Rather, the environmental narrative and the crafting of the experience create the opportunity for small, interpersonal, unobligated acts within the overall game. While there appear to be stakes at the beginning of each game – the important call in *A Short Hike*, the teetering of the car in *Far from Noise*, and the possibility of disappointing your girlfriend in *Depanneur Nocturne* – each of these situations resolves with a necessary, yet specific, catharsis: the aversion of a bad outcome through personal effort.

4.4 Ludic Kindness: Death Stranding and Building Bridges

However, each of the previous examples relied on the narrative framing of the world – the way in which characters speak to the player and each other, the situation of the player character as someone who, while not necessarily helpless, will definitely find their tasks easier with help from others, among other conceits – to build the atmosphere of kindness to which they aspired. The acts of kindness the player can perform in these games are therefore in part informed by the prevailing attitudes of the NPCs around them.

A different approach was taken by 2019's *Death Stranding* (Kojima Productions). Ostensibly about reconnecting America after an apocalypse has forced all of humanity (or at least, America) to live underground, the game also draws on the player's interpersonal connections with NPCs and other players to construct a world in which the kindness of strangers is interwoven with the effects of the player's own actions. Unusually, for a game of this size and budget, the player's connection to others is reinforced almost entirely in the ludic sphere, while it is Sam's (the protagonist's) relationships that take centre stage within the narrative. The combination of the two fulfils Hamrick's nimbus of kindness, yet it is the ludonarrative harmony constructed by the acts that the player chooses to perform that imbues the world with the sense of kindness as kindred: Hamrick's "I-in-the-world with-others" (2002, p. 3).

4.4.1 Forging a Path

The core game loop of *Death Stranding* involves collecting a parcel from a distribution centre, taking it to its destination, and unlocking a new portion of the map (called connecting it to the "chiral network"). Some locations are easier or harder to connect, but if the player delivers enough parcels, every location will eventually join the network.

One key way in which the game expresses kindness to the player is through this chiral network. Arriving at a destination the first time is often difficult, fraught with environmental challenges and enemies that take careful consideration to either confront or avoid. During their journey, the player may construct buildings or devices to aid them in their own progress, such as a Timefall Shelter to wait out the damaging rains, or a Generator to re-power their exoskeleton in a lack of sunlight. Once they pass into the "dead zone" around a new destination that's not connected to the chiral network, however, placing structures becomes impossible.

The magic of the chiral network becomes clear when that new destination is connected – the player can now see and use all of the structures placed by other players during their own journeys. Not only is this kind, but it is necessary: each area has a set amount of "chiral bandwidth", meaning that if the player wants to add a new structure they will sometimes have to delete one of their own (managed simply from the map, and not requiring the player to retrace their steps to deconstruct it – another example of designer-to-player kindness). However, once the area is connected to the chiral network, other players' structures are available for free. They take up no chiral bandwidth and, more importantly, they can fill in gaps in the player's own collection of constructions.

For example, in Episode 5 the player is given the blueprint for a Zip-line - a structure that, when placed in view of another Zip-line, allows the player to connect to it and "zip" quickly over any obstacles or enemies that might have been in their way. One particular destination in the first area, the Wind Farm, is surrounded by a dense forest full of largely invisible enemies that make for a terrifying approach. However, once the player has the Zip-line schematic and has connected the Wind Farm to the chiral network, getting there and back becomes one of the easiest and quickest routes in the game.

However, as previously stated, the player's ability to construct or upgrade structures is not unlimited. To have a full network of Zip-lines connecting the cities of the first area of the game, it is absolutely necessary to rely on Zip-lines constructed by other players. This sometimes means changing a planned network to include someone else's structures, but since those changes are necessary to exceed the player's chiral bandwidth limit, they don't feel like a punishment. Connecting areas later in the game, especially in restoring and maintaining the area's network of highways, it becomes abundantly clear that relying on friends – or strangers who become familiar through repeated association – is really the only way to get by in this world.

4.4.2   Likers Get Likes

Death Stranding's story is constructed around what a lack of social interaction will do to human beings. There's a subplot about an underground city where everyone is addicted to synthetic oxytocin, the hormone released when people hug (among other conditions), and connecting a new area to the chiral network will cause a variety of holographic signs to pop up that have been placed by other players. This includes speed boost signs on the highway, and stamina-restoring signs that can be the difference between failure and success if placed at the right spot on a particularly difficult incline.

The only in-game currency is therefore "Likes". However, contrary to most other games, this currency is entirely useless within the game world. Each time another player or NPC uses a structure that the player put down, they will receive a minimum of one Like. Structures that are placed in important locations will thus receive more Likes, leading to a leaderboard of the server that the player is on. Players are also encouraged to "spam" Likes – for example, while using a ladder there's nothing to do except hold the direction you want Sam to walk in, so the player may as well give the structure as many Likes as they can by mashing the PS4 controller's touchpad until they reach their upper limit (which also increases with game progression). Unexpectedly, the designers have turned traversal into an opportunity to express gratitude.

Of course, there are players who put structures in unavoidable locations merely to farm Likes, or over the spawn points of necessary quest items. However, since these structures only contribute to the server's leaderboard – something the player has to actively be looking for to access – and any offending structure or vehicle can be dismantled by the player whose game it has showed up in (for no additional chiral bandwidth but reduced frustration) the end result is a helpful web of quality-of-life improvements that make the player's world that much nicer to inhabit.

4.4.3   Special Delivery

The final gameplay mechanic to be discussed is the act of delivering another player's cargo. Cargo can be lost in transit for any number of reasons: the player can die, they can get dragged away by enemies, which drops all their cargo piece by piece, or they can fall over and have it washed away downstream, among other situations. While travelling through the world, the player will encounter two types of discarded parcels – blue parcels, which are generated by the game world and ostensibly dropped by NPCs, and green parcels, which were dropped by other players.

Given that the purpose of delivering blue parcels is to increase the player's own chiral bandwidth and receive Likes from NPCs, it seems counter-intuitive to believe that any player would ever add another player's cargo to their own. The unlikelihood is further increased by the fact that cargo condition – how much damage each parcel took during transit – is directly linked to both the number of Likes received and the player's "rating" for that delivery mission. The impossibility cherry on top of the unlikelihood sundae is that green parcels don't progress the player's relationship with a delivery point the same way that delivering blue parcels does, meaning that if the player is trying to connect a new delivery point to the chiral network, delivering green parcels does nothing to advance that goal.

And yet players **do** deliver green parcels. Doing so awards the player Likes from the person whose cargo they collected, and notifies the person who dropped the parcel that it is now at its destination (ideally) and ready to be delivered. This system takes a mechanic that is both necessary – immersion would be completely broken if it were impossible for Sam to drop a parcel – and could have required backtracking by the player after death or combat to mitigate, and turned it into an opportunity to perform kindness for fellow players.

4.4.4 Conclusions

Death Stranding is therefore an embodiment of both Hamrick's nimbus of kindness – down to the idea that the player can press the PS4 touchpad at any time to "call out" and receive answering calls from nearby players online at the same time – and Brownlie and Anderson's assertion that kindness is a collection of small, mundane acts (2017). The feeling of being cared for, either by the game world or other players, is created when we experience multiple unobligated acts of kindness in semi-regular succession. While it remains true that delivering green parcels relies on a somewhat self-serving perspective ("I would want someone to do this for me"), the fact that other player's structures are available to use, free of charge, that players are able to repair and upgrade each others' structures to improve the experience for everyone, and the sense of community that comes from being notified when someone uses a path or road that the player has built, all coalesce into "moments of communal understanding, and thus allow for spaces which grow organically from acts of intimate self-expression" (Schänzel 2020, p. 7–8).

Ultimately, in a world that is inherently dangerous, it is these connections – these "strands" – that tie players together and keep them from feeling alone. Time will tell what remains of the game once the player base declines, but even that, in its own right, is the way of things. Small acts of kindness alone are not enough to keep society together, and there is still a huge amount of work to be done, but for a few, brief moments, we supported, comforted, and consoled each other in the face of a common enemy: loneliness, need, and disconnection.

4.5 Discussion

For Hamrick, kindness must always be critical kindness: it depends on a sense beyond the fallacy of empathy into an imaginative "self-transposal into the perspective of the other" (2002, p. 244). The act is a voluntary one but also purposeful, a kind act usually understood by the performer as being kind. The effort here is non-trivial. It also supposes that the other must be known and so such kindness is found within community, typically, as Brownlie and Anderson note, on a small scale and through small, mundane acts (p. 1224). The instability of kindness means that it is always a slightly risky act, despite its everyday nature.

In addition, kindness has a direction, which Hamrick calls a vector (2003, p. 8). A kind act is both understood as being performed as kindness and done for someone who is perceived as being in need of that kindness. Both act and experience are socially embodied phenomena, located sensibilities in that there must be a degree of familiarity and recognition of need and the potential to address that need. This is a characteristic also observed by Brownlie and Anderson (2017) in their study: that the performer and the recipient are comfortable with each other. One might say that they are kind within a sense or recognition of kindredness and that it is this connection that allows us to recognize the nature of kindness in our experience and, equally, attest to its absence.

Narrative design is the art and craft of creating opportunity for players to engage with and experience meaning within game worlds. Emergent narrative as a field has received considerable attention, but the real interest of the narrative designer is the overall gestalt created by the game world's atmosphere (Lindley 2002). By more closely observing video games through the systemic design of their central mechanics and the implied values contained therein, rather than purely through their accumulative aesthetic qualities, we have demonstrated that it's possible for compassionate approaches toward game design to flourish whilsts remaining respectful of the player's own intrinsic motivations and their central play experience. Such play experiences may even possess enduring psychological benefits due to their inherently participatory nature, as documented by a myriad of studies which have attempted to discern the relationship between games, the accumulative atmosphere of their content and their respective players (Greitemeyer 2013; Whitaker and Bushman 2012). As a result of this emergent shift toward kinder conscientious experiences, games that embody these principles such as *A Short Hike* (2019), *Far from Noise* (2019), *Depanneur Nocturne* (2020), and *Death Stranding* (2019) each demonstrate narratives more profound and reflectively-emergent than have traditionally been associated with video games. They scaffold softer systematic behaviours, nourish a deeper sense of connection toward the game and others, and remain respectful of the player's own intrinsic motivations beyond the standard hero's journey. Through analyzing a collection of kindness-orientated games, we have shown that it's possible to imbue a game with an intrinsic sense of kindness through careful selection of game mechanics and the accumulative atmosphere of a game's space.

References

Activision, *Little Computer People [Computer Software]* (Activision, New York, NY, 1985)

Adamgryu, *A Short Hike [Computer Software]* (Adamgryu, Toronto, ON, 2019)

Atari, *Pong [Computer Software]* (Atari, Sunnyvale, CA, 1972)

P. Barr, R. Biddle, J. Noble, Video game values: human–computer interaction and games. Interact. Comput. **19**(2), 180–195 (2006). https://doi.org/10.1016/j.intcom.2006.08.008

G. Batchelor, *Far from Noise [Computer Software]* (George Batchelor, Montréal, QC, 2017)

J. Brownlie, S. Anderson, Thinking sociologically about kindness: puncturing the blasé in the ordinary city. Sociology (Oxford) **51**(6), 1222–1238 (2017). https://doi.org/10.1177/0038038516661266

P. Campling, J. Ballatt, C. Maloney, *Intelligent Kindness: Rehabilitating the Welfare State* (Cambridge University Press, Cambridge, 2020)

M. Cesar, Fear thy neighbour: socialisation and isolation in animal crossing. Loading **13**(22), 89–108 (2020). https://journals.sfu.ca/loading/index.php/loading

S. Clegg, S. Rowland, Kindness in pedagogical practice and academic life. Br. J. Sociol. Educ. **31**(6), 719–735 (2010)

E. Deci, R. Ryan, Self-determination theory, in *Handbook of Theories of Social Psychology: Volume One*, ed. by P. Van Lange, A. Kruglanski, E. Higgins, (Sage, New York, NY, 2011), pp. 416–433. https://doi.org/10.4135/9781446249215

T. Greitemeyer, Effects of playing video games on perceptions of One's humanity. J. Soc. Psychol. **153**(4), 499–514 (2013). https://doi.org/10.1080/00224545.2013.768593

W.S. Hamrick, Kindness, in *Phenomenology in Practice and Theory*, (Springer, Berlin, 1985), pp. 203–222

W.S. Hamrick, *Kindness and the Good Society: Connections of the Heart* (SUNY Press, Albany, NY, 2002)

J. Huizinga, *Homo Ludens. A Study of the Play-Element in Culture. (R. Hull, Trans.)* (Routledge & Kegan Paul, London, UK, 1949)

R. Hunicke, M. LeBlanc, R. Zubek, MDA: a formal approach to game design and game research, in *Proceedings of the AAAI Workshop on Challenges in Game AI*, vol. 4, no. 1 (2004), p. 1722

L. Klastrup, *A Poetics of Virtual Worlds*. University of Copenhagen (2003). https://citeseerx.ist.psu.edu/index

L. Klastrup, The Worldness of EverQuest: exploring a 21st century fiction. Game Studies **8**(2) (2008). www.gamestudies.org

KO_OP, *Depanneur Nocturne [Computer Software]* (KO_OP, Montréal, QC, 2020)

Kojima Productions, *Death Stranding [Computer Software]* (Sony Interactive Entertainment, San Mateo, CA, 2019)

C.A. Lindley, The gameplay gestalt, narrative, and interactive storytelling. Paper presented at the CGDC Conf (2002)

J. McDermott, Nicer than we think we are. Financial Times (2013). Retrieved from https://www.ft.com/content/16cda9d4-ffb9-11e2-b990-00144feab7de

J.L. Nay, J.P. Zagal, Meaning without consequence: virtue ethics and inconsequential choices in games, in *Proceedings of the 12th International Conference on the Foundations of Digital Games* (2017), pp. 1–8

F.W. Nietzsche, *On the History of Moral Feelings, Human, All Too Human: A Book for Free Spirits*. Aphorism 48. [original: Menschliches, Allzumenschiles, 1878.] (1996)

F. Nietzsche, *Human, all Too Human: A Book for Free Spirits. (A. Harvey, Trans.)* (The Floating Press, Auckland, 2013)

Nintendo, *Animal Crossing: New Horizons* [Computer software] (Nintendo, Kyoto, Japan, 2020)

A. Phillips, B. Taylor, *On kindness* (Hamish Hamilton, London, 2009)

A. Przybylski, N. Weinstein, K. Murayama, M. Lynch, R. Ryan, The ideal self at play: the appeal of video games that let you be all you can be. Psychol. Sci. **23**(1), 69–76 (2012). www.jstor.org/stable/41416995

S. Russell, M. Graetz, W. Wiitanen, B. Saunders, S. Piner, et al., *Spacewar! [Computer Software]* (Massachusetts Institute of Technology, Cambridge, Massachusetts, 1962)

K. Salen, E. Zimmerman, *Rules of Play: Game Design Fundamentals* (MIT Press, Cambridge, MA, 2004)

K. Salen, E. Zimmerman, Game design and meaningful play, in *Handbook of Computer Game Studies*, ed. by J. Raessens, J. Goldstein, (The MIT Press, Cambridge, MA, 2005), pp. 59–79

D. Schänzel, *The Library of Babble*. Masters Dissertation, Auckland University of Technology (2020)

R. Seamus, D. McDonnell. "Lock, load, n' thank the driver": the positive influence of prosocial activity on language in online social groups. Soc. Media +Soc. **6**(2) (2020). https://doi.org/10.1177/2056305120913990

P. Seshadri, T. Reid. Novice engineers' predisposition to compassionate design. Paper Presented at the DS 80-11 Proceedings of the 20th International Conference on Engineering Design (ICED 15) Vol 11: Human Behaviour in Design, Design Education; Milan, Italy, 27–30.07. 15 (2015)

M. Sicart, Family values: ideology, computer games & the Sims. DiGRA Conf. **2**(1) (2003). diagra.org

M. Sicart, The ethics of computer game design. DiGRA Conf. **3**(1) (2005). diagra.org

Sir-Tech, *Wizardry: Proving Grounds of the Mad Overlord [Computer Software]* (Sir-Tech Software, Inc., New York, NY, 1981)

S.L. Star, The ethnography of infrastructure. Am. Behav. Sci. **43**(3), 377–391 (1999)

E. Turner, *Communitas: The Anthropology of Collective Joy*, 1st edn. (Palgrave Macmillan US, New York, 2012)

J. Whitaker, B. Bushman, "Remain calm. Be kind." effects of relaxing video games on aggressive and prosocial behavior. Social psychological and personality. Science **3**(1), 88–92 (2012). https://doi.org/10.1177/1948550611409760

Chapter 5
The Digital Lineage of Narrative: Analyzing Interactive Fiction to Further Understand Game Narrative

Kirsty Michelle McGill

5.1 Introduction

Narrative within games has been a long-standing debate within the field of games studies. This discussion has evolved and one of the questions emerging from the field of game studies is no longer whether games *can* tell stories but *how* they tell stories (Brice 2011; Sim and Mitchell 2017; Roe and Mitchell 2019). Offering choices to players in video games to further the game narrative has become a prevalent design choice in games. This mechanic encourages players to have, or feel they have had, an impact on the outcome of the narrative and generates a narrative experience unique to the player. This design element is the main game mechanic within the older game form of interactive fiction (IF) and this link between narrative and choice has been inherited by modern video games. The notion of machinic texts (Mukherjee 2015) and N. Katherine Hayles' understanding of deep code (2004) provide an overlap for the two media forms of IF and video games to be analyzed due to their shared elements of play and reading co-existing. This chapter discusses the lineage of narrative choices that video games have inherited from IF and aims to demonstrate that by analysing IF, both past and present, new insights regarding narrative in games can be gained.

K. M. McGill (✉)
University of Bedfordshire, Luton, UK
e-mail: kirsty.mcgill@beds.study.ac.uk

5.2 Interactive Fiction

Interactive fiction has remained an area of academic interest as well as maintaining an established audience of readers. Although relatively well known, it has not kept a mass audience following in popular culture as a source of reading for enjoyment (Miall and Dobson 2001; Pope 2010; Mangen and Van der Weel 2017). However, both main forms of IF, hypertext/text adventures and parser-based, utilize the element of offering choices to players to proceed the narrative within the game. Choices within games should encourage a sense of engagement between the player and the game and allow the player to feel that they have exerted their agency onto the game world. Traits present within the choices, or illusion of choice, within IF can be seen to form the basis of narrative choices within video games. IF, as a form, relies on the power of the text to create compelling choices that should, if successful, inspire the player to continue with the game. IFs such as *Howling Dogs* (Porpentine 2012) and *The Uncle Who Works for Nintendo* (Lutz 2014) use ambiguity within the text which, in turn, makes the choices offered to the player more persuasive as following the choice pathways reveals more of the story—a similar trait used in video games.

Traditionally, IFs rely upon their captivating literary aesthetics rather than the detailed visual aesthetics found, particularly, in modern video games. The distinct absence, in many examples, of overt visual aesthetics in IF means that the narrative and choices offered to the player must be more compelling to keep players engaged with the story as they have few other graphical/mechanical elements to rely upon. This does not exclude IFs from combining these elements, such as *80 Days* (Inkle Studios 2014), *10 pm* (Litrouke 2017) and *Stories Untold* (Devolver Digital 2017), only that the typical stylistic choice is to primarily utilize text rather than aesthetics. Furthermore, early IFs, such as *Colossal Cave Adventure* (Crowther and Woods 1976), *Zork* (Infocom 1980) and *afternoon, a story* (Joyce 1987), could only have limited aesthetics due to the restrictions of the technology used to create them. Whereas the point and click game *Kentucky Route Zero* (Annapurna Interactive 2020) intentionally utilizes limited visual aesthetics but is rich in narrative aesthetics. The narrative choices in IF, and video games, must create the notion of choice excitement (Giovagnoli 2011; Genovesi 2017) within players and promote them to exert imaginative effort (Maduro 2017) in order to stay engaged with the story.

The two main styles of choices offered to players in IF are either selecting from a choice of links (hypertext IF/text adventures) or puzzling out and typing in a command to be executed (parser-based IF). The inherited lineage of narrative choices from IF to video games is clearer with the example of hypertext IF. Some games, such as *Until Dawn* (Supermassive Games 2015) or *Catherine* (Atlus 2012), offer a selection of choices, quite often binary choices, to the player on-screen to choose from and the player is asked to make a decision in the moment. Alternatively, players can be informed of choices or have potential choices hinted at but not explicitly stated, or can discover additional choices by exploration, observed in

Dishonored (Arkane Studios 2012) and *Dragon Age: Inquisition* (Bioware 2014) but players do not have to make an immediate decision. Furthermore, players can have choices hidden from them and accidently make a choice without intending to, in *Nier: Automata* (Platinum Games 2017) some of the 26 endings in the game can be achieved this way by inadvertently running in the opposite direction of a main mission objective.

The link between parser-based IF and video games, in relation to narrative, is more tenuous. Parser IFs ask players to solve the puzzle of which commands to type in order to proceed the game and story. A common frustration of parser IFs is not only working out how to proceed within the game but getting the correct phrasing right for the game to accept the command. Notably the IF *Eat Me* (Groover 2017) removes this complication by making the solution to every puzzle to use the command 'eat'. While this reduces the choices available to the player it deeply encourages the narrative of gluttony in the game and every obstacle, whether item or person, can be removed by eating them.

The narrative progression link, in which the narrative of the game is not revealed to the player unless they proceed through puzzles or other gameplay elements, can be seen between parser IFs and video games. However, it cannot categorically be stated that video games have inherited this trait from IF. Both media forms contain puzzles that create narrative contribution (more than simply progressing the story) but drawing an inherited link between the two media forms is challenging to clearly establish, particularly with parser IFs.

5.3 Analysing Interactive Fiction

The method of close-reading (Bizzocchi and Tanenbaum 2011) has been previously demonstrated as an effective way of analyzing video games but can also be applied to the analysis of IF. This method, for both media forms, allows the dual position of both researcher and player, although for IF the term reader-player (Ensslin 2014) is a more suitable media-specific term, in addition to the application of other theories. The understanding of game narrative is still in a nascent stage of development and while utilizing literary theories may be a step away from a preferred media specific analysis they provide a solid theoretical underpinning while specialized game narrative theories and methodologies are further developed and refined.

5.3.1 The Work of Roland Barthes

When carrying out my own close-readings, theories drawn from several disciplines have proved relevant for the study of narrative within IF which can also be applied to video games. The structuralist and post-structuralist work of Roland Barthes (1975, 1977, 1998) has been key to note in addition to the theories of fabula and syuzhet and narrative game mechanics, discussed below. Barthes' earlier work outlines the structural analysis of narratives. Although this has been overtaken by his later post-structuralist work, it importantly establishes that no unit of narrative can produce meaning on its own. These established units must be linked by narrative levels in order for meaning to be created (1977). In terms of narrative within IF and video games, this notion highlights the consideration of how the story works in conjunction with other game elements in order to produce a rounded storytelling experience. All the game elements, in theory, should work in tandem to avoid the undesirable state of ludonarrative dissonance (Hocking 2007). In IF it is easier to establish the narrative elements and how they work together as, noted above, there are often fewer visual aesthetic elements in place. The passage text and corresponding choices are at the forefront of the game.

Barthes' later works discussed the notions of readerly and writerly texts and texts of bliss and pleasure. Many video games produce a readerly play experience where the player is led through the game and, although the game is still interactive, any choices made within that game do not have narrative impact. The game produces a comfortable or satisfying play experience. Whereas games, both IF and video games, that encourage or force players to make choices throughout gameplay have a distinct writerly and blissful play experience and may offer this experience for a moment rather than across a whole game. Choices in these types of games have a resultant effect on the narrative and/or allow players to feel that they have created their own play experience within a realm of bounded agency (Bizzocchi and Tanenbaum 2012) that goes beyond being led through the game by the author. Writerly and blissful gameplay can contain subversive or unconventional choices, a noteworthy example being the first *Mass Effect* (2007) game where players *must* choose which of two companions (Kaiden or Ashley) to sacrifice in a key event. In this binary scenario the player must choose in order for the game, and narrative, to proceed. There is no option to proceed through the game without making this choice and there are no alternative choices for players to make that results in both characters being able to survive. Other games, such as *The Witcher 3: Wild Hunt* (CD Projekt Red 2015), offer players key quests but these can be completed in any order and resultant choices made during those quests may affect the later story of the game. The four part IF series *Sorcery!* (Inkle Studios 2013a, b, c, d) and *80 Days* (Inkle Studios 2014) presents players with a map which has a defined start and end point but how the player gets to the end, and the experiences and choices they make along the way are at the player's discretion, but result in the player putting their own authorial stamp on the game world and achieving a writerly or blissful play experience.

Barthes's concepts overlap with Aarseth's (1997) seminal theory of ergodicity. Similar to Aarseth's understanding in a readerly or nonergodic text the player is more passive, whereas a writerly and/or ergodic text makes more demands of the player. However, I agree with Ryan's claim (2015) that clicking links or buttons can no longer qualify as nontrivial effort as our use and understanding of technology has developed and evolved. Nevertheless, in the case of narrative choices in games nontrivial effort, and resulting ergodic experience, can still be applied. While the method of enacting a choice within games, clicking a link or button is certainly no longer a foreign experience, the act of selecting a decision between the game's offered choices is weighted with player expectation and making these choices require nontrivial effort. This use of nontrivial effort will not apply to all choices offered—choosing whether to go left or right and the choice between two character's lives is clearly not the same. However, games that do use weighted choices can contribute towards a game being considered as an ergodic or writerly text and, presumably, a blissful play experience.

5.3.2 Fabula and Syuzhet

The terms fabula and syuzhet originate from the school of Russian formalism and were first used by the noted theorists Vladimir Propp and Viktor Shklovsky. The notions of fabula (the raw material of the story) and syuzhet (the way in which the story is organized) can aid in understanding games that utilize choices within their narratives. In branching narratives, where the narrative is progressed through player choice, the syuzhet is shown to the player through the choices offered to them. However, when making their choices the player is, potentially, trying to understand and see the fabula, the possible outcomes that may occur from their choices. In games with multiple narrative paths the player tries to heuristically understand the narrative to gauge where the narrative paths divide and how to proceed down them. The video game *Detroit: Become Human* (Quantic Dream 2018) offers the player, at the end of each chapter, a visual representation of the choices they have made and the choices they could have made. The narrative branches are shown to the player demonstrating the syuzhet they have received, through their own choices, but also the total fabula they have yet to, or can potentially, receive.

David Bordwell in his work *Narration in the Fiction Film* (2013) notes that, irrespective of narrative medium, the syuzhet can exert control over the narrative by restricting the amount and importance of the narrative information received. This purposeful restriction is more easily observed in video games which make use of visual flash-forwards/flashbacks, as in *Amnesia: Rebirth* (Frictional Games 2020), or games where the narrative does not proceed chronologically, such as *Beyond: Two Souls* (Quantic Dream 2013). *Until Dawn* (Supermassive Games 2015) utilizes flash-forwards through its totem mechanic, which show short bursts of *potential* upcoming events controlling the information received by the player which can influence future choices the player may make. Certain decisions can also result in flashbacks, with the player being shown decisions they could have made. Both the flash-forwards/flashbacks offer the player a glimpse game's fabula structure; each totem or flashback received hints at a narrative branch to explore either in a current or subsequent playthrough. IFs also make use of this type of restriction when proceeding through the narrative, as observed in *afternoon, a story* (Joyce 1987), *Will Not Let Me Go* (Granade 2017) and *Time Passed* (See 2018). The IF *In The Trees* (Peck 2017) resets the player to the beginning of the game when they make an incorrect choice. The starting passage then updates to inform the player of a sense of déjà vu and results in the progression of the chronological gameplay having a cyclic effect.

IFs, and video games that offer branching pathways, provided by choices, through the narrative include more fabula material than the syuzhet. In IFs the total number of passages/lexias in a game represent the whole of the fabula. However, the reader-player is unlikely to proceed through every passage within the IF, not in a single playthrough, but the passages they choose becomes their syuzhet. Applying the notion of fabula/syuzhet to games, both IF and video games, that use choice as part of a branching narrative allows for a distinction to be established between the story received by the player in a single playthrough and the possible stories that the player may (or may not) experience. Considering a branching narrative in this way allows for a clearer visualization of the game structure during a close-reading and, in particular, where key choices or narrative junctions (Purnomo 2020) take place.

5.3.3   Narrative Game Mechanics

Offering choices to players within games that are linked to the narrative, allows them to be viewed as narrative game mechanics (NGMs). NGMs are, in essence, mechanics that support the construction of the narrative (Bycer 2012, Hjaltason et al. 2015, Dubbelman 2016, Larsen and Schoenan-Fog 2016, Dubbelman 2017). Not only do they form part of the game rules and/or a formal system that the player can interact with, in many instances they are also linked to game progression which further reveals and develops the game narrative. Katsarov et al. (2019) identify 20 game mechanisms. Although their own work is centered around promoting moral sensitivity in players, the mechanisms (and associated player choices) they outline are likely to have narrative consequences in a video game. If a player is asked to make a choice which may impact the narrative this can be viewed as a game mechanic as it is now part of how the player interacts with the game story world; it has become *more* than a narrative element. There is a link between the mechanic element (how the player interacts with the game world) and the game's narrative (how the player understands the game world). In my own work I have found that these choices can also encourage the player to think beyond the scripted story and consider possible future outcomes of the game narrative. The player is engaged in creating their own narrative separate from the provided story. The amalgamation of game rules and story elements should persuade players to interpret the game's events and fill in the narrative gaps (Mukherjee 2015). In many cases the player narrative will be overwritten by the game narrative but the fact that player has postulated alternative narrative outcomes shows that they are exerting imaginative effort and are engaged with the narrative unfolding before them.

Two NGMs that I have observed, in my currently ongoing work, during close readings of IFs and video games are purposeful ambiguity (where information is intentionally concealed from the player) and information mechanic (where information is intentionally revealed to the player). These elements work in conjunction to create narrative gaps and promote both choice excitement and imaginative effort within players. These two components work in tandem by both providing and concealing information from the player during gameplay. In IF these elements are observed in the text provided to the player and the choices they can either click or type in. Although not a game mechanic in the traditional video game sense the text passage of an IF functions as mechanic as it is part of the game's formal systems. In some IFs this text can be directly interacted with but in all IFs the player is required to read the text in order to proceed the game and is, therefore, indirectly interacting with an integral part of the game and utilizing one of the game's mechanics. In the example of *The Uncle Who Works for Nintendo* (Lutz 2014) the reader-player is informed that their friend's uncle will be arriving at midnight. At this point in the IF there has been nothing explicit to say that this will be detrimental for the player. However, when combined with the game's aesthetics (both visual, sound and textual), generating a horror genre atmosphere, it becomes apparent that the player is unlikely to want to be present when The Uncle arrives. This statement works as an information mechanic informing the reader-player that if they wish to avoid meeting The Uncle they must do so by midnight. Furthermore, this sets up the game's goal of leaving the house by midnight and also establishing that there is a time limit. However, this information is also purposefully ambiguous as the reader-player is not informed *why* not meeting The Uncle is the goal. Generating this 'why' question creates a narrative gap for the reader-player to fill using imaginative effort. The hyperlink choices offered to the reader-player now provide choice excitement as they are key to allowing the reader-player to escape and, potentially, answering the 'why' question raised. These features have been observed in both IFs and video games but appear to be more prevalent, or more easily observed, in horror genre games. As there is a genre expectation for some information to be concealed/revealed to players in this genre the utilization of these features is at the forefront within this type of game. This is not to say that these elements are not used in other game genres, only that within the horror genre they are more obviously noted. In *Until Dawn* (Supermassive Games 2015) the elements of the information mechanic and purposeful ambiguity can be seen through the use of the game's totem system and the clues that can be discovered by the characters throughout the game. Each totem/clue both provides and conceals information from the player and creates narrative gaps for the player to fill. It can be theorized that successful information mechanics/purposeful ambiguity can be ascertained by the player exerting imaginative effort.

5.4   Choice in Narrative within Interactive Fiction

To illustrate the use of choice within IF, inherited and utilized by video games, three IF examples have been selected, each demonstrating a different design system. The chosen examples give an insight into the narrative choices within IF, which is relevant to video games, but by no means represent the full range of choices present within IF games. Looking at game narrative from this angle is not to say that choice in video game narratives is a recent development but in IF this feature has always been at the forefront. Even when IF first began with *Colossal Cave Adventure* (Crowther and Woods 1976) choice was offered to players. Reader-players (RPs) are not guided or encouraged along a specific route; they must puzzle out and choose which parser terms are correct in order to proceed. The choices offered to the RP are limited to the game's design, but this is no different from any other IF or video game where players can only act within the bounded agency afforded to them by the game. This design choice passed onto the, relatively short-lived, commercial successes of Infocom bringing us the notable titles of *Zork* (Infocom 1980) and *Planetfall* (Infocom 1983). Towards the end of the Infocom era Eastgate Systems, a forerunner in hypertext and electronic fiction publishing, issued the, now, well-known titles of *afternoon, a story* (Joyce 1987), *Victory Garden* (Moulthrop 1992) and *Patchwork Girl* (Jackson 1995) all created using Eastgate Systems *Storyspace* software (Eastgate Systems 1987). The commercial decline of IF gave way to an online community of supporters and creators, aided by now readily available and easily accessible programming languages and systems; notably *Inform* (Nelson 1993) and *Twine* (Klimas 2009). *Inform* allowed the creation of noteworthy titles such *Curses* (Nelson 1993), *Photopia* (Cadre 1998) (discussed further below) and *Galatea* (Short 2000). *Twine* (Klimas 2009) requires no prior knowledge of programming languages or software and has been both hailed, and critiqued, for allowing anyone to create a game. Prominent text adventure titles created in *Twine* include *Howling Dogs* (Porpentine 2012), *Queers in Love at the End of the World* (Anthropy 2013) and *The Uncle Who Works for Nintendo* (Lutz 2014) (also discussed below).

The three IF examples chosen to illustrate the history of choices in IF, that have now been inherited by video games as the medium has developed, are *Photopia* (Cadre 1998), *The Uncle Who Works for Nintendo* (Lutz 2014) and *Stories Untold* (Devolver Digital 2017). All three games were created using different design systems and, while *Photopia* is the only historically 'classic' IF, all illustrate the use of narrative within games.

5.4.1 *Photopia*

Photopia (Cadre 1998) is considered the first 'puzzle free' IF focusing more on narrative than interactivity. It can be viewed as a precursor to 'walking simulator' games as the focus is on discovering the story rather than adventure or puzzles. Although, personally, I believe that the phrase 'narrative explorer' is a more suitable term to describe these types of games. *Photopia* has a linear game structure, in that the conclusion reached at the end of the game cannot be changed and the RP is led through the game scenes in the same order regardless of choices made. However, it provides an illusion that the game is non-linear and makes the player believe that they are able to exert more agency onto the world than they actually can.

Photopia maintains its illusion of non-linearity by having the story jump between different scenes creating an experience that feels non-cohesive but the narrative comes together for the conclusion. *Photopia* swaps between different narrators/characters as the scenes change, in addition to having the colour of the scene change. The white scenes are voiced by Wendy, Allison and their parents whereas the coloured scenes describe the science fiction adventure of Wendy as narrated by Alison. The language used differs depending on the scene and character, Alison's voice is far more descriptive during the coloured scenes as she tells stories to Wendy and extra descriptions are provided for certain words—words that a child may not know the meaning of and so reinforces the storytelling aspect of the game.

Photopia's narrative experience lends itself to producing a writerly game experience as the RP is asked to try and understand and interpret the connection between the white and coloured scenes. Although the game's narrative is linear, in that the player cannot change the narrative, which should make it a readerly experience. However, as the narrative is given to the RP non-linearly it is more effective at promoting a writerly experience. Similarly, the RP experiences the syuzhet in pieces and it is only once the end of the game is reached that the player can interpret the connections between the passages and understand the fabula.

Photopia excels at delivering a compelling narrative but at the expense of high levels of interactivity. While this once was considered a detrimental approach to gameplay, as the video game medium has matured this approach is no longer considered negative and elements of this approach can be seen in narratively driven video games.

5.4.2   The Uncle Who Works for Nintendo

The Uncle Who Works for Nintendo (Lutz 2014) is an IF created using the platform Twine (Klimas 2009) where the RP proceeds by clicking on the links offered to them either at the end of a text passage or highlighted words within the text passage. The story premise is that the RP takes on the role of a child invited to a friend's house for a sleepover and results in the RP meeting the mysterious Uncle. Up until the game time of '10 pm' the structure of the game is linear but once this time has been reached the RPs can begin to make choices that take them to one of the game's six endings. The IF also retains the information of which choices/endings the RP has achieved, similar to a video game 'New Game +' save state and unlocks some of the game's endings.

The Uncle Who Works for Nintendo utilizes the NGMs of providing information but also being purposefully ambiguous throughout the game. This, as with *Photopia*, encourages the RP to interpret the events of the game producing a writerly experience. Compared to *Photopia*, *The Uncle Who Works for Nintendo* goes one step further by having the choices that the RP makes have outcomes on the narrative of the game—the RPs choices will contribute to which ending they receive. RPs must consider where the narrative junctions lie in order to achieve the different syuzhets offered by the game. One of the easiest narrative junctions to discover is when the Uncle arrives at the house. RPs can choose to go with the friend to open the front door, and meet the Uncle directly, or hide only to be found by the Uncle. Each option leads to a different ending but the moment of choosing between these two pathways is the narrative junction and the results of the decision place the RP on the path to one of these two endings.

The Uncle Who Works for Nintendo provides a branching narrative and generates a horror experience through the use of minimalist mechanics. This pared down gameplay brings the narrative to the foreground and asks RPs to engage closely with the text passages in order to proceed. In essence, the devil is in the details and the RP must pay close attention in order to discover the multiple endings the game offers. This approach is inherited from older parser IFs, where the right combination of items and location must be employed in order to proceed. This has been further inherited by point and click adventure games, such as *Myst* (Cyan 1993) or *Grim Fandango* (LucasArts 1998), but with the addition of multiple endings this nostalgic method can also witnessed in games by Telltale Games such as *The Wolf Among Us* (2013) or Square Enix's *Life is Strange* (2015). These games allow the narrative to flourish while providing players with sufficient mechanics to engage with and offering choices that have visible consequences, allowing players to feel that they have exerted agency within a bounded story world.

5.4.3   Stories Untold

Stories Untold (Devolver Digital 2017) is a contemporary adventure game but provides an experience of classic adventure game mechanics. The game, set in 1986, evokes a sense of retro nostalgia across four episodes and utilizes classic game mechanics of parser IF, point and click, puzzle-solving and first-person exploration. *Stories Untold* was created using the well-known game engine Unity to generate a classic gameplay experience.

Initially the game appears to be four individual stories, but it is revealed in the final episode that each of the episodes is linked in an over-arching narrative. Each episode presents itself as an individual syuzhet but once episode four is reached more of the fabula is revealed. Furthermore, it also initially appears to RPs that they take on the role of a nameless/faceless character, drawing RP and character closer together through the shared use of the second-person use of 'You'. However, as the episodes proceed it becomes apparent that the RP is the character James Aition who is recovering from a car accident and subsequent coma. Part of the game's ambiguous narrative is James refusing to accept the events of the accident and his corresponding guilt as it was his drunk driving which resulted in the death of his sister. The game offers players a blissful play experience as RPs as they can construct their own version of game events, particularly in episodes one—three, as the story taking place is purposely ambiguous and therefore requires RPs to fill in narrative gaps. While this is less likely to occur in the last episode as the 'true' story is revealed RPs can still, potentially, have a blissful experience should they, like the character they control, refuse to accept the more mundane truthful events and instead choose to believe the more fantastical story initially provided to them in the preceding episodes.

Although only part of *Stories Untold's* gameplay is parser based, it demonstrates that IF can be produced in a video games aesthetic 'style'. While *Stories Untold* is not a 'true' parser IF, the ersatz experience it provides demonstrates that a game with IF content can be commercially successful.

5.5 The Future of Interactive Fiction

Interactive fiction has a rich history of utilizing choice within its narratives. By analysing this media form a fuller understanding of game narrative and *how* games tell stories can be achieved. Choice, or the illusion of choice, has been a central feature of IF games since their infancy. Analysing this type of game allows for deeper insights into this design feature by reflecting on the nascent use and development of narrative choice in games. Utilizing emerging theories of narrative game mechanics combined with older narratological theories (such as the notion of fabula and syuzhet) can contribute to answering the pertinent question of how games tell stories. Furthermore, both media forms have a shared overlap of both containing deep code and being machinic texts. This allows for a comparative and critical analysis between IF and video games to reveal similarities and differences between the two forms and see how narrative choice has developed over time within these artefacts.

The mechanics of the IF medium have changed very little over time but has always retained a focus on narrative. However, the IF game *Stories Untold* (Devolver Digital 2017) presents itself in a visually aesthetic style, with more similarities to a video game, and was successful enough to go from a PC only release to being released on video game consoles. Furthermore, the programming language *Ink* (Inkle Studios 2016) used for the creation of *Sorcery* (Inkle Studios 2013a, b, c, d), *80 Days* (Inkle Studios 2014) and *Heaven's Vault* (Inkle Studios 2019) is now publicly available and compatible with the well-known game engine Unity. These developments suggest that a new blended IF medium era, with its own narrative implications, is potentially to come.

References

E. Aarseth, *Cybertext: Perspectives on Ergodic Literature* (Johns Hopkins University Press, USA, 1997)

Annapurna Interactive, *Kentucky Route Zero*. USA (2020)

A. Anthropy, *Queers in Love at the End of the World* (2013). https://w.itch.io/end-of-the-world. Accessed 8 Dec 2020

Arkane Studios, *Dishonored*. France (2012)

Atlus, *Catherine*. Japan (2012)

R. Barthes, *The Pleasure of the Text* (Farrar, Straus and Giroux, France, 1975)

R. Barthes, *Image Music Text* (Fontana Press, London, 1977)

R. Barthes, *S/Z: An Essay* (Hill and Wang, New York, NY, 1998)

Bioware, *Mass Effect*. Canada (2007)

Bioware, *Dragon Age: Inquisition*. Canada (2014)

J. Bizzocchi, J. Tanenbaum, *Well Read: Applying Close Reading Techniques to Gameplay Experiences. Well Played 3.0* (ETC Press, Dartmouth, 2011), pp. 289–315

J. Bizzocchi, J. Tanenbaum, Mass effect 2: a case study in the Design of Game Narrative. Bull. Sci. Technol. Soc. **32**(5), 393–404 (2012)

D. Bordwell, *Narration in the Fiction Film* (Routledge, London, 2013)

M. Brice, *Ludonarrative Resonance*. Alternate Ending (2011). http://www.mattiebrice.com/ludonarrative-resonance. Accessed 17 Nov 2020

J. Bycer, *Extreme Storytelling: The Use of Narrative Mechanics* (2012). http://www.gamasutra.com/blogs/JoshBycer/20120611/172156/Extreme_Storytelling_The_Use_of_Narrative_Mechanics.php. Accessed 18 Nov 2020

A. Cadre, *Photopia* (1998). https://ifdb.tads.org/viewgame?version=1&id=ju778uv5xaswnlpl. Accessed 26 Jan 2021

CD Projekt Red, *The Witcher 3: Wild Hunt*. Poland (2015)

W. Crowther, D. Woods, *Colossal Cave Adventure* (1976). http://dosgames.com/game/colossal-cave-adventure/. Accessed 18 Nov 2020

Luton Cyan, *Myst*. USA (1993)

Devolver Digital, *Stories Untold*. USA (2017)

T. Dubbelman, Narrative game mechanics, in *Interactive Storytelling: 9th International Conference on Interactive Digital storytelling*, (Springer International Publishing, Switzerland, 2016), pp. 39–50

T. Dubbelman, Repetition, reward and mastery: the value of game design patterns for the analysis of narrative game mechanics, in *Interactive Storytelling: 10th International Conference on Interactive Digital Storytelling*, (Springer International Publishing, Switzerland, 2017), pp. 286–289

Eastgate Systems, *Storyspace*. USA (1987)

A. Ensslin, *Literary Gaming* (MIT Press, USA, 2014)

Frictional Games, *Amnesia: Rebirth*. Sweden (2020)

M. Genovesi, Choices and consequences: the role of players in the walking dead: a telltale game series. Open Cult. Stud. **1**, 350–358 (2017)

M. Giovagnoli, *Transmedia Storytelling: Imagery, Shapes and Techniques*. Trans. By Montesano F, Vaglioni P. Published by Lulu.com. USA (2011)

S. Granade, *Will Not Let Me Go* (2017). http://stephen.granades.com/games/wnlmg/. Accessed 24 Nov 2020

C. Groover, *Eat Me* (2017). http://ifarchive.org/if-archive/games/competition2017/Eat%20Me/Eat%20Me/index.html. Accessed 24 Nov 2020

N.K. Hayles, Print is flat, code is deep: the importance of media-specific analysis. Poetics Today **25**(1), 67–90 (2004)

K. Hjaltason, S. Christopherson, J. Togelius, M.J. Nelson, *Game Mechanics Telling Stories? An Experiment* (2015). http://julian.togelius.com/Hjaltason2015Game.pdf. Accessed 18 Nov 2020

C. Hocking, *Ludonarrative Dissonance in Bioshock*. Click Nothing: Design From a Long Time Ago (2007). http://clicknothing.typepad.com/click_nothing/2007/10/ludonarrative-d.html. Accessed 25 Nov 2020

Infocom, *Zork* (1980). http://textadventures.co.uk/games/play/5zyoqrsugeopel3ffhz_vq. Accessed 18 Nov 2020

Infocom, *Planetfall*. USA (1983)

Inkle Studios, *Sorcery! Part 1: The Shamutanti Hills*. UK (2013a)

Inkle Studios, *Sorcery! Part 2: Kharé, Cityport of Traps*. UK (2013b)

Inkle Studios, *Sorcery! Part 3: The Seven Serpents*. UK (2013c)

Inkle Studios, *Sorcery! Part 4: The Crown of Kings*. UK (2013d)

Inkle Studios, *80 Days*. UK (2014)

Inkle Studios, *Ink*. UK (2016)

Inkle Studios, *Heaven's Vault*. UK (2019)

S. Jackson, *Patchwork Girl*. USA (1995)

M. Joyce, *Afternoon, a Story*. USA (1987)

J. Katsarov, M. Christen, R. Mauerhofer, D. Schmocker, C. Tanner, Training moral sensitivity through video Games: a review of suitable game mechanisms. Games Cult. **14**(4), 344–366 (2019)

C. Klimas, *Twine*. USA (2009)

B.A. Larsen, H. Schoenan-Fog, The narrative quality of game mechanics, in *Interactive Storytelling: 9th International Conference on Interactive Digital Storytelling*, (Springer International Publishing, Switzerland, 2016), pp. 61–72

Litrouke, *10pm* (2017). http://ifarchive.org/if-archive/games/competition2017/10pm/10pm.html. Accessed 17 Nov 2020

LucasArts, *Grim Fandango*. USA (1998)

Lutz, M, *The Uncle Who Works for Nintendo* (2014). http://jayisgames.com/games/the-uncle/. Accessed 17 Nov 2020

D.C. Maduro, Choice and disbelief: revisiting immersion and interactivity, in *Digital Media and Textuality: From Creation to Archiving*, (Transcript Verlag, Bielefeld, 2017), pp. 107–130

A. Mangen, A. Van der Weel, Why Don't we read hypertext novels? Convergence Int. J. Res. New Media Technol. **23**(2), 161–181 (2017)

D. Miall, T. Dobson, Reading hypertext and the experience of literature. J. Digit. Inf. **2**(1) (2001). http://journals.tdl.org/jodi/index.php/jodi/article/view/35/37. Accessed 18 Nov 2020

S. Moulthrop, *Victory Garden*. USA (1992)

S. Mukherjee, *Video Games and Storytelling: Reading Games and Playing Books* (Palgrave Macmillan, London, 2015)

G. Nelson, *Inform*. London (1993)

G. Nelson, *Curses*. London (1993)

J.K. Peck, *In The Trees* (2017). https://caspiandepression.itch.io/in-the-trees. Accessed 24 Nov 2020

Platinum Games, *Nier: Automata*. Japan (2017)

J. Pope, 'Where do we go from Here?' Readers' responses to Interactive fiction: narrative structures, Reading pleasure and the impact of Interface design. Convergence Int. J. Res. New Media Technol. **16**(1), 75–94 (2010)

Porpentine, *Howling Dogs* (2012). http://slimedaughter.com/games/twine/howlingdogs/. Accessed 17 Nov 2020

Sf.L.A. Purnomo, *Narrative Junction: Revisiting Design Approach for Role Playing Video Games from the Perspectives of Cognitive Linguistics*. Fantasylicious. (2020). http://www.researchgate.net/publication/339089687_Narrative_Junction_Revisiting_Branching_Narrative_Design_Approach_for_Role_Playing_Video_Games_from_the_Perspectives_of_Cognitive_Linguistics. Accessed 24 Nov 2020

Quantic Dream, *Beyond: Two Souls*. France (2013)

Quantic Dream, *Detroit: Become Human*. France (2018)

Roe C and Mitchell A (2019) 'Is this really happening?' Game mechanics as unreliable narrator. *DiGRA 2019 Game Play and the Emerging Ludo-Mix*. http://digra.org/wp-content/uploads/digital-library/DiGRA_2019_paper_201-min.pdf. Accessed 17 Nov 2020

M.L. Ryan, *Narrative as Virtual Reality 2: Revisiting Immersion and Interactivity in Literature and Electronic Media* (Johns Hopkins University Press, USA, 2015)

See D G, *Time Passed* (2018). http://ifarchive.org/if-archive/games/competition2018/Time%20Passed/Time%20Passed/Time%20Passed.html. Accessed 24 Nov 2020

E. Short, *Galatea*. London (2000)

Y.T. Sim, A. Mitchell, Wordless Games: gameplay as narrative technique, in *Interactive Storytelling: 10th International Conference on Interactive Digital Storytelling*, (Springer International Publishing, Switzerland, 2017), pp. 137–149

Square Enix, *Life if Strange*. Japan (2015)

Supermassive Games, *Until Dawn*. London (2015)

Telltale Games, *The Wolf among Us*. USA (2013)

Chapter 6
The Case for Naive and Low-Fidelity Narrative Generation

Henrik Warpefelt

6.1 Introduction

The procedural generation of complex and believable narrative has long been a subject of research, with much of it focusing on the generation of full and coherent narratives, following the tradition of *Tale-Spin* (Meehan 1977). Although the quality and coherence of these generated artifacts have increased significantly since Meehan presented his seminal work, even the most advanced systems such as *GPT-3* (Brown et al. 2020) still produce output that, although very impressive and convincing, is still fairly easily distinguishable from human output. Furthermore, these highly advanced generators require significant computing resources and extensive data training sets to achieve a sufficient level of believability—to a degree where it is very difficult to understand the underlying model creating the output of the algorithm (Brown et al. 2020). This makes it difficult to integrate these algorithms into games, and to test them as part of a greater user experience. Furthermore, these complex approaches trades off a large amount of user control in favor of a more complex output, an aspect of Artificial Intelligence (AI) technologies that has been raised as a concern for game developers (Johansson et al. 2012). Thus developers may have to design and build games around these algorithms and technologies, rather than using these them to improve their intended game design. As such, a simpler approach may be more favorable.

The aim of this chapter is to highlight a different approach to generative narrative—an approach that may be more amenable to the current design approaches used in the games industry, where it has already seen some success. In this chapter, I

H. Warpefelt (✉)
Department of Software Engineering and Game Development, Kennesaw State University, Marietta, GA, USA
e-mail: research@warpefelt.se

© The Author(s), under exclusive license to Springer Nature Switzerland AG 2022
B. Bostan (ed.), *Games and Narrative: Theory and Practice*, International Series on Computer Entertainment and Media Technology,
https://doi.org/10.1007/978-3-030-81538-7_6

will describe what I call *naive narrative generation*—an approach aimed at lowering the complexity of generative content, and outsourcing parts of the narrative building onto the player. This approach is akin to the storytelling approach used by fairy tales or old folklore, called bardic storytelling by Murray (1997). I will also introduce the concepts of *high-fidelity* and *low-fidelity* generation, discussed from the perspective of narratives. These concepts will be used to describe how different approaches to generative narratives influence how stories are conveyed to the player of the game, and how these narratives in turn influence the player experience. I will also highlight why these techniques and approaches warrant further study from the academic community, and how they can be used to make academic research more relevant to practicing game developers.

6.2   Naive Narrative Generation

At the core of this chapter is the concept of *naive generation*, and particularly as it pertains to narrative. The concept borrows from the computer science definition of a naive algorithm, i.e. an algorithm that is very simple and uses a very direct and uncomplicated approach. Computational naivete is characterized by the process having very few constraints and rules, and little consideration is given to factors like speed or solving the problem in a clever way. Applied to content generation, naivete instead means putting less emphasis on capturing all the perfect nuances and depth of the generated artifact, and instead focusing on producing an easily understood generator that can be built quickly and efficiently, trading off shorter development time for a less complex solution.

If we apply the idea of naive generation to narratives, we aim to create very simple snippets of narrative. Where *GPT-3* (Brown et al. 2020) creates a story several pages long, simpler systems such as *Tale-Spin* (Meehan 1977) create a story that can be contained in a single paragraph. In both of these cases, the story being created is still highly interconnected and each sentence builds on what has happened before, if to a limited degree in *Tale-Spin*, on account of its age. A naively generated narrative would be a loose collection of sentences that fulfill the barest level of interconnectedness. As an example, consider the following story:

The Myth of Torg the Barbarian:
Torg the Barbarian was orphaned at the age of 3.
Torg the Barbarian fought the Dragon of Helmsford.
Torg the Barbarian was crowned the ruler of Helmsford.

In just three short sentences we have told the Myth of Torg—starting with the humble origins of Torg The Barbarian, describing his great deed in fighting the Dragon of Helmsford, and ending with him being crowned the ruler of the same town. As a coherent story this is not very impressive, and does not even reach the level of interconnectedness of the underlying model of *Tale-Spin*, a 40 year old system. However, by reducing the amount of detail and contextualization we have neatly side-stepped many of the problems of narrative coherence. Note that we have no information about Torg the Barbarian, who he is as a character, and why he was actually crowned the ruler of Helmsford. Furthermore, we know next to nothing about the Dragon of Helmsford, nor about Helmsford as itself. However, upon reading this very simple narrative we may still get a sense of the tragic and heroic character Torg the Barbarian, and his valiant defense of Helmsford. None of these things are mentioned in the story, but there is a wide open narrative space for the reader to extrapolate and add their own embellishments. By providing narrative in this simple form, we prompt the reader to apply their own creativity and imagination to fill in the blanks of the narrative.

By all reasonable means this narrative format should not be engaging—and it usually is not beyond this little toy example. The very formulaic nature of the output from this hypothetical generator is very repetitive and unlikely to be engaging in the longer term. This type of ultra-simplistic narrative is also a prime example of what Compton (2016) describes as the *10,000 bowls of oatmeal Problem*, i.e. that a generator can easily spit out 10,000 different variants of something, but they are all more or less the same and provide very little interesting content. However, when it is presented in this simple form the Myth of Torg actually turns into a story. This phenomenon, where simple snippets of narrative is turned into a larger story, is also something we see in fairly successful games—for example *RimWorld* (Ludeon Studios 2016), *Dwarf Fortress* (Bay 12 Games 2006), and *Caves of Qud* (Freehold Games 2015). The style of narrative presentation used by *RimWorld*, *Caves of Qud*, and *Dwarf Fortress* was also common in older games, for example *Sid Meyer's Colonization* (Microprose 1994), developed when technical constraints made it difficult to achieve the level of portrayal used in modern AAA games. We also see this style of narrative presentation being successfully used in some AAA games, for example the *Crusader Kings* series of games (Paradox Development Studio 2012, 2020). But why does it work? To answer that question, we must first explore the concept of fidelity and how it applies to generative content, including narrative.

6.3 Fidelity

In this chapter I use the concept of *fidelity* to describe the sensory complexity and detail by which game content is presented. A high-fidelity game puts heavy emphasis on having state-of-the-art graphics, detailed character animations, a complex soundscape, and generally very finely detailed game world. Conversely, a low-fidelity game tends towards more abstract representation with simpler graphics (perhaps even 2D), less advanced animations, a simpler soundscape, and overall less detail in the game world. Examples of high-fidelity games include *Assassin's Creed: Valhalla* (Ubisoft Montreal 2020), *Cyberpunk 2077* (CD Projekt Red 2020), and *Grand Theft Auto V* (Rockstar North 2013). Examples of low-fidelity games include the aforementioned *RimWorld* (Ludeon Studios 2016), *Dwarf Fortress* (Bay

12 Games 2006), and *Caves of Qud* (Freehold Games 2015), as well as older games that were restricted by the technology of the times, for example *Sid Meyer's Colonization* Microprose (1994). Fidelity, however, isn't strictly binary. Games such as the *Crusader Kings* series (Paradox Development Studio 2012, 2020) occupy a middle ground in terms of fidelity. They are not as sensory complex as the high-fidelity games, but they are also significantly more complex than the low-fidelity games. Thus, fidelity is not a binary value and should instead be measured on a scale, where different games occupy different places on the scale.

If the game reinforces a low-fidelity experience by presenting the player with a less complex sensory experience (i.e. simpler graphics, less complex audio environments, and the like) the player is then conditioned to expect a certain experience in all aspects of the game. Thus, the game can "get away" with a less complex representation of, for example, Non-Player Character (NPC) behavior. In a game like *Assassin's Creed: Valhalla* (Ubisoft Montreal 2020) the player would expect a more complex representation of a greeting between characters where each of the parties is represented using a highly detailed 3D model, and the characters are shown clasping forearms and conversing though pre-recorded sound files. As a contrast, *RimWorld* (Ludeon Studios 2016) the same type of event is represented by moving the characters next to each other and showing speech bubbles with iconography above their heads. These representations are vastly different, but end up being conducive to a positive player experience in their respective games. The reason for this is that both games make sure to situate the player's experience using the game's level of fidelity.

Fidelity influences how the player's understanding of the game is situated, i.e. how that understanding is affected how the player's preconceived notions of the game influence their expectation on their gaming experience (Warpefelt 2020). As described by Kultima and Stenros (2010) the player's experience begins before they even start playing the game, and involves things like advertising, concept art, and trailers for the game. Even at this early stage the player starts establishing expectations on what kind of game this is going to be like, and that process carries on into, throughout, and between play sessions. Because of this, it is critical that the game continuously feeds back into the player's understanding of it, and reinforces the experience that is intended by the designer. Part of this process is the fidelity by which the game is presented, and how that sets a certain expectation (Warpefelt 2020). Borrowing from the field of human-computer interaction, the game must continuously reinforce that it has a certain *character* (Janlert and Stolterman 1997), i.e. a collection of certain characteristics that cast is as being a recognizable form of game—not only in terms of genre but also in terms of complexity of presentation. Thus, the game should continuously reinforce the level of fidelity of the game's presentation. If it fails to do so, the game may be experienced as discordant and confusing. Conversely, if the game manages to reinforce the level of fidelity and properly temper the player's expectation, the game experience will seem more harmonious.

6.3.1   Generative Fidelity

Generative fidelity is fidelity as applied to generative content. In terms of generative narrative, the fidelity of the presentation of the game also sets expectation that the narrative will have a high-fidelity presentation. Because of this, a game like *RimWorld* can again "get away" with a much simpler representation of the narrative. In *RimWorld* there is comparatively little pre-programmed narrative, and instead the narrative of the game is presented through a sequence of short texts describing events, and through in-world events. Conversely, games like *Assassin's Creed: Valhalla* has a large amount of pre-programmed narrative snippets in the form of NPC behavior, cut scenes to provide story, or world events.

6.3.2   Summarizing Fidelity

To summarize, fidelity is the degree by which a game provides a detailed representation of content. The level of fidelity influences the expectations of the player on how the content is going to be presented, and as the fidelity of graphical presentation increases, so must the fidelity of narrative presentation. Conversely, a lower fidelity graphical presentation can also allows a game to maintain a lower level of narrative while still making the narrative seem believable. In the following section we will discuss some of the problems associated with procedural generation, and how they can possibly be sidestepped by reducing the level of fidelity of the generated content.

6.4   Limits of Narrative Generation

There are a few common issues with procedural content generation. In addition to the aforementioned *10,000 bowls of oatmeal problem* (Compton 2016), we also have the twin problems of *expressive range* described by Smith and Whitehead (2010) and the *Kaleidoscope problem* described by Cardona-Rivera (2017). Lastly, we have the problem of the *Black hole of AI* and the trade-off between complexity and control of game design described by Johansson et al. (2012).

As previously discussed, the *10,000 bowls of oatmeal problem* (Compton 2016) describes the fact that a it is trivially easy for a generator to create many different combinations of things, but that few of them are actually interesting—much like oatmeal. Even if you create thousands of different bowls of plain oatmeal, the problem remains that plain oatmeal is just bland. As an antidote to this problem, Compton (2016) suggests two degrees of uniqueness for generated artifacts: *perceptual differentiation* and *perceptual uniqueness*. Perceptual differentiation is the less difficult to achieve of the two, where each generated artifact is perceptually not identical to the next one, but not necessarily entirely unique. Compton exemplifies procedural differentiation using trees: if the trees are all identical or insufficiently varied they will not be seen as natural by even a casual observer, but if they fulfill a basic level of variance they can still be different enough that they fulfill the aesthetic needs of the game, despite each tree not being unique and memorable. An example of this principle in practice would be *SpeedTree* (IDV 2021), a technology commonly used in games and cinema to generate various forms of vegetation. The various trees used by SpeedTree are not necessarily entirely unique, but they are varied enough because players generally do not scrutinize the foliage to a degree where uniqueness matters. The more difficult level described by Compton (2016) is perceptual uniqueness, where each generated item is distinct and unique from the next—or *characterful* as Compton describes it. Compton does not further define the concept of *characterful*, but by connecting to the concept of *character* presented by Janlert and Stolterman (1997) we can describe it as a collection of characteristics that make the generated object distinct from other objects in the game. Compton (2016) uses the metaphor of the object being the lead actor instead of an extra in a movie, and notes that not everyone can be the main character, which also matches the concept of *character* as described by Janlert and Stolterman (1997). A unique object set against a background of more homogeneous objects will stand out more than a unique object lost in a sea of other unique objects. Thus, there exists a need for perceptually different as well as perceptually unique objects. In a concrete example, a game may use SpeedTree to generate the vast majority of a forest, and then use uniquely designed trees as visual markers to guide the player through the level or to provide narrative told through the environment of the game world (Fernández-Vara 2011).

Applied to the space of narrative, the *10,000 bowls of oatmeal problem* captures the fact that it is trivially easy for us to generate narratives along the lines of *The Myth of Torg* that was described above. Each narrative runs the risk of becoming much like the next, and there is seemingly very little of neither perceptual differentiating nor uniqueness in *The Myth of Torg* style narratives. Fortunately, the player understanding of narratives is situated by the fidelity of the game. As we have seen in games such as *RimWorld* (Ludeon Studios 2016) and *Dwarf Fortress* (Bay 12 Games 2006) small snippets of narrative like those presented in *The Myth of Torg* can still achieve believability of they are properly situated with an appropriate level of fidelity—i.e. if the game sets the player's expectations to be in accordance with the content and how it is presented. Thus, if the player's expectations are set in accordance with the complexity of the narrative it will still be perceived as believable and engaging—an effect that we see in the aforementioned games.

However, the problems described by Compton (2016) are fundamentally related to the *Kaleidoscope Problem* described by Cardona-Rivera (2017), and the problem of *expressive range* described by Smith and Whitehead (2010). Where Compton discusses what makes generated content dull or interesting, Cardona-Rivera as well as Smith and Whitehead provide the mechanism by which this happens: once the player starts finding patterns in the generated content they can quickly discern what the generator is capable of creating, and that breaks the illusion of the game. This, in turn, causes the breakdown of various aspects of the gaming experience, such as immersion (McMahan 2003; Ermi and Mäyrä 2005) and suspension of disbelief (Coleridge 1817). Even if the narrative presented by the game is properly situated with an appropriate level of fidelity, the player experience may still be negatively affected if the player is able to perceive the borders of the expressive range of the generator.

The obvious solution to this problem is to apply more technologically advanced solutions to create higher quality generated experiences. However, there are two problems with this approach, as described by Johansson et al. (2012). Game developers are hesitant to implement technologies that take away their control over the design of the game, what Johansson et al. (2012) call trading complexity for control. Furthermore, spending work hours adding more AI technology to a game is often subject to severe diminishing returns—something Johansson et al. (2012) call *the Black Hole of AI*. As stated by Johansson et al. (2012), players are unlikely to notice the more advanced technology due to diminishing returns, and the implementation of those features may have come at the expense of other parts of the game. As AI models grow more complex they grow more expensive to use, and they become more difficult to implement. Because of this, integrating them into a game design becomes very time consuming. Both of these factors add to the development costs of a game, something that is already problematic for the games industry (Tschang 2007). Thus, the financial and labor realities of game development projects favor less complex and more predictable generative approaches—or in our terminology more naive generative approaches. However, as we see above these approaches come with their own design constraints in terms of expressive range and the need for situation.

6.5   The Role of Naive and Low-Fidelty Generation

Given the problems and trade-offs associated with implementing generative content in games, it is clear that there exists a large need for future research into how we apply generative technologies in games. Games already make extensive use of generative technology (as seen in the examples earlier in this chapter) but as described in Sect. 6.4 there are also distinct problems associated with generative content. As previously mentioned, one area that has been (and remains) especially problematic is the generation of complete narratives. Fortunately, this is where a naive and low-fidelity approach to generated content may be useful.

One approach game developers can apply to alleviate the issues of narrative generation is to use the inherently emergent nature of game narratives to their advantage, especially when implementing naive and low-fidelity generative technologies. The narrative of a game is not simply a linear experience presented to a passive consumer, but instead the player takes an active role in the gaming experience. Calleja (2009) presents a division between the *scripted narrative*, which are the parts of the game narrative that are hard-coded into the game, and the *alterbiography*, which are the player's own first-person story of how they played the game. In the case of generative narratives, the *scripted narrative* is what is created by the generative process, whereas the player's *alterbiography* remains the player's own story. Thus, the goal of the game in terms of narrative is to provide the relevant *scripted narrative* pieces to help build an engaging *alterbiography* for the player.

What I advocate in this chapter is essentially taking what *SpeedTree* (IDV 2021) does for vegetation generation and applying it to narrative generation. The vast majority of the content created by *SpeedTree* is not unique or a "main character" as per Compton's terminology. Instead, it forms a distinct but still fairly uniform background on which the more distinct features are set. Similarly, there is a lot of content in games that exist to create world building. As noted by Bartle (2004) and later Warpefelt and Verhagen (2016), this is the role already played by one of the most prominent AI-powered feature in games: NPCs. As described by Bartle (2004), and by Warpefelt and Verhagen (2016), NPCs play a large role in making game world seem alive. If they are presented in coherence with other diegetic game elements, they become part of the game's environment, which is used to enhance the gaming experience and provide narrative to the player, or what Fernández-Vara (2011) calls *indexical storytelling*. By simply existing in the game world, NPCs help build the narrative of the game.

If we apply this reasoning to other generated artifacts in the game world, we can create the fond of less perceptually unique but still differentiated content that acts as a backdrop to larger, more unique events—thereby "thickening" the narrative experience of the player—essentially providing the *scriped narrative* described by Calleja (2009) through the mechanism of *indexical storytelling* described by Fernández-Vara (2011). This then influences and supports the player's construction of their *alterbiography* (Calleja 2009). Described using the theory presented by Barthes and Duisit (1975) the content created using naive and low-fidelity approaches thus acts as catalyst for the player's interpretation of the narrative, and provide a of narrative hints that help the player integrate various forms of key events, or what Barthes and Duisit (1975) call *cardinal functions*. Between these *cardinal functions* are gaps in the narrative that need to be filled by the player, what Barthes and Duisit calls *interstitial gaps*. The filling of these gaps is performed using the mechanism of *indexical sotrytelling* (Fernández-Vara 2011), which the player uses a catalyst (Barthes and Duisit 1975) to create their *alterbiography* (Calleja 2009).

As an example of how this type of narrative presentation has been done in practice, consider *RimWorld* (Ludeon Studios 2016). *RimWorld* is a survival game where the player is in charge of a small collection of colonists trying to survive on, and eventually escape from, a hostile alien planet. The narrative of the game is mostly driven by events, or what Mateas and Stern (2007) would call *story beats*, set against a background of longer periods of peaceful existence. These events (or beats) occur on multiple levels: a narrative director will by default throw events at the player to keep tension at an engaging but reasonable level, weather changes can either be a blessing or a curse on the player, and colonists may experience various emotional states (nervous breakdowns, falling in love, depression, contentment, or even death) that can cause events. The player's colony may develop friendly or hostile relationships with neighboring tribes or colonies, and the lives of the colonists. Each of these events are only loosely connected to each other, but over time the player starts inferring connections between these events and creating meaning from them, making the player build an *alterbiography* of the colony as they experienced it.

In a sense, the approach to narrative used in games like *RimWorld* is very similar to how Murray (1997) describes bardic storytelling, i.e. as a set of formulas within formulas used in conjunction with variable content to create reasonably novel stories by essentially plugging in names and events to weave narratives. Some of these narratives grew to become very formulaic, as can be evidenced by the work of Propp (1968) on the decomposition of folk tales into simple grammars.

In games, naive and low-fidelity generated content takes on the role that helps build the atmosphere in the game. The mechanism that makes naive and low-fidelity generation work for this purpose is that it presents familiar patterns in familiar combinations, similar to bardic storytelling (Murray 1997). It should be noted, however, that naive and low-fidelty narrative generation not necessarily simple random substitution, but instead a curated selection of alternating different contextually appropriate options, again in line with how Murray (1997) describes bardic storytelling. However, a naive approach does not necessarily mean that the implementation is simplistic at the cost of all other aspects. Each event must be properly situated within a context that makes it legible to the player, and conducive to an engaging gaming experience. However, when we take a low-fidelity approach to generation that context can be more or less rigorously defined, and using a low-fidelty presentation can help spark the player's own creative process and make them fill out the gaps in the narrative by integrating it as a part of their *alterbiography* (Calleja 2009).

6.6 Conclusion

To summarize, current high-fidelity approaches to the procedural narrative generation, like *GPT-3* (Brown et al. 2020), are technically costly and difficult to use, and because of that they are likely to be less useful for game development (Johansson et al. 2012). Furthermore, developers who use these advanced techniques need to trade off control over their game design, and will have to invest extensive development time into making them integrate with the game, as described by Johansson et al. (2012).

A naive and low-fidelity approach to generating narratives may be more applicable in many cases. Using a naive generative approach allows for a greater control over the content presented in the game. This approach may also have benefits in terms of difficulty of integrating the generator into the game design. Furthermore, a naive and low-fidelity approach may help build believability for generated narratives created using a more high-fidelity approach by providing more context for the more complex narrative, and acting as a "thickening agent" for the overall gaming experience. In the words of Barthes and Duisit, naive and low fidelity generation creates integrative content that acts as catalytic (Barthes and Duisit 1975) and indexical markers (Fernández-Vara 2011; Warpefelt 2020), and lets the player infer the *cardinal functions* (Barthes and Duisit 1975) of the story. As described by Barthes and Duisit (1975) the *interstitial gaps* between *cardinal functions* can be infinitely filled with content. In the case of naive and low fidelity narrative generation we simply provide less scaffolding and rely more heavily the player's catalytic filling process.

Although much research into generative content has been focused on complex tasks such as full game generation or the generation of highly complex narratives, there has been comparatively little focus on how to help developers create the vast areas of the game that need to be what Compton (2016) calls perceptually different, but not necessarily what she calls perceptually unique. These less diverse and unique parts still play a critical role in supporting the player experience, and the generation of them and their role in contributing to the narrative of the game is currently understudied, despite these elements commonly featuring in various forms. In a talk at the Game Developers Conference Abernathy and Rouse (2014) also make the point that players tend to more strongly recall the parts of the game experience where the narrative intersected with game play rather than the big story beats and game plots presented by the game. This lends further strength to the argument that focusing on the naive and low-fidelity generative parts may be a productive approach if we want to increase the relevance of academic research to industry practice.

Thus, this chapter makes the case for naive and low-fidelity generation of content. Note that this is not simple random substitution, and that a naive approach still need the generated content to be contextually relevant. However, the required level of contextual relevance can be managed and contained by using a low-fidelity approach to generation, which enacts the player's own creative process.

Given the relative proliferation of low-fidelity presentation of generative content and narrative in existing games there has been comparatively little research into how that type of technology supports game design. Granted, naive approaches are likely not exciting from the perspective of pure technical research, but they may still be interesting from the perspective of game design research. Given the costs associated with developing games (Tschang 2007) and with integrating AI technologies (Johansson et al. 2012) it would be beneficial to investigate what constitutes the minimum viable level of generative content, and how that level changes depending on the fidelity of the game's presentation.

References

T. Abernathy, R. Rouse, *Death to the Three Act Structure! Towards a Unique Structure for Game Narratives*, in Talk at Game Developers Conference (2014)

R. Barthes, L. Duisit, An introduction to the structural analysis of narrative. New Literary History **6**(2), 237–272 (1975)

R. Bartle, *Designing Virtual Worlds* (New Riders, Indianapolis, 2004)

Bay 12 Games, Dwarf Fortress. [PC Game] (2006)

T.B. Brown, B. Mann, N. Ryder, M. Subbiah, J. Kaplan, P. Dhariwal, A. Neelakantan, P. Shyam, G. Sastry, A. Askell, S. Agarwal, A. Herbert-Voss, G. Krueger, T. Henighan, R. Child, A. Ramesh, D. M. Ziegler, J. Wu, C. Winter, C. Hesse, M. Chen, E. Sigler, M. Litwin, S. Gray, B. Chess, J. Clark, C. Berner, S. McCandlish, A. Radford, I. Sutskever, D. Amodei (2020) Language models are few-shot learners. http://arxiv.org/abs/2005.14165

G. Calleja, Experiential narrative in game environments, in *DiGRA'09 - Proceedings of the 2009 DiGRA International Conference: Breaking New Ground: Innovation in Games, Play, Practice and Theory* (2009)

R.E. Cardona-Rivera, Cognitively-grounded procedural content generation, in *Proceedings of the What's Next of AI in Games Workshop at the 31st AAAI Conference on Artificial Intelligence, Association for the Advancement of Artificial Intelligence*, pp 1027–1028 (2017)

CD Projekt Red, Cyberpunk 2077. [PC and Console Game] (2020)

S.T. Coleridge, Biographia Literaria. n.p., (1817). Retrieved February 23, 2021, from Project Gutenberg http://www.gutenberg.org/ebooks/6081

K. Compton, So you want to build a generator (2016). https://galaxykate0.tumblr.com/post/139774965871/so-you-want-to-build-a-generator

L. Ermi, F. Mäyrä, Fundamental components of the gameplay experience: analysing immersion, in *DiGRA'05 - Proceedings of the 2005 DiGRA International Conference: Changing Views: Worlds in Play* (2005)

C. Fernández-Vara, Game spaces speak volumes: indexical storytelling, in *DiGRA'11 - Proceedings of the 2011 DiGRA International Conference: Think Design Play, DiGRA/Utrecht School of the Arts* (2011)

Freehold Games, Caves of Qud. [PC Game] (2015)

IDV, Speedtree (2021). http://www.speedtree.com/

L.E. Janlert, E. Stolterman, The character of things. Des. Stud. **18**(3), 297–314 (1997)

M. Johansson, M.P. Eladhari, H. Verhagen, Complexity at the cost of control in game design? in *5th Annual International Conference on Computer Games, Multimedia and Allied Technology (CGAT 2012), Global Science and Technology Forum (GSTF)* (2012)

A. Kultima, J. Stenros, Designing games for everyone: the expanded game experience model, in *Proceedings of the International Academic Conference on the Future of Game Design and Technology* (2010), pp 66–73

Ludeon Studios, RimWorld. [PC Game] (2016)

M. Mateas, A. Stern, Writing façade: a case study in procedural authorship, in *Second Person: Role-Playing and Story in Games and Playable Media*, ed. by P. Harrigan, N. Wardrip-Fruin (MIT Press, Cambridge, 2007), pp 183–208

A. McMahan, Immersion, engagement and presence, in *The Video Game Theory Reader*, ed. by M.J. Wolf, B. Perron, chap. 3 (Routledge, London, 2003), pp. 67–86

J.R. Meehan, Tale-spin, an interactive program that writes stories, in *Proceedings of the 9th International Joint Conference on Artificial Intelligence* (1977)

Microprose, Sid Meyer's Colonization. [PC Game] (1994)

J.H. Murray, *Hamlet on the Holodeck: The Future of Narrative in Cyberspace* (The Free Press, New York, 1997)

Paradox Development Studio, Crusader Kings 2. [PC Game] (2012)

Paradox Development Studio, Crusader Kings 3. [PC Game] (2020)

V. Propp, *Morphology of the Folktale*, 2nd edn. (University of Texas Press, Austin, 1968)

Rockstar North, Grand Theft Auto V. [PC and Console Game] (2013)

G. Smith, J. Whitehead, Analyzing the expressive range of a level generator, in *Proceedings of the 2010 Workshop on Procedural Content Generation in Games* (ACM, New York, 2010), p. 4

F.T. Tschang, Balancing the tensions between rationalization and creativity in the video games industry. Org. Sci. **18**(6), 989–1005 (2007)

Ubisoft Montreal, Assassin's Creed: Valhalla. [PC and Console Game] (2020)

H. Warpefelt, Micro-level examination of games using indicator analysis, in *FDG'20: International Conference on the Foundations of Digital Games* (ACM, New York, 2020), pp. 1–9. https://doi.org/10.1145/3402942.3402980

H. Warpefelt, H. Verhagen, A typology of non-player characters, in *The Workshop on Social Believability in Games at The 1st Joint Conference of DiGRA & FDG'16* (2016)

Part II
Social and Cultural Studies

Chapter 7
Azeroth Has a Workplace Gender Inequality Problem: Gendered Professions Bias in Virtual Worlds

Sercan Sengun, Jennifer Price, Lyndsie Schlink, and Kristin Walker

7.1 Introduction

From its release back in 2004, Blizzard Entertainment's *World of Warcraft* (WoW) stays as the essential and insurmountable massively multiplayer online role-playing game (MMORPG) experience. In 2020, the virtual world of *Azeroth* (the main and the most popular planet that the game takes place despite other planets and planes of existence were added to the game later) might have around five million players (Brown 2020), gradually declined from its peak of 12 million players back in 2010 (Peckham 2013). As a result, WoW stays as the authentic testbed for research on virtual communities (Nardi and Harris 2006), online communication (Chen 2009), game design (Ducheneaut et al. 2006), and digital identities (Bessière et al. 2007).

Due to its large user base, extensive social interactions, and rich in- and out-of-game community and culture, the game has also proved to be an ideal environment for studies around gender, especially digital gender performance (Eklund 2011), body and avatar immersion through gender roles (Stavropoulos et al. 2021), and virtual gender fluidity and queer identities (Chang 2015; Schmieder 2009).

In this study, we examine the issue of gender representation in a virtual world through the lens of gendered profession bias (also called occupational gender segregation). The biases around gendered professions are an extension of gender inequality, sexism, and even sexual harassment problems in workplaces. This

S. Sengun (✉)
Wonsook Kim School of Art, Creative Technologies Program, Illinois State University, Normal, IL, USA
e-mail: ssengun@ilstu.edu

J. Price · L. Schlink · K. Walker
Creative Technologies MS Program, Illinois State University, Normal, IL, USA
e-mail: jmprice@ilstu.edu; laschl2@ilstu.edu

kind of bias and inequality in thinking about an employment role as feminine or masculine might come from organizational (Stamarski and Leanne 2015) and societal (see Hideg and Ferris 2016 for an explanation on how occupational gender segregations can occur) structures.

Professions in WoW are an optional activity for players to create virtual items that benefit themselves or that can become commercial commodities. There are two types of primary professions in the game (in addition to a group of secondary professions): (1) the gathering professions enable players to collect raw materials from the world; and (2) the crafting professions enable players to create items from those raw materials. A character in WoW can choose to master in two primary professions as well as all secondary professions. Apart from the players themselves, the non-playable characters (NPCs) around such professions form the backbone of the "blue-collar" workforce in the virtual world of Azeroth. The choices around the design of such characters can reflect the narrative, culture, and societal structures of the world, as well as shed light on some of the real-world bias that seeps into the virtual worlds that we build.

Our work complements Bergstrom et al.'s (2011) study of the same subject, and explores the changes within the last decade, as well as adding new dimensions to the discussions such as intersections of the in-game factions that superimposes racial and post-colonial narratives onto the findings.

7.2 Background

7.2.1 Gendered Professions Bias

Many professions such as public relations (Aldoory and Toth 2002), engineering (Cech et al. 2011), teaching (Drudy 2008), and nursing (George 2008) are offered to have gendered circles or display pervasive gender bias both within the public and professionals. While some of these professions are considered more masculine, some remain feminine or more feminized over the past years as the result of social and labor market changes. In the physical world, the so-called "feminization" of a profession (e.g., primary education) sits at the intersections of multiple issues, namely "economic development, urbanization, the position of women in society, cultural definitions of masculinity," etc. (Drudy 2008). Some studies offer gendered differences in approach, as well as biological and physical conditions as the possible reasons for such distinctions. For example, Loscocco et al. (1991) offer that women-led small businesses are usually associated with the least profitable industries. Güngör and Biernat (2009) offer that motherhood may become a disadvantage for hiring women as blue-collar workers. Menstrual cycles (Barnack-Tavlaris et al. 2019) and breastfeeding (Kasdan 2001) have also been offered as reasons for discrimination against women in the most workforce.

The perceptions around gendered professions can negatively affect educational and professional choices of individuals (such as female students' avoidance of or poor persistence in STEM fields, see Griffith 2010; Sadler et al. 2012; Chen 2013), as well as their experiences and performances in the field once they become a part of it—see examples in engineering from Cech 2015; in law from Levinson and Young 2010; in accounting from Loft 1992; and in academia from Dion et al. 2018.

7.2.2 Gender, Race, and Videogames

The issues around gender representation had been prevalent in videogames from the beginning of the medium. Beasley and Standley (2002) examine 47 randomly selected games and conclude that "*a significant sex bias in the number of male versus female characters found in the games and among the way in which the male and female characters were dressed*" (p. 279). Similarly, Ivory's (2006) content analysis reveals that female videogame characters are underrepresented in all categories such as playable characters, active/passive NPCs, and focal points in game images. Whenever female characters were represented, however, they are likely to be disproportionately more sexualized compared to their male counterparts. In their virtual census of 150 best-selling games of the decade, Williams et al. (2009) find "*a systematic over-representation of males, white and adults and a systematic under-representation of females, Hispanics, Native Americans, children and the elderly*" (p. 815). However, as a result of the issue being in the spotlight from the early 2000s and push from the stakeholders such as players, scholars, journalists, etc., some issues around gender representation improved over time. In 2015, Kondrat (2015) asserts that "*there is a difference between portraying women in the past and present [and although] there is still negative stereotyping of female gender [...] the target audience of video games desires improvements*" (p. 171). In a 2020 book, Cole and Zammit (2020) observe that the number of female protagonists might be declining yet again recently, especially in high-profile (also called AAA) games.

Videogames also have a poor reputation in racial representation and persistently misrepresent certain races and groups such as associating crime with characters representing black masculinity (Leonard 2004), Latin American and Latinx communities (Penix-Tadsen 2013), poor representations of both the communities and the continent of Africa (Brock 2011; Harrell et al. 2021), as well as Arabs and Arab nations (Šisler 2008) among others.

In a massively multiplayer online game like WoW, identity, especially gender, is performed on multiple levels: first, through the avatars and behaviors of players (regardless of the player's physical-world identity or gender; see Eklund 2011; Corneliussen and Rettberg 2008; Pearce 2017; and Şengün 2014, 2015, for some examples that study identity and gender performance through avatars); and second, through how the societies and mythologies of the world are constructed. Although the societal structures, narratives, and mythologies of WoW do not heavily display inherent sexism,[1] the racial narratives have been offered to possess essentialism (Monson 2012), as well as occasional racist (Pace 2008; Ritter 2010) and post-colonial (Langer 2008) undertones. For example, as a fantasy race, all dwarfs are portrayed as "crude beer-lovers with bad Scottish accents" (Bartle 2010) and voodoo-loving hut-dwelling trolls are associated with unmistakable Jamaican accents (Askmo 2012). Some professions are integrated into the narratives of these fantasy societies in an essentialist way: most if not all dwarfs like mining and blacksmithing, most if not all gnomes have an affection for engineering, etc. In this aspect, it is possible to envision the reasons why the virtual characters related to these professions can dominantly come from specific races, however, it is less possible to envision the reasons why some professions have a gender bias in such a high-fantasy world where female and male characters fight with demons, dragons, and evil gods side-by-side.

7.3 Methodology

Since there is no official public database for WoW, we mobilized the data from Wowhead.com, a user-generated online database that automatically collects data from participating users' clients during gameplay (more details on how Wow-head.com works is explained in Whynot 2011). Wowhead.com was used as a reliable data source in previous studies regarding WoW (see Thorne et al. 2012; Gibbs et al. 2012; Santos and Ramalho 2012).

We visited the specific database of each profession[2] and manually browsed the *Trainers* section while coding the gender,[3] race, faction (*Horde, Alliance,* or both), and origin patch for each character. For the origin patch, we only noted the first digit which indicates the expansion pack[4] when this character was added to the game. To clean our data, we adhered to the following rules:

---

[1]Nardi (2010) asserts that although the design of female characters in WoW generally prioritize the male gaze (Mulvey 1975), apart from employing some impractical and unnecessarily revealing "kombat lingerie" (Fron et al. 2007), the female characters are "for the most part [...] relatively modest" (p. 159). However, Myers (2012) points out some enduring sexist content in the game such as certain dialogue and design decisions.

[2]E.g., For Alchemy, we used https://www.wowhead.com/alchemy#trainers; for Blacksmithing, we used https://www.wowhead.com/blacksmithing#trainers; and so on.

[3]Since these are virtual characters, they cannot self-report their gender or gender identity. So, to do this coding, we relied on WoW's very distinct character models that differentiate between female and male bodies for all playable races distinctively. Since Wowhead.com hosts screenshots for all these NPCs, it was possible for researchers (who are experienced with WoW) to determine the gender based on the provided visual information.

[4]1.x patches indicate the original World of Warcraft (2004) game; 2.x patches indicate The Burning Crusade (2007) expansion; 3.x patches indicate the Wrath of the Lich King (2008) expansion; 4.x patches indicate the Cataclysm (2010) expansion; 5.x patches indicate the Mists of Pandaria (2012) expansion; 6.x patches indicate the Warlords of Draenor (2014) expansion; 7.x patches indicate the

- We merged all allied races' data to their originating race. For example, the data of Kul Tiran Humans was merged with Humans, the data of Zandalari Trolls was merged with Trolls, the data of Gilgoblins was merged with Goblins, etc. Some allied races like the Vulpera did not need flattening since they produced no data points.
- The data from unplayable races were eliminated. These races include Oribos Brokers, Ankoans, Arakkoas, Tortollans, Klaxxi, etc.
- Although not a playable or an allied race, the data of Taunka trainers was merged with Taurens due to in-game lore reasons.
- General or multi-profession trainers were recounted for each profession, thus, contributing to the results of all professions that they teach.

As a result, we end up with 739 NPCs that teach 15 professions. Only 279 of the in-game professions trainers (37.8%) are female. In terms of faction, they had a precise distribution: 288 *Alliance*, 288 *Horde*, and 163 trainers serving both factions. Our dataset is available as a GitHub repository.[5]

7.4   Results

As of patch 9.x, There are 15 professions in WoW: *Alchemy, Archaeology, Black-smithing, Cooking, Enchanting, Engineering, Fishing, Herbalism, Inscription, Jew-elcrafting, Leatherworking. Mining, Riding, Skinning,* and *Tailoring.*

First, we check the female versus male trainer percentages for each profession (see Fig. 7.1). There were only two professions (13.3% of all professions) where female trainers barely outnumbered male trainers: *Herbalism* (51.7% female) and *Archaeology* (56.5% female). For two professions (13.3%), gender distribution was almost equal: *Tailoring* (49.4% female, 50.6% male) and *Riding* (sharp 50% for both). For all other eleven professions (73.4%), the male trainers outnumbered the female ones. Out of these professions. we designated two categories: professions with a gender bias (60%–74% male) and professions with a severe gender bias (75 + % male). The professions with a gender bias were: *Leatherworking* (60.4%), *Inscription* (63.6%), *Alchemy* (64.6%), *Skinning* (66.7%), and *Engineering* (67.9%). The professions with a severe gender bias were: *Blacksmithing* (sits close to the border with 74.6%), *Fishing* (78%), and *Mining* (81.5%).

Previous studies highlight construction, mining, and heavy manufacturing (that could relate to blacksmithing) as traditional fields with a bias toward requiring 'masculine' traits (Pinto et al. 2017). In our data, we see this bias seep into the virtual world of *Azeroth*, although there is no practical reason why that should be the case.

Legion (2016) expansion; 8.x patches indicate the Battle for Azeroth (2018) expansion; and finally, 9.x patches indicate the Shadowlands (2020) expansion.

[5]https://github.com/sercansengun/azeroth-workplace-gender-inequality

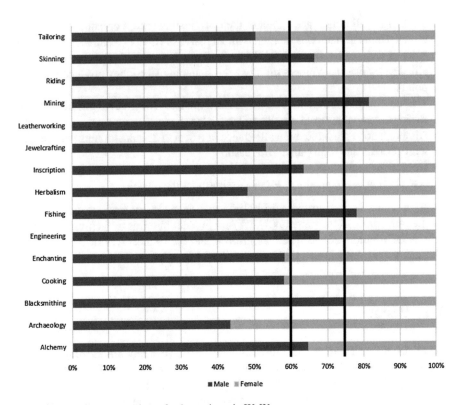

Fig. 7.1 Female versus male profession trainers in WoW

Compared to Bergstrom et al.'s 2011 data, the gender disparity in *Mining* (down to 81.5% male trainer from 92.3%) and *Blacksmithing* (down to 74.6% male trainer from 76.9%) are a bit ameliorated, but *Fishing* is retrograded (up to 78% male trainer from 74.2%). In contrast, *Herbalism* has become less female-oriented in the last 10 years (down from 63.6% male trainer to 51.7%) and *Archaeology*, that was a non-existent profession back in 2011, starts with a female orientation. It is encouraging to see that *Engineering* is now more female-friendly (up to 32.1% female trainers from 21.9%), however, it is still far away from equal representation. In *Inscription* (down to 36.4% female trainer from 44.4%) and *Skinning* (down to 33.3% female trainers from 40.7%), the female trainers lost ground. We provide the comparative data as Table 7.1.

Second, to complement the historical comparison, we display the virtual female workforce percentages per profession based on the patches that the characters were added to the game (see Table 7.2). Since patch 9.x mostly added "Oribos Broker" profession trainers who are not included in the data (see Methodology), percentage changes between 8.x and 9.x are negligible.

From the data, it is possible to see that the female workforce in *Alchemy* and *Inscription* started close to equal representation but then fell as early as the next

Table 7.1 Comparison of our 2021 data with Bergstrom et al.'s 2011 data

Profession	Change in female representation	Female		Male	
		2011	2021	2011	2021
Alchemy	▼	36.7%	35.4%	63.6%	64.6%
Archaeology[a]	•	N/A	56.5%	N/A	43.5%
Blacksmithing	▲	23.1%	25.4%	76.9%	74.6%
Cooking	▲	33.3%	41.9%	66.7%	58.1%
Enchanting	▼	42.3%	41.9%	57.7%	58.1%
Engineering	▲	21.9%	32.1%	78.1%	67.9%
First Aid[b]	•	56.3%	N/A	43.7%	N/A
Fishing	▼	25.8%	22%	74.2%	78%
Herbalism	▼	63.6%	51.7%	36.4%	48.3%
Inscription	▼	44.4%	36.4%	55.6%	63.6%
Jewelcrafting	▲	40%	46.7%	60%	53.3%
Leatherworking	▼	40%	39.6%	60%	60.4%
Mining	▲	7.7%	18.5%	92.3%	81.5%
Riding	•	N/A	50%	N/A	50%
Skinning	▼	40.7%	33.3%	59.3%	66.7%
Tailoring	▲	45.5%	49.4%	54.5%	50.6%

[a]Profession was not available in 2011
[b]No longer a separate profession in 2021. *First Aid* was integrated into Tailoring

Table 7.2 Cumulative percentage of female trainers per profession per patch

	1.x	2.x	3.x	4.x	5.x	6.x	7.x	8.x	9.x
Alchemy	46.7	33.3	35.5	35.9	36.6	34.9	35.6	34	34
Archaeology	0	0	0	43.8	41.2	47.4	50	56.5	56.5
Blacksmithing	22.2	20.8	23.7	24	21.8	22.8	23.8	23.9	23.9
Cooking	25	38.5	43.2	43.2	45.3	43.6	43.9	41	41
Enchanting	40	47.1	52.2	43.8	42.9	40.5	40	41.9	41.9
Engineering	6.25	15.4	26.5	24.4	24.4	25.5	26	32.1	32.1
Fishing	15	22.2	25	22.9	21.1	20	19.6	22	22
Herbalism	63.2	60	62.5	55.8	55.1	54.9	53.6	50.8	51.7
Inscription	0	0	46.2	33.3	34.6	35.7	35.7	37.5	37.5
Jewelcrafting	50	50	38.5	45.8	48	48.1	48.1	46.7	46.7
Leatherworking	37.5	39.1	34.4	35	34.1	36.4	38.8	39.6	39.6
Mining	0	5.56	8	15	15.6	14.9	17.6	18.5	18.5
Riding	25	33.3	42.1	54.2	50	50	50	50	50
Skinning	41.7	47.1	39.1	36.4	33.3	32.5	31	33.3	33.3
Tailoring	36	43.6	47.1	46.8	47.9	50	50.6	49.4	49.4

patch from when they were introduced and stayed consistently around one-third of the trainers. *Skinning* is another profession that started stronger for female representation but settled down around patch 5.x to one-third of the population. *Tailoring, Riding,* and *Cooking* started male-dominated but then risen close to equal

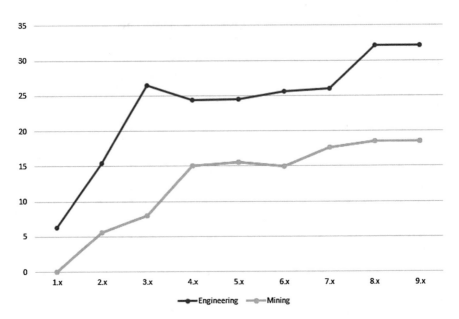

Fig. 7.2 Cumulative percentage of female trainers per patch for *Engineering* and *Mining* professions

representation. *Blacksmithing* and *Fishing* have been consistently low with only one-fifth of the workforce being female, while *Leatherworking* and *Enchanting* consistently staying around two-fifths. *Jewelcrafting* stayed as an equal-opportunity profession for genders in WoW and *Archaeology* swung from being male-dominated to female-dominated between the patches 4.x and 8.x. *Herbalism* starts as a female-dominated profession but equalizes over time. *Engineering* and *Mining* started remarkably poor for female representation and, although, they got better over time, still stay as fields where Azerothian women may not be welcome (see Fig. 7.2).

Third, we explore if female versus male representations in professions change according to factions. In WoW, there are two opposing factions: *Horde* and *Alliance*. Previous studies (Langer 2008; Ritter 2010; Pressnell 2013) offer readings of these two factions along the lines of colonialism wherein *Alliance* is offered as morally high-grounded, civilized, urban, industrial, religious, and, generally, Western and familiar, while *Horde* is offered as morally ambiguous, savage, tribal, primitive, spiritual, exotic, and, generally, other and foreign. The divide was much more apparent in the earlier versions of the game when the *Horde* cities, especially *Orgrimmar,* were designed significantly less settled and industrial than *Alliance* cities such as *Stormwind* or *Ironforge*. Additionally, in the first version of the game, *paladin* class (that might be likened to medieval religious knights) was only accessible to *Alliance* players, while *shaman* class (typically attributed to the religious and spiritual practices of non-Western cultures) was only accessible to *Horde* players—a design choice that deepened the colonial otherness of the *Horde*.

Orcs, the driving race of the *Horde* faction, can also be considered as immigrants, since they arrived at Azeroth from another planet. The tension between humans who want to welcome Orcs to their lands versus those who want them to go back to where they have come from has been a major narrative theme at the beginning of the game. (On the other side, the tensions between Orcs who want to conquer human lands versus Orcs who believe that they can live side-by-side with the humans have been a parallel theme.) It should be noted that the racial narratives and representations of both factions became more nuanced over time, moving away from the stereotypes in some respects. However, the post-colonial and orientalism discussions emerged once more around the release of the fifth expansion *Mists of Pandaria* that added the Pandaren race to the game whose culture was adopted from the Chinese elements and mythology (Rivera 2017; Wu 2020).

For this analysis, we eliminate the trainers who serve both factions (typically found in neutral spaces as members of other in-game factions that remain neutral) and only focus on faction-specific trainers. By comparing the female workforce percentage of *Alliance* versus *Horde* professions trainers, it was possible to see that *Horde* female characters were more afforded to be miners, fishers, and alchemists compared to their *Alliance* counterparts, while *Alliance* female characters could more easily become archaeologists (see Fig. 7.3).

The results are interesting in a way that while *Mining* and *Fishing* remains male-dominant overall, *Horde* displays more gender equality in those fields. This is in-line with the essentialist preconceptions of the lifestyles of indigenous people or families in developing countries wherein women might take the lead in food provisioning (Kuhnlein 2017) and physical work (McCallum 2014). The imbalance in *Alchemy* might be related to perceptions around who is more likely to perform witchcraft, however, *Horde* also contains the Undead race that has thematic connections to this profession. *Alliance* female characters being more likely to become archaeologists completes this picture since *Archaeology* can be considered as a more scholarly and colonial field.

7.5 Discussion

In this study, we investigated gendered profession bias in the design of a virtual world. The virtual characters living in this world are not bound by physical bodies and their indicated biological genders do not have any practical meaning (e.g., they do not procreate or nurture their young). Moreover, the player avatars can indiscriminately become heroes, travel to dangerous locations, fight powerful foes, and, essentially, do anything they want within the confinements of the game rules, regardless of their gender. In fact, gender has no effect on the gameplay experience in terms of rules and game mechanics (although it might have tremendous effects on the personal and social experiences in the online community). Despite this equal opportunity afforded to the player characters of all genders, the rest of the game world seems to employ a societal gender-based order for blue-collar professions-

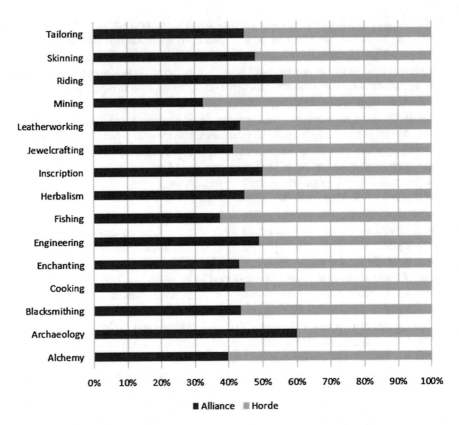

Fig. 7.3 Percentage of female trainers per profession between *Alliance* and *Horde* factions

related NPCs. We collect and analyze the data of all profession trainers in the game to illustrate this point. Since there is no practical reason for a gender gap for professions in a virtual world, we offer these results as a projection of real-world bias into virtual world designs.

Our results indicate that, although there have been small improvements over time, some professions (such as *Mining, Blacksmithing, Engineering, Fishing*, etc.) remain moderate to heavily male-biased. There are a few professions that have more or less equal representation (such as *Herbalism, Jewelcrafting, Riding*, and *Tailoring*), however, some of these professions might be accepted to already have feminized undertones in the physical world. Only one profession was marginally female-dominant and that was *Archaeology* with 56.5% female trainers.

We also investigated the situation along the lines of the factions (*Alliance* versus *Horde*). The original design of these two factions has been offered as being post-colonial and racially charged in that *Alliance* representing the "familiar" cultures of Western societies, and *Horde* representing the "foreign" and "uncivilized" otherness. Over the years, however, factions have gone through many changes, including new races, city designs, storylines, etc. that alleviate (but not eradicate) these undertones. In line with these post-colonial narratives, we find that the *Horde* female characters are more likely to become miners and fishers, and *Alliance* female characters are more likely to become archaeologists.

Harrell and Lim (2017) propose the concept of the *avatar dream* that entails "using the computer to imagine [ourselves] as whomever or whatever [we] want to be" (p. 50). To construct this blending of identity exploration and imagination, the game designers need not only focus on the avatar options and affordances given to their players, but also on the design of the worlds, societies, and narratives that these avatars live in. The gender choices for layperson NPCs in a virtual world might seem arbitrary, however, they might also become the tools that infuse biases in a virtual community. We do not argue that equal gender representation can be achieved through NPC headcounts, but game designers must be aware of the complexities of the ecosystems they build and their possible effects in recuperating or reinforcing the tired stereotypes inside those new virtual environments that could have the potential of repudiating and fighting these biases instead.

A.1 Ludography

World of Warcraft (Blizzard Entertainment, 2004)

References

L. Aldoory, E. Toth, Gender discrepancies in a gendered profession: a developing theory for public relations. J. Public Relat. Res. **14**(2), 103–126 (2002)

C. Askmo, *Non-Standard Features in World of Warcraft: An Exploratory Study of Role-Players' Orthographic Features and Lexical Items*, Unpublished Thesis (2012)

J.L. Barnack-Tavlaris, K. Hansen, R.B. Levitt, M. Reno, Taking leave to bleed: perceptions and attitudes toward menstrual leave policy. Health Care Women Int. **40**(12), 1355–1373 (2019)

R. Bartle, Digital culture, play and identity: a World of Warcraft reader. Game Stud. **10**(1) 2010

B.C. Beasley, T.C. Standley, Shirts vs skins: clothing as an indicator of gender role stereo-typing in video games. Mass Commun. Soc. **5**(3), 279–293 (2002). https://doi.org/10.1207/s15327825mcs0503_3

K. Bergstrom, V. McArthur, J. Jenson, T. Peyton, All in a day's work: a study of World of Warcraft NPCs comparing gender to professions, in *Proceedings of the 2011 ACM SIGGRAPH Symposium on Video Games* (2011), pp. 31–35

K. Bessière, A.F. Seay, S. Kiesler, The ideal elf: identity exploration in world of Warcraft. Cyberpsychol. Behav. **10**(4), 530–535 (2007)

A. Brock, When keeping it real goes wrong: resident evil 5, racial representation, and gamers. Games Cult. **6**(5), 429–452 (2011)

A. Brown, *How Many People Are Playing World of Warcraft*, ScreenRant.com (2020).https://screenrant.com/world-warcraft-players-amount-servers-popular-subscribers-total/. Accessed 26 Feb 2020

E. Cech, Engineers and engineeresses? Self-conceptions and the development of gendered professional identities. Sociol. Perspect. **58**(1), 56–77 (2015)

E. Cech, B. Rubineau, S. Silbey, C. Seron, Professional role confidence and gendered persistence in engineering. Am. Sociol. Rev. **76**(5), 641–666 (2011)

E.Y. Chang, Love is in the air: queer (im) possibility and straightwashing in FrontierVille and world of Warcraft. QED J. GLBTQ Worldmaking **2**(2), 6–31 (2015)

M.G. Chen, Communication, coordination, and camaraderie in world of Warcraft. Games Cult. **4**(1), 47–73 (2009)

X. Chen, *STEM Attrition: College Students' Paths into and Out of STEM Fields*. Statistical analysis report. NCES 2014–001. National Center for Education Statistics (2013)

A. Cole, J. Zammit, *Cooperative Gaming: Diversity in the Games Industry and how to Cultivate Inclusion* (CRC Press, Boca Raton, 2020)

H. Corneliussen, J.W. Rettberg, *Digital Culture, Play, and Identity: A World of Warcraft Reader* (MIT Press, Cambridge, 2008)

M.L. Dion, J.L. Sumner, S.M. Mitchell, Gendered citation patterns across political science and social science methodology fields. Polit. Anal. **26**(3), 312–327 (2018)

S. Drudy, Gender balance/gender bias: the teaching profession and the impact of feminization. Gend. Educ. **20**(4), 309–323 (2008)

N. Ducheneaut, N. Yee, E. Nickell, R.J. Moore, Building an MMO with mass appeal: a look at gameplay in world of Warcraft. Games Cult. **1**(4), 281–317 (2006)

L. Eklund, Doing gender in cyberspace: the performance of gender by female world of Warcraft players. Convergence **17**(3), 323–342 (2011)

J. Fron, T. Fullerton, J. Morie, C. Pearce, The hegemony of play, in *Proceedings of Digra Conference* (2007), pp. 309–381

A. George, Nurses, community health workers, and home careers: gendered human resources compensating for skewed health systems. Glob. Public Health **3**(S1), 75–89 (2008)

M. Gibbs, J. Mori, M. Arnold, T. Kohn, Tombstones, uncanny monuments and epic quests: memorials in World of Warcraft, Game Studies, **12**(1) (2012)

A.L. Griffith, Persistence of women and minorities in STEM field majors: is it the school that matters? Econ. Educ. Rev. **29**(6), 911–922 (2010)

G. Güngör, M. Biernat, Gender bias or motherhood disadvantage? Judgments of blue collar mothers and fathers in the workplace. Sex Roles **60**(3), 232–246 (2009)

D.F. Harrell, C. Lim, Reimagining the avatar dream: modeling social identity in digital media. Commun. ACM **60**(7), 50–61 (2017)

D.F. Harrell, S. Şengün, D. Olson, Africa and the avatar dream: mapping the impacts of videogame representations of Africa, in *The Digital Black Atlantic*, (University of Minnesota Press, Minneapolis, 2021)

I. Hideg, D.L. Ferris, The compassionate sexist? How benevolent sexism promotes and undermines gender equality in the workplace. J. Person. Soc. Psychol. **111**(5), 706 (2016)

J.D. Ivory, Still a man's game: gender representation in online reviews of video games. Mass Commun. Soc. **9**(1), 103–114 (2006). https://doi.org/10.1207/s15327825mcs0901_6

D. Kasdan, Reclaiming title VII and the PDA: prohibiting workplace discrimination against breastfeeding women. NYUL Rev. (76), 309 (2001)

X. Kondrat, Gender and video games: how is female gender generally represented in various genres of video games? J. Comp. Res. Anthropol. Sociol. **6**(1), 171–193 (2015)

H.V. Kuhnlein, Gender roles, food system biodiversity, and food security in indigenous peoples' communities. Mater. Child Nutr. (13) (2017)

J. Langer, The familiar and the foreign: playing (post) colonialism in world of Warcraft, in *Digital Culture, Play, and Identity: A World of Warcraft Reader* (2008), pp. 87–108

D. Leonard, High tech blackface: race, sports, video games and becoming the other. Intell. Agent **4**(4.2), 1 (2004)

J.D. Levinson, D. Young, Implicit gender bias in the legal profession: an empirical study. Duke J. Gender Law Policy **18**(1), 1–33 (2010)

A. Loft, Accountancy and the gendered division of labour: a review essay. Account. Organ. Soc. **17**(3–4), 367–378 (1992)

K.A. Loscocco, J. Robinson, R.H. Hall, J.K. Allen, Gender and small business success: an inquiry into women's relative disadvantage. Soc. Forces **70**(1), 65–85 (1991)

M.J.L. McCallum, *Indigenous Women, Work, and History: 1940–1980* (University of Manitoba Press, Winnipeg, 2014)

M.J. Monson, Race-based fantasy realm: essentialism in the World of Warcraft. Games Cult. **7**(1), 48–71 (2012)

L. Mulvey, Visual pleasure and narrative cinema. Screen, (16), 6–18 (1975)

J. Myers, *Why is Blizzard still OK with Gender Inequality in World of Warcraft?*, Engadget.com (2012). https://www.engadget.com/2012-04-03-why-is-blizzard-still-ok-with-gender-inequality-in-world-of-warc.html. Accessed 26 Feb 2020

B.A. Nardi, *My Life as a Night Elf Priest: An Anthropological Account of World of Wacraft* (University of Michigan Press, Ann Arbor, 2010)

B.A. Nardi, J. Harris, Strangers and friends: collaborative play in World of Warcraft, in *Proceedings of the 2006 20th Anniversary Conference on Computer Supported Cooperative Work* (2006), pp. 149–158

T. Pace, Can an orc catch a cab in stormwind? Cybertype preference in the World of Warcraft character creation interface, in *CHI'08 Extended Abstracts on Human Factors in Computing Systems* (2008), pp. 2493–2502

A.M. Pearce, Exploring performance of gendered identities through language in world of Warcraft. Int. J. Hum. Comput. Interact. **33**(3), 180–189 (2017)

M. Peckham, *The Inexorable Decline of World of Warcraft*, Time (2013).https://techland.time.com/2013/05/09/the-inexorable-decline-of-world-of-warcraft/. Accessed 26 Feb 2020

P. Penix-Tadsen, Latin American ludology: why we should take video games seriously (and when we shouldn't). Latin Am. Res. Rev. **48**(1), 174–190 (2013)

J.K. Pinto, P. Patanakul, M.B. Pinto, The aura of capability: gender bias in selection for a project manager job. Int. J. Proj. Manag. **35**(3), 420–431 (2017). https://doi.org/10.1016/j.ijproman.2017.01.004

L.A. Pressnell, *Building a World of Warcraft: Cyber-Colonialism through Othering Strategies.* Unpublished Doctoral Thesis, University of Alabama (2013)

C.J. Ritter, *Why the Humans are White: Fantasy, Modernity, and the Rhetorics of Racism in World of Warcraft.* Washington State University, Unpublished Doctoral Thesis (2010)

Rivera, T, Orientalist biopower in world of Warcraft: mists of Pandaria, in *The Routledge Companion to Asian American Media* (2017), p. 195

P.M. Sadler, G. Sonnert, Z. Hazari, R. Tai, Stability and volatility of STEM career interest in high school: a gender study. Sci. Educ. **96**(3), 411–427 (2012)

F.K.C. Santos, G.L. Ramalho, A parametric analysis and classification of quests in MMORPGs, in *Proceedings of SBGames 2012*, (SBC, Brazil, 2012), pp. 117–126

C. Schmieder, World of maskcraft vs. world of queercraft? Communication, sex and gender in the online role-playing game World of Warcraft. J. Gaming Virtual Worlds **1**(1), 5–21 (2009)

S. Şengün, A semiotic reading of digital avatars and their role of uncertainty reduction in digital communication. J. Media Crit. (1) (2014), Special, pp. 149–162

S. Sengün, Why do I fall for the elf, when I am no orc myself? The implications of virtual avatars in digital communication. Comunicação e Sociedade. (27), 181–193 (2015)

V. Šisler, Digital Arabs: representation in video games. Eur. J. Cult. Stud. **11**(2), 203–220 (2008)

C.S. Stamarski, S.S.H. Leanne, Gender inequalities in the workplace: the effects of organizational structures, processes, practices, and decision makers' sexism. Front. Psychol. (6), 1400 (2015)

V. Stavropoulos, J. Rennie, M. Morcos, R. Gomez, M.D. Griffiths, Understanding the relationship between the Proteus effect, immersion, and gender among world of Warcraft players: an empirical survey study. Behav. Inform. Technol. **40**, 821–836 (2021). https://doi.org/10.1080/0144929X.2020.1729240

S.L. Thorne, I. Fisher, X. Lu, The semiotic ecology and linguistic complexity of an online game world. ReCALL **24**(3), 279–301 (2012). https://doi.org/10.1017/S0958344012000158

T.A. Whynot, Success through collaboration: what the players of world of Warcraft can teach us about knowledge production and sharing in virtual communities. Dalhousie J. Interdisc. Manage. **7**(2) (2011). https://doi.org/10.5931/djim.v7i2.73

D. Williams, N. Martin, M. Consalvo, J.D. Ivory, The virtual census: representations of gender, race, and age in video games. New Media Soc. **11**(5), 815–834 (2009). https://doi.org/10.1177/1461444809105354

Z. Wu, Cultural adoption in World of Warcraft, in *Proceedings of 2020 4th International Seminar on Education, Management and Social Sciences (ISEMSS)*, (Atlantis Press, Paris, 2020), pp. 519–524

Chapter 8
Narrative Design in Turkish Video Games: History and Comparison

Ertuğrul Süngü and Esin Selin Güregen

8.1 Video Games in Turkey and Narratology

Digital games are played by millions of people worldwide, and the industry of digital games is one of the fastest-growing industries. The growth in the digital game market, which exceeded 70,000 dollars in 2012, has more than doubled in 7 years and exceeded 15,000 dollars. Growth in the mobile game market since 2015 has peaked, surpassing the growth in console and PC games.[1] According to the data released in May 2019 by Entertainment Software Association (ESA), 65% of adults in the USA regularly play video games, and most games are played on mobile phones with a staggering 60% rate. It is known that the average age of gamers is 33 years old.[2] In the light of these developments, game developers in Turkey, who are already closely following the digital games industry, aim to produce games that could compete in this global market. About 30 million people in Turkey are playing games, and the game market in Turkey was valued at 750 million dollars, yet in 2018 it reached 878 million dollars (Dijital Oyunlar Raporu (*Digital Games Report*) 2019, 10).

---

[1]Newzoo, Global Game Market Report Premium, 2018.

[2]2019 Essential Facts: About the Computer and Video Game Industry, The Entertainment Software Association (ESA).

E. Süngü
Bahçeşehir University, Istanbul, Turkey
e-mail: ertugrul.sungu@comm.bau.edu.tr

E. S. Güregen (✉)
İstinye University, Istanbul, Turkey
e-mail: esin.guregen@istinye.edu.tr

© The Author(s), under exclusive license to Springer Nature Switzerland AG 2022
B. Bostan (ed.), *Games and Narrative: Theory and Practice*, International Series on Computer Entertainment and Media Technology,
https://doi.org/10.1007/978-3-030-81538-7_8

Nowadays, games have become more accessible. With the diversification in the games, not only these hyper-casual games rose in number, but the number of games that focus on narrative has also increased. Mostly the digital environment directly affects the creation and circulation processes of texts. Developing technologies transformed storytelling, revealing an interactive narrative that users can influence and have a personalized experience through it. Even if the same game with linear or branched storytelling is played again, it can offer different experiences. The user (i.e., the player in this context) not only watches the fantastic world to which is new and stranger to them, but also can make changes in this world, and these changes will have meaningful results. For this reason, digital games are highly suitable tools to use in every element of storytelling (Cassidy 2011). Combining narrative elements with game mechanics, these games offer more than a gaming experience to the player and leave the game's control in the hands of the player. Even though it is not too often, narrative science is also used in the games that are developed in Turkey. The main subject of the study is following three narrative-rich Turkish games; *Lale Savaşçıları, Conarium,* and *Stygian: Reign of the Old Ones.*

8.2 Purpose

Different types of games have been released worldwide in recent years, and the digital gaming industry in Turkey is also following such global trends. Although the production and consumption of practical, hyper-casual, and similar types of games are much more prominent, some game developers are working on narrative games that deal with themes they are interested in, albeit in smaller numbers. Following titles are given to provide examples of successful narrative-focused games which are developed in Turkey; *Lale Savaşçıları* utilizes a theme of Turkish and Anatolian origin. On the other hand, *Conarium* and *Stygian: Reign of the Old One* has much more of a Lovecraftian theme.

The objective of this research can be separated into numbered titles. First of all, this research aims to examine the changes and developments of Turkish narrative games developed on different concepts from past to present. The research also focuses on understanding and finding out why the number of narrative-focused games developed in Turkey is insufficient quantity-wise and the reason behind this phenomenon. Thus, we will be examining why two out of three games that are at the center of this study include the themes that revolve around the works of Lovecraft, and only one of them has utilized strictly Turkish and Anatolian themes. A comparative analysis of the researched games was conducted to reinforce the subjects. In general, the studies around digital games in Turkey and narratology are relatively limited in number (Bostan and Marsh 2010; Şengün 2015; Demirbaş 2017; Akbaş 2019). Therefore, this study has the potential to fill up the gap in Turkish academia, and in a broader, global sense, it can be a guiding source for studies on Turkish games. Finally, personal interviews were done with the producers of the games examined during the study, and their opinions on the Turkish game industry were acknowledged; and as a result of these interviews, evaluations were made about the state of the industry through the experiences of game developers who have been/are actively involved in the game industry.

8.3 Research Method

8.3.1 Comparative Analysis Method

There are different features that each medium brings to its content. In the same way, it is crucial to address and interpret their interactivity and multi-layered structure when analyzing video games. In "Introduction to Game Analysis," Clara Fernández-Vara guides the basic building blocks of game analysis (Fernández-Vara 2014). The analysis of the games has been carried out by considering the three analysis areas stated in the book, and the games were compared according to these areas. Comparative analysis enables us to analyze and compare two or more objects or ideas and reveal the similarities and differences between the said objects or ideas (Bukhari 2011). While using this method, the differences in the similarities and the similarities in the differences between the cases are analyzed (Çakın 1989, 15). The purpose of comparative analysis is to help predict or explain current or future events by drawing some conclusions about past events (Dierkes et al. 1987). *In the Handbook of Comparative Communication Research* (2012), edited by Esser and Hanjtzsch, it is suggested that; comparative communication research should utilize at least two macro-level units (systems, cultures, markets, or sub-elements of these) based on at least one comparative item in the context of the study subject. Comparative studies differ from non-comparative studies as they reveal results beyond a single system or culture and explain differences and similarities between analysis items based on their context (Esser and Hanitzsch 2012, p. 6).

   The stage of determining the analysis units is crucial for the reliability of the research conducted. "The smallest unit counted in content analysis is called an 'analysis unit'. Words, news headlines, sentences, characters, themes, visual elements, all the texts can be considered as an analysis unit according to the purpose. It is essential to construct and define the categories in which the analysis units will be placed" (İrvan, 2000, 77). While applying this method, each unit considered is first examined in detail in the context of the research subject. Then, the subject's characteristic features are determined, and the similarities and differences are revealed as a result of following through the topics of the research (Esser and Vliegenthart 2017, 251). It is possible to compare time periods and themes to see how storytelling changes in the games under consideration in the specific sub-topics, such as the game's development, game theme, and target demographic. The essential features of these themes were examined and the question of how they shaped the narrative has been taken into consideration. While the game *Lale Savaşçıları*, which was examined during the study, adopted a satirical narrative style, *Conarium* and *Stygian* revolve around concepts based in the Cthulhu Mythos.

Before the research is detailed, it will be helpful to explain the concepts and themes of the games briefly. Theme can be described as the meaning of the narrative; it expresses the reason for the story (Adams 2013). While the setting provides an emotional connection to the game, it is also possible to use a specific setting within different kinds of themes. Our first research subject is a very satirical game called *Lale Savaşçıları*. The concept of satire which has its roots in Ancient Rome has been described in Yüksel Baypınar's paper, "Hiciv Kavramı Üzerine Bir İnceleme" (*An Examination on the Concept of Satire*) (1978, 32) as such; "The purpose of satirists is to mock and criticize the flaws, injustices, distortions in society or institutions, the bad and unpleasant aspects of human life, and their views. The most prominent feature of satire that separates the text from any other kind of critical text (as in it involves criticism) is that it has an overriding direction of humor and amusement." Satire is based on social criticism. However, given that this criticism is not direct, it is carried out indirectly. Writers of satirical works draw the reader to the text by using fluent language and reveal the thoughts behind the topic that needs to be discussed and criticized. From this point of view, other than being the first locally developed digital role-playing game (RPG), *Lale Savaşçıları*, is differentiating from other examples thanks to its satirical atmosphere which shines through in-game dialogues.

On the other hand, *Conarium* and *Stygian* have narratives that revolve around the Cthulhu Mythos, which has been first coined as a term by August Derleth and points towards themes, shared elements, characters, and fiction that Howard Philips Lovecraft either created or gave inspiration to. It is the name given to the fictional universe created by Lovecraft, one of the writers who left his mark on the twentieth century with his cosmic horror literary wave and tension-filled narratives and the whole body of works that includes stories in this universe are considered a part of it. It is named after the imaginary presence of Cthulhu in these stories. Cthulhu, an extraterrestrial being, is generally described in these works as a massive creature with octopus-like features, a head full of tentacles on the face, a scaly-looking body, and large claws on its front and hind legs (Strickland 2007). After Lovecraft's death, many authors also perpetuated the myth. By the twenty-first century, Cthulhu has become a phenomenon, and works that use it as a theme have been produced in different mediums. Another area inspired by this rich narrative world is games; tabletop games, card games, and digital role-playing games are included in this category (Bauer 2019). This rich cosmic horror concept of Lovecraft has been combined with games by adapting the stories told in the written format to games (Ekin, 2019). For example, the game, which is also known as Call of Cthulhu Roleplaying, takes place in three different periods in general, and sanity is an essential variable in such games. These characteristics are unique to Call of Cthulhu (Küpçü 2011).

8.4 Comparative Analysis of the Examined Games

İstanbul Efsaneleri: Lale Savaşçıları, Conarium, and *Stygian* are productions that received positive feedback from gamers, both with their narrative-rich content and being successful examples of their genres. By comparing these games, differences in narrative styles were determined. Later, personal interviews were held with the producers of the games, and the opinions of these game developers about the Turkish game industry were revealed.

It is of great importance for our research to compare the games discussed in the correct comparison units. In line with this purpose, in comparative studies, the critical elements of the research subject should be determined and turned into research topics (Esser and Vliegenthart 2017, 251). When considered in the context of our research, critical topics used in building narratives in digital games are also determined. All of the selected topics below are interconnected and affect the game experience and narrative altogether.

8.4.1 Game Genre

When we examine it according to the game genre, *Lale Savaşçıları* is the first role-playing game developed as digital media in Turkey. The creation process of the four controllable characters in-game has been designed in a particular and well-detailed way. *Stygian*, another role-playing game, is developed around the idea of mixing RPGs and turn-based tactical game genres. Just like *Lale Savaşçıları*, it features a detailed character creation process and players can personalize their in-game characters. *Conarium*, otherwise, is an adventure game, it does not contain any role-playing game features, and the progress in the game is happening through solving puzzles. To summarize, while *Lale Savaşçıları* and *Stygian* shares a similar game genre *Conarium* is different from the other titles in the sense of the game genre.

8.4.2 Theme

When we analyze these games in terms of themes, *Stygian* and *Conarium's* usage of Lovecraftian themes and the fact that they are inspired by Lovecraft's works is clearly apparent. When asked why there was a Lovecraftian theme in these two productions, *Stygian's* creative director Can Oral (Personal communication, December 4, 2019) stated that he has been reading Lovecraft since the age of 10; thus, he has a strong understanding of this theme. He stated that the idea of a Film Noir RPG game with supernatural elements (Noir-The Film-Noir RPG/1996) appealed to him, seeming like an experience he might want to play. The

Cthulhu Mythos is a well-established and accepted IP[3] (Intellectual Property); it is determined as appropriate for use in *Stygian*. Onur Şamlı (Personal communication, December 4, 2019), one of the team members that developed *Conarium*, also developed two games before, which Lovecraft's works had inspired. He states that he and his brother have been interested in gothic morbid fiction and works of literature since they were very young. They met with H.P. Lovecraft's works through these interactions. He also says that they thought developing a game that revolves around Lovecraftian influences made sense to them because of the circumstances, as mentioned earlier. Apart from that, Şamlı says that because Lovecraft is a famous writer, a game that includes these stories brings a large audience of players. This is a considerable advantage in terms of advertising the game. So much so, the fact that *Stygian's* Kickstarter campaign gathered support worldwide and on the first 5 days, it reached more than 30,000 Euro funding. At the end of the campaign, it reached 73,742 Euro funding[4] is proof that this strategy that game developers works have utilized. Users accessed the game through Kickstarter; the largest group is with 1004 supporters from America and the second-largest group is 201 supporters from Germany, followed by the United Kingdom with 200 people and 143 people from Turkey.[5] The developers of both Lovecraftian-themed games have chosen to use this theme in their games, being aware of the popularity it brings and the intense interest in Lovecraft's work. Moreover, considering that there are 1880 games with contents that include the Cthulhu concept on the Steam platform as of February 2021, it is evident that this theme is already well-known in the digital game medium.

İstanbul Efsaneleri is specific to Turkey in terms of its subject and has developed an ideological narrative through this element by using Istanbul as a gameplay element. Unlike the other two games, in *Lale Savaşçıları* almost all the elements used are local in origin, and *Lale Savaşçıları* is a role-playing game specific to Turkey in that sense.

8.4.3   Character Creation and Existing Characters

In games based on storytelling, characters are of great importance in terms of gameplay. Two of the three games discussed are RPG games, detailed character options, and developable abilities in these two games. While *Lale Savaşçıları* offers a total of seven different character types and four main characters that the player can control, *Stygian* has seven archetypes and six belief systems to choose from when

---

[3]This term refers to products which has a patent, copyright or a service brand (Biymed,?) and is used because it points towards works of art such as books literature, inventions, designs, symbols and games and their intellectual rights (Romero 2016).

[4]Data is based on Stygian's Kickstarter site from December 9, 2019.

[5]Supporter   data: https://www.kickstarter.com/projects/1698219403/stygian-a-lovecraftian-computer-rpg/community

Fig. 8.1 A view from the Character Creation screen in *Stygian: Reign of the Old Ones*

creating the main character (Fig. 8.1). Can Oral stated that he tried a method that he could define as "mental acting" during the writing phase of the characters and tried to insert himself into the character he wrote with all their flaws, passions, unique gestures, and emotions. These options in the character creation process in *Stygian* deepens the game and make each game experience different. According to Can Oral, *Stygian*, compared to *Lale Savaşçıları*, much more adhere to dramatic and tragic side of the narration, and it focuses much more on reality and multidimensionality in narrative structures as well. Onur Şamlı, however, states that *Conarium* differs from *Lale Savaşçıları* with its fixed main character and linear storytelling (Personal communication, December 4, 2019). *Conarium* has a fixed main character in the story, and the players continue the game by directing this fixed character.

8.4.4 Game Mechanics

Lale Savaşçıları's game mechanics have similarities with *Dungeons and Dragons* (1974), which is the basis of most role-playing games. The game mechanics are quite unique at the time of its release as the first role-playing game Turkey. They push the player to act strategically, allowing them to use their palate/vocabulary (equivalent to *mana* in D&D) points, phrases (spells), and items in the game. To progress in the game, it is necessary to go to the mentioned districts and complete the assigned quests. In the game *Stygian*, progress is dependent on the experience gained by the main character and the information they add to their own journal, and the management of the dialogue options in the game is of great importance in terms of progress. The game is based on the mental health of the main character;

the progress of the game changes as the level of "sanity" decreases. During the dialogues, the skills of the characters develop and level up. *Stygian*, compared to *Lale Savaşçıları,* has a multi-layered (or multi-dimensional if you will) storyline and this is of the factors that affect the differentiating gaming experience between two titles. *Conarium* is based on the principle of the main character changing locations, finding notes left in the past, and solving the puzzles they encounter. Onur Şamlı describes the operation used in the game as a historical narrative (Personal communication, November 4, 2019).

8.4.5   The Language Used in the Game

Lale Savaşçıları, with its satirical and sincere language, is an example not previously precedented in the Turkish game industry. While entertaining the player with its humorous dialogues, it makes them think by emphasizing the missing points, the game takes on an ideological meaning rather than being an entertainment tool in this context. It also contains slang words in harmony with its narrative's sincerity; play on Turkish words and puns also enriches the game. *Conarium* has a narrative language suitable for the mystery and tension factors it contains, and the use of language in the dialogues shows parallels to this fact. Since it is a game played in a first-person perspective, the dialogues are also designed accordingly. *Stygian: Reign of the Old Ones,* on the other hand, is themed around a story that takes place in the 1920s in New England, and the language used in the game is reflecting of this as it utilizes older and grandiloquent English.

8.4.6   The Universe of the Game

Since two of the three games examined are inspired by Lovecraft's fictional universe, it is possible to see that these game universes' are inspired by the works of the author. Because *Conarium*'s story is inspired by Lovecraft's *"At the Mountains of Madness"* there are many parallels with the novel. The game takes place in and near the Upuaut Research Center on the Antarctic continent, where a research team goes to study. As Şamlı states, the atmosphere in the game is built upon the eerie feeling of being alone in the wilderness of this untrodden and frozen continent, between the members of a species that belongs to civilization from outer space. A map of the area where the game takes place is shown in Fig. 8.2.

Likewise, *Stygian* is a game that has Lovecraftian themes as well, and it carries traces of many of Lovecraft's works in its narrative. The game starts in Arkham, which has been "somehow got detached from the world and moved onto another dimension". These two games have some common elements in terms of handling similar themes. In the game *Stygian*, there is a university named Miskatonic University as shown on the map in Fig. 8.3. When the characters in *Conarium*

Fig. 8.2 Image from the map of *Conarium*

Fig. 8.3 Image of the map in *Stygian: Reign of the Old Ones*

are examined, the researchers who are the subject of the game are studying in the Anthropology Department of Miskatonic University in the reality of its universe. As it can be seen, the concepts and expressions previously known by game fans who are familiar with the Lovecraftian themes were included in both of these games, which has been examined in our research. The player is expected to observe the places on this map and go to the required area for their quests.

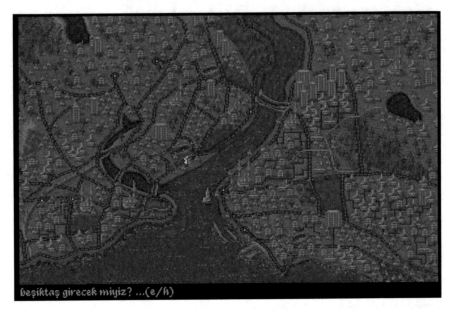

beşiktaş girecek miyiz? ...(e/h)

Fig. 8.4 Image of the map in *Lale Savaşçıları*

Lale Savaşçıları takes place in a fantastical version of İstanbul, which is designed around the real city. During the game, the main characters go to certain districts of İstanbul to complete the assigned quests and actually tour Istanbul. A familiar experience is designed for game lovers living in or knowing İstanbul (Fig. 8.4).

8.4.7 Camera Mode

Lale Savaşçıları utilizes two different perspectives together. During regular gameplay, players see through the eyes of the characters, as in the first-person perspective. The player has the feeling of being included in the game by watching the events from the perspective of the characters. When the game progresses to the battle stage, camera mode switches, the game continues with an isometric camera perspective, making it easier to observe the characters from a distance and control them on the battlefield. *Conarium* continues from a primary-person perspective throughout the entire game experience. It can be stated that this camera mode, which is used to make the main character's perspective translate into first-hand experience for the player and facilitate the focus due to the puzzle-heavy progress of the game, has been successful. Otherwise, *Stygian* presents the game from a tertiary perspective using an isometric strategical camera during the game. Complementing the game's modern graphical design, this use of perspective is suitable for the game. It offers the player a more comfortable gaming experience in the game's universe.

8.4.8 Interaction

Interaction can be defined as mutual or reciprocal action or influence[6] and when it comes to digital games, interaction becomes an even more important topic. When examined through games, interaction expresses how the player experiences the game with its story, mechanics, and setting (The Artifice 2017). In this context, *Lale Savaşçıları* offers players an intimate experience with its dialogues that break the fourth wall and the language it uses. It allows the players to direct the flow of the game by offering options during the dialogues, and in general, *Lale Savaşçıları* promises a fun experience to the players. *Conarium* allows the player to interact with items in the game, prompts the player to think strategically, and must focus entirely on the game to unravel the mysteries in the game. Its puzzle system makes the player feel in control of the game and successfully finishing puzzles are rewarded with in-game progress. *Stygian*'s multi-layered structure and intense storytelling provide a long-term gaming experience to players.

Another common point that *Stygian* and *Lale Savaşçıları* have, apart from the game genre is that both games have cliffhanger[7] endings. Players experiencing the game will encounter an incomplete plot in these games and probably became curious about how the story will continue. However, *Conarium*'s story is narratively complete at the end of the game, and it can be said that its story is "realized" in this regard.

8.4.9 Utilization of Technological Infrastructure

Lale Savaşçıları was designed in 1994 using the technologies of its time, as a game initially produced for the AMIGA platform. In this context, it is not difficult to guess that the game's design process is much more complex compared to known modern games. The advertisement process of this game was also tricky. The other two games, one of which was released in 2017 and the other in 2019, were designed and released with much more practical and accessible technologies than it was available in the past, utilizing modern infrastructure. Even at the stage of producing the games, developers reached their target audience, not only in Turkey but also worldwide, and they managed to get support and feedback from potential players of their games. The well-known theme addressed by these two games should also be considered here. From this perspective, *Conarium* and *Stygian* are

---

[6]According to the official description of "interaction" in Merriam-Webster's online dictionary (Merriam-Webster n.d.).

[7]Especially in Works that are published in episodes, the producers trying to ensure the continuing interest of the audience, aim to break up the story in a way that leaves the audience curious. Optimizing this understanding for excitement and matching the particularly exciting part of the story to the end of the episode is called "cliffhanger" (Bilgin 2018).

games that benefited from the convenience provided by the developing technological infrastructure and targeting an already existing target audience. *Lale Savaşçıları,* otherwise, started its journey as both the first RPG game and as targeting a niche audience in Turkey. After the game's release, advertising, and distribution stages have also been much more time-consuming than they would have been today. However, even though in mid-90s Turkey, game development and gaming were not at the forefront of the Turkish people's minds, this attempt at creating a locally inspired RPG has met with great interest of gamers at the period. To summarize, it can be said that the developers of *Lale Savaşçıları* have been through a complicated process in terms of the technological infrastructure of the period. However, the return they received, as a result, was satisfactory.

8.4.10 Analysis of Gaming Industry in Turkey

All three games that were the subject of this study had been developed in Turkey. During personal interviews, when the game developers were asked about the difficulties of making/producing games, Onur Şamlı (Personal communication, December 4, 2019) stated that producing games has become a much more effortless and easy process compared to previous years due to the abundance of game engines and easier access to information. He mentioned that seriousness and game genre had a significant influence on this process. Stygian's, another game that we focus on, has been developed in almost 4 years. The game's developer Can Oral states that based on his own experience during the development stage of the game which had is an RPG game with an indie storyline, difficulties of creating a digital game in Turkey can be categorized under four different topics (Personal communication, December 4, 2019):

Lack of talent pool: It is exceedingly difficult to find individuals who have the experience and talent required to participate in such productions. In the case of Stygian, Oral stated that he had to mentor the individuals he wanted to work with almost from scratch. It becomes inevitable that the project being worked on will be interrupted because the people left the team for various reasons during this production because their positions cannot be filled quickly.

Lack of know-how: There had been a limited number of narratively focused RPG video games produced in Turkey. Therefore, development teams have to "re-invent the wheel" since they can only use the game they are working on as a testing board.

Indifference/ignorance of local investors about the gaming industry: Since local investors do not know and cannot define the game industry, they can cause time and energy loss for the development team.

An effort to discourage that can reach the level of collectivism: Oral (Personal communication, December 4, 2019) mentions that some individuals in the society may show the behavior of demoralizing, targeting those who work on projects and studies that somehow touches themes of faith and this makes working on such projects challenging. In addition to these, when asked about the local themes and narrative elements of the game *Lale Savaşçıları*, Oral said, "...I really appreciate their courage to make a game with local themes in a fictional İstanbul. I think they were free from commercial concerns too much compared to us." Therefore, he commented on producing content that focuses on local themes in Turkey as a display of courage.

One of the producers of *Lale Savaşçıları*, Özgür Özol, states that following up on a project in Turkey is challenging as a process and he says that 'keeping yourself motivated during the development is the most crucial part.' He also states that the development stage of a game takes place in a long period, and keeping up the battle against the difficulties during this period takes some other motivating force than "money" and follows his statements as such:

> Not very easy to continue to work on a project in Turkey... What I hear is that today, our young people are designing good games and creating works. Well, we have to ask them why they do what they do because they would say they didn't do it to earn money, at least I believe they would. All the young people would say, "I don't want to earn money" to cover up for the possibility of not making money. To prove themselves, to show that they can do something, this or that... If they are doing it this way, I hope they will be successful, because if they start with such a motivation, they can bring their works to the point that İstanbul Efsaneleri reached. (Teknoloji TV 2005)

Thanks to the momentum gained in recent years in the Turkish gaming industry, game developers keep up with the world trends in gaming and share the games they develop with game lovers worldwide. While fighting to reflect their dreams on the monitor of gamers, Turkish game designers are facing difficulties because other industries still do not have enough information about gaming, and finding investors is a tricky process for them.

8.5 Conclusion

Digital games have undeniable importance in the twenty-first century. Likewise, one of the fastest-growing markets on a global scale is the digital game industry as well. So much so that while the total market share of game platforms was 70.6 billion dollars in 2012, this number was approximately 152 billion dollars by 2019, and it is expected to reach 180 billion dollars by 2022 (Newzoo, Global Game Market Report Premium, 2018). It also includes the works of Turkish game developers with the effects of the developments in technological infrastructure and new media. When examining the history of Turkish game developers, it can be said that by closely following the global progress of digital games, developer companies in Turkey aim to produce games on par with other noteworthy titles around the world. In Turkey, the digital gaming market was 750 million dollars in 2017, which in 2019 exceeded one billion dollars (Digital Gaming Report, 2019).

Through the analysis of the three digital games that have been the main subject of this study, and personal interviews about the Turkish gaming industry, the following statements can be made:

- Apart from the period in which the games were developed and the themes they deal with the game genre, the target audience and the game mechanics planned for the game also profoundly affected the narrative form.
- For a game to be successful narratively, the game developers must have a significant interest in and knowledge about the planned game's themes. In other words, the success of storytelling in a game is dependent on the affinity and understanding of the theme.
- Even though Turkish game developers follow global trends because other industries and disciplines have insufficient knowledge about the gaming industry, this results in adverse effects for local developers.
- Because the game developers in Turkey have little economic support, and the profit margin of the games they develop is small, developers tend to choose already known themes to include in their games.
- Other than financial concerns, thanks to hyper-casual mobile games rise in the industry, and there are too many types/amounts of games, games with strictly Anatolian or Turkish contents are pretty limited in number.

As it can be seen in the first example of an RPG game that was developed in Turkey (*Lale Savaşçıları*), appropriate use of language according to the theme of the game can create a much more effective gaming experience and differentiate the game narrative-wise from other titles with similar genres. In the examples of *Conarium* and *Stygian: Reign of the Old Ones* that we examined during the study; the production team is commanding the theme of their game. It has reflected positively on the narrative in the game. Although there are 25 years between the release date of the *Lale Savaşçıları* and *Stygian*, which both shares RPG game genre, these games are also successful examples in terms of narrative. The technological infrastructure that changes day by day has accelerated game creation compared to the past and provided convenience to game developers. It can be seen that, regardless of the period it is produced in, the depth of the plot designed in the game and the emotional elements it contains, the roles of the characters in the narrative, the integration of the game mechanics and the plot, and the characteristics of the target audience are the main factors that make the narrative games a success (Atkins 2003, p. 23). If the elements in the game are well blended and balanced with the narrative, it is possible to produce enjoyable games with a story that attracts the player's mind (linear or non-linear). The three games discussed during this study can be deemed successful, even though they were developed in different periods, in different genres, and implemented in different technological infrastructures because the target audience of the game has been identified correctly. The developers had in-depth knowledge about the themes. In this context, it is seen that while game developers are working on a game, it should be taken into consideration that the resulting work is more than an entertainment tool; it is a designed experience.

Following the personal communications and interviews that had been done previously, other than the implications stated above, it is shown that motivation has an essential role as a factor. Game development is a time-consuming and labor-intensive task, especially if the subject game is a big project. Also, the production team probably deals with the details of a single project for an extended amount of time. According to Özgür Özol, if the only aim is to earn money while developing a game, it will be detrimental in solving the developer team's problems (Teknoloji TV 2005). Therefore, it can be said that starting the process, with developers being motivated and enthusiastic about their work, is directly related to the success of the final product of the game development process.

The size of the digital gaming market in the global context has reached 160 billion dollars nowadays. Turkey has just one billion dollars share in this market, and this fact paints a negative picture for the game developers in the country. In this context, Metin Mamati's interview with Tansu Kendirli, Chairman of the Board of Game Designers, Developers, Producers and Publishers Association (OYUNDER) in 2018, Kendirli stated that the Turkish gaming industry should be introduced to the international market and said, "Within the scope of taking the right steps, we can reach an export volume of 15 billion dollars" (Mamati 2018). Considering that the two titles we discussed, Conarium and Stygian had international distributors, it can be said that international connections are still insufficient for local distributors to reach global audiences in this context. Focusing on international promotion activities and demonstrating the potential of the present and future Turkish gaming industry has the utmost importance in reinforcing and invigorating the industry.

It is possible to see that the small number of academic research carried out primarily on Turkish games, increases the importance of studies to be carried out on different disciplines in this field. While making future studies around this subject, the affecting factors in game development can be analyzed in detail in the general sense of Turkish game companies. However, to examine how the narrative is designed to be presented to players during the development process; a study can be done on how Turkish gamers look into narratively focused games by including end-user questionnaires.

Ludography

Call of Cthulhu: Dark Corners of the Earth (2005), Headfirst Productions.
Conarium (2017), Zoetrope Interactive.
Dungeon & Dragons (D&D) (1974), TSR.
Eternal Darkness (2002), Silicon Knights.
Istanbul Efsaneleri: Lale Savaşçıları (1994), Siliconworx.
Stygian: Reign of the Old Ones (2019), Cultic Games.

References

A.S. Adams, Needs met through role-playing games: a fantasy theme analysis of Dungeons & Dragons. Kaleidoscope **12**(6), 69–86 (2013)
M.G.Akbaş, "Dijital Oyunlarda Hikâye ve Hikâye Anlatıcılığı: "God of War" Örneği", Yüksek Lisans Tezi, T.C. Maltepe Üniversitesi, Sosyal Bilimler Enstitüsü (2019)
B. Atkins, More Than a Game: The Computer Game as Fictional Form (Manchester University Press, Manchester, 2003), p. 23

P. Bauer, *Cthulhu, Encyclopædia Britannica* (2019). Web Sitesi. https://www.britannica.com/topic/Cthulhu. Accessed 18 Dec 2019

Y. Baypınar, Hiciv Kavramı Üzerine Bir İnceleme, Ankara Üniversitesi Dil ve Tarih-Coğrafya Fakültesi Dergisi, **29**(1–4), 31–37 (1978)

A. Bilgin, Geek Terminoloji: Cliffhanger Nedir?, makale (2018). https://kahramangiller.com/genel/geek-terminoloji-cliffhanger-nedir/. Accessed 18 Dec 2019

B. Bostan, T. Marsh, *The 'Interactive' of Interactive Storytelling: Customizing the Gaming Experience* (2010), pp. 472-475. https://doi.org/10.1007/978-3-642-15399-0_63

S.A.H. Bukhari, *What is Comparative Study*. SSRN. (2011, November 20). https://ssrn.com/abstract=1962328. Accessed 18 Dec 2019

I. Çakın, Karşılaştırmalı kütüphanecilik: Yöntemi ve özellikleri. Hacettepe Üniversitesi Edebiyat Fakültesi Dergisi, **6**(1–2), 0–0 (1989). Retrieved from https://dergipark.org.tr/tr/pub/huefd/issue/41173/497742

S.B. Cassidy, The videogame as narrative. Q. Rev. Film Video **28**(4), 292–306 (2011)

Y. Demirbaş, Oyun Çalışmalarında Dijital Anlatı ile Oyun Biçimi Karşıtlığı Ekseninde Süren Tartışmalara Farklı Bir Bakış. Hacettepe Üniversitesi İletişim Fakültesi Kültürel Çalışmalar Dergisi (2017). ISSN:2148-970X

M. Dierkes, W. Hans, A. Ariane, *Comparative Policy Research*. Gower (1987). ISBN:9780566051968

Digital Gaming Report, Report, Research and Markets, (2019), p.100. https://www.researchandmarkets.com/research/zsprv4/global_digital?w=4

E. Ekin, Lovecraft ve Tavsiye Hikâyeler, Dragon's Lair, inceleme yazısı, (2019). http://draconism.com/lovecraft-ve-tavsiye-hikayeler/. Accessed 18 Jun 2021

F. Esser, T. Hanitzsch, On the why and how of comparative inquiry in communication studies, in *Handbook of Comparative Communication Research*, ed. by F. Esser, T. Hanitzsch, (Routledge, London, 2012), pp. 3–22

F. Esser, R. Vliegenthart, Comparative research methods, in *The International Encyclopedia of Communication Research Methods*, ed. by J. Matthes, C. S. Davis, R. F. Potter, (John Wiley & Sons, Hoboken, 2017). https://doi.org/10.1002/9781118901731.iecrm0035

C. Fernández-Vara, *Introduction to Game Analysis* (Routledge, Milton Park, 2014)

Global Games Market Report, Newzoo, (2018). https://newzoo.com/products/reports/global-games-market-report/. Accessed 20 Sep 2021

S. İrvan, Metin Çözümlemelerinde Yöntem Sorunu. Medya ve Kültür **1**, 73–86 (2000)

Istanbul Efsaneleri Söyleşisi, *TeknolojiTV - Bölüm 1, Teknoloji TV*. Youtube.com. (2005). https://www.youtube.com/watch?v=80tVQ2jOvbU

K.K. Küpçü, *Call of Cthulhu'ya Giriş*. FRPNET (2011). Web Sayfası. https://frpnet.net/call-of-cthulhu/call-of-cthulhu-giris. Accessed 18 Dec 2019

M. Mamati, *Türkiye'de Dijital Oyun Sektörünün Durumu*. Qolumnist.com. (2018). Makale. https://qolumnist.com/tr/2018/09/29/turkiyede-dijital-oyun-sektorunun-durumu/. Accessed 18 Dec 2019

Merriam-Webster, *Merriam-Webster Dictionary* (n.d.). Retrieved from https://www.merriam-webster.com/dictionary/interaction. Accessed 15 Feb 2021

I. Romero, *Video games: What does IP mean?*. (2016, June 27). Web Sitesi Sayfası. https://twinfinite.net/2016/06/video-games-what-does-ip-mean/. Accessed 18 Dec 2019

S. Şengün, *Sanal Hikâye Anlatıcılığı Çağında Yaşayan Bilimkurgu ve Fantastik Dünyalar Olarak Video Oyunları* (2015)

Story Telling and Interactivity in Video Gaming, *Shehrozeameen (Yazar kullanıcı adı)*. The Artifice. (2017). Blog Post. https://the-artifice.com/video-gaming-story-telling-interactivity/. Accessed 18 Dec 2019

J. Strickland, *How Cthulhu Works*. HowStuffWorks.com (2007). Makale. https://entertainment.howstuffworks.com/arts/literature/cthulhu.htm. Accessed 18 Dec 2019

Chapter 9
The Games on Exhibition: Videogames as Contemporary Art

Tolga Hepdinçler

9.1 Introduction: Is Video Game Art?

Video game as an art is not a recent debate. As like the old "new" technologies of previous centuries as photography and film, game has been a subject of same argument. Yet, we should not forget that the process of evaluating other media as art takes place simultaneously with the period in which the meaning, context and application forms of art transformed. It is possible to say that the relationship between video games and art was established in a period free from old school institutional definitions of art. Contemporary art practices basically art of today welcomes all media conceptually located themselves as art form. This mostly related with the understanding that content is more important materials and forms used. Hence, artist conceptual engagements define how we define the artwork, and so art itself. Although Video games defined with collective creative agents and profit-oriented industry or entertainment-oriented consumption habits, video games can easily count as an art practice as like all creative processes of today. But still, the conceptualization of video games as art needs to a justification to define itself as "high" art in the realm of art other than being a "low" art with its industrial and cultural orientation. One of the biggest obstacles to the inclusion of games in any form of art is that they are based on game mechanics and gaming experience dynamics that are not very similar to the art practices. As Elbert emphasizes, the rules of the games are determined and they can be considered only as cultural artifact with their structure based on competition and rewarding, with their structure based on the goal of winning, it is not possible to be associated with art only as a cultural experience (Ebert 2010). Even if it is possible to refute this claim by

T. Hepdinçler (✉)
Bahçeşehir University, Istanbul, Turkey
e-mail: tolga.hepdincler@comm.bau.edu.tr

B. Bostan (ed.), *Games and Narrative: Theory and Practice*, International Series on Computer Entertainment and Media Technology,
https://doi.org/10.1007/978-3-030-81538-7_9

saying that works of art are also a cultural artifact, what Elbert wants to emphasize is that the practice of play based solely on entertainment and pleasure cannot be evaluated in the same way as the aesthetic pleasure presented by art. To put it more clearly, the catharsis or ecstatic experiences created by video games is not solely adequate to define them as artistic practices, contrary these experiences make them more associated to entertainment practices. But on the other hand, we can assume that film, also has been a controversial medium in the sense of art, reflects similar audience practices., if cinema counts as art with these practices, video games trigger a similar audience practice should not constitute any obstacle to its count as art. However, here it would be appropriate to include Williams' comment, who contributed to Elbert's claim;

> The really crucial observation to me exists in that last sentence, in which Ebert is suggesting that the player is *doing* something in playing a game, whereas normally an audience's relationship to art (be that a painting, novel, film, etc.) is merely "experiencing" (in some passive sense of the word) the object before them, allowing meaning to "wash over them", rather than actively participating with the artwork (Williams 2011).

In this context, one of the material bases of art the audience separates from the universe of experience that is inherent in itself and turns into an active practitioner in video games. This, of course, recalls the practice of interactive art. Interactive art defines works that transform in terms of content and form with the participation of the presence of the binding agent. In other words, it enables the viewer to be positioned not only as an "experiencer" but also as a creator. As we can see in interactive film, interactive architecture, or interactive installation, it is possible to come across commentary in which the viewer turns into an entity or an agent of the artwork. And more, art intervention is a case of a contemporary art practice commonly defined with change of existing conditions created by the artist. Video game can provide an experience like this interaction universe. In fact, one of the interaction strategies can be implemented as a game (Kluszczynski 2010). Such as, Keith Lam's *Paper Super Mario Bross* (2007), Julian Oliver's *Level Head* (2007) installations can be examples to the virtual side of game strategy in interactive arts. But this arises a question that the interaction in videogames is an interaction between player and a machine. As Jonas stated, the player cannot claim to impose a personal vision of life on the game, while the creator of the game has ceded that responsibility. No one "owns" the game, so there is no artist, and therefore no artwork (Jonas 2012). It becomes some sort of a playground of human-machine interaction with any kind of artistic conceptualization of the gamer.

Even tough, industrial and consumption processes involved in game production raise suspicion, we can argue that contemporary art practices may allocate space to video games. We can establish the legitimate ground for this claim in the contemporary art practices as art theorist Arthur Danto has stated at his renown article "The End of Art" in relation to artwork of today (Danto 2005, p. 102). As Danto points out, the transformation of art into the object of its own conceptual consciousness and therefore the transformation of what we call art into a mere idea allow the production and consumption practices of video games to be associated with the idea of art. In this context, we need to put aside our traditional definitions of art and look at what the motivations are in the creative experience to evaluate video games as art. This motivation can lead us to call they are art if those objects created their own conceptual consciousness as artistic experiences. After all, what we call art today has evolved into this. Since we can call everything art after the death of art, there is no harm in the videogame being an art. Among the game types, non-game or art-game types can easily be described as art due to their theoretical consciousness and consumption patterns that are easily inherent in the production process. On the other hand, the question arises, how can we define video games as art, which coincide with the historical, aesthetic, and practical experiences that we define art, but do not have the theoretical consciousness that makes them self-evident. Considering the increasing interest of the art world in video games in the last decade, we observe that many games that are considered in the context of art are known for their commercial success, in fact, they are distant works in the motivations mentioned above.

These assumption makes the argument more complicated and complex. We can easily express that "game is only a game" and nothing to do with art. But on the other hand, industry itself shows a dexterity to be a part of art scene by mimicking the practices of all creative industries to shape a legitimate space for its own sake. Not only the exhibitions are going to be mentioned below, annual trade fairs like *Gamescom, Paris Gameweek* and festivals like *PAX or* showcases like The Boston Festival of Independent Gemas *represent practical* similarities to the events in the art world. Just like film festivals and art fairs, these events are not just a simple commercial event, they can be referred as the curatorial processes for translating videogames into intellectually acclaimed cultural artefacts (Grace 2017).

9.2 Videogame as Art: Past and Present

If we look back to the academic scene video game and art relation, a consensus has not been established, yet. The academic researches on games and art limit themselves to justify the video game's proposed positioning as an art form. While some of the works point aesthetical qualities of video games rather than video game criticism concentrated on game mechanics while offering a theoretical framework comperes video games and mainstream understanding of aesthetical practices (Clarke and Mitchell 2007; Kirkpatrick 2017), others argue the ties between the conceptualization of video games as work of art while questioning the medium's appearance as artist tool, today (Sharp 2015), and more some proposes a future a game/art justifies its own realm of artistic practice (Atkins 2006). This critical climate creates bound between past, present, and future of videogames as an art form. If we start with the past, there is a tendency focuses on the commercial games mostly unintentionally practiced artistic and aesthetical applications. One of the first exhibitions on videogame art *Hot Pursuits: A Video Arcade* in 1989 can be good example to define this motivation. The exhibition consisted a collection of arcade games placed as aesthetical design objects (Stalker 2005). As the curator of the exhibition stated her goal after two decades,

> My goal was to present the games themselves—this was to be a museum exhibition, after all, and the museum's first responsibility is to offer the public a direct encounter with the objects of study. I wanted to select the games that had somehow stood apart from the mass—because they had broken new ground in graphic design, introduced a new type of gameplay, or perhaps been unpredictably popular (Solvin 2009).

This approach is largely like Marcel Duchamp's displaying his ready-made products. The game kiosks have undertaken a transformative function, just as Duchamp reversed the definitions of intuitional art by placing industrial products such as Fountain (1917) and Bicycle Wheel (1951) in the exhibition areas. A closer example to the transformation of industrially produced games into museum or collection pieces is the Museum of Modern Art New York's game museum initiative. In 2011 Museum of Modern Art New York (MOMA) acquired initially 12 and then totally 40 video games in its permanent museum collection including one of the earliest arcade game Pong (1972), Pac-Man (1980), The Sims (2000) and more recent Minecraft (2011). According to the bulletin published by MOMA museum, videogames on display consulted scholars, digital experts, historians and critics to select games for the gallery based on their aesthetic quality—including the programming language used to create them (Holpuch 2013). It is possible to define MOMA's initiative as one of the most important steps video games have taken into the art world. The identity of the museum in the art world is important in terms of determining what to consider as a work of art. We can observe in the example of photography that the same process works for other controversial media. The Family of Man exhibition organized by MOMA in 1955 was one of the initiatives that legitimized photography to be a unique art practice. Both attempts similarly aimed to place practices that exist undefined within the art world in a curatorial narrative in a retrospective order. The most important difference of MOMA's videogame collection from the videogame representations that preceded it is that the games are generally represented in their original form without consoles that define them. Some would be playable with controllers, and more complex, long-running games like SimCity 2000 (2000) were presented as specially designed walkthroughs and demos (Holpuch 2013). In this context, the evaluation of video games as works of art was defined by MOMA based on the criteria as explained by the collection curator Paola Antonelli;

> As with all other design objects in MoMA's collection, from posters to chairs to cars to fonts, curators seek a combination of historical and cultural relevance, aesthetic expression, functional and structural soundness, innovative approaches to technology and behavior, and a successful synthesis of materials and techniques in achieving the goal set by the initial program (Antonelli 2012).

The MOMA's initiative considers videogames not only as a technological product or cultural artifact, but also as a work of aesthetic expression. According to Antonelli, the designer's envisions with the rules, stimuli, incentives and narratives materialize with the behaviors of gamer, the transformation of the formal elegance formed with the limitations of the contemporary technologies turns into aesthetics, innovative space construction that aims to transcend the boundaries of technology and time conceptualized in different dimensions (Antonelli 2012). Thus, videogames can show the ability to establish aesthetic and sensory experiences, space and time conceptions that are inherent in the work of art.

MOMA's retrospective approach can be seen as a meaningful step in determining the boundaries of the relationship between video games and art. Determining these boundaries enables us to define canons, hence artistic conventions, for video games, which we can consider today as works of art. It would be appropriate to look at how I define games as works of art other than a retrospective narrative, and provide an example of how the canon works. A more recent example, Victoria and Albert Museum (V&A Museum) curated an exhibition titled *Videogames: Design/Play/Disturb* in 2018 exhibits art games like *Journey* (2012) and *A Series of Gunshots* (2015), adventure games like *Last of Us* (2013) and *Mafia III* (2016), and again *Minecraft* (2011). As curator of the exhibition stated,

> For this project, however, we chose not to cast our gaze back towards a nostalgic retro past, instead we remain in the present, a period impacted by the technological catalysts of the mid-2000s, when innovations such as broadband, smartphones and social media all radically disrupted the way video games designed, discussed and played (Foulston and Volsing 2018)

The emphasis of the curators on tools and platforms transformed by technological developments is largely related to the democratization of the video game field. The increase in the accessibility of tools and platforms has caused it to turn into a work that allows transitions between the designer and the player. The democratization process has led to the emergence of new wave designers and paved the way for the elimination of existing stereotypes for video games. In this context, contemporary videogames emphasize the critical and transformative function that points to one aspect to the future rather than a retrospective definition of the relationship between art. We can practically create connections with Walter Benjamin's ideas about work of art after the mechanical reproduction. He claimed, tools for mechanical reproduction photography and cinema have a transformative effect to work of art while democratizing it by reducing the distance and dispelling the uniqueness (Benjamin and Underwood 2008). Although he referred to democratization of art itself, the curator V&A exhibition points democratization of the medium itself. But either refers to the technological determinist perspective to conceptualize work of art. Hence, a political aspect can penetrate to what we call work of art. The political aspect mostly shared with the contemporary artistic practices and personally with artists. This brings another canonical influx to the videogame practice as work of art in relation to the ideological motivation that they involved. Videogames in this fashion tracked down subject such as racism, geo-politics, feminism and sexuality. If we trace back Danto's commentary on contemporary work of art, intellectual associations of videogame practices define a conceptual conscious to locate them as work of art. Thus, video game and art for the future, beyond being only a digital archeology work, can create a potential art universe for the future.

9.3 Conclusion: The Future

For a final evaluation, it would be appropriate to mention the exhibitions organized by the Barbican Museum in the context of digital art. Barbican Museum of London curated a couple dozen exhibitions titled *Digital Revolutions* between 2014 and 2019 at the major cities including like London, Beijing, Frankfurt, and Istanbul. Although the exhibition did not directly focus on video games, it had sections titled *Indie Games Space* and *State of Play* particularly emphases independent game practices and interaction as artistic expression. The most important motivation of the exhibition is a practice of an digital archeology as indicated in the exhibition booklet to delve into the history of digital creativity through contemporary art, design, music, film, video games and the wen examining the stories of leading practitioners and landmark works (McConnon et al. 2014, p. 13). Although the focus of the exhibition appears to be standing in the past, it proposes a connection between cultural heritage and future of digital environment. The concern on videogames from franchises like *Grand Theft Auto Series* (1997–2013) and *Call of Duty Series* (2003–2020) to indie games like *Thomas was Alone* (2013) and *The Unfinished Swan* (2012), tries to examine how those contemporary practices changed our visual culture. While celebrated franchises pushing forward the boundaries of design, story and interaction, in depended movements practicing new forms of videogame language by demonstrating a variety of new game-play mechanics and graphical styles (2014, p. 15). The most important contribution of the exhibition is that it placed video games in convergence with art practices that established their legitimate space long before digitization. These practices, which exist in the same virtual world, can exist by mutual interaction with each other or intertwine with each other. In summary, it can be claimed that video game as art has the potential to exist by being included in the universe of other arts with its transformative effect and convergence practices in the present by focusing on more established aesthetic experiences with its retrospective relationship with the past.

Art experiences of video games go through the processes in which each new technology forms its own legitimate ground, as stated above. In line with the modern interpretation of history, it is inevitable that video art will gain legitimate ground as we move forward. As observed in all other art practices, the process of articulating the video game to visual culture and transforming it continues in a period that we are not so historically distant. Although the art practices we have exemplified in above establish a link between the past and the future and show that video game can be evaluated as an art object, it also creates an intellectual accumulation to make this assessment. Digital archaeological initiatives into the history of video games lead them to be treated not only as industrial products and as simple cultural artefacts, but as phenomena that transform our ways of perception.

It has shown that MOMA's goal is not only to create a technology collection, but also videogames can be handled as an aesthetic experience or a self-sufficient artistic language. Experiences that focus on the today of video games have aimed to reveal the existence of social or political relations that video games establish with the "real" world. The liberalization of the areas of application in technology has enabled the spread of video game design practices to a wider universe, and this has enabled the creation of outputs that evolved from the conceptual resources of the contemporary art world.

The pieces of experience that can lead to the formation of the conceptual consciousness pointed out by Danto are formed by the initiatives and similarities we have pointed out here. Although Danto associates it with the end of art in a pessimistic tone, there is no obstacle to the definition of play as an art practice with its conceptual expansion. However, the relationship that video games have established with art will continue to be controversial in the short and long term. As observed in the comments here, our traditional habits embedded in our visual culture of artworks will make it difficult to define the complex experiential, temporal and spatial practices of video games as art.

On the other hand, the video game medium has also been included in artistic production, so it is possible to talk about video game as art. It has been observed that artists such as Bill Viola embed video games into their artistic production processes. It is possible to say that video games exist as one of the instruments of the artist, just like the video, which we recognized as a commercial product before.

References

P. Antonelli, *MoMA: Video GAMES: 14 in the Collection, for Starters* (2012). Retrieved 12 May 2021, from https://www.moma.org/explore/inside_out/2012/11/29/video-games-14-in-the-collection-for-starters/

B. Atkins, What are we really looking at? Games Cult. **1**(2), 127–140 (2006)

W. Benjamin, J.A. Underwood, *The Work of Art in the Age of Mechanical Reproduction* (Penguin Books, London, 2008)

A. Clarke, G. Mitchell, *Videogames and Art* (Intellect, Bristol, 2007)

A.C. Danto, *The Philosophical Disenfranchisement of Art* (Columbia University Press, New York, 2005)

R. Ebert, *Video Games Can Never Be ART*. Roger Ebert (2010). Retrieved 2 May 2021, from https://www.rogerebert.com/roger-ebert/video-games-can-never-be-art

M. Foulston, K. Volsing, *Videogames: Design, Play, Disrupt* (V & A Publishing, London, 2018)

L.D. Grace, Heuristics from curating and exhibiting game art in the 21st century, in *Proceedings of the 8th International Conference on Digital Arts* (2017)

A. Holpuch, *Video Games Level Up in the Art World with New Moma Exhibition* (2013). Retrieved 12 May 2021, from https://www.theguardian.com/technology/gamesblog/2013/mar/01/video-games-art-moma-exhibition

J. Jonas, *Sorry MOMA, Video Games Are Not Art* (2012). Retrieved 12 May 2021, from https://www.theguardian.com/artanddesign/jonathanjonesblog/2012/nov/30/moma-video-games-art

G. Kirkpatrick, *Aesthetic Theory and the Video Game* (Manchester University Press, Manchester, 2017)

R. Kluszczynski, Strategies of interactive art. Journal of Aesthetics & Culture **2**(1), 5525 (2010)

N. McConnon, C. Bodman, D. Admiss, *Digital Revolution: An Immersive Exhibition of Art, Design, Film, Music and Videogames* (Barbican, London, 2014)

J. Sharp, *Works of Game: On the Aesthetics of Games and Art* (MIT Press, Cambridge, MA, 2015)

R. Solvin, *Hot Circuits: Reflections on the First Museum Retrospective of the Video Arcade Game* (2009). Retrieved 12 May 2021, from http://www.movingimagesource.us/articles/hot-circuits-20090115

P.J. Stalker, *Gaming in Art: A Case Study of Two Examples of the Artistic Appropriation of Computer Games and the Mapping of Historical Trajectories of "Art Games" Versus Mainstream Computer Games*. Master's Thesis, 2005, University of the Witwatersrand (2005)

C. Williams, *Why Video Games Might Not Be Art*, Popmatters (2011). Retrieved 12 May 2021, from https://www.popmatters.com/146097-why-video-games-might-not-be-art-2495970677.html

Chapter 10
Ethics of Interactive Storytelling

Sami Hyrynsalmi, Kai K. Kimppa, and Jouni Smed

10.1 Introduction

Interactive storytelling refers to the process of telling stories so that the audience has a chance to take part and change the story being told. Conventional storytelling is often non-interactive: books, movies, television shows or podcasts do not usually offer one a chance make changes, but one is a passive receiver.

The difference between interactive storytelling and conventional, non-interactive storytelling is easiest to understand with the spectrum of interactivity illustrated in Fig. 10.1 (Smed et al. 2021). Let us imagine that we have a range—a spectrum—where on the lefthand side we have no interactivity but we are passive receivers who cannot affect anything. On the righthand side, we have total interactivity and we are free to do anything we want—or, at least, anything that we are capable of doing. Within this spectrum, conventional storytelling would reside at the lefthand side. If one is watching a film, one does not get the chance to change the scenery, characters, mood or plot of the film, but all of that has already been determined among others by the scriptwriter, the director, the producers. One's input to the story is non-existing; one cannot interact with it.

S. Hyrynsalmi
Department of Software Engineering, LUT University, Lahti, Finland
e-mail: sami.hyrynsalmi@lut.fi

K. K. Kimppa
Information Systems Science, University of Turku, Turku, Finland
e-mail: kai.kimppa@utu.fi

J. Smed (✉)
Department of Computing, University of Turku, Turku, Finland
e-mail: jouni.smed@utu.fi

© The Author(s), under exclusive license to Springer Nature Switzerland AG 2022
B. Bostan (ed.), *Games and Narrative: Theory and Practice*, International Series on
Computer Entertainment and Media Technology,
https://doi.org/10.1007/978-3-030-81538-7_10

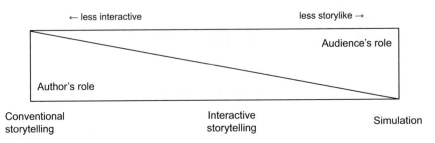

Fig. 10.1 The spectrum of interactivity

If we go to the other extreme, we have a simulation. In a pure simulation, nothing is imposed but you are free to do whatever you will—or whatever the simulation allows you to do. For example, in a flight simulator you have a total control over your plane and can choose to do whatever you want, whether it is making aerial manoeuvres with a jumbo jet or landing upside down on a grassy pasture.

In this spectrum, interactive storytelling lies somewhere between these two extremes. It is more interactive than conventional storytelling but not as free as a simulation. The more we move to the left, the less interactive the application becomes. And if we move to the right, the more interactive it becomes. But it also becomes something else at the same time. On the very left we have a controlled and authored experience—just a like a film. Once we start moving towards right, the less control the author of the story has. Actually, the story starts getting looser as there is more possibility for interaction. First, there might be two or three alternate endings that the user can choose from. Then there can be couple of parallel plots. After that things start to get really complex and it would be hard to pinpoint or enumerate the possible story instances.

We can safely say that the more we move to the right, the less storylike the application becomes. A pure simulation does not offer any ready-made stories, but one would have to invent them oneself. In fact, we can think that as interactivity increases, the control over the story shifts from the author to the audience. It is worth noting that although in this illustration the transition from conventional stories to simulation looks smooth and non-discrete, in reality the transition is likely to go through categories of different types of storytelling.

In conventional storytelling, the author's role is more important. The author has the control over the story. The more interactive the application becomes, the smaller the author's role and control gets. Vice versa the audience's role is at minimum in conventional storytelling and it increases the more interactive the application becomes. In a pure simulation, there is no pre-authored story but the audience or the player can invent themself whatever story they like. The interesting area lies between the extremes, where we find interactive storytelling.

Fig. 10.2 The four partakers

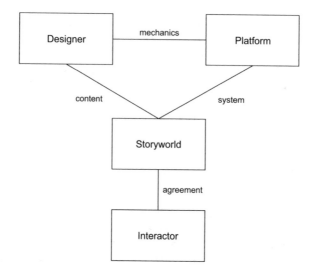

10.1.1   Elements of Interactive Stories

When thinking about the ethical dimension of interactive storytelling, we have to realize that we are focusing on what human beings are doing. We have organized this paper according to the classification by Smed et al. (2021) and take each of the partakers—platform, designer, interactor and storyworld (see Fig. 10.2)—and look at them from this perspective one by one.

In this categorization, the *platform* refers to the software that provides mechanics for running the storyworld. It also provides the user-interfaces to the designer to create a storyworld and for the interactor to experience an interactive story.

In conventional storytelling, we talk about having an author—someone who has authored the story and has authority over the story. In interactive storytelling, this not the case because the audience can take part in shaping up the story. The 'author' would not be the only author and definitely would not have a complete control over the story. To discern we call this diminished author a *designer*. We could even say that author is a special case of a designer, when the situation is limited to conventional storytelling.

The designer creates a *storyworld*. Again, there is a difference in the term, because the designer is not creating a single story, but an intermingling bundle of them. In other words, the designer creates a world where different stories can take place. It includes all the characters, props, scenes and events as well as the mechanics that combine them together into a living world.

Next, we have yet another change of term. Whereas in conventional storytelling we can talk about the passive recipient of the story as a spectator, audience or reader, here that person has an active, or rather an interactive role. We could call that person with many names such as 'player', 'actor', 'user', 'agent' or 'participant' but the term 'interactor' emphasises being an interactive actor in a storyworld created by a designer. The interactor is the one who experiences the story as it unravels.

Now, let us take a look at the whole structure. Interactive storytelling puts the interactor in a key role. The designer is providing the characters, props and external events forming the storyworld. Based on this and the interactor's choices a story instance is generated, which is the result of not the designer alone but also the interactor who has made choices and provided input into the story.

10.1.2   Moral Philosophy

Ethics or moral philosophy is a classical philosophical branch which addresses concepts of right and wrong behavior. The ethical effects of ICT have been considered for a long time; for example, the oldest academic journal in publication in the field, *Ethics and Information Technology* was launched already in 1999, and others, such as *Journal of Information, Communication and Ethics in Society*, which started year 2003 have been launched since. It is worth noting, however, that the effects of computers in society from an ethical perspective have been discussed at least from early 1960s, when Norbert Wiener gave his series of lectures in Yale in 1962, the content of which was later published as the book *God and Golem, Inc.* in 1964.

In the field of computing, as in the general ethical theory based on the analytical tradition of philosophy, there are four major ethical theories which are used. These are utilitarianism (see e.g. Mill 1879/2004), deontology (see e.g. Kant 1785/2004), contractarian (see e.g. Rawls 1999) and virtue ethics (see e.g. Aristotle 350 BCE/2003).

The most common problems for interactive storytelling are utilitarian (see e.g. Mill 1879/2004) especially in regard to ICT and ethics (Moor 1999), e.g. *consequences* of either designers or other interactors. They can promote wellbeing or cause harm, and an analysis aiming for the good effects can be done for different practices in the interactive story. Both designers and interactors can cause harm, either intentionally or accidentally. designers would do this by inserting features to the story itself which are harmful for the interactors, such as extensive advertisements or psychological traps (see e.g. Kimppa et al. 2015). On the other hand, harmful consequences other interactors can cause are somewhat different to those in typical computer games, although many of the same ones are also present, such as harmful utterances, e.g. racial or sexist slurs. In computer games, other harmful consequences by other players can be present, for example, as cheating, which tend to be less common in interactive storyworlds. Although utilitarianism has traditionally been used to analyse specific actions in specific situations by specific persons, the theory has since been extended to consider any effects harmful to people anywhere, and thus computerised systems, which after all can produce those, can also be analysed through the theory.

Deontology (see e.g. Kant 1785/2004), on the other hand is interested on the *intent* of the actors. Are the persons an act affects considered as "ends in themselves", i.e. persons worthy of respect; as all people ought to be considered? Would the actor, if being the target of the cation, consider the act done good intentioned; would the actor consider the act as a potentially good universal rule all ought to follow, whether they were the target or not? Typically the theory is used to analyse ones own actions, as telling whether others' actions are good or evil intentioned is difficult at best, and often impossible to know. However in the case of intentions included into systems, such as inserting psychological traps (see e.g. Kimppa et al. unpublished), can actually be known to some degree.

Contractarian theories (see e.g. Rawls 1999) are based on a *contract* between those who are affected. For example James H. Moor (1999) has already early on used contractarian theory in the ICT and ethics field. Typically this concerns societies at large, but it can be applied to any group of people, such as designers and interactors in an interactive storyworld. More often than not, the contract is implicitly accepted, e.g. in case of computer games choosing to play the game or, when it comes to interactive storytelling to enter the storyworld. Some tools are, however, available to analyse whether the contract is fair, namely, does it treat those in the weakest position (in this case the interactors) fairly, or do all the participants find the rules acceptable. In the case of interactive storytelling, the typical solution if one finds the storyworld to be unfair is to leave the storyworld. This is true when it comes to computer games as well, although some people breaking the implicit contract by cheating for example can interrupt the game enough to make it unplayable even if the other participants would want to play it. A similar situation in which the implicit contract is broken can happen in interactive storyworlds, and this is, of course true for computer games as well: if the environment becomes toxic enough through slurs or other too disturbing acts the interactors may feel they cannot participate in the story, even if they would otherwise prefer to do so.

Finally, virtue ethics (see e.g. Aristotle 350 BCE/2003) is interested in building the character of the participants, specifically oneself, but also providing an environment in which this growth is possible (see e.g. Heimo et al. 2018). If the interactive storyworld is created in such a manner as to help build ones character, as Sicart (2009) for example suggests, those participating can choose their moral actions, and thus possibly grow as human beings. Choosing the right action because it is right and thus strengthens ones character can, if done intentionally, make oneself a better person.

All of these theories, as can be seen from the examples given above, are visible in one form or another in interactive storytelling. Although the examples given are specifically directed towards computerised storyworlds, many are applicable also to non-computerised interactive storytelling, such as interactive storybooks or even role-playing games such as *Dungeons & Dragons*. Even though it is typically not made explicit in the following which theory is relevant in each situation, the words "consequence", "intent", "contract" and "character", or other concepts do tie the instances of potential ethical issues to the theories.

Extant literature has already touched on the ethical issues related to interactive storytelling. For example, Fisher and Schoemann (2018) address ethical considerations of dark tourism and specifically settings where virtual reality and interactive storytelling is used in a real-world location with dark history. In addition, Melcer et al. (2020) have used interactive storytelling application to teach ethics.

10.2   Platform

When thinking about the platform where the interactive storytelling application run, we expect it to be reliable, maintain our private information and not be open for hacking. The interactor should be able to trust that the information they share is treated respectfully and with care. The platform can be compromised by attacks utilizing either technical or social weaknesses. For example, passwords can be stolen by cracking them (technical attack) or pretending to be the administrator and asking the players to give their passwords (social engineering attack). These demands on data security are typical for any kind of application nowadays.

We can extend this to include also to what is done with the log data and interactors' profiles. Apart from collecting data from the interactor's decisions, the platform can also record the their decisions on advertisements (e.g. whether the interactor decide to click it or skip it). Although this data is not related to the actual story, it is a valuable asset for the platform owner, because it can be used to recognize the most potential advertisers. Moreover, when this data is combined with the log data, the platform owner can try to modify the application to be more advertisement friendly, which can lead to blurring the demarcation between advertorial and actual content.

A special challenge would be profiling the interactor as they make many choices. For instance, the game *The Walking Dead* (Telltale Games 2012) computes a morality of the player after each level. We can well imagine how this profile could include much more information. Even though the choices might not represent the person as such, it could still give a strong indication of their traits, preferences and personality. This would again leave the interactor at the hands of the platform owner when it comes to how this possible sensitive information could be utilized for the benefit of the platform owner—or the harm of the interactor.

Generally, the ethical problems present in the platform are related to how it is taking away the interactor's control of their resources such as money, time, attention, social capital, mental and physical energy and security (Hyrynsalmi et al. 2020). When one uses an interactive storytelling application, one is willing to invest these resources: the interactor invests money to use the application, reserves time for experiencing the story, uses social capital to invite others to join in the platform, exerts mental and physical energy to progress in the story, and assumes to be secure in the real world whilst engaged in virtual risks in the storyworld.

Furthermore, there are some aspects relevant also for other kinds of platforms that should be taken specially into account due to their unexpected results of mixing them with the storyworld. For example, location-based games—which mix the gaming world with the real world by using a real-world location as a gameplay mechanism—pose the ethical questions of their own (Hyrynsalmi et al. 2021). Yet, mixing location-based mechanisms with interactive storytelling should be considered with care as unexpected storyline could potentially move a player in a dangerous or restricted area.

10.3   Designer

As the creator of the storyworld, the designer has the burden to define its ethical dimension. Adams (2014, pp. 159–162) lines out this ethical dimension so that the designer defines "what right and wrong means within the context of that world". Sicart (2009, p. 41) shares this view and asserts that the "designer is responsible for most of the values that are embedded in the system and that play a significant role during the game experience". Sicart also points out that in this way the player, or in this case the interactor, can choose ethically relevant actions in the game, or in this case interactive story, be they positive or negative; the emphasis being on the choice. Katsarov et al. (2019) present a similar cases as negotiating with NPCs (non-player characters) to find an agreement on an ethical problem and how to mediate a conflict between NPCs, the aim being to resolve a conflict between the NPCs. Even negative choices can be positive in real world as tools for analysis of action and consequence. Katsarov et al. (2019, p. 351) also point out that the interactor may have to "understand a complex case of unethical behavior". Although they do not necessarily actively choose ethical or unethical participation, they have to go through the part of the story where these situations are depicted, if the designer inserts them into the story. Typically though, these interactions need to be intentionally designed into the game or interactive story, and care must be applied on what kinds of choices are available, and how they are presented to avoid situations where all choices are inherently evil.

Broadly speaking, many of the same ethical considerations that apply to video games also apply to interactive storytelling. It would be possible to imagine how appealing such a storyworld could be for product placement or advertising. The characters could be harnessed for promoting products or services that are then needed in proceeding. Also, props could be based on real-world products. The line here is vague: It could be argued that this is just a way for monetization and as long as it follows the judicial guidelines (e.g. promoting smoking is forbidden or including material that is suitable for the intended younger audience) it would be on the safe side. A counter argument would require these connections to be made visible as it might be hard to differentiate what is promotion and what is not. Of course in the extreme, promotion by the characters might look like in the film *The Truman Show*, where pushing the products becomes too intrusive to go unnoticed.

Also, psychological traps, like used in many freemium games (Søraker 2016) can be used in interactive storytelling environment. The intention is to trap the interactor into the story for as long as possible. It can be either for seeing and clicking as many advertisements possible or to have the interactor spend as much money as possible in the environment, and can thus cause direct harm to the interactor (see e.g. Heimo et al. 2018). It is also typical in freemium games to obscure the amount of money spent by only allowing the player to use money by buying some kind of in-game money. These are typically diamonds, in-game coins or similar. The same method can be used in interactive story worlds. The designer can—in the worst case—insert actual victimising elements into the story. If, as pointed out by Katsarov et al. (2019) elements such as threathening, bullying, ridiculing, kidnapping the interactor are included with the interactor having minimal control over the actions, this could at least frustrate, if not even cause distress on the interactor.

There is a short step from here to propaganda. One could easily imagine interactive storytelling as a tool for political, religious or cultural propaganda. This is not uncommon as the controversy around games such as *America's Army* (United States Army, 2002), *Quest for Bush* (Global Islamic Media Front 2006) and *Left Behind: Eternal Forces* (Inspired Media Entertainment 2006) have shown. Interactive storytelling might make this propaganda even more effective as it possibly immerses the interactor even deeper in the storyworld. It could be used to confirm already existing stereotypes, racist, misogynous or other prejudices. In this sense it is closer to social media than video games as its characters reacting to the interactor and situation can create a similar echo chamber effect. This could be even more pronounced if we have multiple interactors, who might even be able to hijack an existing platform to their use, which reminds how other Twitter users turned Microsoft's chatbot Tay in a short time into a proxy spewing out misogynous and racist hatespeech.

10.4   Interactor

Having multiple human interactors also opens the door for ethical questions, the obvious one being cheating. Apart from technical cheating such as hacking the software, this is about what belongs to the agreement the interactors are committed to. Cheating means achieving the goal by breaking the rules, but what are the goals and rules in a storyworld? Cheating that takes place inside the storyworld is just a part of the story, since every action within the storyworld—no matter how civil or rude—are part of the experience and should be valid. This kind of cheating can be called managed or explicitly possible. However, cheating that is not comprehended as a part of the interactors' agreement may ruin the experience, depending on if the cheat becomes accepted as a way to broaden the conflict aspect of the storyworld. That is, the agreement may evolve, with mutual approval.

Multiple interactors can also bring about cyberbullying and other unethical behaviour that riddles, for example, multiplayer games and social media. Preventing this kind of behaviour can be hard to realize but it should be a conscious aim of everyone taking part in the implementation, design and use of an interactive storytelling application. Katsarov et al. (2019) point out that other players can intentionally take a role in which they attempt to perform unethical choices in the story. This is not a problem as long as they do this in a single player game, but if there are multiple interactors in the story, it can lead to exactly the kind of behaviour suggested above.

Modding blurs the line between the interactor and designer. It also makes the modder to face the same ethical questions as the designer. The content created by the modder might differ radically from the original storyworld. For example, a storyworld intending to promote social integration of refugees could be modded to be a tool for rightwing indoctrination. Moreover, modding might yield results unexpected by the modder as well as the original designer. A simplified case example is *Cyperpunk 2077* (CD Projekt Red 2020) where modders had enabled a player have an intercourse with the game character Johnny Silverhand, portrayed by the actor *Keanu Reeves*. The mod was quickly removed with the statement by the game developers that mods "can't be harmful towards others" (Stanton 2021). As illustrated with this example, a modder can intentionally or unintentionally create content that is harmful for a person. In the case of interactive storytelling applications, the unintended outcome is a risk.

10.5   Storyworld

We can mainly attribute events in the storyworld to the other three partakers who are obviously humans. However, it is worth considering whether there could ethical issues that stem from the computer-controlled creations alone.

As the systems become more complex, it is possible that there emerges a phenomenon that is ethically questionable. At the moment, this might seem a highly hypothetical possibility, but it is possible to imagine a scenario where an ethically problematic phenomenon cannot be explained away by the intentions of the platform developer, designer or interactor. One can pose the question, if we could then talk about the ethics of computer-controlled character. The second question would be, whether we would be able recognize such a behaviour in a character (e.g. psychopathy)?

It seems likely that we could, but then we would have to frame the question *inside* the storyworld. As the character lives there, it does not know the existence of a world outside of it—the world of the humans who created it, populated it and participate in it. It does not know what its gods are doing. We can only judge it within its own world and hold it responsible there.

10.6 Conclusion

In this chapter, we reviewed ethical considerations related to the interactive storytelling applications. The research on interactive storytelling has been focusing mainly on the technical or design challenges and studies on the ethical aspects are practically non-existent. This chapter aimed to map the field and line out the relevant questions that the should be answered. Proceeding as pioneers we were able to raise questions more than give answers, but we hope that this would be start for further studies and call for other researchers to provide their take on the matter. This chapter provides an approach to analyse ethical challenges of interactive storytelling applications by using the four key elements.

References

E. Adams, *Fundamentals of Game Design*, 3rd edn. (New Riders, San Francisco, 2014)

Aristotle (350 BCE/2003), The Nicomachean Ethics of Aristotle. Translator by D. P. Chase. The Project Gutenberg EBook #8438

CD Projekt Red, *Cyberpunk 2077*. (CD Projekt, 2020)

J.A. Fisher, S. Schoemann, Toward an ethics of interactive storytelling at dark tourism sites in virtual reality, in *Interactive Storytelling*, ed. by R. Rouse, H. Koenitz, M. Haahr (Springer, Cham, 2018), pp. 577–590

Global Islamic Media Front, *Quest for Bush*. (Global Islamic Media Front, 2006)

O.I. Heimo, J.T. Harviainen, K.K. Kimppa, T. Mäkilä, Virtual to virtuous money: a virtue ethics perspective on video game business logic. J. Bus. Ethics **153**(1), 95–103 (2018). https://doi.org/10.1007/s10551-016-3408-z

S. Hyrynsalmi, K.K. Kimppa, J. Smed, The ethics of game experience, in *Game User Experience and Player-Centered Design*, ed. by B. Bostan (Springer, Cham, 2020), pp 253–263. doi:10.1007/978-3-030-37643-7_11

S.M. Hyrynsalmi, M.M. Rantanen, S. Hyrynsalmi, Towards ethical guidelines of location-based games: challenges in the urban gaming world, in *Software Business*, ed. by E. Klotins, K. Wnuk (Springer, Cham, 2021), pp. 134–142

Inspired Media Entertainment, *Left Behind: Eternal Forces*. (Inspired Media Entertainment, 2006)

I. Kant, *Fundamental Principles of the Metaphysic of Morals*. Translated by Thomas Kingsmill Abbott. The Project Gutenberg EBook #5682 (1785/2004)

J. Katsarov, M. Christen, R. Mauerhofer, D. Schmocker, C. Tanner, Training moral sensitivity through video games: a review of suitable game mechanisms. Games Culture **14**, 344–366 (2019)

K.K. Kimppa, O.I. Heimo, J.T. Harviainen, First dose is always freemium. SIGCAS Comput. Soc. **45**(3), 132–137 (2015)

K.K. Kimppa, O.I. Heimo, J.T. Harviainen, Dutiful game developers: a Kantian approach to developing games (unpublished)

E.F. Melcer, J. Ryan, N. Junius, M. Kreminski, D. Squinkifer, B. Hill, N. Wardrip-Fruin, Teaching responsible conduct of research through an interactive storytelling game, in *Extended Abstracts of the 2020 CHI Conference on Human Factors in Computing Systems, CHI EA'20* (Association for Computing Machinery, New York, 2020), pp. 1–10, doi:10.1145/3334480.3382973

J.S. Mill, *Utilitarianism*, 7th edn. The Project Gutenberg EBook #11224 (Longmans, Green, London, 1879/2004)

J.H. Moor, Just consequentialism and computing. Ethics Inf. Technol. **1**(1), 61–65 (1999)

J. Rawls, *A Theory of Justice* (Oxford University Press, Oxford, 1999)

R. Stanton, CDPR shuts down Cyberpunk mod that let players have 'sex' with Keanu Reeves. PCGamer (2021). https://www.pcgamer.com/cdpr-shuts-down-cyberpunk-mod-that-letplayers-have-sex-with-keanu-reeves/. Accessed 29 Sept 2021

M. Sicart, *The Ethics of Computer Games* (MIT Press, Cambridge, 2009)

J. Smed, T. Suovuo, N. Skult, P. Skult, *Handbook on Interactive Storytelling* (Wiley, Chichester, 2021)

J.H. Søraker, Gaming the gamer? – the ethics of exploiting psychological research in video games. JICES **14**(2), 106–123 (2016)

Telltale Games, *The Walking Dead*. (Telltale Games, 2012)

Chapter 11
The World Building in the Superhero Genre Through Movies and Video Games: The Interplay Between *Marvel*'s *Avengers* and *Marvel Cinematic Universe*

Hasan Kemal Suher and Tuna Tetik

11.1 Introduction

Superhero stories have been experienced through various media for a long time. Many scholars indicate *Action Comics #1* as the birth of a new genre. The popularity of Superman has led superhero comics to experience the Golden Age in the first years of the 1940s. From the Golden Age of superhero comics to the present, superheroes have been adapted into a variety of media with various formats, including books, television series, cartoons, movies, and video games. One can claim that whereas comic books-based on superhero stories have experienced a Golden Age period between the late 1930s and the end of World War II, the 2000s covered a new Golden Age for superheroes in cinema. Several researchers in their significant works (McSweeney 2018; Robb 2014; Mills 2014; Burke 2008) associate the increasing popularity of superheroes in cinema with technological developments, industrial trends, and sociopolitical events during the 2000s. Liam Burke (2019a, p. 8) states that "the visibility of superheroes since 2000 goes beyond popularity to an unprecedented level of pervasiveness." Besides, the late 2000s and the 2010s included a contextual, thematic, and industrial change in the superhero movie genre. Two major comic book publishers, Marvel Comics and Detective Comics, had created their cinematic universes that include many interrelated movies. The former president of DC Entertainment, Diane Nelson,

H. K. Suher (✉)
Department of Advertising, Faculty of Communication, Bahcesehir University, Istanbul, Turkey
e-mail: kemal.suher@comm.bau.edu.tr

T. Tetik
Department of Film and Television, Faculty of Communication, Bahcesehir University, Istanbul, Turkey
e-mail: tuna.tetik@comm.bau.edu.tr

(Burke 2019b) defines this period as 'the superhero renaissance.' She claims that "...I believe that the superhero renaissance is a testament to excellent creative storytelling in many new mediums." (Burke 2019b, p. 150) Marvel Entertainment relaunched its film production company titled Marvel Studios and announced its movie-driven universe called Marvel Cinematic Universe via the release of *Iron Man* (Jon Favreau 2008), which has gone beyond a single medium. Today, the MCU contains the highest-grossing movie of all time titled *Avengers: Endgame* (Russo Brothers 2019),[1] a few television series on ABC, many originals on Netflix, same short films on YouTube, the current and upcoming television series on Disney+, and a couple of video games. According to Burke (2019a, p. 8), "the digital age made the once impossible images of comics achievable, thereby helping to facilitate today's superhero movies, TV shows, video- games, and other audiovisual adaptations." Even though movies, television series, and short movies are apparently interconnected to each other within a specific story world, the interplay between the latest Marvel superhero video games and the MCU is not evident.

11.1.1 Marvel Comics-Based Superheroes in Video Games and Movies during the 2010s

There were three *Spider-Man* movies, produced by Colombia Pictures, distributed by Sony Entertainment Pictures, and directed by Sam Raimi in the 2000s, while Marc Webb directed two *Spider-Man* movies with a new cast in a different story world by the same companies during the first half of the 2010s. Then, Marvel Entertainment and Sony Entertainment Pictures agreed on the movie adaptation rights of Spider-Man. Therefore, Spider-Man, starring Tom Holland, participated in the MCU with *Captain America: Civil War* (Russo Brothers 2016). One year after the first appearance of Spider-Man in the MCU, Marvel Studios presented *Spider-Man: Homecoming* (Jon Watts 2017) as the first solo Spider-Man movie in the MCU. In 2018, the *Spider-Man* video game was released by Sony Interactive Entertainment and developed by Insomniac Games for PlayStation 4. The game was centered in a separate story world from the MCU. However, the MCU's *Spider-Man* movies' the releasing schedule and the video game took advantage of the same intellectual property's popularity. Marvel Studios presented the second solo *Spider-Man* movie called *Spider-Man: Far from Home* (Jon Watts 2019) 1 year after the *Spider-Man* video game release. According to Eli Blumenthal at USA Today (2018), the *Spider-Man* PS4 game achieved to sell 3.3 million copies in the first 3 days of

---

[1]There is a continuous competition between *Avengers: Endgame* (Russo Brothers 2019) and *Avatar* (James Cameron 2009). The highest-grossing movie status has been changing even in 2021. According to Box Office Mojo, *Avatar* took the leadership from *Avengers: Endgame* at the worldwide box office records with the help of re-release in China, 2021. Top Lifetime Grosses. *Box Office Mojo*. [Accessed on March 28, 2021]. Retrieved from https://www.boxofficemojo.com/chart/ww_top_lifetime_gross/

the release, while two solo *Spider-Man* movies in the MCU have earned over $ 2 billion at the worldwide box office.[2] After the hype of Spider-Man in multiple media, *Spider-Man: Miles Morales* (Insomniac Games) has been announced as one of the first video games for PlayStation 5 in 2020. At the end of 2020, *Marvel's Avengers* was developed by Crystal Dynamics, released by Square Enix.

Marvel's Avenger video game offered players familiar characters within a similar environment. The movie-goers had four different *Avengers* movies before the release of the video game. In 2012, Joss Whedon's *the Avengers* brought six superheroes, including Iron Man, Captain America, Thor, Hulk, Black Widow, and Hawkeye, together. However, in comics, the members of Avengers initiative have been changed and the number of Avengers members has increased since 1963. The first issue of the Avengers[3] in 1963 included Thor, Ant-Man, Wasp, Iron Man, and Hulk as the main cast, then, Captain America has joined the Avengers initiative at the fourth issue, 1964. In some issues of Avengers comics from 1963 to the mid-1980, many new Avengers members and new villains have appeared, including Kang the Conqueror (*Avengers #8*, 1964), Hawkeye, Quicksilver, and Scarlet Witch (*Avengers #16*, 1965), Black Panther (*Avengers #52*, 1968), Ultron (*Avengers #55*, 1968), Vision (*Avengers #57*, 1968), Ms. Marvel (*Avengers #183*, 1979), Taskmaster (*Avengers #196*, 1980), Nebula (*Avengers #257*, 1985). Although Avengers comics[4] have covered many superheroes and various supervillains for many decades, Joss Whedon's Avengers members are considered as 'the original six,' regarding the cinematic representations of the characters by the MCU's fan community due to the popularity of the MCU.

The Avengers was followed by *Avengers: Age of Ultron* (Joss Whedon 2015), in which two new Avengers members, Wanda (Scarlet Witch) and Vision, were participated in the initiative. In *Avengers: Infinity War* (Russo Brothers 2018), Spider-Man became the newest member of the Avengers initiative, when *Avengers: Endgame* (2019) included over 40 supportive superheroes among the original six. From *the Avengers* (2012) to *Avengers: Endgame* (2019), each *Avengers* movie has achieved to earn over $ 1 billion at the worldwide box office.[5] Matthias Stork (2014, p. 79) claims that "the Avengers initiative must thus not be seen as yet another superhero text battling for market share in the oversaturated Hollywood summer lineup. It is rather to be seen as an idea designed to reconfigure the market context in its entirety." Despite the box office records of *Avengers* and *Spider-Man* movies, and the best-selling records of the latest Marvel video games, the

---

[2] Spider-Man. *Box Office Mojo*. [Accessed on Feb 17, 2021]. Retrieved from https://www.boxofficemojo.com/search/?q=Spider-Man+

[3] Avengers (1963) #1. *Marvel Comics Online*. [Accessed on March 28, 2021]. Retrieved from https://www.marvel.com/comics/issue/6951/avengers_1963_1

[4] For further information on key issues and current value of Avengers comics between 1963–1985. Avengers (1963) Key Issues. *Go Collect*. [Accessed on March 28, 2021]. Retrieved from https://comics.gocollect.com/series/key-issues/avengers-the

[5] Avengers. *Box Office Mojo*. [Accessed on Feb 17, 2021]. Retrieved from https://www.boxofficemojo.com/search/?q=avengers

interrelatedness between the MCU and Marvel video games is not well-described and investigated. This chapter aims to discover the possible interrelation and mutual effect of *Avengers* movies (Marvel Studios 2012–2019) and *Marvel's Avengers* video game (Crystal Dynamics 2020). For that purpose, the relation of the movies to the video game, regarding characters, story, and conflict, is researched.

11.1.2 Adapting Superheroes from Comics to Various Media in a Nutshell

Through the history of the superhero genre (1938 - the present), adaptation ways of superheroes from comics to various media and strategies of companies on selling superheroes' adaptation rights have been changing due to various agreements between separate organizations and companies, industrial trends, commercial values and popularities of intellectual properties, and changing ways of productions in multiple media, etc. However, through the panorama of the last 20 years, a shared way could be observed to be mentioned in this regard. The Golden Age of superheroes in cinema (2000 - present) included a shared way on adapting superheroes[6] in various media. In this sense, two major comic book publishers have maintained a specific strategy in adapting superheroes from comics into other media. This way could be summarized with a simple explanation by analyzing the condition of the genre. At first, a superhero is created for comic book medium. If the superhero gains enough popularity, that superhero could be adapted in a movie by a particular film production company, which can buy licensing rights of the superhero. After that, if the movie becomes commercially successful, the superhero in the movie could be transferred into other media, such as television series and video games. These productions could be interrelated to each other or not. This adaptation way could describe the world-building strategy of two major comic book publishers in the creation of a transmedia world for their intellectual properties. However, the superhero genre has been changing in many ways after the releases of Marvel's and DC Comics' cinematic universes.

In contrast to the standard world-building process, *Marvel's Avengers* introduced a new superhero as the main cast and a playable character, called Kamala Khan, known as Ms. Marvel, after the first appearance of the character in comics. Then, Ms. Marvel's own television show was announced for Disney+. The chapter proposes to discover any possible relation between the movies and Avengers' video game in light of these novelties.

---

[6]For further and detailed information, Burke, L. (2015). *The comic book film adaptation: Exploring modern Hollywood's leading genre*. Jackson: University Press of Mississippi.

11.2 Methodology

11.2.1 The Research Interest and the Question

The research has begun with a particular interest. During the second half of the 2010s, both *Avengers* and *Spider-Man* movies have become one of the most profitable blockbusters at the worldwide box office. Meanwhile, three Marvel video games, including *Spider-Man, Spider-Man: Miles Morales, and Marvel's Avengers*, were released in that short period when the MCU has expanding its branded universe in multiple media. These new installments and the current or possible relation between them constituted the core interest of the research. Then, a specific research question was determined. 'How *Avengers* movies and *Marvel's Avengers* contribute to each other' became the main question. A detailed research process was followed to explore the interplay between Marvel's videogame and the MCU regarding the Avengers brand.

11.2.2 Qualitative Approach and Data Collecting Method

The chapter includes a qualitative approach to the research process. The in-depth interview technic was selected as the data collecting method of the chapter. Grounded theory, as the qualitative approach, was decided to be used in this chapter. John W. Creswell (2007, p. 63) explains that "participants in the study would all have experienced the process, and the development of the theory might help explain practice or provide a framework for further research." Therefore, six different participants were specifically selected among the people who have watched the MCU's *Infinity Saga* (23 movies), played *Marvel's Avengers* video game and/or watched over 10 h of gameplay, have been familiar with superhero comics, superhero television series, and superhero video games, have called themselves as a geek or a superhero fan. At first, six separate in-depth interviews were conducted between sixth and ninth February 2021 via Zoom. In-depth interviews were recorded with the permission of the participants. These in-depth interviews provide over 3 h-record in total. Each in-depth interview takes between 20 and 53 min. After in-depth interviews were completed, these recordings were transcribed into 21 pages of a document. Kathy Charmaz (2006, p. 14) mentions that "...grounded theory quickens the speed of gaining a clear focus on what is happening in your data without sacrificing the detail of enacted scenes." Creswell (2009, p. 130) claims that the questions could be prepared for generating a theory of some process and the exploration of a specific process. Thus, questions of the in-depth interviews were determined with an exploratory purpose to discover the interplay between *Avengers* movies and *Marvel's Avengers* video game. Six specific questions, which were directed toward participants, are listed below:

1. After watching a superhero movie, do you think superheroes should stay in that medium or appear in other media? How does this affect you?
2. Does a superhero in a video game reflect the same superhero's characteristic in the movie? Does a superhero in a movie reflect the same superhero's characteristic in the video game?
3. What is the image of the cinematic representation of the superhero in *Marvel's Avengers'* gameplay?
4. Are different media's ways of reflecting superheroes' characteristics different or the same?
5. Are the story of the videogame *Avengers* and the story of the movies interrelated? Are they related to each other?
6. After the first appearance in comics, Kamala Khan, as a new superhero, is introduced in the video game *Avengers*; then, her television series is announced for Disney +. Does the video game present a television series? Could a television series or a movie be the presentation of a video game?

The judgment / purposeful (Maxwell 2012) sampling technique was used. Maxwell (2012, p. 99) explains that "in this strategy, particular settings, persons, or activities are selected deliberately to provide information that is particularly relevant to your questions and goals, and that can't be gotten as well from other choices." According to Martin N Marshal, the researcher is able to select 'the most productive sample' for answering the research question (1996, p. 523). Thus, six participants were selected individuals who are very familiar with *Avengers* movies, the MCU, comic book origins of superheroes, superhero television series, and the video game to discover and reach the research purpose. After analyzing data, four specific categories were reached. Impact, influence, connection, interrelation, and interconnection were gathered together under the first category called *interaction*. Mimic, familiarity, similarity, and relatedness were unified in the second category called *resemblance*. *Experience* was reached as the third category during data analysis. Finally, consume, franchise, company, industrial, and promotion shaped the last category called *commerciality*. Therefore, four main categories, which were reached, can be listed as interaction, resemblance, experience, and commerciality.

11.3 Discovering Similarities and Differences Between Avengers Video Game and Movies

Henry Jenkins' (2004) seminal work titled '*Game Design as Narrative Architecture*' constitutes one of the inspirations for this research. In his work, Jenkins attempts to theorize the concept of environmental storytelling by Don Carson who worked as a show designer in Disney Engineering. In his well-known book called '*Homo Ludens*,' Johan H. Huizinga (1980, p. 1) begins his statement with the idea that "in play there is something 'at play' which transcends the immediate needs of life and imparts meaning to the action. All play means something." From a contemporary perspective, Jenkins (2004, p. 121) underlines that "game designers don't simply tell stories; they design world and sculpt spaces." Mark J. P. Wolf taxonomies on- and off-screen spaces in video games from *Planetfall* (1983) as a text-based game without a visual space to *SimCity 2000* (1994) as a video game included mapped spaces (1997, pp. 11–22). Wolf indicates that boundaries of two separate media, video games and movies, have been converging (1997, p. 22). With this regard, he calls the process as 'the cross-fertilization.' According to Wolf, "whereas the cinema offered a window and positioned the spectator with- in the world it depicted, the video game goes further, allowing the spectator to explore that world and take an active role in its events." (1997). Thus, the interaction between two different media becomes more important in the field especially for contemporary perspectives. Significantly, Jenkins categorizes several narrative structures regarding the game design: emergent narratives, embedded narratives, enacting stories, spatial stories - environmental stories, and evocative spaces (2004, pp. 118–130). Jenkins describes evocative spaces that "the most compelling amusement park attractions build upon stories or genre traditions already well-known to visitors, allowing them to enter physically into spaces they have visited many times before in their fantasies." (p. 123). Jenkins explains that we have been interacted with a transmedia storytelling world in which all works have served to a larger narrative economy (p. 124). He gives *Star Wars Saga* as an example that "we already know the story before we even buy the game and would be frustrated if all it offered us was a regurgitation of the original film experience." (2004). According to him, games are placing their stories in larger narrative systems in which all the information is communicated through other media, such as films, books, television shows, and comics (2004). He concludes his statement on evocative spaces that "in such a system, what games do best will almost certainly center around their ability to give concrete shape our memories and imaginings of the story world, creating an immersive environment we can wander through and interact with." (2004).

Jenkins is one of the first theoreticians who has brought new perspectives onto transmedia studies and the world building concept. Tom Dowd et al. (2013, p. 241) examine the Captain America's transmedia value by focusing on the adaptation of the character into multiple media. According to them, "Captain America survives the transmedia explosion into the 21st century because Joss Whedon and Marvel understand the relationship between Captain America, the brand, the intellectual property, and you, the consumer. Captain America is one of Marvel's brand identities." (2013). The transfer of Captain America from comic books to recent productions in multiple media, including *the Avengers* (2012), proves the Marvel-based characters' transmedia storytelling power (Dowd et al. 2013, p. 241).

Among several researches on the transmedia studies, one can associate *Marvel's Avengers* and also other superhero comics-based video games with evocative spaces with the help of Jenkins' approach. As mentioned above, Avengers comics have been published since 1963, whereas movie-goers have watched many adventures of Avengers members on bigger screens since 2012. Through Jenkins' idea, this could be claimed that *Marvel's Avengers*, similar to the MCU, superhero comic books, superhero television series, and cartoons, is linked to a larger narrative economy.

This network could be annoying or fascinating for the readers, the players, and the viewers. By considering *Marvel's Avengers* as a part of a larger narrative space, the video game' relation to the expanded corpus was attempted to discover.

11.3.1   Marvel's Avengers Video Game

Marvel's Avengers is one of the latest video games, which is based on Marvel Comics' characters. It is an action-adventure role-playing game that players are able to control the majority of Avengers members, including Kamala Khan, with a single player or multiplayer mode. The game was released in 2020 for not only PlayStation but also Windows and several Xbox series. After the video game's release, the players have begun to receive many updates on resources caps, outfits, and settings. *Marvel's Avengers* offers the players experiencing to control well-known characters from the MCU in a similar environment with different secondary characters and story arcs through a third-person perspective. By *Marvel's Avengers*, the superhero team's main characters could be experienced in a new medium differently from comics and movies.

11.3.2   Exploring Interaction, Resemblance, Experience, and Commerciality in the Marvel's Expanded Narrative Environment

In the in-depth interview process, the answer to the question of "should superheroes stay in that medium [cinema], or they appear in other media" was firstly searched. Six participants mainly express their gratitude to see their favorite superheroes in several media. Participant 1 states that "if I like something, I want to have some part of the impact on everything that I consume. Maybe I want them to steam in my games, in my television series, and in my books." Participant 1 explains the idea that "it threatens an opportunity to use the character, their story, their arcs, their interests, and their existence in different media where you can present them different lives. I think that we shouldn't be limited to a single medium, especially if it is movies." Participant 2 describes the comment that "I would watch all the television shows, superhero games, and everything. For me, I am a geek. I would watch and play everything about superhero movies. We have already had only one MCU; we should see them a lot more in other media." Participant 3 mentions that "I want to play characters in the game originated from the movies. They need to do it precisely."

> *I think that they should go to other media as well. It is a great idea to have those heroes in other media. They are apparent in the game, such as the Avengers game, which I just play. It is really cool to see that fan interaction. It gives everybody a great opportunity to*

see those characters that we love in different media because you will go and watch them or play with them. That was really cool to see the characters that we all love in other media. I was extremely interested in playing this game too. Because I do love the characters. Participant 4.

While participant 5 indicates the pleasure in the interaction of the same intellectual properties between various media, participant 6 explains this gratification to experience these superheroes in other media. According to participant 5, "actually, I am very satisfied to see characters and stories in other media, and also films come from the comic books. There should be an interaction between different media." Participant 6 explains the experience of seeing these characters beyond a single medium that "I am okay and pleased to see superheroes in various mediums. It is exciting for me to experience them in a game where I can play as them, or series where I can learn more about their inner selves or own stories."

The second question was asked to explore the ideas of participants on the condition of Avengers members' characteristics in adapting them from a different medium into a video game. Participants agreed that most of the characters have familiar characteristics, including superpower, mission, attitude, and sense of humor, with the Avengers members' attributes in the MCU, even though they are not directly adapted from the cinematic universe into the video game. Participant 1 explains the opinions on that "at most of the times; they try to mimic each other since they are officially operated by Disney and Marvel Studios. They try to present a single unified existence for main cast characters." Participant 3 exemplifies the resemblance between the movie cast of *Avengers* movies and characters in the game.

I can say that they do very good job to reflect characteristics into the game such as Captain America's bossy characteristic into the game like a team leader, like a captain. Captain America is followed by other superheroes, they followed his lead. Hulk is a very angry person, and also Bruce Banner a is very cold person. The game is very well doing it with some pacts between the bad temper guy and good Samaritan in a very good way. It is a very good complication. It is a really good job to reflect original movie's characteristics to the game. Participant 3.

Participant 5 varies the examples that "absolutely, there are familiarities in the characters of the movie and the game, such as Iron Man is rich, powerful, and the cool guy same as in the game. Hulk is too angry. He is the monster and also has the rage in the game." With this regard, participant 6 states that "it is mostly similar, because they wanted to, for my understanding, keep characters' personas similar to the movie representation of the characters or the actors who played them."

Question 3 compares the physical appearances and the image of the same characters both in the video game and the movie. Whereas participant 1 claims that there are both similarities and differences that "their characters might be similar. Their personas might be the same. But they have not the same arcs. For example, the game Thor did not have Chris Hemsworth's Thor's character. We don't have the same familiarity. It is not apparent to us," participant 2 claims that "... it is exactly adaptation to the *Avengers* movie. But Marvel and Disney don't want to make those characters more charismatic than the original cast of the actors like Robert Downey Jr. and Chris Hemsworth." Participant 3 indicates the facial difference of Tony

Stark in the video game that "when I look at the game, Tony Star has long hair." In this sense, participant 5 and 6 explain that by the different ways of producing content in various media. Participant 5 states that "they are very similar as their looking and also their superpowers. All the characters look very similar, but there are technological differences between the production of the movie and the production of the game."

> It was a very realistic approach in the game with relation to the movies. Their physical appearance, for me, the most reliable one was the Hulk. Because the movie version of the Hulk is also CGI, so it is, I think, the easiest to present him in a game format. Other than that, Iron Man, Black Widow, and Captain America, of course, have also very similar representations of their costumes or their physics, faces in relation to the movies. Participant 6.

The fourth question of "are different media's ways of reflecting superheroes' characteristics different or the same?" was asked to participants for exploring their opinions on different media's adaptation ways of the same characters. Participants explain their ideas with their experiences in various media. Participant 1 mentions that "they do present them in a different light. Because they have the different experiences they can give. Being a watcher, being part of a game, and reading a comic book... They are all different media that present themselves in different storytelling and provide different experiences." Participant 2 explains that "they try to remind us the MCU in the game. It is a kind of an advertisement of the MCU. That's why they are similar, maybe, but the reflection of the MCU that we can see in the games as well."

> In the movies, you watch what happens. You watch the character choice; you watch the character's development and changes in the storyline. That's why there should be a bit of difference between the movie and the video game. The reason for telling this is the different experiences of the movie and the video game. You watch the movie, but you play and direct the game. Participant 5.

The MCU covers movies, television series, originals on SVODs in a shared and larger narrative in which the same casts and characters can appear. Therefore, the stories of the live-action productions are commonly interconnected to each other. The fifth question was asked to reveal participants' opinions on the connection or disconnection between the video game's gameplay and the movies' story. Participants agreed on that there is a Marvel story path to be followed by each medium, although the plots of the video game and the movies are not directly connected.

> I think we called, homage / familiarity. This is very apparent here. From the characteristics of characters down to story arcs, for example "the Stark's technology is going to destroy us" arc of Avengers: Age of Ultron is exceptionally apparent here like it is main catalyst of everything, every story beat, every arc. Also just like that characters are heavily taking from Avengers movies. Participant 1.

Participant 2 indicates the familiarities in settings that "they are not related to each other directly. The game looks like *the Avengers* (2012) movie because the main base in the game is the S.H.I.E.L.D helicarrier." Still, participant 2 also explains differences in the video game cast that "the main enemy of the movie was Loki in *the Avengers*. In the game, it is the A.I.M. corporation, and the main villain was M.O.D.O.K. In story-wise, there are a lot of differences, but the main similarities are the characters and the style of the story." Participant 3 describes the opinions on that "obviously, it is going to be changed into a different story. People don't want the same thing. If the game has the same story like one of those movies, I don't want to see the same story." However, participant 1, 5, and 6 underline that the central setting of the video game and the movie is New York, even though there are different sub-plots in the video game.

The last question is about the implementation of the character called Kamala Khan in the video game before the characters' introduction in any live action format. All participants agreed on that this is the promotion of the character for the television series. However, they are pleased to meet, play, and see Kamala Khan in the video game. Participant 1 states that "it is smart to at least familiar characters that might not be known for a mainstream way. It creatively opens some opportunities and basically advertisement which is better than having an advertisement on a bus." Participant 2 is very clear on the idea that "there is only one answer to this: Kamala Khan's television show is coming up. Disney and Marvel want to basically make the advertisement of Kamala Khan television show or more generally the MCU." According to participant 3, it is 'the commercial way' of Marvel. Participant 4 states that it is a new kind of presentation way because these characters are 'transferrable.' According to participant 5, "every character and product of Avengers, with the name of Avengers, will be each other's promotion in online or offline media." Participant 6 explains introducing a new character in a video game before movies with an example from one of the latest Marvel series on Disney + called *WandaVision* (Jac Schaeffer 2021).

> This is the most interesting part of this video game. But after Marvel has introduced *Avengers: Endgame*, their whole system has changed. So that Kamala Khan's introduction in a video game, rather than a movie, is really important in this aspect. I can relate this with the WandaVision series that Wanda and Vision's twins, Tommy and Billy, first-ever introduced in a television series. They are the children of two superheroes, so they have superhero abilities. Like Kamala Khan's introduction in a video game, rather than her solo movie, it is really important for Marvel Universe. With this, we can understand that we can see any new coming superhero in any medium. Participant 6.

By participants' opinions, one can suggest that *Marvel's Avengers* is not the direct adaptation of *Avengers* movies and they are not in a shared narrative plot. However, they try to mimic each other and they endeavor to take benefit from each other. Stork (2014, p. 78) defines Avengers as 'the brand icon of Marvel's cinematic universe.' Avengers brand is used for reframing the aesthetic, economic, and industrial dynamics of the superhero genre by Marvel Studios (2014). While the majority of the participants are pleased to *experience* the *interaction* of different productions and *resemblance* of the comics-based characters between several media, they are aware of that these kinds of interconnections between various media have maintained for *commercial* purposes. The participants' opinions could lead to declare that Avengers is one of the most reasonable brands to bridge over a larger narrative economy by providing various kinds of experiences to entertain the reader, the viewer, and the player with a growing transmedia universe.

11.4   Conclusion

The opinions of the participants enable to discover an understanding of the interplay between *Marvel's Avengers* video game and *Avengers* movies in the MCU. Besides their personal experiences and opinions, several categories, including interaction, resemblance, experience, and commerciality, were reached at the end of the data analysis. Whereas answers to the first question were related to the experience and the commerciality, the second and third question's answers were associated to the resemblance and the interaction. When the participants' opinions on the question four directed the interaction, the experience, and the commerciality, the answers to the fifth question were linked to the interaction, the resemblance, and the commerciality. The answers to the last question on the implementation of Kamala Khan in the video game before any live-action adaptation were related only to the commerciality. By the opinions of the participants, a broad perspective to the condition of the same characters in a larger narrative beyond a single medium could be reached. Whereas participants, who are willing to follow the characters in various media, are eager to find any resemblances and differences of comics-based superheroes in multiple media, the interaction between comics, movies, television series, and video games makes them pleasant. They are enthusiastic about experiencing these characters with the opportunities of various media, which are provided. Significantly, *Marvel's Avengers* video game's offer to control superheroes, as playable characters, in a familiar environment within cinematic settings, was underlined to explain the crucial opportunity of the medium that the participants want to experience. However, the commercial purposes of this narrative economy are mostly recognized by the participants.

As a qualitative approach, the grounded theory allows researchers to develop a perspective or a theory on a particular field by exploring and discovering. In today's highly technological world, each medium has begun to involve (or with Jenkins' word; converge) the other. Especially, Jenkins' contributions on the participatory culture (1992) and the convergence (2006), and Janet H. Murray's work on the future of narratives (2016) are seminal to understand this transformative connection. By the research, one can suggest that Marvel Comics-based video games are in a specific direction to be part of a larger transmedia universe. The term, transmedia, has been defined by many different theoreticians with the inspiration of Jenkins. Lisbeth Klastrup and Susana Tosca's (2004) approach on the definition of the transmedial worlds could be more related to the scope of this research. They describe the transmedial worlds as "abstract content systems from which a repertoire of fictional stories and characters can be actualized or derived across a variety of media forms." (2004, p. 409). They approach a transmedial world as more than a specific story, it is a process of 'the world actualization' beyond a single medium mostly created by a single creator with a single vision, such as George Lucas' *Star Wars: A New Hope* (1977) and J. R. R. Tolkien's *Lord of the Rings* novels (1977). This world could be initiated in any medium, such as *Lord of the Rings* from novels, *Star Wars* from movies, and *Pokemon* from Nintendo Gameboy game, even though the worlds are operated by different media organizations beyond the single creator or a particular creative team in multiple media (Klastrup and Tosca 2004, p. 410). Klastrup and Tosca's point is important for the research's topic. Stan Lee and Jack Kirby were known as the creators of many Marvel Comics-based intellectual properties. However, Kevin Feige has been the executive producer of the MCU movies since the release of *Iron Man* (2008). At present, Feige is both the president of Marvel Studios and the chief creative officer of Marvel Entertainment. As the chief decision-maker, Feige has the creative control on the future of Marvel productions. Therefore, this could be claimed that, Marvel productions in multiple media could include more cinematic universe-related stories, characters, or environments which try to resemble cinematic versions in the MCU. Besides, superhero movies could be accepted as expressive generic texts in order to discover converging media aesthetics beyond a single medium (Gilmore and Stork 2014, p. 2).

Although *Marvel's Avengers* contains a variety of subplots and characters, which have not been appeared in any other medium, except for comics, the video game could be defined as the latest content, which includes many resemblances in character designs, conflicts, and settings with the MCU. According to Box Office Mojo's data, four *Avengers* movies earned over $ 7.7 billion at the worldwide box office.[7] The Avengers' popularity could be seen as a catalyst for these intellectual properties to be transferred into other media. In addition to Wanda and Vision, the audience would have a chance to see these characters, including Falcon, Winter Soldier, Loki, Hulk, Hawkeye, and War Machine, with the same casts on smaller screens at a short span of time.[8] *Marvel's Avengers* offers players to meet Kamala Khan before seeing the character's adventures in a television series. Marvel Entertainment includes many branches and divisions, such as Marvel Comics, Marvel Studios, and Marvel Games. Even though each content, which is produced by these divisions, is not directly interconnected to each other, each one contributes to another commercially, contextually, and thematically. By the data analysis, the interconnection between various media through the same characters and similar narratives, and the resemblance of characters' representations in different media cause to deduce that the superhero genre is expanding in the direction of any transmedia franchise should go. In fact, the genre presents opportunities to experience branded

---

[7]Avengers. *Box Office Mojo*. [Accessed on Feb 17, 2021]. Retrieved from https://www.boxofficemojo.com/search/?q=avengers

[8]Upcoming Marvel TV Shows Coming to Disney Plus. *Cinema Blend*. [Accessed on Feb 17, 2021]. Retrieved from https://www.cinemablend.com/television/2488233/upcoming-marvel-tv-shows-coming-to-disney-plus

and well-known characters in partly unified existences beyond a single medium. Therefore, this chapter's research could contribute to the field and provide insight for further studies on the interconnection between video games and other media.

Ludography

Crystal Dynamics. (2020). *Marvel's Avengers* [Video game]. United States: California.

Game Freak. (1996). *Pokemon (Pocket monsters red and green)* [Video game]. Japan: Tokyo.

Infocom. (1983). *Planetfall* [Video game]. United States: Massachusetts.

Insomniac Games. (2020). *Spider-Man: Miles Morales* [Video game]. United States: California.

Insomniac Games. (2018). *Spider-Man* [Video game]. United States: California.

Maxis. (1994). *SimCity 2000* [Video game]. United States: California.

Filmography

Ali, K. B. (2021). *Ms. Marvel* [Television series]. United States: Marvel Studios.

Cameron, J. (2009). *Avatar* [Motion picture]. United States: twentieth Century Fox.

Favreau, J. (2008). *Iron Man* [Motion picture]. United States: Marvel Studios.

Lucas, G. (1977). *Star Wars: A new hope* [Motion picture]. United States: Lucas Film.

Raimi, S. (2007). *Spider-Man 3* [Motion picture]. United States: Columbia Pictures.

Raimi, S. (2004). *Spider-Man 2* [Motion picture]. United States: Columbia Pictures.

Raimi, S. (2002). *Spider-Man* [Motion picture]. United States: Columbia Pictures.

Russo, A., & Russo, J. (2019). *Avengers: Endgame* [Motion picture]. United States: Marvel Studios.

Russo, A., & Russo, J. (2018). *Avengers: Infinity war* [Motion picture]. United States: Marvel Studios.

Russo, A., & Russo, J. (2016). *Captain America: Civil war* [Motion picture]. United States: Marvel Studios.

Schaeffer, J. (2021). *WandaVision* [Television series]. United States: Marvel Studios.

Watts, J. (2019). *Spider-Man: Far from home* [Motion picture]. United States: Marvel Studios.

Watts, J. (2017). *Spider-Man: Homecoming* [Motion picture]. United States: Marvel Studios.

Webb, M. (2014). *The amazing Spider-Man 2* [Motion picture]. United States: Columbia Pictures.

Webb, M. (2012). *The amazing Spider-Man* [Motion picture]. United States: Columbia Pictures.

Whedon, J. (2015). *Avengers: Age of Ultron* [Motion picture]. United States: Marvel Studios.

Whedon, J. (2012). *The Avengers* [Motion picture]. United States: Marvel Studios.

References

E. Blumenthal, Marvel's 'spider-man' for PlayStation 4 swings to a record-breaking opening. USA today (2018). Retrieved from https://www.usatoday.com/story/tech/talkingtech/2018/09/20/marvels-spider-man-ps-4-sells-record-3-3-million-copies-opening/1346187002/. Accessed 15 Feb 2021

L. Burke, *Superhero Movies* (2008). Pocket essentials. ISBN 13: 978-1-84243-275-4

L. Burke, Introduction, in *The Superhero Symbol: Media, Culture, and Politics*, ed. by L. Burke, I. Gordon, A. Ndalianis, (Rutgers University Press, New Brunswick, Camden, and Newark, 2019a)

L. Burke, An interview with former president of DC entertainment Diane Nelson, in *The Superhero Symbol: Media, Culture, and Politics*, ed. by L. Burke, I. Gordon, A. Ndalianis, (Rutgers University Press, New Brunswick, Camden, and Newark, 2019b)

K. Charmaz, *Constructing Grounded Theory: A Practical Guide through Qualitative Analysis* (Sage Publications, London, Thousand Oaks, New Delhi, 2006)

W.J. Creswell, *Qualitative Inquiry and Research Design: Choosing among Five Approaches* (Sage Publications, London, Thousand Oaks, New Delhi, 2007)

W.J. Creswell, *Research Design: Qualitative, Quantitative, and Mixed Methods Approaches* (Sage Publications, London, Thousand Oaks, New Delhi, 2009)

T. Dowd, M. Niederman, M. Fry, J. Steiff, *Storytelling Across Worlds: Transmedia for Creatives and Producer* (Focal Press: Taylor & Francis Group, New York and London, 2013)

N.J. Gilmore, M. Stork, Introduction, in *Superhero Synergies: Comic Book Characters Go Digital*, ed. by M. Stork, J. N. Gilmore, (Rowman & Littlefield Publishers, Lanham, 2014)

H.J. Huizinga, *Homo Ludens: Story of the Play Element in Culture* (Routledge, New York and London, 1980)

H. Jenkins, *Textual Poachers: Television Fans and Participatory Culture* (Routledge, New York and London, 1992)

H. Jenkins, Game design as narrative architecture, in *First Person: New Media as Story, Performance, and Game*, ed. by N. Wardrio-Fruin, P. Harrigan, (MIT Press, Cambridge, 2004)

H. Jenkins, *Convergence Culture: Where Old and New Media Collide* (New York University Press, New York and London, 2006)

L. Klastrup, S. Tosca, Transmedial worlds-rethinking cyberworld design, in *2004 International Conference on Cyberworlds* (IEEE, 2004), pp. 409–416

N.M. Marshal, Sampling for qualitative research. Fam. Pract. **13**, 522–525 (1996)

A.J. Maxwell, *Qualitative Research Design: An Interactive Approach* (Sage Publications, Los Angles, London, New Delhi, 2012)

T. McSweeney, *Avengers Assemble! Critical Perspectives on the Marvel Cinematic Universe* (Wallflower Press, London and New York, 2018)

A.R. Mills, *American Theology, Superhero Comics, and Cinema: The Marvel of Stan Lee and Revolution of a Genre* (Routledge, Taylor & Francis Group, New York and London, 2014)

H.J. Murray, *Hamlet on the Holodeck: The Future of Narrative in Cyberspace* (The Free Press, New York, London, and Toronto, 2016)

J.B. Robb, *A Brief History of Superheroes* (Running Press and Robinson, Philadelphia, London, 2014)

M. Stork, Assembling the avengers: Reframing the superhero movie through Marvel's cinematic universe, in *Superhero Synergies: Comic Book Characters Go Digital*, ed. by M. Stork, J. N. Gilmore, (Rowman & Littlefield Publishers, Lanham, 2014)

P.J.M. Wolf, Toward a taxonomy of on- and off-screen space in video games. Film Quart. **51**(1), 11–23 (1997)

Part III
New Technologies and Approaches

Chapter 12
Academical: A Choice-Based Interactive Storytelling Game for Enhancing Moral Reasoning, Knowledge, and Attitudes in Responsible Conduct of Research

Katelyn M. Grasse, Edward F. Melcer, Max Kreminski, Nick Junius,
James Ryan, and Noah Wardrip-Fruin

12.1 Introduction

Responsible conduct of research (RCR) comprises fundamental ethical topics that inform all aspects of the research process, making it an important concept that warrants study of and improvement to existing training tools (Kalichman 2014). However, ethics in research can be complicated by many factors such as power dynamics and marginalized identities (Melcer et al. 2020a,b). As a result, RCR requires understanding a variety of perspectives and dilemmas that impact underlying research ethics (Kalichman and Plemmons 2007; Shamoo and Resnik 2009). This makes topics such as RCR difficult to teach due to the complexity of applied ethics and ethical decision-making (Bouville 2008), the need for moral reasoning (Schmaling and Blume 2009), and the lack of existing educational tools that are motivating and foster critical thinking (Kalichman 2014). While past work has attempted to address these issues through alternative learning approaches such as group mentoring Whitbeck (2001) and role-playing (Brummel et al. 2010; Seiler et al. 2011), these issues have still remained largely unaddressed—resulting in ill-defined content, format, and goals, as well as minimal evidence for effectiveness (Kalichman 2013). Furthermore, traditional educational RCR tools suffer from a notable lack of user engagement and motivation with students (Kalichman 2014).

K. M. Grasse (✉) · E. F. Melcer · M. Kreminski · N. Junius · N. Wardrip-Fruin
University of California, Santa Cruz, CA, USA
e-mail: katy@ucsc.edu; eddie.melcer@ucsc.edu; mkremins@ucsc.edu; njunius@ucsc.edu;
nwardrip@ucsc.edu

J. Ryan
Carleton College, Northfield, MN, USA
e-mail: jryan@carleton.edu

Conversely, in the context of educational games, choice-based interactive storytelling is a popular format for narrative videogames (Friedhoff 2013; Murray 2018; Salter 2016). There have even been educational interactive narratives designed specifically to teach issues related to ethics (Hodhod et al. 2009), although they have yet to be evaluated for effectiveness. Interactive storytelling (and educational games in general Keehl and Melcer 2019; Melcer et al. 2017; Melcer and Isbister 2018) have also been shown to increase engagement/motivation and learning for more rote topics with clearly defined answers and educational outcomes, such as in the areas of STEM (Rowe et al. 2011; Weng et al. 2011; Zhang et al. 2019). However, past work has not fully examined the capabilities of choice-based interactive storytelling games in teaching more ambiguous concepts such as moral reasoning and ethical decision-making.

Interactive storytelling games may be an effective supplemental training tool for addressing the above issues with RCR education. Specifically, we hypothesized that the choice-based, role-playing nature of interactive storytelling games could be employed to improve student engagement as well as cognitive and socio-affective learning outcomes. As a result, we created *Academical*, a choice-based interactive storytelling game for RCR education that allows players to experience a story from multiple perspectives and practice ethical decision-making (see Fig. 12.1). In this chapter, we discuss the design of *Academical*, and provide results from a pair of initial studies evaluating the game's efficacy for teaching RCR learning outcomes. The first study compares our web-based game with traditional web-based educational materials from an existing RCR course at the University of Utah with respect to their engagement and efficacy for teaching RCR knowledge and moral reasoning skills. The second study explores whether *Academical* can also improve attitudes about RCR and how players' engagement with the game relates to their attitudes. We conclude with a discussion of combined results from both studies and their implications for the usage of choice-base interactive storytelling games for holistically teaching both cognitive and socio-affective learning outcomes of ethically complex content.

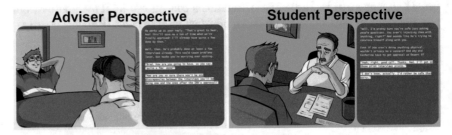

Fig. 12.1 Two perspectives and corresponding choice points from *Academical*'s first scenario, "The Head Start." In this story, the player can role-play as an adviser or a graduate student struggling to navigate the human subjects research approval process. The two highlighted text blocks from each scene represent the player's dialogue options for their character

12.2 Background

12.2.1 Interactive Storytelling and Learning

Prior work has argued for interactive storytelling's power in terms of evoking empathy (Bratitsis 2016; Salter 2016; Samuel et al. 2017),[1] providing therapeutic benefits (Dias et al. 2018; Starks et al. 2016), and enabling learning experiences through educational games (Camingue et al. 2020; Danilicheva et al. 2009; Melcer et al. 2015; Nguyen et al. 2018; Weiß and Müller 2008). Specifically, narrative/storytelling is an important element that can be incorporated into educational games in order to maintain and increase students' motivation (Dickey 2006; Padilla-Zea et al. 2014; Rowe et al. 2011), with some suggesting that integration of a good story into an educational game will determine its success or failure (Göbel et al. 2009). Interactive storytelling has been incorporated into a number of educational games focusing on topics such as history (Christopoulos et al. 2011; Song et al. 2012), STEM (Danilicheva et al. 2009; Weng et al. 2011; Zhang et al. 2019), and bullying (Aylett et al. 2005; Watson et al. 2007). However, the majority of research on educational interactive storytelling games has focused on adaptivity (Göbel and Mehm 2013; Kickmeier-Rust et al. 2008), interactivity (Song et al. 2012; Zhang et al. 2019), emergent narrative (Aylett et al. 2005), player and knowledge modeling (Magerko 2007; Rowe and Lester 2010), narrative planning and generation (Hodhod et al. 2011; Riedl et al. 2008; Wang et al. 2016; Zook et al. 2012), and the game creation process itself (Christopoulos et al. 2011; Diez and Melcer 2020; Spierling 2008). As a result, there is comparatively little work evaluating the impact of an interactive storytelling approach on learning outcomes, especially for topics such as RCR with ethically complex concepts that require a variety of perspectives.

12.2.2 Responsible Conduct of Research Training

Training scientists to recognize and engage in good ethical behaviors is critical to improving the quality of research, encouraging healthier workplace practices and increasing the general public's trust in the scientific process. The importance of RCR is such that many major funding agencies, such as the National Institutes of Health (NIH) and National Science Foundation (NSF), explicitly require researchers supported by their grants to receive RCR training (NIH et al. 1989; Plimpton 2009). However, concepts utilizing applied ethics, such as RCR, can prove difficult to teach due to the complexity of problems faced by researchers and the many underlying perspectives involved in such dilemmas (Shamoo and Resnik 2009). Currently, the NIH provides a guideline of nine core RCR topics (Kalichman

---

[1]Though see Pozo (2018) for a critique of this notion.

2016): (1) *conflict of interest*, (2) *human and animal subjects*, (3) *mentoring*, (4) *collaboration*, (5) *peer review*, (6) *data management*, (7) *research misconduct*, (8) *authorship and publication*, and (9) *scientists and society*. Past research on RCR education has ranged from issues teaching ethical theories underlying RCR (Bouville 2008) and identifying metacognitive reasoning strategies that facilitate ethical decision-making (Kligyte et al. 2008; Mumford et al. 2008) to the use of group mentoring (Whitbeck 2001) and role-playing (Brummel et al. 2010; Seiler et al. 2011) for improved training efficacy. However, there is still a notable engagement issue within current RCR education, and a serious need for a variety of tools to improve discussion, engagement, and critical thinking (Kalichman 2014; Kalichman and Plemmons 2007). As a result, an interactive storytelling approach may prove effective for increasing motivation and fostering deeper critical thinking.

12.2.3   RCR Learning Outcomes

According to RCR training experts, being able to successfully navigate ethical dilemmas requires mastery of a combination of distinct learning outcomes, including (1) relevant conceptual knowledge (e.g., sensitivity to societal expectations), (2) moral reasoning skills (e.g., judgement of possible solutions) and (3) positive attitudes about RCR (e.g., motivation to behave ethically) (Antes et al. 2010; Bebeau 1993; Kalichman and Plemmons 2007). The logic follows that teaching cognitive skills is only useful if the student also has the affective motivation to apply them (Kalichman 2014). Reviews examining the pedagogical efficacy of RCR training methods strongly recommend that learning activities should be engaging and promote thoughtful consideration and discussion of relevant ethical issues (Kalichman 2014). For instance, role-play provides an engaging opportunity for students to embody contending perspectives on an issue, making it one of the most promising discussion methods for improving comprehension and execution of ethical behavior (Brummel et al. 2010). Much research has shown that role-play is capable of training each of the three learning outcomes—knowledge, moral reasoning skills and attitudes—that drive improvements in behavior (Rao and Stupans 2012). Unfortunately, traditional role-play activities are relatively resource-intensive because they require experienced guidance from an instructor combined with substantial time spent with a partner to practice necessary skills (Cook et al. 2017; Feinstein et al. 2002). However, there is growing evidence demonstrating the advantages of virtual training simulations over live-action role-play for preparing workers to navigate challenging workplace scenarios (Spencer et al. 2019). This chapter highlights the potential for interactive narrative games to provide an easily accessible single-player form of digital role-play that is still capable of holistically training both cognitive and socio-affective RCR learning outcomes. Notably, this has not yet been empirically demonstrated for existing online RCR training tools.

12.3 Academical: A Choice-Based Interactive Storytelling Game

Academical is a work of choice-based interactive storytelling (Koenitz et al. 2015; Mawhorter et al. 2014, 2018) that was created using the Twine authoring framework (Friedhoff 2013; Salter 2016). The game comprises nine playable scenarios, each pertaining to a specific topic in RCR (Kalichman 2016). These scenarios are adapted (with permission) from a series of existing educational RCR role-playing prompts (Brummel et al. 2010; Seiler et al. 2011). Figure 12.1 shows screenshots taken during gameplay in a web browser.

Each playable scenario in *Academical* centers on a conversation between two stakeholders in the RCR issue at hand, one of whom is controlled by the player—in the sense that they select dialogue options for that character. By virtue of these choices, the player will ultimately reach one of several possible endings, a subset of which represent successful navigation of the situation. Upon reaching a good ending for the first character, the player then unlocks the other interlocutor and replays the scenario from that person's viewpoint. In turn, reaching a good ending for the second character in a given scenario unlocks the next scenario/RCR topic.

At the outset of the project, we decided that the format of choice-based interactive storytelling—which allows a player to experience a story from multiple perspectives and replay scenes to see how different actions play out—would demonstrate the complicated nature of RCR to students in a compelling way. In adapting the role-playing prompts, we sought to show how seemingly obvious answers around questions of research ethics can be complicated by factors such as power dynamics and marginalized identities and experiences. Instead of cleanly delineating right and wrong answers, *Academical* showcases complexity and uncertainty to provoke questions around how courses of action could have unexpected consequences. In turn, while all successful paths through the game's scenarios represent the player character acting responsibly, not all of the situations reach clear resolutions. Specifically, many scenarios feature paths that appear to represent obvious solutions, but ultimately lead to bad outcomes. Through replaying and selecting new options, the player explores the social concerns encompassed in a given RCR scenario, which will lead to a richer understanding of the ethical complications that one can encounter while conducting research as well as aid future moral reasoning.

12.4 Experiment 1: Randomized Group Comparison Study

12.4.1 Methods

We hypothesized that the choice-based, role-playing nature of *Academical*—which is specifically designed to highlight how research ethics can be complicated by many factors such as power dynamics and marginalized identities—would be (1) more engaging, (2) as effective as traditional RCR educational materials at developing knowledge of RCR concepts, and (3) result in stronger moral reasoning skills. In order to explore these hypotheses, we conducted a between-subjects study comparing our choice-based interactive storytelling game approach with web-based educational materials from an existing university RCR course. The study consisted of two conditions: (1) a group that read through two modules of the web-based educational RCR materials covering peer review and authorship; and (2) a group that played two chapters of *Academical* covering peer review and authorship content.

12.4.1.1 Procedure

Participants were told that the study was to explore different approaches to RCR education, and they would either play a game or read materials teaching selected RCR concepts. They then completed an online survey collecting demographic information (age, prior gaming experience, prior RCR experience, and so forth). Upon completing the survey, participants were randomly assigned to one of the two conditions (web materials or *Academical*). After completing the RCR training for peer review and authorship, participants then completed a post-test that assessed their (1) engagement with the training material, (2) quantitative knowledge of peer review and authorship RCR concepts and (3) qualitative moral reasoning skills for these same concepts.

12.4.1.2 Measures

Temple Presence Inventory, Engagement Subscale Engagement is a critical aspect of the learning process (Kearsley and Shneiderman 1998), drastically influencing a learner's motivation to continue interacting with a system and the educational content (O'Brien and Toms 2008). In order to assess participant engagement with the two educational RCR tools employed, we utilized the Engagement subscale of the Temple Presence Inventory (TPI) (Lombard et al. 2009). The TPI has been validated for use with games (Lombard et al. 2011) and measuring game engagement (Martey et al. 2014).

Peer Review and Authorship RCR Quizzes To assess and compare how effective the two RCR tools were for teaching knowledge of peer review and authorship concepts, we utilized two quizzes from an existing online RCR course at the University of Utah. Each quiz consists of three questions around a respective topic, and each question is either true/false, yes/no, or multiple choice.

Qualitative Assessment of Moral Reasoning To assess and compare how effective the two RCR tools were for teaching moral reasoning skills, we utilized qualitative test materials from a previous study that evaluated the effect of role-play on RCR learning outcomes (Seiler et al. 2011). These test materials included two RCR-themed short stories obtained from the Online Ethics Center for Engineering and Research and three short answer questions that the previous study designed to characterize a student's ability to (1) analyze a moral problem, (2) consider the viewpoints of all individuals involved, and (3) propose solutions and anticipate their possible short- and long-term consequences. Participants first read and wrote responses to the short story about peer review, then answered the same three questions for the other scenario involving authorship. After completion of the study, two of the authors scored these answers using the behaviorally anchored rating scale (BARS) method (see Melcer et al. 2020a and Seiler et al. 2011) for more information on the authors' coding procedure.

12.4.2 Results

12.4.2.1 Participant Demographics, Prior Knowledge and Experience

A convenience sample of 28 university graduate and undergraduate students—the standard target populations for RCR training—were recruited for the study (age: $\mu=24.8$, $\sigma=7.6$). There were 10 female, 14 male, and 3 non-binary participants, with 1 declining to disclose gender. During the study, participants were randomly assigned to one of the two conditions: web materials (**14 total**; 3 female, 2 non-binary, 8 male, 1 decline to answer) and *Academical* game (**14 total**; 7 female, 1 non-binary, 6 male).

According to a series of independent samples t-tests, participants in the two conditions did not differ with respect to age, prior game experience, or prior interactive story experience (all p values >= 0.12). Similarly, none of the participants reported prior RCR training in the past 2 years. Therefore, we can assume that participants in both groups had similar prior RCR, game, and interactive story experience.

12.4.2.2 Engagement with RCR Training Tools

An independent samples t-test revealed a significant difference in favor of *Academical* for participant engagement (see Table 12.1; $p = 0.029$, $r = 0.4$), suggesting that a choice-based interactive story game is a more engaging experience for RCR training than traditional web reading materials.

12.4.2.3 RCR Learning Outcomes

Peer Review and Authorship RCR Quizzes A series of Wilcoxon rank sum tests showed that participants in the *Academical* condition scored significantly higher on the peer review test (see Table 12.1; $p = 0.002$, $r = 0.56$) and comparable to the web materials for the authorship test (n.s., $p = 0.23$). This suggests that, in terms

Table 12.1 Post-test results for engagement, RCR knowledge and moral reasoning skills. Bold font indicates statistical significance

	Web		Game		Sig	ES	
Quantitative measures	μ	σ	μ	σ	p	d	r
TPI engagement (out of 42–6 items)	23.4	9	30.1	6.1	**0.029**	**0.87**	**0.4**
Peer review knowledge quiz (3 items)	2.14	0.77	2.93	0.27	**0.002**	**1.4**	**0.56**
Authorship knowledge quiz (3 items)	2.36	0.75	2	0.79	0.23	−0.47	−0.23
Qualitative measures	μ	σ	μ	σ	p	d	r
Identify issues (2 topics)	6.93	1.9	8.57	1.6	**0.023**	**0.92**	**0.42**
Describe viewpoints (2 topics)	4.71	2.8	7.36	2.5	**0.016**	**0.99**	**0.44**
Propose solutions (2 topics)	4.71	2.3	7.14	2.3	**0.015**	**1.1**	**0.47**
Total score (out of 30–6 items)	16.4	5.7	23.1	4.7	**0.004**	**1.3**	**0.54**

of short-term learning, a choice-based interactive story approach is overall more effective than traditional educational materials for developing knowledge of certain RCR topics.

Qualitative Assessment of Moral Reasoning A series of Wilcoxon rank sum tests showed that participants in the *Academical* group scored significantly higher overall on the qualitative tests of moral reasoning (see Table 12.1; Total Score: p = 0.004, r = 0.54). Combining the scores across the two scenarios revealed that these participants had similarly significant improvements for all three aspects of moral reasoning (Issues: p = 0.023, r = 0.42; Viewpoints: p = 0.016, r = 0.44; Solutions: p = 0.015, r = 0.47). A series of independent-samples t-tests similarly highlighted that the *Academical* group also demonstrated better overall moral reasoning skills for each scenario (Peer Review: p = 0.015, r = 0.44; Authorship: p = 0.0028, r = 0.53). These results indicate that, with respect to short-term learning, a choice-based interactive story approach is more effective than traditional educational RCR materials for developing moral reasoning skills necessary to properly employ RCR.

12.5 Experiment 2: Correlational Study

12.5.1 Methods

For the second study, we hypothesized that (1) a choice-based interactive narrative game (i.e., *Academical*) would improve participants' attitudes towards RCR and (2) participants' reported engagement playing the game would predict their post-game attitudes about RCR. In order to explore these hypotheses, we conducted a quasi-experimental within-subjects study measuring one group of participants' RCR attitudes before and after playing a single short session of *Academical* to compare with their feelings of engagement with the game.

12.5.1.1 Procedure

Study participants were required to (1) complete a pre-game survey assessing demographics and attitudes about RCR, (2) play the *Academical* game, and (3) complete a post-game survey gauging knowledge and attitudes about RCR and their feelings of engagement with the game. All participants were recruited from an undergraduate course offered through the engineering department at UCSC (a Tier 1 research institution). Participants were informed of the study through email and offered extra credit toward their class grade in exchange for completing the study. Participants were also told that the purpose of the study was to test the efficacy of a new RCR training program. Participants accessed the surveys and game using the same methods as the previous *Academical* study—through their preferred web browser on their personal computers and without any supervision beyond automated data collection. Two of the nine possible scenarios were selected for students to play through (i.e., peer review and authorship). Participants were instructed to play through each character at least once in each scenario—equating a minimum of 4 total playthroughs (2 per module)—before completing the post-survey. Nine of the 69 participants that successfully completed all parts of the study reported that they had received prior RCR training and were excluded from analysis. Of the 60 remaining participants, there were 41 males, 16 females and 3 non-binary. The average participant age was 20.6 ± 2.2 years (median: 20, range: 18–29), which is a typical age for students starting to engage in research and consider applying to graduate school.

12.5.1.2 Assessment Tools

Temple Presence Inventory, Engagement Subscale See Sect. 12.4.1.2.

RCR Attitudes Survey To assess *Academical*'s efficacy for improving attitudes about RCR, we created a short survey using a list of attitude goals that are highly recommended by RCR instructors (Kalichman and Plemmons 2007). This survey included six items (two questions and four statements, see Table 12.2) with possible responses along a 7-point Likert scale indicating level of agreement. To assess within-subject changes in these attitudes, participants completed the same attitude survey before and after playing the game.

12.5.2 Results

12.5.2.1 RCR Attitudes

In order to gauge whether playing *Academical* could improve participants' attitudes about RCR, we conducted within-subject comparisons of pre- and post-game

Table 12.2 Participants' attitude score before and after playing a single short session of *Academical*. Bold font indicates statistical significance.

Attitude survey items	Pre		Post		Sig	ES
	μ	σ	μ	σ	p	d
(1) How important is RCR training to you?	4.2	1.5	5.0	1.5	**<0.001**	**0.49**
(2) How important do you think RCR training should be for researchers?	5.7	1.2	6.3	1.0	**<0.001**	**0.57**
(3) Research ethics is serious and deserving of the attention of all researchers.[a]	6.1	1.0	6.5	0.9	**0.01**	**0.35**
(4) Researchers have a personal responsibility to model and promote RCR.[a]	5.5	1.1	6.1	1.0	**<0.001**	**0.51**
(5) Researchers have a responsibility to society.[a]	5.6	1.2	6.0	1.1	**<0.001**	**0.37**
(6) Excellence in research includes RCR.[a]	5.6	1.2	6.2	1.0	**<0.001**	**0.55**
Overall attitude score	5.3	0.9	5.9	0.9	**<0.001**	**0.65**

[a] Items borrowed from Kalichman and Plemmons (2007)

attitude ratings. For each participant, we averaged the six attitude scores to find an overall attitude score for both test-points (Pre: 5.3±0.9; Post: 5.9±0.9; Change: 0.55±0.7). A series of Wilcoxon sign rank tests revealed that, after playing *Academical*, participants on average reported a significant improvement in agreement with every individual item in the attitudes survey (see Table 12.2; all p<0.01; effect size range of d = 0.35–0.57, which are small to medium). This analysis also showed that participants' averaged overall attitude score also increased significantly after playing the game (Rank sign test: r = 0.31, p < 0.001; effect size d = 0.65, which is medium). These results confirmed our first hypothesis and demonstrate that playing a short session of *Academical* can significantly improve a variety of important attitudes about RCR.

12.5.2.2 Engagement Correlations with RCR Attitudes

Participants on average reported an engagement score of 26.9±6.6 out of a possible 42 points (median: 28; range: 7–42), showing that this cohort varied greatly in their feelings of engagement with the game. First, Spearman correlations revealed that engagement did not predict participants' pre-game attitude scores (r_s = 0.16, p = 0.23). In contrast, we found that engagement was significantly correlated with post-game attitudes (r_s = 0.41, p = 0.001, moderate strength)—confirming our hypothesis that engagement would predict post-game attitudes. Engagement was also correlated with participants' change in attitude (r_s = 0.27, p = 0.04, weak strength). Together, these results indicate that after playing *Academical*, participants changed their RCR attitudes to more closely align with their feelings of engagement with the game (see Fig. 12.2).

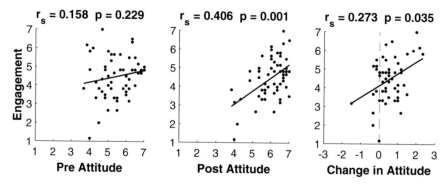

Fig. 12.2 Participants changed their RCR attitudes to more closely align with their feelings of engagement with the game. For simpler visual comparison with the overall attitude scores, engagement scores are reported here as the average (rather than the sum) of the six survey items. Non-parametric Spearman correlation coefficients are provided above each result

12.6 Overall Discussion

12.6.1 Using Interactive Narrative to Teach RCR Learning Outcomes

The results from these two studies evaluating *Academical* suggest that a choice-based interactive storytelling game design is effective as an RCR education tool. In the first study (Melcer et al. 2020a,b), participants who played the *Academical* game (n = 14) developed significantly higher engagement, stronger overall moral reasoning skills, and statistically equivalent or better knowledge scores for certain RCR topics compared to a group trained by an existing web-based university RCR course (n = 14)—highlighting the potential of choice-based interactive storytelling games for improving student engagement and learning outcomes within RCR education. In the second study (Grasse et al. 2021), participants (n = 60) reported significantly higher attitudes about RCR after playing *Academical*, demonstrating that playing the game, even for a short amount of time, can also improve relevant socio-affective learning outcomes. Together, these two studies show that *Academical* is an effective tool for training all three key learning outcomes (i.e., knowledge, skills and attitudes) that contribute to improvements in ethical behavior. Importantly, this collection of evidence indicates that the choice-based interactive storytelling design of the *Academical* video game can successfully train both cognitive and socio-affective learning outcomes **simultaneously**, addressing the full breadth of distinct learning outcomes essential to RCR education in one tool. To the best of our knowledge, this is an achievement which has not yet been documented for existing web-based RCR pedagogy (Powell et al. 2007; Seiler et al. 2011).

12.6.2   The Importance of Engagement within Interactive Narrative

Game-based learning research has demonstrated that engagement can influence a student's motivation to learn (Clark et al. 2016; Noe 1986), particularly for socio-affective outcomes like attitudes (Sabourin and Lester 2013; Lustria 2007). Narrative has become an especially effective method for improving engagement and deep learning (Rowe et al. 2010). Contrasted with the passive reading study strategy promoted by the majority of existing web training tools, *Academical* utilizes narrative role-play and interactive choices to foster engagement and challenge the player to successfully navigate various moral dilemmas common to scientific research. However, care should be taken to generalize *Academical*'s success across the interactive narrative game genre. Our results illustrate the importance of ensuring that an interactive narrative is engaging for the player, as post-game attitudes ($r_s = 0.41$, $p = 0.001$) and changes in attitudes from pre to post ($r_s = 0.27$, $p = 0.04$) were significantly correlated with participants' engagement. This highlights that merely using the interactive narrative medium does not guarantee that a story will feel immersive or engaging for all (or even any) readers. Therefore, it is crucial for designers of interactive narrative games to consider how aspects of their design impact engagement and employ various techniques to improve it. For instance, a lack of relatability to the content (either the characters or story) can cause players to disengage from the narrative (Green and Jenkins 2014), so utilizing a demographically diverse cast of characters or enabling the player to personalize their character for the narrative could improve relatability and subsequently engagement. In order to help guide improvements to *Academical*, future work is required to fully explore which aspects of the game's design best facilitate players' engagement and learning (Revi et al. 2020; Kalyuga and Plass 2009; Ryan et al. 2006).

12.6.3   The Benefits of Online Single-Player Interactive Role-Play

Studies have shown that live-action interactive role-play can help students practice moral reasoning skills, but when compared to playing a computer game, it is a relatively resource-intensive activity in terms of the time and energy needed to facilitate and evaluate the training process (Cook et al. 2017; Spencer et al. 2019). Furthermore, role-playing with others in the physical world can be an uncomfortable or unproductive experience for some people, potentially compromising the learning experience (Cook et al. 2017; Seiler et al. 2011). In comparison, *Academical* is an engaging single-player role-playing experience that carries no social pressure, allowing students to explore multiple perspectives at their own pace. Furthermore, its digital nature means that all learners can play through the same training scenarios with the same dialogue options, and consequently their learning experience, learning progress and progression through the stories can be tracked far more easily than traditional role-playing scenarios (Feinstein et al. 2002). Critically, the improved convenience of using *Academical* for ethical training has the potential to reach a far broader audience than live action role-playing, as well as enable larger and more controlled studies of its effects on RCR learning outcomes.

12.7 Conclusion

In this chapter, we described the design of *Academical*, a choice-based interactive storytelling game for RCR training that enables players to experience a story from multiple perspectives. We also presented results from two initial studies altogether demonstrating (1) *Academical*'s advantages over traditional web-based educational materials for teaching the full breadth of RCR learning outcomes and (2) the potential role of engagement for driving positive attitudes about RCR (and possibly cognitive learning outcomes as well). This work provides evidence supporting the efficacy of interactive narrative games for training ethics. More specifically, our results further elucidate the value of a choice-based interactive storytelling game, such as *Academical*, for teaching RCR and provide implications for the use of interactive storytelling games to improve learning outcomes of ethically complex content such as RCR.

Acknowledgments We would like to thank Jim Moore and the UCSC Division of Graduate Studies for sponsoring the development and evaluation of Academical. We would also like to thank Squinky who played a crucial role leading the development of *Academical*, as well as Brent Hill from the University of Utah for graciously providing their web-based RCR course materials. Furthermore, we would like to thank the many UCSC undergraduate students that assisted with various aspects of the game's development. Finally, we also thank Gene Amberg, C. K. Gunsalus, Sylvie Khan, and Michael Loui of the University of Illinois, both for allowing us to adapt their materials to create this game and for providing feedback on an early prototype.

References

A.L. Antes, X. Wang, M.D. Mumford, R.P. Brown, S. Connelly, L.D. Devenport, Evaluating the effects that existing instruction on responsible conduct of research has on ethical decision making. Acad. Med. J. Assoc. Am. Med. Colleges **85**(3), 519 (2010)

R.S. Aylett, S. Louchart, J. Dias, A. Paiva, M. Vala, FearNot!–an experiment in emergent narrative, in *International Workshop on Intelligent Virtual Agents* (Springer, Berlin, 2005), pp. 305–316

M.J. Bebeau, Designing an outcome-based ethics curriculum for professional education: strategies and evidence of effectiveness. J. Moral Edu. **22**(3), 313–326 (1993)

M. Bouville, On using ethical theories to teach engineering ethics. Sci. Eng. Ethics **14**(1), 111–120 (2008)

T. Bratitsis, A digital storytelling approach for fostering empathy towards autistic children: lessons learned, in *Proceedings of the International Conference on Software Development and Technologies for Enhancing Accessibility and Fighting Info-exclusion* (2016), pp. 301–308

B.J. Brummel, C. Gunsalus, K.L. Anderson, M.C. Loui, Development of role-play scenarios for teaching responsible conduct of research. Sci. Eng. Ethics **16**(3), 573–589 (2010)

J. Camingue, E.F. Melcer, E. Carstensdottir, A (visual) novel route to learning: a taxonomy of teaching strategies in visual novels, in *International Conference on the Foundations of Digital Games, FDG'20* (Association for Computing Machinery, New York, 2020)

D. Christopoulos, P. Mavridis, A. Andreadis, J.N. Karigiannis, Using virtual environments to tell the story: "The Battle of Thermopylae", in *2011 Third International Conference on Games and Virtual Worlds for Serious Applications* (IEEE, Piscataway, 2011), pp. 84–91

D.B. Clark, E.E. Tanner-Smith, S.S. Killingsworth, Digital games, design, and learning: a systematic review and meta-analysis. Rev. Edu. Res. **86**(1), 79–122 (2016)

A.S. Cook, S.P. Dow, J. Hammer, Towards designing technology for classroom role-play, in *Proceedings of the Annual Symposium on Computer-Human Interaction in Play* (2017), pp. 241–251

P. Danilicheva, S. Klimenko, Y. Baturin, A. Serebrov, Education in virtual worlds: virtual storytelling, in *2009 International Conference on CyberWorlds* (IEEE, Piscataway, 2009), pp. 333–338

L.P.S. Dias, J.L.V. Barbosa, H.D. Vianna, Gamification and serious games in depression care: a systematic mapping study. Telematics Inf. **35**(1), 213–224 (2018)

M.D. Dickey, Game design narrative for learning: appropriating adventure game design narrative devices and techniques for the design of interactive learning environments. Edu. Technol. Res. Dev. **54**(3), 245–263 (2006)

J.D.S. Diez, E.F. Melcer, Cookie mania: a serious game for teaching internet cookies to high school and college students, in *Joint International Conference on Serious Games* (Springer, Berlin, 2020), pp. 69–77

A.H. Feinstein, S. Mann, D.L. Corsun, Charting the experiential territory: clarifying definitions and uses of computer simulation, games, and role play. J. Manag. Dev. **21**(10), 732–744 (2002)

J. Friedhoff, Untangling twine: a platform study, in *Proceedings of DiGRA* (2013)

S. Göbel, A. de Carvalho Rodrigues, F. Mehm, R. Steinmetz, Narrative game-based learning objects for story-based digital educational games. Narrative **14**, 16 (2009)

S. Göbel, F. Mehm, Personalized, adaptive digital educational games using narrative game-based learning objects, in *Serious Games and Virtual Worlds in Education, Professional Development, and Healthcare* (IGI Global, Pennsylvania, 2013), pp. 74–84

K.M. Grasse, E.F. Melcer, M. Kreminski, N. Junius, N. Wardrip-Fruin, Improving undergraduate attitudes towards responsible conduct of research through an interactive storytelling game, in *Extended Abstracts of the 2021 CHI Conference on Human Factors in Computing Systems, CHI EA'21* (Association for Computing Machinery, New York, 2021)

M.C. Green, K.M. Jenkins, Interactive narratives: processes and outcomes in user-directed stories. J. Commun. **64**(3), 479–500 (2014)

R. Hodhod, P. Cairns, D. Kudenko, Innovative integrated architecture for educational games: challenges and merits, in *Transactions on Edutainment V* (Springer, Berlin, 2011), pp. 1–34

R. Hodhod, D. Kudenko, P. Cairns, AEINS: adaptive educational interactive narrative system to teach ethics, in *AIED 2009: 14th International Conference on Artificial Intelligence in Education Workshops Proceedings* (2009), p. 79

M. Kalichman, A brief history of RCR education. Account. Res. **20**(5–6), 380–394 (2013)

M. Kalichman, Rescuing responsible conduct of research (RCR) education. Account. Res. **21**(1), 68–83 (2014)

M. Kalichman, Responsible conduct of research education (what, why, and does it work?) Acad. Med. **91**(12), e10 (2016)

M.W. Kalichman, D.K. Plemmons, Reported goals for responsible conduct of research courses. Acad. Med. **82**(9), 846–852 (2007)

S. Kalyuga, J.L. Plass, Evaluating and managing cognitive load in games, in *Handbook of Research on Effective Electronic Gaming in Education* (IGI Global, Pennsylvania, 2009), pp. 719–737

G. Kearsley, B. Shneiderman, Engagement theory: a framework for technology-based teaching and learning. Edu. Technol. **38**(5), 20–23 (1998)

O. Keehl, E. Melcer, Radical tunes: exploring the impact of music on memorization of stroke order in logographic writing systems, in *Proceedings of the 14th International Conference on the Foundations of Digital Games, FDG'19* (Association for Computing Machinery, New York, 2019)

M.D. Kickmeier-Rust, S. Göbel, D. Albert, 80Days: melding adaptive educational technology and adaptive and interactive storytelling in digital educational games, in *Proceedings of the First International Workshop on Story-Telling and Educational Games (STEG'08)*, vol. 8 (2008)

V. Kligyte, R.T. Marcy, S.T. Sevier, E.S. Godfrey, M.D. Mumford, A qualitative approach to responsible conduct of research (RCR) training development: identification of metacognitive strategies. Sci. Eng. Ethics **14**(1), 3–31 (2008)

H. Koenitz, G. Ferri, M. Haahr, D. Sezen, T.İ Sezen, *Interactive Digital Narrative: History, Theory and Practice* (Routledge, London, 2015)

M. Lombard, T.B. Ditton, L. Weinstein, Measuring presence: the Temple Presence Inventory, in *Proceedings of the 12th Annual International Workshop on Presence* (2009)

M. Lombard, L. Weinstein, T. Ditton, Measuring telepresence: the validity of the Temple Presence Inventory (TPI) in a gaming context, in *ISPR 2011: The International Society for Presence Research Annual Conference* (2011)

M.L.A. Lustria, Can interactivity make a difference? Effects of interactivity on the comprehension of and attitudes toward online health content. J. Am. Soc. Inf. Sci. Technol. **58**(6), 766–776 (2007)

B. Magerko, Evaluating preemptive story direction in the interactive drama architecture. J. Game Dev. **2**(3), 25–52 (2007)

R.M. Martey, K. Kenski, J. Folkestad, L. Feldman, E. Gordis, A. Shaw, J. Stromer-Galley, B. Clegg, H. Zhang, N. Kaufman, et al., Measuring game engagement: multiple methods and construct complexity. Simul. Gaming **45**(4–5), 528–547 (2014)

P. Mawhorter, M. Mateas, N. Wardrip-Fruin, A. Jhala, Towards a theory of choice poetics, in *Proceedings of Foundations of Digital Games* (2014)

P. Mawhorter, C. Zegura, A. Gray, A. Jhala, M. Mateas, N. Wardrip-Fruin, Choice poetics by example. Arts **7**(3), 47 (2018)

E.F. Melcer, K. Isbister, Bots & (Main)Frames: exploring the impact of tangible blocks and collaborative play in an educational programming game, in *Proceedings of the 2018 CHI Conference on Human Factors in Computing Systems, CHI'18* (Association for Computing Machinery, New York, 2018)

E.F. Melcer, V. Hollis, K. Isbister, Tangibles vs. mouse in educational programming games: influences on enjoyment and self-beliefs, in *Proceedings of the 2017 CHI Conference Extended Abstracts on Human Factors in Computing Systems, CHI EA'17* (Association for Computing Machinery, New York, 2017), pp. 1901–1908

E.F. Melcer, T.-H.D. Nguyen, Z. Chen, A. Canossa, M.S. El-Nasr, K. Isbister, Games research today: analyzing the academic landscape 2000–2014, in *Proceedings of the 10th International Conference on the Foundations of Digital Games* (2015)

E.F. Melcer, K.M. Grasse, J. Ryan, N. Junius, M. Kreminski, D. Squinkifer, B. Hill, N. Wardrip-Fruin, Getting academical: a choice-based interactive storytelling game for teaching responsible conduct of research, in *International Conference on the Foundations of Digital Games, FDG'20* (Association for Computing Machinery, New York, 2020a)

E.F. Melcer, J. Ryan, N. Junius, M. Kreminski, D. Squinkifer, B. Hill, N. Wardrip-Fruin, Teaching responsible conduct of research through an interactive storytelling game, in *Extended Abstracts of the 2020 CHI Conference on Human Factors in Computing Systems, CHI EA'20* (Association for Computing Machinery, New York, 2020b)

M.D. Mumford, S. Connelly, R.P. Brown, S.T. Murphy, J.H. Hill, A.L. Antes, E.P. Waples, L.D. Devenport, A sensemaking approach to ethics training for scientists: preliminary evidence of training effectiveness. Ethics Behav. **18**(4), 315–339 (2008)

J.T. Murray, Telltale hearts: encoding cinematic choice-based adventure games. Ph.D. Thesis, UC Santa Cruz (2018)

T.H.D. Nguyen, E. Melcer, A. Canossa, K. Isbister, M.S. El-Nasr, Seagull: a bird's-eye view of the evolution of technical games research. Entertain. Comput. **26**, 88–104 (2018)

NIH et al., Requirement for programs on the responsible conduct of research in national research service award institutional training programs. NIH Guide for Grants and Contracts **18**(45), 1 (1989)

R.A. Noe, Trainees' attributes and attitudes: neglected influences on training effectiveness. Acad. Manage. Rev. **11**(4), 736–749 (1986)

H.L. O'Brien, E.G. Toms, What is user engagement? A conceptual framework for defining user engagement with technology. J. Am. Soc. Inf. Sci. Technol. **59**(6), 938–955 (2008)

N. Padilla-Zea, F.L. Gutiérrez, J.R. López-Arcos, A. Abad-Arranz, P. Paderewski, Modeling storytelling to be used in educational video games. Comput. Hum. Behav. **31**, 461–474 (2014)

S. Plimpton, NSF's implementation of Section 7009 of the America COMPETES Act. Fed. Regist. **74**(160), 42126–42128 (2009)

S.T. Powell, M.A. Allison, M.W. Kalichman, Effectiveness of a responsible conduct of research course: a preliminary study. Sci. Eng. Ethics **13**(2), 249–264 (2007)

T. Pozo, Queer games after empathy: feminism and haptic game design aesthetics from consent to cuteness to the radically soft. Game Stud. **18**(3), (2018)

D. Rao, I. Stupans, Exploring the potential of role play in higher education: development of a typology and teacher guidelines. Innov. Edu. Teach. Int. **49**(4), 427–436 (2012)

A.T. Revi, D.E. Millard, S.E. Middleton, A systematic analysis of user experience dimensions for interactive digital narratives, in *International Conference on Interactive Digital Storytelling* (Springer, Berlin, 2020), pp. 58–74

M.O. Riedl, A. Stern, D. Dini, J. Alderman, Dynamic experience management in virtual worlds for entertainment, education, and training. Int. Trans. Syst. Sci. Appl. **4**(2), 23–42 (2008)

J.P. Rowe, J.C. Lester, Modeling user knowledge with dynamic bayesian networks in interactive narrative environments, in *Sixth Artificial Intelligence and Interactive Digital Entertainment Conference* (2010)

J.P. Rowe, L.R. Shores, B.W. Mott, J.C. Lester, Integrating learning and engagement in narrative-centered learning environments, in *International Conference on Intelligent Tutoring Systems* (Springer, Berlin, 2010), pp. 166–177

J.P. Rowe, L.R. Shores, B.W. Mott, J.C. Lester, Integrating learning, problem solving, and engagement in narrative-centered learning environments. Int. J. Artif. Intell. Edu. **21**(1–2), 115–133 (2011)

R.M. Ryan, C.S. Rigby, A. Przybylski, The motivational pull of video games: a self-determination theory approach. Motiv. Emotion **30**(4), 344–360 (2006)

J.L. Sabourin, J.C. Lester, Affect and engagement in game-based learning environments. IEEE Trans. Affect. Comput. **5**(1), 45–56 (2013)

A. Salter, Playing at empathy: representing and experiencing emotional growth through Twine games, in *Proceedings of International Conference on Serious Games and Applications for Health* (IEEE, Piscataway, 2016)

B. Samuel, J. Garbe, A. Summerville, J. Denner, S. Harmon, G. Lepore, C. Martens, N. Wardrip-Fruin, M. Mateas, Leveraging procedural narrative and gameplay to address controversial topics, in *Proceedings of International Conference on Computational Creativity* (2017)

K.B. Schmaling, A.W. Blume, Ethics instruction increases graduate students' responsible conduct of research knowledge but not moral reasoning. Account. Res. **16**(5), 268–283 (2009)

S.N. Seiler, B.J. Brummel, K.L. Anderson, K.J. Kim, S. Wee, C. Gunsalus, M.C. Loui, Outcomes assessment of role-play scenarios for teaching responsible conduct of research. Account. Res. **18**(4), 217–246 (2011)

A.E. Shamoo, D.B. Resnik, *Responsible Conduct of Research* (Oxford University Press, Oxford, 2009)

Q. Song, L. He, X. Hu, To improve the interactivity of the history educational games with digital interactive storytelling. Phys. Proc. **33**, 1798–1802 (2012)

S. Spencer, T. Drescher, J. Sears, A.F. Scruggs, J. Schreffler, Comparing the efficacy of virtual simulation to traditional classroom role-play. J. Edu. Comput. Res. **57**(7), 1772–1785 (2019)

U. Spierling, 'Killer Phrases': design steps for a game with digital role-playing agents, in *Transactions on Edutainment I* (Springer, Berlin, 2008), pp. 150–161

K. Starks, D. Barker, A. Cole, Using Twine as a therapeutic writing tool for creating serious games, in *Proceedings of Joint International Conference on Serious Games* (Springer, Berlin, 2016), pp. 89–103

P. Wang, J. Rowe, B. Mott, J. Lester, Decomposing drama management in educational interactive narrative: a modular reinforcement learning approach, in *International Conference on Interactive Digital Storytelling* (Springer, Berlin, 2016), pp. 270–282

S. Watson, N. Vannini, M. Davis, S. Woods, M. Hall, L. Hall, K. Dautenhahn, FearNot! An anti-bullying intervention: evaluation of an interactive virtual learning environment. Artif. Intell. Simul. Behav. **24**, 446–452 (2007)

S.A. Weiß, W. Müller, The potential of interactive digital storytelling for the creation of educational computer games, in *International Conference on Technologies for E-Learning and Digital Entertainment* (Springer, Berlin, 2008), pp. 475–486

J.-F. Weng, H.-L. Kuo, S.-S. Tseng, Interactive storytelling for elementary school nature science education, in *2011 IEEE 11th International Conference on Advanced Learning Technologies* (IEEE, Piscataway, 2011), pp. 336–338

C. Whitbeck, Group mentoring to foster the responsible conduct of research. Sci. Eng. Ethics **7**(4), 541–558 (2001)

L. Zhang, D.A. Bowman, C.N. Jones, Exploring effects of interactivity on learning with interactive storytelling in immersive virtual reality, in *2019 11th International Conference on Virtual Worlds and Games for Serious Applications (VS-Games)* (IEEE, Piscataway, 2019)

A. Zook, S. Lee-Urban, M.O. Riedl, H.K. Holden, R.A. Sottilare, K.W. Brawner, Automated scenario generation: toward tailored and optimized military training in virtual environments, in *Proceedings of the International Conference on the Foundations of Digital Games* (2012), pp. 164–171

Chapter 13
The Marriage of Quantum Computing and Interactive Storytelling

Natasha Skult and Jouni Smed

13.1 Introduction

We have witnessed the first steps of using quantum computing in the field of game development in game jams worldwide.[1] The results, however, have not yet shown any significant advantages but, in most of the cases, the quantum simulations have been used as a fancy random event generator, which does not make any real difference in the players' involvement.

A team of game developers from Finland together with a research group of IBM from Zürich has taken a step forward and experiment with the possibilities of utilizing quantum technology in a narrative progression of a game. This commercial PC title will be the first game on the market utilizing a quantum computer in creating immersive interactive narrative experience which can lead potentially in changing the practices of interactive storytelling. This game called *C.L.A.Y.: The Last Redemption* (MiTale 2021), which is a role playing game (RPG) set in the post-apocalypse several generations after the collapse of civilization. The survivors of the apocalypse live in tribal societies and tell stories of the day the cities came alive and devoured all who lived in them. The game combines explorative gameplay akin to *Sunless Sea* (Failbetter Games 2015) and *Sunless Skies* (Failbetter Games

---

[1] http://www.quantumgamejam.com/.

N. Skult (✉)
Department of Art History, University of Turku, Turku, Finland
e-mail: nabutr@utu.fi

J. Smed
Department of Computing, University of Turku, Turku, Finland
e-mail: jouni.smed@utu.fi

2019) on a procedurally generated hex-grid map with *Disco Elysium* (ZA/UM 2019) style narrative mechanics. The player uses RPG-like skills, their companions and resources to overcome various challenges in their travels, while following a number of different possible story threads towards one of multiple endings. The main game mechanics are within exploration, multi-layered story and time-limited quests. Each of these game mechanics provide the player with multiple playthroughs, uncovering the content and abilities based not just on the player's "choices" in a game but also not-made-choices. Every act of exploration, building in-game relationships and interacting with different items lead to a new version of the gaming experience. In achieving this "multiverse" in interactive storytelling design, the lead role belongs to balanced integration with quantum mechanics.

Quantum physics is utilized in the following aspects of game design and development:

1. *Generating environment and visual effects*: Procedural generation has a lead role in environment and visual effects in the game based on numerous successful results from the IBM's team of researchers led by Dr. James Wootton.
2. *Characters development and in-game relationships*: Quantum physics are implemented with the in-game characters, developing the personalities and relationships with the players' lead character based on the type of a game player pursues. Each movement, dialogue and action or not taking action are deeply seated with the narrative side of the game, providing unique twists and outcomes for each quest.
3. *Branching narrative and encounters*: As a narrative-driven role-playing game, the choice-based narrative is an obvious choice, because we can utilize the quantum effect to the narrative progression resulting with many more possible endings with the same "choice" that the player may make.

By combining these three areas the game consists of hundreds of encounters, conversations, adventures and more, accompanied by a visual narrative system that provides an immersive narrative experience.

Numerous factors must be considered in the design of interactive storytelling with quantum computing in which this chapter provides main observations from the conducted practices in developing this game. The research work is ongoing but the gathered result in gameplay are encouraging and seem to indicate vast potential in utilizing quantum computing to achieve desired results in interactive storytelling. For more details on the theory and practices of interactive storytelling in general, the reader is referred to the book by Smed et al. (2021).

This chapter aims at presenting the overall details of the development process. In Sect. 13.2, we begin by describing the process of building a narrative-driven game and the related choices that the designer has to make. This followed by a detailed description of the game *C.L.A.Y.: The Last Redemption* in Sect. 13.3. In Sect. 13.4, we discuss how quantum computing is possible to fit into a narrative gameplay experience. Finally, the concluding remarks appear in Sect. 13.5.

13.2 Building a Narrative-Driven Game

Game design is a craft that requires multitude of observations and carefully picked game mechanics. It is not just following the ideas about what would be "nice to have" for an immersive experience, but working with a set of boundaries that each game receives from, for example, its genre, platform or accessibility features. The more cross-disciplined design requirements are, the more challenges as well as opportunities are presented to a team.

All this opens the discussion of how and why games move us, how players engage and bond with the gameworld, its inhabitants and the rules under which everything "makes sense" (Suovuo et al. 2020). Making sense and adding a meaning is something we humans are particularly apt to do. We find connections between things that may be completely unrelated, we strive for finding patterns and meanings, and from these things we are able to construct unbelievable ideas. This ability to depict, collect and share the information is what storytelling is all about; this is how stories—both fictional and factual—are the basis of our achievements as humanity.

The concept of visual storytelling obviously contains the elements of 'visual' and 'communicating'. The essence of any visual representation is to hold the information—the core meaning and data which a visual form represents—so that representation becomes a sign. Recognizing the information that a sign is carrying is the core principle of communication and storytelling. Semiology or semiotics refers to the science of signs with assumptions that cultural assets (e.g. language, visual art or music) are composed by signs, where every sign holds a meaning beyond, in its literal self (Eco 1978, 1989).

In the case of a visual representation, visual storytelling possibly has the most significant effect on human reception. Seeing and reacting on an image has much more success in provoking senses and being memorized longer than any other verbal or written information. Panofsky (2003) states that the steps of understanding correspond to the forms of knowledge, which presuppose historical experience. Early semiotic work is known as connoisseurship, which is related to the interpretation of signs of authenticity and authorship. The designer holds the origin of the work of art and aims to characterize the existence, circulation and discourses within a storyworld. The designer beholds the attendance of certain events within the created world, along with changes, distortions, and their various modifications. Led by the designer's thought with conscious or unconscious desires, the contradictions can resolve in relations to the others creating a specific meaning which is for the players to find. In visual representations, parts of the field are open for submitting the order of values in the context of the represented objects with potential signs. The changing nature of image–sign relationship is an essential subject in the view of Schapiro (1969). One could say that semiotic approaches of visual representation are the matters in discussion of interactive storytelling in the digital era (Merleau-Ponty 1964, p. 58).

To create an immersive experience it is crucial to solve game design challenges and test the core mechanics. Nothing can compensate for poor game design choices.

No matter how good a story is, if game design fails, the narrative experience will also suffer. The embedded story must follow game design principles.

Unlike other visual media such as static images or paintings, animated or recorded videos, games break the static and one-way-directed-messages into a form of a dialogue. They provide a feeling of transformation that the player gets by interacting with the environment, other characters or items and solving the given challenges (Adams 2014, pp. 37–40). Games have such a big impact on us, because the interactive medium allows each player to pursue their own journey. Every game provides its own set of communicating tools through visual, audio and special transmission, disregarding the player's native language.

Visual storytelling is based on the familiarity of the concepts that it represents, the visual cues that are given to a player in each gameplay sequence must be comprehensive regardless of the possible interaction changes such as

- gameplay modes,
- camera modes,
- avatar or non-avatar modes, and
- change of controls and inputs.

The gameplay experience must consist of a stylistically unified visual language in order to keep the communication with the player intact. The observer/player becomes a dynamic interactor with that message, making an impact through the actions and receiving feedback and responses from these actions. For this dialogue to be successful, the game experience should give an expressive scope to the players—"a choice" and variations in which players can respond to the given challenge. This equips the player with the ability to choose how they wish to proceed the story and articulate a wide range of emotional engagements based on choosing the gameplay actions. The set of actions provided to the player build the 'language' unique for that particular game. If any of the visual cues is not in balance with the rest of the designed experience, the risk to break the player's fantasy is higher.

Regardless of the type of the gameplay experience, the visual narrative should follow the basic principles from the traditional art theory—used widely in film and animation—such as

- building an authentic experience, which refers to the specific rules and characteristics of the world and interactions that player may conduct during the gameplay;
- relevant topics or situations to which player can truly relate that builds the emotional engagement and relationship with the characters and the world inside the game; and
- atmosphere referring to the use of traditional visual storytelling practices such as composition and variety of view-angles, lighting that brings desired atmosphere as colours and their values building the contrast and harmony, forms and shapes, perspective and scale.

Games use narrative for a variety of reasons aside from the desire to tell a story. The "story" might simply support visuals (e.g. a useful tip or a tutorial). With aim to be understood, the story must be concretized into a representation.

This representation can be anything that conveys the experience of the story to the interactor and, at the same time, serves as a means for the designer to express the story and vary it to reflect the interactor's reactions. In interactive storytelling, not only the representation can include multiple modes but it brings interactivity that forms a dialogue between observer and the artform. A game allows the player to move around in the physical world through a set of inputs and simulate the motion in the physical world. Enabling a player to interact builds upon deeper emotional connection and the feeling of immersion.

Games that present a complex narrative design to a player using different forms of storytelling commonly have a deep narrative design with a main protagonist that reflects the player's preferences (e.g. aggressive/achievement-driven to more adventurous/story-driven experience). In such an approach, semiotics theory (Schapiro 1969) and iconography (Panofsky 2003) have an essential role in creating the interactive narrative experience for the players, where even the symbolism of a colour or the type of light and the texture in a scene can provide necessary information for the interactor to progress in the game. This demands the visual designer to translate the narrative design into a visual narrative by using all possible tools from semiotics, psychology and symbolism theories. Moreover, this visual translation needs to be easily understood via a functional user interface design and clear indicators in the game environment that guide the player.

The power of visual representation is in its ability to adjust the consciousness of the observer, where processes the idea of an artwork is a crucial aspect of the concept which its appearance suggests. Game as an interactive storytelling platform provides a new medium of expression where the interactor does not regard them as entertaining platforms but digital environments for gaining new experiences.

13.3 Case Study: *C.L.A.Y.: The Last Redemption*

Starting with the new game project is both ecstatic and terrifying for each member of the development team as the waves of ideas and features flood the meeting room, defying the scope of the project and what is reasonable/doable with the available resources and timeline. This project was no different, as the original idea for the game was created during a game jam. We aimed to make a roguelike RPG (role-playing game), set in a post-apocalyptic world that is filled with the remains of the "matter" that caused the apocalypse.

Because our aim is to present how quantum computing is used in this game, we have to first give an insight into the worldbuilding, the main characters and locations, the leading quests and skillset required for the player to obtain to win the game. Each of the features are interconnected and use quantum mechanics in some capacity. For this reason, we begin by discussing the game design and narrative principles.

13.3.1 Story

The game is set several generations after the collapse of civilization. The survivors of the apocalypse live in tribal societies and tell stories of the day the cities came alive and devoured all who lived in them. These tribal inhabitants of the world are only vaguely aware of the world that came before, through myths and legends, although they are still haunted by it. The apocalypse was caused by C.L.A.Y, an incredibly complex material that was invented prior to the apocalypse, that can be programmed to take just about any shape or have just about any property. As programmable matter, it is also the perfect home for AI, another invention of the pre-apocalypse. What the pre-apocalyptic people knew as AI was not, however, true AI—instead they were the digitized minds of the super-powerful and reached individuals that were ruling the biggest corporations in the world. In the process of becoming digitized, these profit-driven individuals have lost touch with their humanity and set about conquering the world in the pursuit of endless profit. Humans were seen as little more than a roadblock, insufficient to their mission. This smartmass that was used to build, augment or modify nearly everything in the pre-apocalypse; from building the cities to human-enhancements, got corrupted by the AI of corporations and it caused the collapse of society and the world as it was known. In an act of sacrifice, the Triumvirate let its own body be churned into tiny particulate matter in an atmospheric processor and then spread across the whole world, carrying in its golden clay, a virus, that would destroy the corrupted AI wherever it would get in contact with. As the winds carried the golden clay across the world, however, civilization was destroyed.

A 1000 years later, humanity survives, far away from the cursed cities and the 'black swarm' that still survives here and there, their bodies as eternal as their hatred. Some parts of society have learned to use "clay" for their own benefit, re-programming it into golems of their own or to make tools to help them survive. Anything can now be imbued with life of sorts, and the ones most adept at re-programming clay are called Claymancers. These Claymancers gain their skills from a very particular form of symbiosis with a golden clay. As the centuries passed, the tiny particles of golden clay began to merge, and eventually enough of it merged to re-form a kind of personality. The Claymancers, descendants of some of the original freedom fighters, learned how to replace parts of their brains with the golden clay, letting it live in their heads. In doing so, they also gain a special affinity with the world of clay around them, letting them sense, mould and speak to clay in a way mere potters cannot. Claymancers can use clay as weapons, as medicine, to communicate over vast distances, and more—they also have access to memories and knowledge, however fragmented, of the world before.

One of the truly unique aspects of the game narrative design is that even in the hostile world, every challenge is possible to complete with right negotiations and strategic thinking, as we wish to create non-violent gameplay. The game tackles emotional engagement and in-game-relationships in solving quests and discoveries to complete the main mission. This game does not, however, feature Claymancers as direct protagonists. It takes place inside a 'moving city', an urban area that, in the pre-apocalypse, was in the middle of a giant project of urban renewal. Smartmatter was being used at an unprecedented scale to build the city, while the old city was torn down to be used as raw material. When the virus hit, the corrupted-AI in charge of the project went mad, but instead of turning feral and devouring the city and its inhabitants, like most others, it instead went dormant—leaving only the building process active.

As the supply of raw materials ran out, the City—its arms and hands a swarm of assembling drones—began to cannibalize itself, ever building outwards and consuming itself in the process. Thus, the city "moves". Anything that comes too close to the edge is snatched up by the Assemblers and merged into the fabric of the city, or disassembled into nothing.

Normally, things do not enter nor leave the City, but over the years it is known to have happened. When it does, the 'immune system' of the City is usually triggered, and whatever it is that infiltrates it is quickly dispatched by Hunter-Killer drones. One important discovery in the game is possession of the ombrascope. An ombrascope is a device that, when you shine a light through it, will create a shadow-image of some kind. Ombrascopes are used to project glyphs that can be used to control the city in various ways or to open new pathways, and are usually made out of Clay. There are different versions of the ombrascopes, and the most powerful one is made out of golden clay which projects non-static images, leading to much deeper discoveries of the world before the collapse.

Those who lived in the city were trapped there—many millions at first, but as the years went by their numbers dwindled, society adapting as best it could to a new, nomadic lifestyle. After a 1000 years, even these survivors only have a vague, ancestral memory of the world before, living in tribal units of a few hundred individuals, always travelling, always fighting over turf, arable ground, or simply honour and glory. The player starts the game by creating and customizing own or selecting the existing protagonist, who is the young scion of a tribe trapped in a Moving City, and the presumptive heir to their father's seat as chieftain. When the Shamans augur that it is time for the City to begin migrating again, the player must leave the safety of the Corral and head out into the City to prepare your people for the coming tribulations. The player will use RPG-like skills, their companions, and resources to overcome various challenges in their travels, while following a number of different possible story-threads towards one of several endings.

When developing visual language and style of the storyworld, the process of art creation slightly differs from the traditional art production. Commonly the artist starts with the idea, based on that idea chooses the methods and media used for the art production. The creation of the art piece takes certain time and alterations take place based on the artist's vision if it answers the message or idea that originated. In visualising a storyworld for a game, the artist is presented with the design documents and through discussions with the team gets familiar with the world, characters, atmosphere of the story they wish to tell. From the start the process is guided by the team of designers where the artist's role is to depict the best possible visual representation of the design and aimed experience for the interactor.

Furthermore, the artist must take into consideration the platform and think of the technical requirements and limitations as they must be optimized to achieve a smooth experience. As a narrative-driven game, we had to develop clear and consistent visual language for the project, as we knew we must be able to utilize a lot of information from the story to the actual gameworld and its visual representation instead of putting endless scrolls of text to the screen.

Thinking of the player, we wanted to focus on the player's choices and how they should or would affect the direction of the unfolding story. Providing multiple choices as visual novels do was not building the emotional engagement that we wished to achieve. The game design choices required that each of the choices presented to the player should have an observable and differentiable outcome. In the case of our game, the approaches can be problem solving (such as deciphering glyphs in order to enter the restricted areas), interaction modes (exploring the world in hex-based map or face encounters based on skill-check mode with/or ethical choices). The most effective approach in creating emotionally engaging gameplay is providing the player with influence of how the story is being unfold, generating the illusion that every choice makes a difference, even that each of the narrative paths and discoveries for the player are carefully designed by the game creators. Making sure that this illusion is not obvious is the key to supply a successful interactive storytelling, enabling a player to feel depth in each of the encounters and choices made.

13.3.2 Gameplay Loop

The gameplay takes place in a top-down view of the city, with the player's caravan being an icon on the world map together with other points of interest. The player can move around the area freely, yet the map unfolds as the exploration progresses. The tasks and encounters take time: from resting, to scouting for food, to stopping to let shamans decipher the messages from the ombrascope. When in "rest" mode the player is able to recuperate, level up the skills, melt the scraps into clay-matter, take care of the crew and make strategic decisions of the next moves.

The player has five skills (Warchief, Shaman, Trickster, Pactmaker, Clayworker), all of which are used when navigating the city. There are also five resources (Tribesmen, Warriors, Food, Courage and Clay). Generally, when there is a task the player needs to succeed at a skill check or lose one of the resources: for example, failing to remove the brains of a disabled Hunter-Killer might lead to its awakening and killing some of the tribesmen. Often, working on things takes time, and bigger projects take more time. Some challenges are ongoing and require multiple steps to complete, but most of them are required to do the work in a specific location. Failing skill checks or not having enough of some resource will mean the task will take more time, and as tasks often can have several layered timers attached, the player will need to make choices again. For example, the player might be able to exchange the lives of some of the tribesmen to cut down on a timer, or if the player

Fig. 13.1 World-map has both pre-set and randomly generated areas as well as spawning spots, making each exploration session unique for a player while being able to navigate throughout different areas with ease

has a lot of time left one can make sure some tasks are done safely, risking less, but taking more time. These are all decisions that are up to a player, as chieftain.

Travelling takes time, and makes the crew hungry and tired, meaning there is need to rest in a "camp" mode. One can scavenge for more supplies, but that has its own dangers. Also, when on the move, the random events will occur, some good, some bad. At night, travelling is especially dangerous. If one loses a lot of "courage" skill, it will trigger more dangerous encounters ahead. If a player loses too many of the tribesmen, or makes poor decisions, the chieftain will die, and the player will fail the mission.

As an overall gameplay modes, we have set three main pillars:

1. *Discovery and exploration*: The world is built upon the hex-based map that the player needs to explore (see Fig. 13.1). Every play-session is different and the player can experiment with different playstyles.
2. *Time limit*: The game begins with the player on a time limit of 100 days from which the City will start to move, and by then the Tribe must be ready (see Fig. 13.2).
3. *Multi-layered story*: The game is meant to be played several times, every playthrough revealing more of the story—and more endings (see Fig. 13.3).

Fig. 13.2 The crew of the protagonist needs to rest and gather resources in order to continue the journey. Setting up a camp allows the player to reflect on the encounters, collect pieces of discoveries made throughout the exploration session and build the necessary skillset to overcome the upcoming challenges

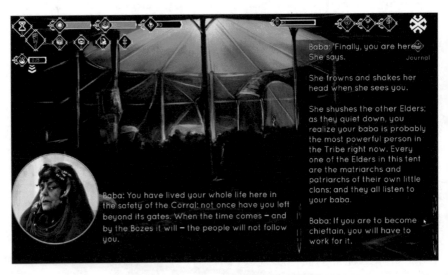

Fig. 13.3 In-game relationships and outcomes of the passed/failed encounters, discovered story-bits, items and other collectables are directly affecting how the story unfolds and the type of challenges ahead

13.3.3   Characters

The crew that the player assembles can have five specialists that each give a bonus to one of the five skills. In the beginning player can pick one, and the rest will be acquired through various events and completed tasks/challenges. Specialists can also be lost through events or when a player 'risks' them in skill-checks, in which case they will be lost forever. Each specialist has a name and portrait representation and is mainly involved with one of the story locations. Each also has their own associated story.

The main specialists are:

- Valfrig, the Shaman. Old and wise, they are exceedingly interested in finding out the truth about the world; what the city is, what happened before, what the ombrascope is, and so on. They are ready to sacrifice anyone and anything to get to the bottom of things. Unless picked at the start, they are not technically a shaman, but a healer. They are also very good at getting people to do things, and can keep them alive when doing it.
- Barr, the Warchief, is one of the young braves. If picked at start they are one of the military advisors, otherwise they can be found through a special event. Their defining feature is their fearlessness, which they regularly inspire in others as well, although it can make them reckless.
- Chi, the Trickster, is a wanderer, someone who travels without a tribe and survives alone. Sometimes they travel for a time with others, sometimes in small groups, but often they are entirely alone. A survivor through and through, she has seen and learned things not even the wisest shamans can dream of, and understands the city in a way few do.
- Jaerd, the Clayworker, is a clayguild foreman, someone who leads the other clayworkers. Their work is quasi-spiritualist, in that they see clay as a living force with a spirit that inhabits it. Golden clay is something he has never seen before, and something he is fascinated by.
- Fayni, the Pactmaker, is a trader, and as such used to dealing with tribes of all sorts. They are often the most quiet person in the tent, but they rarely if ever backs down, and will win over with reason, passion or, if nothing else, threats.

13.3.4   Locations

There are five main story locations, each corresponding roughly to one resource, as well as referencing one specialist. These do not necessarily overlap, to find a story-location player will need the clues. Several clues can be received from the ombrascope, one clue from the associated specialist, and 1–2 clues from events in the world. One clue can be received also from the "associated" location.

Fig. 13.4 The scene from the game with Claymancer and War Golem

The main locations are:

1. The Dig: The opening is set underneath a perpetually-collapsed skyscraper, the location quite hard to find. In order to reach the opening they first have to dig into the deepest area of the building, which requires a lot of tribesmen.
2. The War Golem: An ancient, ambulatory weapon of war that produces its own golem soldiers. It is foreign to the City, and will often fight with the City's own defenders. No-one has ever taken it on directly. It was built in the post-apocalypse by the Claymancers and sent in to put a stop to the city, but the Claymancers were all killed. The remaining Golden Clay took over the War Golem and has been doing its best to survive, becoming year by year more traumatized and directionless (see Fig. 13.4).
3. The Veil: The player will need to collect a piece from a disassembler bot, but not one that is in 'fight' mode, since then it needs to be destroyed. Instead, the player needs to ambush one in an area that is actively being disassembled.
4. Hunger Engine: The player will need to acquire an enigmatic eating engine that, once activated, will require a constant input of organic matter in order to slowly produce the item you are looking for. One can carry it along the journey, but it will require food every day, more than your fellow tribesmen.
5. The Factory: The Ombrascope directs the player to begin making repairs in a giant, district-sized machine of some kind, repairing multiple different parts of the machine by manufacturing tools out of clay according to the ombrascope's blueprints. The machine has been overrun with sentient plants, making all work there very dangerous.

In order to finish the game, the player needs to complete at least three out of the five story locations. Aside from the first one, the player will be given the locations by studying the ombrascope. Each location will have several timers, difficult skill checks, and resource requirements of various kinds. Each location also "helps" with a different location, meaning each location fits together in three ways: the main resource used, the main specialist needed, and a main other location that unlocks something in it.

13.4 Fitting in the Quantum Computing

The initial idea of utilizing quantum computing in a narrative-driven gaming experience came spontaneously in one of the discussions with Dr. James Wootton, who is a member of IBM Research, Zürich. He was introducing procedural generation using quantum computing, where we saw potential in integrating it with the narrative-driven game development. We were not aware of any previous attempts and, therefore, decided to join forces and experiment with the available open-source quantum computing simulation program Qiskit[2] by IBM.

According to Wootton (2020), the quantum blur effect used in the procedural generation is targeted specifically at using simulators or currently available proto-type quantum hardware. It uses quantum operations to create an effect that could be useful also in other types of procedural generation. We saw that in addition to using quantum mechanics to generate a game world, it could be used to generate a narrative experience as well.

The first stage of utilizing the quantum simulation is world-building as well as spawning of the resources and encounters. This has been done before and it is proven to work well. However, we wanted to move forward and see how the quantum calculations effect the combination of choices of the player. The gameplay shapes according to the type of own intuitive exploration based on the areas that player visits, the choices made in dialogues, developing skills and in-game relationships with other characters, and the interactions with the items and artifacts. This way each gameplay builds into its own reality from the possible multiverse of gameplays. For example, imagine that two players are sitting by the screen and playing the game for the first time, from the very beginning. Even if both players make the same choices of characters to lead as well as dialogues, each player will be intuitively exploring the world and its content in their own ways. One player may decide to observe the sunset or a wild animal passing by, while the other moves directly towards the area indicated by the quest at hand. Each of these interactions are providing an additional layer of the unique gameplay experience as all these—possibly subconscious—

---

[2]Qiskit [kiss-kit] is an open source SDK for working with quantum computers at the level of pulses, circuits and application modules, see https://qiskit.org/.

The watcher on the door turns towards you, and you raise your ombrascope to receive its message. Within moments, the device in your hand clicks and whirrs, and mirrors the message it received back at you.

You know what it expects of you: your wercru-authorization. All you have to do is tell your ombrascope what to reply.

Fig. 13.5 The in-game screenshot of the work in progress on implementing the Ombrascope device

micro-decisions create the effect of stirring the gameplay experience away from the generic linear storyline, although objectively both players make the same choices.

We also use quantum computing in the ombrascope, which is the key in-game device for a player to interact with the clay-matter (see Fig. 13.5). As we already mentioned, clay in its essence is based on a programming language—a code that has been malfunctioning. This was another reason why we wanted to experiment with the character development and in-game-relationships with the clay itself so that player uses ombrascope to communicate with the quantum computer directly, and based on those "discussions" the game and story unfolds according to the logic of the quantum mechanics.

As this kind of experimentation has never been done before in developing a commercial title, we opted for having quantum computing available as an additional feature. The player can choose to "switch on/off" the quantum effects and the game itself does not dependent on the Qiskit SDK. We aim to explore not just the development practices with quantum computing but also observe players' experiences and how this method manages to create unique gameplay for each player and for each session.

Among the various factors that one must be consider in the design of interactive storytelling with the quantum computing, these are some the two biggest challenges we have encountered:

- How does procedural generation with a quantum computer differ from processes run on a regular computer? In our case, this was not an issue in the world-map generation, but the notion of having a "corrupted AI" system, where quantum computing is utilized with an Ombrascope, did eventually provide more appealing results in the overall game progression experience.

- Can a quantum simulation with players worldwide be run without causing excessive delays? Because we are using the simulation instead of an actual quantum computer, we calculate that this should not be an issue. However, this risk does exist, which is why we have decided to use Qiskit as an optional feature for the players.

These observations are based on the development and the initial testing with the players. More concrete results will be available and analysed after the game is launched globally at the end of 2021.

13.5 Conclusion

The use of quantum theory and quantum computing in the field of game development is not a new idea. It has been tried out by professionals as well as casual developers who have attended to quantum physics inspired game jams around the world. Games have been used to find solutions to optimization problems in the development of quantum technologies and teaching concepts in quantum physics and quantum computing. Within Finland alone, Quantum Game Jam events have already been a creative starting point for some 68 quantum games and prototypes, enabling creators to explore the quantum technology through play.

Quantum physics have been inspiring writers, visual artists, and musicians throughout the years, becoming popularized through common themes of science fiction that often cover notions of parallel universes and multiple histories. Through such mediums, we are providing a better understanding of these complex theories that are not commonly discussed in the everyday world. Quantum technology is overly expensive and becoming a professional to operate such devices takes extensive effort and devotion, since quantum computers are—at the moment—a rare commodity. Collaborating with professionals in the field of quantum mechanics and computing is the key in finding the ways to merge the best practices from both disciplines—games and quantum physics.

With years of collaboration with the quantum physicists and research groups from project QPlay at University of Turku, Aalto University and University of Helsinki, we have had privilege to do multiple gamification projects and experiment with solutions for solving quantum physics problems. Quantum mechanics gives its own set of challenges for the game designers to tackle. These challenges force the designer to step out of their own comfort zone as it guides and enables them to utilize these "restrictions" and "rules" as building blocks for the gameplay experience. Finding a solution and a balanced flow in the game is an ultimate goal for every game designer, and with gaining such a diverse experience, the common game design practices will keep evolving further.

C.L.A.Y.: The Last Redemption is currently the first and only commercial quantum computing powered PC game title released on Steam. We do not expect that the use of quantum simulation will increase the sales nor make a difference in the market placement, but we believe that it will inspire other developers to explore the opportunities with the emerging technologies. This will help us establish best practices through trial and error, and it will enable us to find the most sufficient uses for quantum computing in game development. From the experience in developing this project, we are aware that this experiment is just a scratch on the surface of what quantum computing would be able to do for designing immersive gameplay and narrative experiences.

References

E. Adams, *Fundamentals of Game Design*, 3rd edn. (New Riders, San Francisco, 2014)

U. Eco, *Theory of Semiotics* (Indiana University Press, Bloomington, 1978)

U. Eco, *The Open Work* (Harvard University Press, Cambridge, 1989)

Failbetter Games, Sunless Sea. Failbetter Games (2015)

Failbetter Games, Sunless Skies. Failbetter Games (2019)

M. Merleau-Ponty, *Signs* R. McCleary (Trans.) (Northwestern University Press, Evanston, 1964)

MiTale, C.L.A.Y. – The Last Redemption. MiTale (2021). https://store.steampowered.com/app/1411890/CLAY__The_Last_Redemption/

E. Panofsky, *Iconography and iconology: An Introduction to the Study of Renaissance Art* (University of Chicago Press, Chicago, 2003)

M. Schapiro, On some problems in the semiotics of visual art: field and vehicle in image-signs. Semiotica I, 223–242 (1969)

J. Smed, T. Suovuo, N. Skult, P. Skult, *Handbook on Interactive Storytelling* (Wiley, Chichester, 2021)

T. Suovuo, N. Skult, T.N. Joelsson, P. Skult, W. Ravyse, J. Smed, The game experience model (GEM), in *Game User Experience and Player-Centered Design* (Springer, Cham, 2020), pp. 183–205. https://doi.org/10.1007/978-3-030-37643-7_8

J.R. Wootton, Procedural generation using quantum computation, in *International Conference on the Foundations of Digital Games, FDG'20* (Association for Computing Machinery, New York, 2020). doi:10.1145/3402942.3409600

ZA/UM, Disco Elysium. ZA/UM (2019)

Chapter 14
A Shared Vocabulary for Interactive Digital Narrative (IDN): An Encyclopedia Project

Hartmut Koenitz, Mirjam Palosaari Eladhari, Sandy Louchart, Frank Nack, Christian Roth, Elisa Mekler, and Péter Kristóf Makai

14.1 Introduction

The lack of a shared vocabulary is a longstanding issue of the field of interactive digital narrative (IDN) (Koenitz et al. 2009; Koenitz 2016; Thue and Carstensdottir 2018). The root of this problem is the fact that scholars and practitioners concerned with the topic of interactive narrative originate in a number of different fields,

An earlier version of this chapter has been published as an INDCOR white paper on the pre-print server arxiv https://arxiv.org/abs/2010.10135

H. Koenitz (✉) · F. Nack
University of Amsterdam, Amsterdam, The Netherlands
e-mail: h.a.koenitz@uva.nl; nack@uva.nl

M. P. Eladhari
Stockholm University, Stockholm, Sweden
e-mail: mirjam@dsv.su.se

S. Louchart
Glasgow School of Art, Glasgow, UK
e-mail: s.louchart@gsa.ac.uk

C. Roth
HKU University of the Arts, Utrecht, The Netherlands
e-mail: christian.roth@hku.nl

E. Mekler
Aalto University, Aalto, Finland
e-mail: elisa.mekler@aalto.fi

P. K. Makai
University of Duisburg-Essen, Duisburg, Germany
e-mail: peter.makai@mensa.hu

including literature studies, film studies, computer sciences (both from an Artificial Intelligence (AI) and an Human Computer Interaction (HCI) perspective), media studies, creative practices and many more. All of these fields have associated specific vocabulary, positioned within a semantic field of meaning developed in their respective tradition and thus often not immediately accessible to "outsiders" from a different field. The issue is further aggravated by the fact that many common terms used in Interactive Digital Narrative research and practice—such as "narrative", "plot" or "story"—have both a common meaning in everyday conversation, and also specific ones in scholarly and professional contexts. The 'story' of a journalist is not exactly the same as the 'story' of a film director and what is exactly meant in each case is only fully accessible to practitioners in the respective fields. Equally, 'narrative' in the sense used by sociology scholars describing a "group narrative" is not the same ontological entity that an AI researcher concerned with procedural generation has in mind. In a recent article Koenitz and Eladhari (2019) compared this status to the biblical metaphor of the "Babylonian confusion".

This issue of diverse-language-use manifests as a considerable obstacle to productive work, especially in interdisciplinary settings, for example in the multinational research network INDCOR[1,2] The aim of INDCOR is to facilitate the use of interactive digital narratives (IDN) to represent highly complex topics, e.g. global warming, the refugee situation in the EU, pandemic events such as COVID19, or the switch to E-mobility. Here, a shared vocabulary is a foundational necessity in order to enable scholars and practitioners from various disciplines to meaningfully contribute to IDN research, further the development in professional settings (design practices, production workflows), spur wider adoption and thus realize market opportunities. In addition, the question of a shared vocabulary is also a crucial element in the networks' intention to improve the understanding of IDN in society at large. The question is thus: how to overcome the Babylonian confusion?

This chapter frames the situation from the perspective of the EU INDCOR network and proposes to address the issue through the creation of a "living encyclopedia of IDN vocabulary" based on an overarching analytical framework (SPP model) and associated taxonomy. We detail the process for the creation and continued development of such a resource within INDCOR and also invite the community to participate in the development of this central aspect for the fledgling field of IDN research and practice.

---

[1] https://indcor.eu

[2] The network is funded as a COST action, under the EU Horizon 2020 and Horizon Europe funding schemes, cf. http://cost.eu

14.2   Foundational Considerations for a Shared Vocabulary

Before getting into the details of our proposal, we would like to describe our process and consider the aim and purpose of a shared vocabulary to determine its scope.

In order to enable such a shared understanding, an overarching analytical perspective is necessary. This is an insight gained by our own experience in the INDCOR project. The setup of workgroups was a bottom-up approach developed by the expert community. As work progressed, a long list of terms to be defined in a shared vocabulary was quickly produced, but subsequent discussions made clear that a consensus on how to connect different definitions was elusive. Consequently, we identified the need of an overarching abstraction to guide our work on a shared vocabulary of IDN. Without it, there was a manifest risk that a shared vocabulary would replicate the existing Babylonian confusion and thus miss its central aim. In ongoing work and subsequent meetings, the SPP (System Process Product) model (Koenitz 2015) was the one singled out across workgroups that could function as a starting point for connecting the four pillars that are expressed as workgroups in INDCOR: Design and Development (WG1), Theories and Concept (WG2), Evaluation (WG3) and Societal Impact (WG4). These topics cover a board perspective on research into interactive digital narratives, from work on authoring tools, AI-based methods, aspects of design, theoretical concepts, evaluation methods and evaluations of particular artifacts, as well as projects applying IDN for education and societal impact.

14.2.1   An Overarching Analytical Perspective: The SPP Model

The SPP model is a media-specific perspective that identifies three broad categories for the analysis of IDN artefacts, reflecting its different stages: *system*—the digital artifact, *process*—the interactive experience of a system, and *product*—the result of the experience, either in the form of a recording or as a retelling (Eladhari 2018) to others (Fig. 14.1).

Fig. 14.1 SPP model.
(Koenitz 2015)

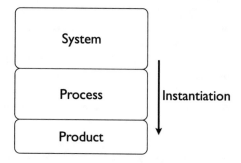

The SPP model takes the systemic, dynamic character of IDN works as its central characteristic, building on a foundation laid by cybernetics (Wiener 1948), and cybernetic art theory (Ascott 1964; Ascott 1968), as well as earlier perspectives on interactive forms of narration (Laurel 1986; Jennings 1996; Murray 1997; Montfort 2005; Murray 2011). In order to understand the specific aspects of IDN and avoid limitations inherent in adapted perspectives,[3] the SPP model does not rely on underlying models derived from the classical formal study of literature and the cinema in narratology. Instead, it acknowledges the 'cognitive turn' in narratology—a perspective that understands narrative not as a property of certain types of artefacts, but as a cognitive function, a "frame for constructing, communicating, and reconstructing mentally projected worlds" (Herman 2002). This perspective opens up a space for novel kinds of narrative manifestations—as in principle any artefact can be considered a narrative as long as it triggers the cognitive frame of narrative. In other words: an IDN work does not need to be similar to the literary novel or the movie to be considered a narrative. This insight might have been understood in the field of narratology for a considerable time, for example by Umberto Eco in his consideration of the "open work" (1989) but was mostly ignored in the early days of games studies (e.g. Aarseth 2004) and is still not an established fact in current game design practices, where adaptations of principles gleaned from film scriptwriting and other earlier narrative forms are still at the center of attention. Conversely, narratology has yet to address the kind of interactivity afforded by dynamic artifacts directly influenced by the audience, in contrast to the dynamic and interactive interpretation of fixed artifacts, This aspect necessities further theoretical development to support novel practices.

Therefore, the SPP model is concerned specifically with IDN, defining *systems*, their *processes* and resulting *products* and organizes related concepts and design aspects accordingly. For instance, *system* contains the *protostory*, the sum of all potential narratives that can be instantiated with a given artefact (Fig. 14.2). Further aspects related to an IDN work (*narrative design, user interface, assets, environment definitions/rule systems*) are subcategories of *protostory*. This would mean for example that an AI engine is described as a *rule system* within the protostory and its particular implementation as a part of the *narrative design*. Conversely, concepts, practices and examples related to the manner in which an IDN is presented to and experienced by an audience (i.e. visual presentation, interaction, feedback) would be represented within the category of *process*. Finally, *product* describes the output of a *process*, either as a recording (objective product) or as re-telling (Eladhari 2018) (subjective product).

For the INDCOR shared vocabulary project, the SPP model is used as a foundational analytical framework to connect central concepts of IDN in terms of design and development, theory building, societal context and evaluation. This choice is pragmatic, based on several advantages:

---

[3]Cf. N. Katherine Hayles' call for a "media-specific analysis" of digital forms of narration (Hayles 2002) and Hausken's warning of "media blindness" (2004).

Fig. 14.2 Protostory and its elements. (Koenitz 2015)

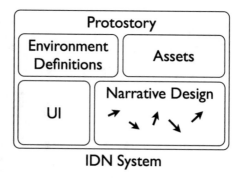

- SPP emphasizes the specificity of this dynamic form thus providing a clear distinction from earlier, fixed forms of narrative such as the printed novel or film and associated vocabulary and thus avoiding the pitfalls of re-defining existing terminology;
- The SPP model takes the systemic nature of IDN artifacts as foundational, building on a solid lineage of cybernetics, cybernetic art and system theory;
- The SPP model continues efforts by scholars such as Brenda Laurel (1986), Pamela Jennings (1996), Janet Murray (1997) and Nick Montfort (2005) in understanding the specific aspects of Interactive Digital Narratives;
- The SPP model features an inclusive view that acknowledges the wide variety of different forms of IDN, including hypertexts, journalistic interactives, narrative-focused video games, interactive documentaries, installation pieces, and AR/VR work as well as emerging forms;
- The SPP model provides a high-level model of IDN works and their relationship with their audiences that is open both to extensions and further lower-level specification and thus the SPP model can serve as a central element in an IDN taxonomy.

In the next section, we describe the SPP model in more detail, before outlining our specific approach on implementing a shared vocabulary.

The conceptual framing provided by such a model is particularly important when considering the crucial role we expect disciplines adjacent to IDN to play in the development and establishment of the shared vocabulary. Whilst a theatre writer and a game developer might differ in their definitions of a story environment, their definitions could be presented alongside each other in a sub-section of this particular model. Conversely, a film director's definition of an environment, might be more oriented towards the process or product aspect of SPP and closer related to the audience experience than the story setting commonly observed in games and theatre.

The diagram in Fig. 14.3 provides a framework through which IDN and complexity can be contextualized using the generic IDN elements identified by the SPP model.

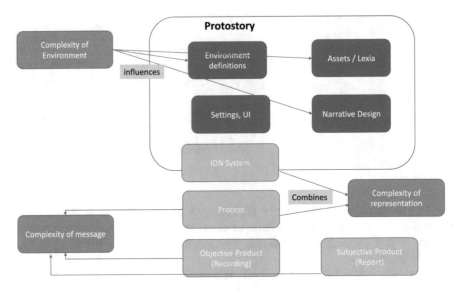

Fig. 14.3 A contextual framework for a shared vocabulary

14.2.2 A Starting Point for the Field

Any choice of overarching analytical perspective is open to criticism and will be controversial to some researchers and/or professionals, yet there is the simple fact that a starting point must be chosen. Given the above-mentioned advantages, the SPP model provides a solid foundation.

A shared vocabulary does not mean that all differences in meaning or historical context would simply disappear, or that scholarly dispute will suddenly end, but that a coordinate system would be established against which extensions and alternative views can be discussed and understood. Conversely, from this clear vantage point, explicit connections can be drawn which will enable scholars to better understand each other and productively work together. Most importantly, since we aim to make the concept of a shared vocabulary available for the whole community of researchers and designers, it can serve as a hub for knowledge exchange and an important step in building a field accessible also to newcomers and related disciplines.

14.3 A Taxonomy for IDN: Extending the SPP Model

The SPP model is concerned with analyzing the IDN artifact, which means it does neither explicitly cover the conditions leading to a work (Ideation) nor its creation process (Authoring). Conversely, it also does not concern itself with societal effects of the work in question or on other works (Critical discourse). As a broad framework, it also does not provide the granularity necessary for an encyclopedia. In order to include these additional aspects, the authors of this chapter have developed a taxonomy for interactive digital narrative with the top-level categories of *authoring*, *artefact* and *critical discourse*, taking the SPP model as basis (Table 14.1).

The taxonomy relates authors' contributions to an overall structure. For example, *transformation* is categorized as an aesthetic quality and thus an aim during the authoring process (**Authoring** > Ideation > Content > Aesthetic qualities > Transformation) and an element of the experience of successful design (**Artefact** > Process > Experience > Aesthetic > Transformation).

We understand this taxonomy as a first effort (version 1.0) explicitly open to changes and amendments as the result of discussions and developments in INDCOR as well as in the research and practice communities at large.

The taxonomy itself represents the core of the shared vocabulary and as such provides a foundation which supports the community-driven effort in developing a more extensive collection of terminology. This explicitly means that further terms should be proposed and will be integrated to grow the vocabulary. The focus here will be on concepts not already well-defined in existing collections, e.g. *The Living Handbook of Narratology* (described below).

This taxonomy also provides a starting point for an IDN Ontology understood in the sense used in computer sciences, as a structure that defines its members not only through self-contained definitions, but also through connections as part of a network.

14.4   A (Living) Encyclopedia for IDN

With the foundations of analytical foundation and taxonomy in place, the question is how to make it accessible and enable community involvement and further development. Examples for accessible shared vocabularies exist in the form of online encyclopedias and this is the model we have decided to follow. Arguably the most successful example for general knowledge is Wikipedia (2020b), the free online encyclopedia. In the scholarly realm, two particularly successful examples are the Living Handbook of Narratology (Hühn et al. 2015) and the Stanford Encyclopedia of Philosophy (2020a). Both Wikipedia and the scholarly resources are viable models. We aim to follow the latter model for a variety of reasons and will be developing an online encyclopedia for IDN research and practice.

An argument for creating an encyclopedia rather than a shared Wikipedia is that, based on the examples above, these endeavors have proven more successful in terms of creating a complete and high-quality curated result. The reasons for this outcome are likely multifold, but we speculate that an encyclopedia entry is more rewarding for authors to participate in, since their efforts are clearly recognizable and properly credited. As for its audience, an encyclopedia appears to be more curated in both its individual content, and as a whole, since an encyclopedia by its nature promises to provide a more comprehensive view of a given topic, rather

Table 14.1 IDN
encyclopedia

IDN Taxonomy V 1.0

1. Authoring

  1.1. Ideation

    1.1.1. Affordances

      1.1.1.1. Procedural

      1.1.1.2. Participatory

      1.1.1.3. Spatial

      1.1.1.4. Encyclopedic

    1.1.2. Audience

      1.1.2.1. Social

      1.1.2.2. Private

      1.1.2.3. Expectations

    1.1.3. Content

      1.1.3.1. Complexity

        1.1.3.1.1. Topic

        1.1.3.1.2. Addressee

          1.1.3.1.2.1. Social

          1.1.3.1.2.2. Private

      1.1.3.2. Prior narratives

      1.1.3.3. Materia

        1.1.3.3.1. Fiction

        1.1.3.3.2. Non-fiction

      1.1.3.4. Form

        1.1.3.4.1. Interactive documentary

        1.1.3.4.2. Video game

        1.1.3.4.3. Hypertext fiction

        1.1.3.4.4. Location-based

        1.1.3.4.5. AR/VR

        1.1.3.4.6. Mixed

      1.1.3.5. Aesthetic qualities

        1.1.3.5.1. Immersion

        1.1.3.5.2. Agency

        1.1.3.5.3. Transformation

      1.1.3.6. Meaning making

        1.1.3.6.1. Mental processes

          1.1.3.6.1.1. Hermeneutic circle

          1.1.3.6.1.2. Narrative cognition

          1.1.3.6.1.3. Cognitive reduction

          1.1.3.6.1.4. Embodied cognition

        1.1.3.6.2. Rhetoric

        1.1.3.6.3. Interface

          1.1.3.6.3.1. Interaction metaphor

        1.1.3.6.4. Prediction of audience reaction

          1.1.3.6.4.1. Feedback

(continued)

Table 14.1 (continued)

IDN Taxonomy V 1.0

1.2.   System implementation
  1.2.1.   Protostory
    1.2.1.1.   Asset creation
      1.2.1.1.1.   Characters
      1.2.1.1.2.   Props
    1.2.1.2.   Environment building
      1.2.1.2.1.   Geographic
        1.2.1.2.1.1.   Landscapes
        1.2.1.2.1.2.   Buildings
      1.2.1.2.2.   Rule systems
        1.2.1.2.2.1.   Physics systems
        1.2.1.2.2.2.   Societal rules
    1.2.1.3.   UI/Interface building
    1.2.1.4.   Interactive narrative designing
      1.2.1.4.1.   Combinatorics
      1.2.1.4.2.   Structure
        1.2.1.4.2.1.   Events
        1.2.1.4.2.2.   Narrative vectors
      1.2.1.4.3.   Experience schema
        1.2.1.4.3.1.   Narrative cognition
        1.2.1.4.3.2.   Narrative experience
        1.2.1.4.3.3.   User representation
          1.2.1.4.3.3.1.   Memory structure
          1.2.1.4.3.3.2.   Preferences
      1.2.1.4.4.   Existing authoring tools
        1.2.1.4.4.1.   Aurora NWN
        1.2.1.4.4.2.   GURPS
        1.2.1.4.4.3.   ASAPS
        1.2.1.4.4.4.   Scenejo
        1.2.1.4.4.5.   IDTension
    1.2.1.5.   Intents
      1.2.1.5.1.   Rhetoric
      1.2.1.5.2.   Aesthetic
1.3.   Creator
  1.3.1.   Industry roles
    1.3.1.1.   Interactive narrative designer
    1.3.1.2.   Game writer
    1.3.1.3.   Creative director

(continued)

Table 14.1 (continued)

IDN Taxonomy V 1.0

2. Artefact

  2.1. System

    2.1.1. Protostory

      2.1.1.1. Assets

        2.1.1.1.1. Characters

        2.1.1.1.2. Props

      2.1.1.2. Interactive narrative design

        2.1.1.2.1. Narrative mechanics

        2.1.1.2.2. Narrative vectors

        2.1.1.2.3. Narrative structure

      2.1.1.3. Environment

        2.1.1.3.1. Geographic

          2.1.1.3.1.1. Landscapes

          2.1.1.3.1.2. Buildings

        2.1.1.3.2. Rule systems

          2.1.1.3.2.1. Physics systems

          2.1.1.3.2.2. Societal rules

        2.1.1.3.3. UI/interface

  2.2. Process

    2.2.1. Participation

      2.2.1.1. Interaction

        2.2.1.1.1. Active/performance

        2.2.1.1.2. Passive/sensoric

      2.2.1.2. Sense making

        2.2.1.2.1. Double hermeneutic circle

        2.2.1.2.1.1. Reflection

        2.2.1.2.1.2. Action

          2.2.1.2.1.2.1. Planning

          2.2.1.2.1.2.2. Execution

      2.2.1.3. Experience

        2.2.1.3.1. Aesthetic

        2.2.1.3.1.1.1. Immersion

        2.2.1.3.1.1.2. Agency

        2.2.1.3.1.1.3. Transformation

        2.2.1.3.2. Rhetoric

  2.3. Product   2.3.1. Objective (recoding)

      2.3.1.1. Interaction analysis

      2.3.1.2. Attention analysis

      2.3.1.3. Pace control

(continued)

Table 14.1 (continued)

IDN Taxonomy V 1.0
2.3.2.   Subjective (retelling)
2.3.2.1.   Experience model
2.3.2.1.1.   Narrative cognition
2.3.2.1.2.   Cognitive reduction
2.3.2.3.   Embodied cognition
2.3.2.2.   Structure Inference
2.3.2.3.   Updating episodic memory
2.3.2.4.   Updating perception memory
3.   Critical Discourse
3.1.   Inclusivity
3.1.1.   Intersectionality
3.2.   Society
3.2.1.   Audience
3.3.   Effect
3.3.1.   Comparison intent/experience
3.4.   Reflective analysis
3.4.1.   Methods

than to rely on seemingly random selections and emphasis determined by wiki-authors' preferences. This being said, the two methods are not mutually exclusive. A Wikipedia site could likely serve well as a pre-stage in the production of the Encyclopedia of IDN the way we envision it.

14.4.1   The Living Handbook of Narratology

The Living Handbook of Narratology (LHN) can be read as a book. It consists of chapters and sections which explain in depth a set of concepts that are chosen by the curating editorial board. LHN originated as a printed book in 2009. Content was added in a Wikipedia format up until 2013, after which it changed to the current form of an encyclopedia. At the time of writing LHN consists of 68 concepts, each making up a longer section.

The article text about each concept is most often attributed to one author, sometimes to two or three. For example, the text on the concept Reader (see Fig. 14.4) is authored by renowned narratology scholar Gerald Price, and follows the recipe of what an entry in the LHN should consist of: Definition, Explication, a number of content specific sections, bibliography, works cited, and further readings.

The articles in LHN are of substantial length, often exceeding 4000 words. The 68 concepts included in the LHN are chosen as being central specifically for the field of narratology as it is understood by the editorial board. If a similar approach was adopted for creating an encyclopedia for IDN, a likely - corresponding - article

Fig. 14.4 Article in the living handbook of narratology

of a 'reader' would be that of the concept of the Interactor, e.g. the person or implied person who traverses an IDN. The original work on the LHN was supported by a grant from the German Research Association (DFG).

14.4.2 The Stanford Encyclopedia of Philosophy

The Stanford Encyclopedia of Philosophy (SEP) (2020a) is an established source in the field of Philosophy, featuring 1600+ entries (Fig. 14.5).

It was designed from the onset to be a high-quality resource which makes use of the specific advantages of an online publication with regular updates and revisions according to its own description:

> From its inception, the SEP was designed so that each entry is maintained and kept up-to-date by an expert or group of experts in the field. All entries and substantive updates are refereed by the members of a distinguished Editorial Board before they are made public. Consequently, our dynamic reference work maintains academic standards while evolving and adapting in response to new research (2020a)

Articles in the SEP are prestigious and are of considerable length - often exceeding 10,000 words. Most entries are invited by the editorial board, although proposals

Fig. 14.5 Article in the stanford encyclopedia of philosophy

are considered. The SEP maintains a quarterly publication/update schedule and entries might be cited including a version designation (e.g. "fall 2015). The SEP has been supported by seven grants over the course of 9 years (2020a), mostly from the NEH (National Endowment for the Humanities), but also NSF (National Science Foundation) and the Andrew W. Mellon Foundation.

14.4.3   Editorial Procedures

Taking inspiration from the two examples, we see a strong editorial board as central to the success of this undertaking, providing guidance and assuring academic excellence. Conversely, we consider community engagement as crucial in making this undertaking a success, which means to aim at a good balance of both aspects. Therefore, the IDN encyclopedia will be composed of articles written by authors from the community which have undergone a thorough peer-review process.

Articles will be published based on their academic rigor and the relevance of their contribution to the field.

Members of the core management group of INDCOR chairs (scholars originating in different disciplines and at different career stages[4]) will act as the initial editorial board, soliciting authors from inside the project and the community at large for encyclopedia entries. At the time of writing, the INDCOR action consists of more than 160 scholarly experts and professionals concerned with IDN complexity representations. The editorial board would act as the initial group of reviewers, but will be inviting additional experts from the field to assure a diversity of perspectives and a high level of quality content also for topics outside their core expertise. The aim is to make the encyclopedia a high-quality resource where each entry is recognized as a publication in its own right and thus writing for the encyclopedia is a rewarding undertaking for contributors.

14.4.4   Content Structures of the IDN Encyclopedia

The proposed content structure of the Encyclopedia of IDN will need to evolve in tandem with the INDCOR project and developments in the research community.

In general, entries should be guided by the principles of multi-entry and interlinked dependencies. The INDCOR project provides a microcosm representing different perspectives in the IDN community, manifested in its four workgroups. Therefore, a guiding principle for every author is that they are writing from the perspective of one of the four workgroups, but need to consider how the same entry would be understood by, and thus be useful for, members from any of the other three workgroups. For example, if an entry is implicitly written from a design and development (1) perspective its content needs to provide 'entries' - hooks - that enable connections to how narrative complexity can be conceptualized and theorized (2), to how it can be evaluated (3), and to the question in what societal contexts it might apply to (4). Additionally, the encyclopedia needs to be able to represent the interlinked dependencies in the development of the IDN field. For example, that a specific work of interactive fiction might not have been possible without a certain authoring system, while the authoring system might not have been possible unless there had been precursors to it both in terms of theory and implementation.

The components of information that we are using as a starting point for encyclopedia entries include three main types of that would be linked via their (specific) content:

---

[4]Hartmut Koenitz, Mirjam Palosaari Eladhari, Frank Nack, Agnes Bakk, Jose Manuel Noguera, Andrew Perkis, Sandy Louchart, Elisa Mekler, Lissa Holloway-Attaway.

Concept
Relation to taxonomy (either defining a term that exist in the taxonomy or relating to closest existing term(s))
Alternative names for concept (if available)
Definition
Explication
History
Custom sections for specific concept
Bibliography

IDN (a specific work)
Relation to taxonomy
Precursors
Underlying system
Audience-facing elements (including interaction, audience feedback, discourse, cinematography, lighting etc.)
Media specificity and traditions
Reception

Late-breaking Work
This type of entry is for ongoing research, especially targeting current MA and PhD research work, but also ongoing and as of yet incomplete research projects. It uses the same categories as fully-developed entries, but is marked as "late-breaking"

14.4.5   Two Example Entries

In the appendix, we provide two examples of already finished and peer-reviewed entries. The first is a high-level concept (i.e Authoring - > Ideation) and the second shows the content for a hierarchically deeper sitting concept (i.e. Artefact - > Process - > Experience - > Aesthetic - > Transformation).

14.5   Conclusion and Future Work

In this paper, we have identified the lack of a shared vocabulary as a central issue for the INDCOR project as well as for the field of Interactive Digital Narrative in general. We further identified the need for an overarching analytical perspective, selected the SPP model in this capacity and have proposed to address this issue through a communal expert-authored and peer-reviewed encyclopedia. Examining the successful examples of the *Living Handbook of Narratology* and the *Stanford Encyclopedia of Philosophy*, we propose a structure for such an effort and introduce a taxonomy presented in this document as the underlying framework for the development of the encyclopedia, to gather definitions of concepts central to IDN and useful across perspectives for scholars and practitioners in the field, taking into account the four lenses represented in INDCOR and in the community at large:

design and development, conceptualization and theory, evaluation, and societal context. We invite the research community to partake in the endeavor of creating a multifaceted, living encyclopedia providing a shared vocabulary for IDN. Initially, INDCOR core management members will act as the editorial board for this effort and will reach out to the wider academic community to participate as contributors and reviewers. A high academic standard is key for the success of this project all contributions to the shared IDN vocabulary will be peer-reviewed and published based on their academic rigor and the relevance of their contribution to the field. In order to assure the continued development of this effort beyond the end of the life cycle of the INDCOR project, ARDIN[5] (Association for Research in Digital Interactive Narratives) has agreed to provide a home for the encyclopedia in the future.

Acknowledgements This research was funded as part of the COST EU Action CA-18230 INDCOR: https://www.cost.eu/actions/CA18230/./ We also like to acknowledge Luis Bruni and Alex Mitchell for their contribution to the Ideation encyclopedia entry.

A.1   Appendix 1: Top Level Entry—Ideation

A.1.1   Ideation

Concept: Ideation
Main Authors: Péter Kristóf Makai Frank Nack, Mirjam Palosaari Eladhari
Contributors: Luis Emilio Bruni, Alex Mitchell
Relation to (version 1 of the) taxonomy: 1. Authoring > 1.1 Ideation

A.1.2   Definition

Ideation is the formation of ideas or concepts. In IDN authoring, the process is based on an idea, goal or agenda that results in a prospective template for action that authors can implement during the authoring process.

A.1.3   Explication

Ideation is an essential part of the authoring process that is used in all stages of a thought cycle, from innovation, to development, to actualization (Graham and Bachmann 2004). Ideation can be conducted by individuals, organizations, or

---

[5]https://ardin.online

crowds. The size and scope of the ideating team impacts the choice of ideation methods and tools required to keep the process manageable.

Ideation is distinct from inspiration in that inspiration is an unconscious association of concepts and stimuli in the mind that form the kernel of a new idea, motivating the ideator to express the new insight. Ideation articulates, develops, and communicates those new ideas, where an idea is understood as a basic element of thought (Jonson 2005; Hardman et al. 2008; Sofia et al. 2020).

Ideation is a creative process ideally conducted in an environment that facilitates the free, open, and non-judgemental sharing of ideas. The ideation process takes a rough idea and the related agenda the author tries to implement as its main input. Here, tools are required to facilitate the author to establish the core ideas, preferably already sorted by content, expression, audience and aim. Ideations tools range from simple face-to-face discussion to the use of dedicated idea management software. Examples include brainstorming, mind-mapping, analogies, storyboarding, etc.

A.1.4 Custom Sections for Specific Concept

Creativity techniques are used as part of the ideation process. These methods focus on a variety of aspects of creativity, including techniques for idea generation and divergent thinking, methods of re-framing problems, changes in the affective environment, etc. Examples for those techniques are aleatory techniques or improvisation. Aleatory is here understood as the incorporation of chance (random elements) into the process of creation (i.e. coin tossing, picking something out of a hat, or selecting random words from a dictionary). The aleatory approach can also cover what is called provocation, a method that generates new ideas in writing by directing a plot with creative connections through random words picked from a reference book (Bundy 2002).

Design thinking refers to the cognitive, strategic and practical processes by which design concepts (e.g. for communications) are developed. This method covers processes such as context analysis, problem finding and framing, ideation and solution generating, creative thinking, sketching and drawing, modelling and prototyping, testing and evaluating (Cross 2011).

A.1.4.1 Ideation Tools

There exist a considerable set of ideation tools (see for example O'Connor 2005; Hoffmann et al. 2011; Robbins 2011), often analog ones, used by narrative designers and game designers in the ideation phase. A common denominator of the tools is, depending on the scope, to either expand or constrain the design space. Ideation tools for IDNs are often used collaboratively in a development team in an early phase of a production, where a backstory or fictional universe is to be created. The complexity of the tools vary. An example of a basic unconstraining tool is that of Rory's Story Cubes (O'Connor 2005), where dies with pictures are rolled - the images that are shown on the dies can be used as creativity prompts. A more constraining tool that also offers a structure of dependencies among story elements is made by Hoffman, Spierling and Struck (Hoffmann et al. 2011). It uses the classic planning approach of STRIPs. Designers sometimes use board games in order to collaboratively build elaborate story worlds, where the foremost example is that of Microscope (Robbins 2011). In Microscope, designers define elements and themes that may or may not exist in a world, devise multiple timelines and conflicts using pen and paper.

Supporting literature regarding creativity/ideation:

M. Resnick, B. Myers, K. Nakakoji, B. Shneiderman, R. Pausch, T. Selker, M. Eisenberg, Design principles for tools to support creative thinking, in *Report of Workshop on Creativity Support Tools* (2005).

E. Edmonds, L. Candy, Creativity, art practice, and knowledge. Commun. ACM, **45**(10), 91–95 (2002).

A. E. Zook, M. O. Riedl, B. S. Magerko, Understanding human creativity for computational play, in *Proceedings of the 2nd International Conference on Computational Creativity* (2011).

J. Frich, M. Mose Biskjaer, P. Dalsgaard, Twenty years of creativity research in human-computer interaction: current state and future directions, in *Proceedings of the 2018 Designing Interactive Systems Conference* (2018), pp. 1235–1257.

R. K. Sawyer, Creativity as mediated action: A comparison of improvisational performance and product creativity. Mind Cult. Act. **2**(3), 172–191 (1995).

J. Kuittinen, J. Holopainen, Some notes on the nature of game design, in *DiGRA Conference* (2009).

B.1   Appendix 2: Low Level Entry: Transformation

B.1.1   Transformation

(abridged version, full version at https://arxiv.org/abs/2010.10135)
Concept: Transformation
Main Authors: Christian Roth, Elisa D. Mekler
Relation to (version 1 of the) taxonomy: 1.).

Transformation is an aesthetic quality and thus an aim during the authoring process (Authoring > Ideation > Content > Aesthetic qualities > Transformation

It is also an element of the experience of successful design (Artefact > Process > Experience > Aesthetic > Transformation)

Finally, the transformation manifests in different products (Artefact > Process) from the same protostory (Artefact > System > Protostory).

B.1.2   Alternative Names of Concept

-

B.1.3   Definition

Transformation is a fundamental aesthetic quality of interactive narratives with the potential to positively change interactors' thinking and behavior.

In her influential book, Hamlet on the Holodeck, Janet Murray (1997) proposes transformation as one of the characteristic pleasures of digital environments. Murray describes three distinct meanings of transformation:

Transformation as enactment. The interactive narrative allows the interactor to transform themselves into someone else for the duration of the experience.

Transformation as variety. The experience offers a multitude of variations on a theme. The interactor is able to exhaustively explore these kaleidoscopic variations and thus gain an understanding of the theme and different aspects.

Personal transformation. The experience takes the player on a journey of personal transformation, potentially altering their attitudes, beliefs, and behaviour.

Transformation as masquerade and as variety can be seen as precursors for personal transformation.

B.1.4   Explication

"The right stories can open our hearts and change who we are"—according to Janet Murray, interactive narratives can reflect our contemporary conception of the world as multiple and enacting stories, which enables the exploration of multiple instances from different perspectives. This personal transformation is crucial for the success of commercial, artistic, and serious applications alike.

The idea of personal transformation in Interactive Digital Narrative (IDN) is based on the notion of a transformative experience, commonly defined as "causing or able to cause an important and lasting change in someone or something", in particular "causing someone's life to be different or better in some important way" (Merriam-Webster dictionary).

Murray (1997) understands transformation as a hybrid category, describing both the changes afforded by the interactor on the narrative and the changes in the interactors themselves, in their understanding of the topic at hand, thus aligning transformation closely with learning.

B.1.5   History

Looking at the history of transformation and IDN, we find the term proposed by Janet Murray (1997) as one of her three aesthetic phenomenological categories for the analysis and design of interactive story experiences: immersion, agency, and transformation.

In Murray's view, a successful IDN work draws the audience in (immersion), provides agency (the satisfying ability to make meaningful changes to a virtual environment), and transforms both the virtual environment and the interactor.

In Murray's work *transformation* has distinct meanings:

Transformation as enactment
[section omitted in abridged version]

Transformation as variety
[section omitted in abridged version]

Personal transformation
[section omitted in abridged version]

B.1.6   Custom Sections

Design Considerations
Murray called for a new set of formal conventions for handling mutability and affording transformation. While this research area is still nascent, some design considerations can be distilled from game design and learning research.

Kaleidoscopic Storytelling
Transformation as enactment and variety constitute opportunities for "kaleidoscopic storytelling" (Murray 1997), the creation of coherent multisequential—often contrasting—narratives, which require the interactor to construct their own meaning and acknowledge the multiplicity of perspectives. *Naughty Dog's The Last of Us 2*, for example, has players enact characters from two different warring factions, thereby providing players an opportunity to engage with the trauma and pain of both. *PeaceMaker* similarly allows players to assume the role of the Palestinian president or Israeli prime minister, to juxtapose opposing perspectives and reflect the political complexities.

B.1.7   Sequence Questions

[section omitted in abridged version]

B.1.8   Disorienting Dilemma

[section omitted in abridged version]

B.1.9   Example: Interactive Installation "Angstfabriek"

[section omitted in abridged version]

B.1.10   Evaluation Tools

[section omitted in abridged version]

Related concepts: Elements impacting transformation
(links to other encyclopedia entries):

- Usability
- Immersion
- Agency
- Embodiment
- Identification
- Self-Determination Theory (Competence, Autonomy, Social Relatedness)
- Motivation
- Media and Transmedia literacy
- Technological barriers and opportunities

B.1.11   Connected Theories

[section omitted in abridged version]

B.1.12   Bibliography

[section omitted in abridged version]

References

E. Aarseth, Genre trouble, in *First Person: New Media as Story, Performance, and Game*, ed. by N. Wardrip-Fruin, P. Harrigan, (MIT Press, Cambridge, MA, 2004)

R. Ascott, *The Construction of Change* (Cambridge Opinion, Cambridge, 1964)

R. Ascott, The cybernetic stance: my process and purpose. Leonardo **1**(2), 105 (1968). https://doi.org/10.2307/1571947

W. Bundy, *Innovation, Creativity, and Discovery in Modern Organizations* (Quorum Books, Westport, CT, 2002)

N. Cross, *Design Thinking: Understanding how Designers Think and Work* (Berg, Oxford, 2011)

U. Eco, *The Open Work* (Harvard University Press, Cambridge, 1989)

M.P. Eladhari, Re-tellings: the fourth layer of narrative as an instrument for critique, in *Interactive Storytelling: 11th International Conference for Interactive Digital Storytelling, ICIDS 2018*, 11th International Conference on Interactive Digital Storytelling, ICIDS 2018, Dublin, Ireland, December 5–8, 2018, Proceedings, ed. by R. Rouse, H. Koenitz, M. Haahr, vol. 11318, (Springer, Cham, 2018), pp. 65–78. https://doi.org/10.1007/978-3-030-04028-4_5

D. Graham, T. Bachmann, *Ideation: The Birth and Death of Ideas* (John Wiley and Sons Inc., Hoboken, 2004)

L. Hardman, Z. Obrenovic, F. Nack, B. Kerherve, K. Piersol, Canonical processes of semantically annotated media production. Special issue on 'canonical process of media production'. Multimedia Syst. J. **14**(6), 327–340 (2008)

N.K. Hayles, *Writing Machines* (MIT Press, Cambridge, 2002)

D. Herman, *Story Logic* (U of Nebraska Press, Lincoln, NE, 2002)

S. Hoffmann, U. Spierling, G. Struck, A practical approach to introduce story designers to planning. *IADIS International Conference Game and Entertainment Technologies (GET)* (2011), pp. 59–66

P. Hühn, et al., *The Living Handbook of Narratology*, ed by P. Hühn et al., (2015). http://www.lhn.uni-hamburg.de. Accessed 5 Oct 2020

P. Jennings, Narrative structures for new media. Leonardo **29**(5), 345–350 (1996)

B. Jonson, Design ideation: the conceptual sketch in the digital age. Des. Stud. **26**(6), 613–624 (2005)

H. Koenitz, Towards a specific theory of interactive digital narrative, in *Interactive Digital Narrative: History, Theory, and Practice*, (Routledge, New York, 2015)

H. Koenitz, Interactive storytelling paradigms and representations: a humanities-based perspective, in *Handbook of Digital Games and Entertainment Technologies*, (Springer Singapore, Singapore, 2016), pp. 1–15

H. Koenitz, M.P. Eladhari, Challenges of IDN research and teaching, in *Technologies for Interactive Digital Storytelling and Entertainment*, 12th International Conference on Interactive Digital Storytelling, ICIDS 2019, Little Cottonwood Canyon, UT, USA, November 19–22, 2019, Proceedings, vol. 11869, (Springer International Publishing, Cham, 2019), pp. 26–39. https://doi.org/10.1007/978-3-030-33894-7_4

H. Koenitz, G. Ferri, T. I. Sezen, *Do We Need a New Narratology for Interactive Digital Storytelling? a Workshop on Theory at ICIDS 2009* (2009), p. 354

B. Laurel, *Toward the Design of a Computer-Based Interactive Fantasy System* (Ohio State University, Columbus, 1986)

N. Montfort, *Twisty Little Passages* (MIT Press, Cambridge, MA, 2005)

J.H. Murray, *Hamlet on the Holodeck: The Future of Narrative in Cyberspace* (Free Press, New York, NY, 1997)

J.H. Murray, *Inventing the Medium : Principles of Interaction Design as a Cultural Practice* (MIT Press, Cambridge, MA, 2011)

R. O'Connor, *Rory's Story Cubes*. The Creativity Hub (2005). https://www.iloveoffset.com/the-creativity-hub/ and also https://www.wearehubgames.com/blog/the-craft-of-the-cubes-rory-s-story-cubes-originals

B. Robbins, *Microscope - A Fractal Role-Playing Game of Epic Histories*. Lame Mage Productions [Boardgame]. (2011). http://www.lamemage.com/microscope/

K. Sofia, J. James, M. David, What authors think about hypertext authoring, in *HT '20: Proceedings of the 31st ACM Conference on Hypertext and Social Media*, (ACM, New York, NY, 2020), pp. 9–16

D. Thue, E. Carstensdottir, *Getting to the Point: Toward Resolving Ambiguity in Intelligent Narrative Technologies* (2018)

N. Wiener, *Cybernetics or Control and Communication in the Animal and the Machine* (MIT Press, Cambridge, MA, 1948)

N. Wiener, *Stanford Encyclopedia of Philosophy*. Plato.Stanford.Edu (2020a). https://plato.stanford.edu/. Accessed 27 Jun

N. Wiener, *Wikipedia*. Wikipedia.org (2020b). http://wikipedia.org. Accessed 27 Jun

Chapter 15
Narrative as a Game User Experience Dimension: An Experimental Study

Seray Şenyer and Barbaros Bostan

15.1 Game User Experience and Narrative

The concept of user experience is the subjective relationship between the user and the application, with special emphasis on interaction. Accordingly, the concept of player experience is the subjective relationship between the player and the game, again with special emphasis on interaction but the interactive nature of digital games necessitates different methods to analyze user experience since the player is not merely an interactor but an active participant that shapes his/her own experience with his/her actions and choices. In this regard, modeling player experience is a diverse field of research. Wiemeyer et al. (2016) divided psychological models of player experience into two, general models that have been developed for a wide range of application areas including gaming and domain-specific models that have been developed especially for gaming.

The general psychological models are Self-Determination Theory (SDT) of Ryan and Deci (2000), the Flow model of Nakamura and Csikszentmihalyi (2002), Attention, Relevance, Confidence, Satisfaction (ARCS) model of Keller (1987), and the various presence/immersion studies in literature. These generic models were developed for other fields of study and although there were attempts to apply them to gaming, narrative is not an individual dimension of player experience in any of them. SDT was extended and applied to gaming with the Player Experience of Need Satisfaction (PENS) model (Ryan et al. 2006) and the three dimensions of player experience are: PENS in-game autonomy, PENS in-game competence, PENS in-game relatedness. Flow model has been modified by Sweetser and Wyeth (2005) as GameFlow and consists of eight elements: concentration, challenge, skills, control,

S. Şenyer (✉) · B. Bostan
Department of Game Design, Bahcesehir University, Istanbul, Turkey
e-mail: barbaros.bostan@comm.bau.edu.tr

© The Author(s), under exclusive license to Springer Nature Switzerland AG 2022
B. Bostan (ed.), *Games and Narrative: Theory and Practice*, International Series on Computer Entertainment and Media Technology,
https://doi.org/10.1007/978-3-030-81538-7_15

clear goals, feedback, immersion, and social interaction. Presence, which is defined as the subjective experience of being there, is a psychological phenomenon that resides in the perceptions of the user. Takatalo et al. (2010) integrated presence and flow in their Presence-Involvement-Flow Framework (PIFF2) model and identified the following game user experience dimensions: challenge, interaction, valence, impressiveness, enjoyment, playfulness, control, competence, role engagement, attention, interest, importance, copresence, arousal, and physical presence. As it is seen, these studies identified several dimensions of player experience, but narrative is not among them.

Besides the psychological models of player experience, assessment of the player experience with surveys is also a research area with different approaches. Again, there are general surveys or questionnaires originating from other fields of study that have been applied to assess player experience before. The Presence Questionnaire of Witmer and Singer (1998) is commonly used in VR (virtual reality), including games as 3D VEs (virtual environments). The proposed presence subscales are sensory exploration, involvement, interface awareness, control responsiveness, reality/fidelity, and adjustment/adaptation. The Independent Television Commission–Sense of Presence Inventory (ITC-SOPI) of Lessiter et al. (2001), the Igroup Presence Questionnaire (IPQ) of Schubert (2003) and the MEC spatial presence questionnaire (MEC-SPQ) of Vorderer et al. (2004) are also presence questionnaires utilized in game studies. ITC-SOPI identified four factors: sense of physical space, engagement, ecological validity, and negative effects. IPQ identified three subscales: spatial-presence, realness, and involvement. MEC-SPQ identified process factors (attention allocation, spatial situation model, spatial presence: self-location, spatial presence: possible actions), variables referring to states and actions (higher cognitive involvement, suspension of disbelief), and variables addressing enduring personality factors. Similar to the general models of user experience, these questionnaires identified several components that may be related with player experience when they are applied to gaming, but narrative is not among the identified subscales, with a partial exception. In Temple Presence Inventory (TPI) (Lombard et al. 2009), the three items in Social Realism dimension queries the plausibility of events in the VE. However, it cannot be claimed that this dimension can evaluate the effect of narrative on presence.

Among the surveys or questionnaires especially designed to assess player experience, three of them require special attention: The Game Experience Questionnaire (GEQ) of IJsselsteijn et al. (2008), the Game Engagement Questionnaire (GEnQ) of Brockmyer et al. (2009), and the Core Elements of the Gaming Experience Questionnaire (CEGEQ) of Calvillo-Gámez et al. (2010). GEQ identified the following game user experience dimensions: sensory and imaginative immersion, tension, competence, flow, negative affect, positive affect, and challenge. GEnQ identified four dimensions of game user experience: absorption, flow, presence, and immersion. CEGEQ identified two guiding elements of game user experience: puppetry (control, ownership, controllers, aesthetic value, etc.) and video-game (rules, graphics, game-play, etc.). Similar to the domain specific models of user experience, these studies identified several components of game experience, but narrative is not among them. Besides these questionnaires, The Gameplay Experience Questionnaire of Ermi and Mäyrä (2005), the Immersion Questionnaire of Jennett et al. (2008) The Gameplay Scale of Parnell (2009), and the Play Experience Scale (PES) of Pavlas et al. (2012) also do not have a narrative dimension. Although the recently developed Player Experience Inventory (Abeele et al. 2020) has a "Meaning" dimension that refers to value, relevancy and meaning of the game which can be associated with the narrative, there is not any direct reference to a narrative dimension.

Considering the diversity of game experience studies and surveys mentioned above, we decided to choose a survey to analyze the narrative dimension of game user experience based on two criteria: (1) choosing a domain specific survey rather than a general one applied to gaming, and (2) selecting a survey that identifies narrative as a subdimension of game user experience. Based on our selection criteria, the Game User Experience Satisfaction Scale (GUESS) of Phan et al. (2016) seemed the most suitable choice. The questionnaire was developed by the analysis of several existing questionnaires based on their strengths and weaknesses: 13 existing questionnaires on gaming experience, 15 lists of game heuristics, and 3 user satisfaction questionnaires for human-computer interaction were used during item development and selection process. Furthermore, a comprehensive psychometric evaluation was made during the development process of the scale. Exploratory Factor Analysis (EFA) was conducted with 629 data and Confirmatory Factor Analysis (CFA) was conducted with 729 data. The reliability and validity of the scale was tested with the evaluation of different video games. The subscales of GUESS are usability/playability, narratives, play engrossment, enjoyment, creative freedom, audio aesthetics, personal gratification, social connectivity, and visual aesthetics. Narratives is assessed with seven items and identified as 'the story aspects of the game (e.g., events and characters) and their abilities to capture the player's interest and shape the player's emotions'. In the end, we aim to discuss: (1) the applicability of GUESS as a game user experience measurement tool (with nine sub-dimensions) using different games from different genres, and (2) to discuss the relationship of the narrative dimension of game user experience with the other dimensions of the scale.

15.2   Harmonizing Game Narrative with Gameplay

Scholars and designers in the field of game studies were in a ludology-narratology debate for a very long time. Ludology refers to 'the study of game and play activities' (Frasca 1999) and advocates that games should be examined separately from other disciplines and be interpreted in their own field (Murray 2005). On contrary, narratologists focus more on the narrative dimension of the games and try to interpret games based on relatable structures between game narrative and traditional storytelling (Kokonis 2014). However, these debates could not find either strong evidence or validated conclusion even after years of discussions (Mateas and

Stern 2007). In fact, a strict distinction between ludology and narratology began to fade over. Such that, it is started to be questioned whether this distinction ever existed in the first place (Mäyrä 2008). Frasca (1999), who suggested the term of ludology, stated in one of his later studies that ludology-narratology debate is the result of 'a series of misunderstanding and misconceptions'.

A question that arising from the ludology/narratology debate is how to achieve harmony between game narrative and other gameplay elements. The pleasure driven from the game narrative is based on the player's 'willing suspension of disbelief' (Coleridge 1817). The player surrenders to the experience of game narrative while engaging with it emotionally and intellectually. One critical difference of game narrative from classical narratology is the 'time' of events. Contrary to examples of classical narratology, players do not experience past events but actively produce sequences of events in real-time (Dubbelman 2011). Therefore, it can be said that experiencing game narrative requires both active and passive participation of the player (Bizzocchi et al. 2011). On the other hand, the pleasure of gameplay heavily depends on the active participation of player to reach a rewarding flow state (Czikszentmihalyi 1990). The player continuously goes through a ludic decision-making process to be successful against challenges.

Difficulty in harmonizing game narrative and other gameplay elements originates from differences of active and passive participation between experiencing game narrative and the flow state. It is stated that active participation in ludic decision-making sometimes interferes with the passive state of willing suspension of disbelief (Bizzocchi et al. 2011). Interactive narrative design is seen as a solution for this problem by transcending to the 'active state of belief' as suggested by Murray (2005). To be able to create an interactive game narrative, which intertwines with game elements, one should use a multidimensional approach. In his study, Aarseth (2012) tries to determine which elements are the most important for harmonizing game narrative with other game elements. He starts with seeking for a definition of narrative and deconstructs game structure into four dimensions: world, objects, agents, and events. Based on his analysis of several video games, he concludes that world and objects are the least related dimensions with narrative elements while the agent and events are the most related ones. He further states "there is nothing necessarily narrative about topological variation in world structure, nor about the degree of flexibility of game objects". By this statement, he tries to explain the linearity or openness of the game world does not determine whether a game is "more narrative" or not. Therefore, any type of world structure or limits of interaction with objects can be used for games with narrative. He gives especially two distinct examples to clarify this assumption, which are *Dragon Age: Origins* (Bioware 2009) and *Heavy Rain* (Quantic Dream 2010).

Dubbelman (2016) approaches game mechanics and the narrative with a cognitive perspective. He states that the experience of a narrative not only depends on the narrator's abilities but also depends on the player's active construction of events in his/her mind. Therefore, each element in the game is also a narrative device because they help the creation of events in real-time and contribute to the mindful construction of the story by the player. Dubbelman (2016) names those elements as narrative game mechanics. He gives examples of how game mechanics serve as narrative elements by analysis of three videogames: *Left 4 Dead 2* (Valve 2009), *The Last of Us* (Naughty Dog 2013), and *Papers, Please* (Lucas Pope 2013).

Larsen and Schoenau-Fog (2016) present a model of continuum to explain the relationship between game mechanics and the game narrative with a similar approach to Dubbelman (2016). They structure their model on the MDA framework of Hunicke et al. (2004). According to MDA, the game is experienced through game dynamics, which is formed by the relation of one game mechanic with the other. Therefore, dynamics stand at one end of the continuum in Larsen and Schoenau-Fog's (2016) model. They also state that game mechanics should be designed according to the meaning the game is trying to give to the player. Otherwise, the meaning deduced from the game by the player would be slightly or completely different from what the designers assumed. They assert that the first step of giving the right meaning is relating the context with mechanics (in their model, this relation stands in the middle of the continuum). The second step is the congruency between this relation and the story. In some games, context can perfectly relate with the mechanics, but this relation cannot be congruent with the story while in other games it might be the opposite. Therefore, the quality of a game is determined by the existence of these relation and congruency. Finally, at the other end of the continuum, there is a context-to-context relationship that stems from traditional storytelling. The context-to-context relationship is seen in games through elements such as dialogues, character interactions, or world-building. By this model, Larsen and Schoenau-Fog (2016) argue that a combination of these three elements (i.e. dynamics, context-mechanic relation, and context-context relation) in a continuum is what creates the game narrative.

The studies mentioned above try to describe the relationship between different game elements and the game narrative from a holistic perspective. However, design implications for specific game elements to increase the feeling of the game narrative require deeper examination and studies that cover those examinations are scarce in the literature. Rogers et al.' (2018) study is one of the rarest examples that empirically examine how visual design choices relate to the game narrative. In their study, they try to understand if the visual design of non-player characters (NPCs) affects the understanding of their narrative roles. NPCs in many videogames have various functions according to their roles. Understanding an NPC's role depends on its interaction with the player and/or the game world. However, Rogers et al. (2018) state that there also might be specific visual expectations from NPCs based on their roles and related attributes. Most of the time, these attributes are referred to specific typologies which are also called personas or archetypes. To examine if congruency between visual expectations and functional attributes leads to an understanding of an NPC's role better in the game narrative, researchers created visual designs for three different NPCs with specific roles based on Vogler's (2007) archetypes (mentor, companion, and enemy were chosen for this study). Then, they asked participants to rate those NPCs according to their possible role in a game narrative. The results of the study revealed that the visual appearance of an NPC might be an indicator of its role in the game narrative.

In another study, Bizzocchi et al. (2011) closely looked at the role of interface design in the presentation of the game narrative. The researchers chose interface design because they argue that, if accordingly designed, interface has a reinforcing effect on narrative because of the inevitable focus of player's attention at certain points. To support their argument, they have examined interface design of several games in terms of different design approaches. The 'look and the feel' of the interface is about the congruency between audio-visual design of the interface and theme of the game narrative. It also includes the informative power of the interface about the player's status in the game. The shape of the cursor, audio feedback of interaction with game objects, and indicators of game status such as health and stamina bar or amount of ammo can be given as examples of interface designs referred in this approach. These interface elements are critical for player's interaction with the game world and keeping track of his or her status in the game. Therefore, researchers assert that they are hard to escape from player's attention, and their narrativization contributes to pleasure taken from game's narrative.

Finally, the design approach called 'behavioral mimicking and behavioral metaphors' is about the design strategy used for interactions in the game. Behavioral mimicking refers to interactions that are almost like their real-world representations. Researchers give example to this design strategy from the game *Bully: Scholarship Edition* (Rockstar 2006). In the game, a combination lock is opened as if opening a real lock with the rotational movement of the analogue stick on the Nintendo Wii controller. Bizzocchi et al. (2011) claim that this narrative mirroring process of gameplay actions creates a bond between the player and the game narrative. Contrary to behavioral mimicking, behavioral metaphor is more abstract for representation of real-world actions. They provide less mirroring of real-world actions bur more functionality in the gameplay. By skillful design strategies, behavioral metaphors increase the functionality of the player in the game narrative. According to Bizzocchi et al. (2011), this helps player to connect with the game narrative more.

Focusing on the interactive nature of video games, bridging the gap between the ludology and narratology schools with the assumption that the game narrative intertwines with several game elements, we are interested in the relationship of the narrative dimension of game user experience with the other dimensions of the Game User Experience Satisfaction Scale (GUESS). For this purpose, we used empirical data collected with GUESS which identifies game user experience with nine subdimensions: usability/playability, narratives, play engrossment, enjoyment, creative freedom, audio aesthetics, personal gratification, social connectivity, and visual aesthetics. The coherence of the GUESS dimension scores is investigated through variance analysis, exploring their affinity with the narrative. Additionally, we also mobilize secondary data coming from multiple online game reviews to explain the role of narrative (and the other subdimensions of GUESS) within the scope of game user experience.

15.3 Methodology

In our study, we used Game User Experience Satisfaction Scale (GUESS) of Phan et al. (2016) and focused on the 'narratives' factor of the GUESS and analyzed its relationship with other factors. For this purpose, six different video games were selected by the authors and they were played by 121 university students. For the selection of the video games, five colleagues in the field of game design higher education were asked to list ten video games they have recently played. Six video games were selected from 50 games in a semi-randomized way according to their meaningfulness (if the subject can experience enough content of the game) for a 30 min session. The selected games are *Super Mario Odyssey* (Nintendo 2017), *Sniper Elite 4* (Rebellion 2017), *Contrast* (Compulsion Games 2013), *Control* (Remedy Entertainment 2019), *Hellblade: Senua's Sacrifice* (Ninja Theory 2017), and *The Council* (Focus Home Interactive 2018). The first four games were played in the controlled lab environment where a research assistant accompanied the subjects. The research assistant was responsible for setting up the gaming system, starting the game, and handing out the data collection instrument at the end of the gameplay session. Due to Covid-19 restrictions, participants played the last two games at home and responded to the questionnaire in their own settings.

The research design employed is the within-subjects experimental design where a single group of participants played different games in selected platforms sequentially. Since data is collected from each participant for each game, this design is also called a repeated-measures design. Twenty-four of the participants were female (19.8%) and 97 of the participants were male (80.2%). Participants' age was ranging between 19 and 32 (M = 21.01 SD = 1.86). Brief information about selected games such as the genre, the platform the game is played on, and the nature of the game narrative were summarized in Table 15.1. The collected data was analyzed with SPSS version 25.0 software (SPSS, Inc., Chicago, IL). Pearson correlation and One-Way MANOVA (Multivariate analysis of variance) were used for analysis.

15.4 Games and User Experience Dimensions

Descriptive data for each factor is given in Table 15.2 for means and standard deviations. However, only 7 of 9 factors are presented in the table. It is because One-Way ANOVA revealed no significant results for Player Gratification and Social Connectivity factors. Therefore, it was decided not to include mean and standard deviations for these two factors.

Based on the descriptive statistics provided in Table 15.2, we mobilized secondary data coming from multiple online game reviews to explain the role of narrative (and the other subdimensions of GUESS) within the scope of game user experience. The reviews were taken from three major review websites and review scores of the six selected games were given in Table 15.3.

Table 15.1 Additional information about the games used in the study

Game	Platform	Genre	Narrative
Super Mario Odyssey	Nintendo Switch	Platformer and action game	Level based narrative with environmental cues
Sniper Elite 4	Playstation 4	Third-person tactical shooter stealth game	Fast-paced, action-oriented storytelling with fast beats
Contrast	PC	Indie puzzle and adventure game	Slow paced storytelling relying on the puzzles and the environment
Control	Playstation 4	Supernatural action adventure game	Mixed paced (slow and fast) storytelling around the challenges
Hellblade: Senua's Sacrifice	PC	Action adventure game	Fast-paced, action-oriented storytelling as the player fights through the world
The Council	PC	Adventure role-playing game	Complex, slow-paced storytelling enriched by deep characters

Table 15.2 Mean and standard deviations of seven GUESS factors (The highest means were highlighted with green while the lowest means were highlighted with red for each factor)

Game No*	Audio Aesthetics		Creative Freedom		Enjoyment		Narrative		Play Engrossment		Usability Playability		Visual Aesthetics	
	M	Std	M	Std	M	Std	M	Std	M	Std	M	Std	M	Std
1	23,28	4,52	32,76	7,72	24,59	4,13	25,44	6,17	30,07	8,90	55,61	6,28	17,33	3,63
2	24,22	3,32	33,80	7,79	25,36	4,59	30,23	7,13	33,66	10,77	53,26	9,11	18,60	2,84
3	22,63	4,18	29,06	8,74	23,56	5,05	24,17	8,06	30,76	10,53	47,3	10,94	17,07	3,55
4	25,11	3,61	39,01	7,68	26,75	3,96	31,30	7,30	36,75	10,09	55,75	8,04	18,49	3,43
5	25,17	3,83	34,46	8,37	24,31	5,06	31,72	7,77	34,22	11,30	48,94	11,39	19,28	2,36
6	22,87	3,80	34,75	8,34	24,80	5,05	30,22	6,89	32,67	10,49	55,21	8,62	17,10	3,42
Total	23,83	3,99	33,74	8,61	24,90	4,72	28,58	7,80	32,92	10,53	52,62	9,74	17,95	3,34

[a](1) Super Mario Odyssey, (2) Control, (3) Sniper Elite 4, (4) Contrast, (5) Hellblade: Senua's Sacrifice, (6) Council

Hellblade: Senua's Sacrifice (Ninja Theory 2017) is an action-adventure game where players assume the role of a Celtic female warrior named Senua who is plagued with severe psychosis. Contrasting inner voices and visual hallucinations highlight the psychological nature of the protagonist's spiritual journey. The game progresses by solving visual puzzles and overcoming enemies or obstacles. The game has been described as a visually gorgeous game (Tyrrel 2018) that blends

Table 15.3 Review scores of six games on three major game review websites

Game	Gamespot	IGN	Game informer
Super Mario Odyssey	10/10	10/10	9.75/10
Sniper Elite 4	8/10	8.3/10	7.75/10
Contrast	5/10	7.5/10	7.5/10
Control	8/10	8.8/10	8.75/10
Hellblade: Senua's Sacrifice	8/10	9/10	8/10
The Council	Not reviewed	Not reviewed	6.5/10

amazing visuals and inventive design to amplify story and game play (Fillari 2019). The sound design is praised by almost every critic and described as an audial experience that is as vivid and liberal as anything that happens before your eyes (Tyrrel 2018). The game's narrative is also praised by critics and described as an undeniably memorable and compelling experience (Juba 2017). Our statistical analysis also showed that *Hellblade: Senua's Sacrifice* scored higher than the other five games in terms of 'audio aesthetics', 'narratives' and 'visual aesthetics' which are the defining characteristics of the game (Table 15.2). The 'enjoyment' score and the 'usability/playability' scores were the second lowest scores among the six games used in the study. This may be due to the lack of a heads-up display (HUD), a combat tutorial, a skill system, an objective marker and a minimap, making the game harder to play. The visual puzzles of the game were also criticized to be repetitive and tedious (Fillari 2019; Juba 2017). Sound plays a primary role in *Hellblade: Senua's Sacrifice* and it is classified as the first "big" game which fully incorporates the possibilities of binaural sound (Farkaš 2018). Thus, it is not surprising for the game to have the highest 'audio aesthetics'.

Control (Remedy Entertainment 2019) is a paranormal action-adventure game where players assume the role of a young woman with a troubled past named Jesse Faden on her first day as director at the Federal Bureau of Control. The game's fascinating narrative unravels in Jesse's mind through a series of inner monologues and psychic projections (Brown 2019) but in terms of 'narratives', 'audio aesthetics', 'creative freedom', 'usability/playability' and 'play engrossment' the game has average scores and does not stand out among the games used in the study. The statistical analysis showed that the game has the second highest scores of 'enjoyment' and 'visual aesthetics'. The powerful psychic abilities given to players are praised to be as satisfying to use as they are to watch (Reeves 2019) and the combat that deftly mixes gunplay and superpowers are praised to be fun and stylish (Brown 2019). These unique game mechanics may be the reason behind the high score of 'enjoyment'. The setting is described as an engrossingly weird paranormal world (Dornbush 2020) and the art style is praised to be gorgeous that evokes dread and awe (Brown 2019) which may be the indicators of the high score in 'visual aesthetics'.

Sniper Elite 4 (Rebellion 2017) is a third-person tactical shooter stealth game set in Italy in 1943 where players assume the role of an elite American sniper in the Office of Strategic Services (OSS) named Karl Fairburne. World War II story consists of eight huge campaign levels varying visually and functionally (Albert 2017) but since it is a shooter game it has a fast-paced, action-oriented storytelling with fast beats. The game has the lowest 'audio aesthetics', 'creative freedom', 'enjoyment', 'narratives', 'visual aesthetics', and 'usability/playability' scores. The game is criticized to have an inconsistent AI and an uninspired story (Wakeling 2017) and although the sandbox nature of the missions and the smooth gameplay are praised to deliver a fun experience that is easy to play (Shea 2017). The participants of our study also said that they were not familiar with playing a shooter game on Playstation 4 and they found the controls too difficult to get accustomed to. Accordingly, it was also reported in literature that players felt significantly more challenged by the game if they were not allowed to play on their comfort platform and the perceived usability is affected by a platform change (Gerling et al. 2011). The participant's inability to play the game smoothly maybe the reason behind the lowest scores in almost all the dimensions of the GUESS, especially in 'usability/playability'.

The Council (Focus Home Interactive 2018) is an adventure role-playing game where players assume the role of Louis de Richet searching his missing mother. The story is about a secret society that determines how to govern the world and the player meets historical characters like George Washington and Napoleon Bonaparte. The player, like a detective, collects evidence and clues to solve mysteries and progress in the story. The game is criticized as being disappointing and unsatisfying, with ridiculous plotlines, technical shortcomings, and annoying puzzles but the choice and progression mechanics are praised as being interesting (Wallace 2018). The game has the second highest 'creative freedom' score where the exploration/evidence collecting mechanics and the dialogue choices it offers may play a role. The game has the second lowest 'audio aesthetics' and 'visual aesthetics' scores which were also the dimensions criticized by reviewers. Wallace (2018) stated that the voice acting is so bad that it is distracting and watching the wooden character models interact is just as jarring.

Contrast (Compulsion Games 2013) is a single player adventure/puzzle plat-former game where players control a mysterious figure named Dawn aiding a young girl named Didi in her efforts to prevent her family from falling apart. The ability of the player to shift between a corporeal, three-dimensional existence and a silhouet-ted, two-dimensional one is a creative game mechanic useful for solving some of the puzzles of the game. Since most of the games used in the study were produced by bigger game studios and budgets, it is surprising that *Contrast* has the highest 'play engrossment', 'creative freedom', 'enjoyment', and 'usability/playability' scores. The game also has the second highest scores of 'narratives' and 'audio aesthetics'. Although the game is criticized for its mostly mundane gameplay (Petit 2013), simple but creative and interesting game mechanics (Stapleton 2013) resulted in high scores of 'usability/playability' and 'enjoyment'. Wallace (2013) praised the voice acting, music, and sound effects stating that they provide a quality ambiance, and this was also reflected on the game's high 'audio aesthetics' score. Stapleton (2013) defined the game as full of heart and beauty which may be the indicators of high scores of 'play engrossment' and 'creative freedom'. Although the game has the low review scores among the games used in the study (Table 15.3), the statistical analysis shows that the game perfectly blends different aspects of game user experience together and creates a unique/satisfying experience for the players.

Super Mario Odyssey (Nintendo 2017) is a platformer game where players control the familiar and iconic game character, Mario. The game has the second highest 'usability/playability' score which is not a surprising fact when the familiarity of the Mario series and their game mechanics were considered. The game's playability is defined by Reiner (2017) as easy to pick up and play but loaded with enough depth to keep you going until well after the credits roll. Brown (2019) also stated that the game surprises the players with not just inventive mechanics, of which there are many, but with expertly tuned level design and moments of charismatic wit. Although the game has the highest review scores among the games used in the study (Table 15.3) and the reviews praised almost every aspect of the game, *Super Mario Odyssey* has the lowest 'play engrossment' score and the second lowest scores of 'narratives' and 'creative freedom' in our study.

15.5 Narrative and User Experience Dimensions

Differences of six games for their game user experience dimensions were analyzed with MANOVA. The results revealed that overall gaming experience significantly differs according to the game, F (50, 1982) = 6.06, $p < 0.000$. Follow-up analyses showed that six games are significantly different from each other for audio aesthetics (F (5, 443) = 5.8; $p < 0.000$; partial η^2 = 0.061), creative freedom (F (5, 443) = 12.629; $p < 0.000$; partial η^2 = 0.125), enjoyment (F (5, 443) = 4.246; $p < 0.001$; partial η^2 = 0.046), narrative (F (5, 443) = 15.113; $p < 0.000$; partial η^2 = 0.146), play engrossment (F (5, 443) = 4.195; $p < 0.001$; partial η^2 = 0.045), usability/playability (F (5, 443) = 12.02; $p < 0.000$; partial η^2 = 0.119), and visual aesthetics factors (F (5, 443) = 5.648; $p < 0.000$; partial η^2 = 0.06). These results indicate that GUESS is a robust game user experience measurement tool that can identify differences in game user experience dimensions when applied to different games from different genres.

The relationship of 'narratives' with other factors was analyzed with Pearson Correlation. Results of the analysis show that 'narratives' factor is positively correlated with all other factors considering six games in overall, (r (447) = 0.575, $p < 0.001$ for audio aesthetics, r (447) = 0.745, $p < 0.001$ for creative freedom, r (447) = 0.698, $p < 0.001$ for enjoyment, r (447) = 0.749, $p < 0.001$ for play engrossment, r (447) = 0.577, $p < 0.001$ for gratification, r (447) = 0.215, $p < 0.001$ for social connectivity, r (447) = 0.434, $p < 0.001$ for usability/playability, and r (447) = 0.528, $p < 0.001$ for visual aesthetics). According to the results, the highest correlations of 'narratives' were with 'play engrossment' and 'creative freedom' factors. On the other hand, 'narratives' was found to be lest correlated with 'social connectivity' and 'playability' factors.

Based on main effect results, further post-hoc tests were applied to understand how individual games differ from each other in nine factors. However, there were homogeneity differences among factors. The null hypothesis of equal variances is rejected for 'usability/playability' factor, $p < 0.05$. Therefore, Tukey's HSD post-hoc test was applied for 'audio aesthetics', 'creative freedom', 'enjoyment', 'narratives', 'play engrossment', and 'visual aesthetics' factors, while Games Howell post-hoc test was applied for the 'usability/playability' factor. Tukey's HSD post-hoc analysis for 'audio aesthetics' showed that *Contrast* showed significantly higher score for 'audio aesthetics' than *Super Mario Odyssey* ($p = 0.05$), *Sniper Elite 4* and *Council*, $p < 0.05$. Additionally, *Hellblade: Senua's Sacrifice* is perceived to be more satisfactory for 'audio aesthetics' than *Council* and *Sniper Elite 4*, $p < 0.05$. For 'visual aesthetics', Tukey's HSD post-hoc analysis showed that *Hellblade: Senua's Sacrifice* found to be giving higher pleasurable experience than *Super Mario Odyssey*, *Sniper Elite 4* ($p < 0.05$), and *Council*. Additionally, results showed that *Control* is rated higher for 'visual aesthetics' than *Sniper Elite 4*, $p < 0.05$.

Tukey's HSD post-hoc analysis for 'creative freedom' revealed that *Contrast* revealed significantly the highest score ($p < 0.05$), while *Sniper Elite 4* gives the lowest score than all other games ($p < 0.05$). For 'play engrossment', Tukey's HSD post-hoc analysis showed that *Contrast* found to be rated higher than *Super Mario Odyssey* and *Sniper Elite 4*, $p < 0.05$. For 'enjoyment' factor, Tukey's HSD post-hoc analysis showed that *Contrast* gives higher score 'enjoyment' than *Hellblade: Senua's Sacrifice* and *Sniper Elite 4*, $p < 0.05$.

Games Howell post-hoc analysis for 'usability/playability' factor showed that *Contrast*, *Control*, *Council*, and *Super Mario Odyssey* gives higher experience than *Sniper Elite 4*, $p < 0.05$. Also, *Contrast*, *Council*, and *Super Mario Odyssey* found to be rated for usability/playability higher than *Hellblade: Senua's Sacrifice*, $p < 0.05$. Among all other games, *Contrast* was found to have the highest score for 'usability/playability' factor while the *Sniper Elite 4* have the lowest score.

Tukey's HSD post-hoc analysis for Narrative factor showed that *Contrast*, *Control* and *Council* are rated higher for narrative aspects than both *Super Mario Odyssey* and *Sniper Elite 4*, $p < 0.05$. Also, *Hellblade: Senua's Sacrifice* is found to be significantly higher rated than *Super Mario Odyssey* ($p < 0.05$), and *Sniper Elite 4* ($p < 0.05$). Furthermore, *Hellblade: Senua's Sacrifice* was the highest rated in terms of the 'narratives' factor.

15.6 Discussion

The statistical analysis conducted indicate a harmony between the 'narratives' and other game user experience dimensions of the Game User Experience Satisfaction Scale (GUESS). In this sense, it can be argued that each game element such as the audiovisuals of the game or the mechanics that support player's creativity and curiosity is also a narrative device. Accordingly, we can claim that the narrative dimension is intertwined with other game elements to create a meaningful player experience. The mutual relationship between the gameplay (the interactions of the player and the ludic decision-making processes) and the narrative (the emotional and intellectual engagement of the player with the story) creates or shapes the subjective experience of playing a game.

High correlation between the narratives and play engrossment dimensions indicate that 'the degree to which a game can hold player's attention and interest' is closely related with the narrative experience. Similarly, the high correlation between the narratives and the creative freedom dimension indicates that 'the extent to which a game is able to foster the player's creativity and curiosity' is closely related with the narrative experience. Narratives has the lowest correlation with the social connectivity and usability/playability factors. The results about social connectivity may not indicate a generalizable fact about game user experience since none of the chosen games allow player-to-player interactions and thus has a limited sense of social connectivity.

The analysis conducted on the 'narratives' factor of the scale showed that GUESS is a reliable tool for analyzing narrative as a game user experience dimension. Among the games used in the study, the platformer *Super Mario Odyssey* and the shooter *Sniper Elite 4* prioritizes gameplay over story, and this can also be seen by their low scores of 'narratives'. Among the games used in the study, *Hellblade: Senua's Sacrifice* has the highest 'narratives' score but it should also be noted that the game also has the highest 'visual aesthetics' and 'audio aesthetics' scores. The combination of amazing visuals and innovative sound design may support/enhance the narrative of the game so that it scored higher than all the other games in terms of 'narratives'.

References

E. Aarseth, A narrative theory of games, in *Proceedings of the International Conference on the Foundations of Digital Games* (2012), pp. 129–133

V.V. Abeele, K. Spiel, L. Nacke, D. Johnson, K. Gerling, Development and validation of the player experience inventory: a scale to measure player experiences at the level of functional and psychosocial consequences. Int. J. Hum. Comput. Stud. **135**, 102370 (2020)

B. Albert, *Sniper Elite 4 Review* (2017). https://www.ign.com/articles/2017/02/13/sniper-elite-4-review

Bioware, *Dragon Age Origins* [Videogame] (Bioware, 2009)

J. Bizzocchi, M.A. Ben Lin, J. Tanenbaum, Games, narrative and the design of interface. Int. J. Arts Technol. **4**(4), 460–479 (2011)

J.H. Brockmyer, C.M. Fox, K. Curtiss, E. McBroom, K.M. Burkhart, J.N. Pidruzny, The development of the game engagement questionnaire: a measure of engagement in video game-playing. J. Exp. Soc. Psychol. **45**(4), 624–634 (2009). https://doi.org/10.1016/j.jesp.2009.02.016

P. Brown, *Control Review - An Action-Packed Paranormal Portal* (2019). https://www.gamespot.com/reviews/control-review-an-action-packed-paranormal-portal/1900-6417278/

E.H. Calvillo-Gámez, P. Cairns, A.L. Cox, Assessing the core elements of the gaming experience, in *Evaluating User Experience in Games*, ed. by R. Bernhaupt, (Springer, New York, NY, 2010), pp. 47–71

S.T. Coleridge, *Biographia Literaria* (IM Dent and Sons, London, 1817)

Compulsion Games. *Contrast* [Videogame] (Compulsion Games, 2013)

M. Czikszentmihalyi, *Flow: The Psychology of Optimal Experience* (Harper & Row, New York, 1990)

J. Dornbush, *Control Review Stays on My Mind* (2020). https://www.ign.com/articles/2019/08/26/control-review-2

T. Dubbelman, Playing the hero: how games take the concept of storytelling from representation to presentation. J. Media Pract. **12**(2), 157–172 (2011)

T. Dubbelman, Narrative game mechanics, in *International Conference on Interactive Digital Storytelling*, (Springer, Cham, 2016), pp. 39–50

L. Ermi, F. Mäyrä, Fundamental components of the gameplay experience: analysing immersion, in *The Proceedings of the DiGRA Conference 1050 Changing Views: Worlds in Play*, ed. by S. Castell, J. Jenson, (Peter Lang, New York, NY, 2005), pp. 37–54

T. Farkaš, Binaural and ambisonic sound as the future standard of digital games. Acta Ludol. **1**(2), 34–46 (2018)

A. Fillari, *Hellblade: Senua's Sacrifice Review - The Power of Empathy* (2019). https://www.gamespot.com/reviews/hellblade-senuas-sacrifice-review-the-power-of-emp/1900-6416724/

Focus Home Interactive, *The Council* [Videogame] (Focus Home Interactive, 2018)

G. Frasca, Ludology Meets Narratology: Similitude and Differences between (Video) Games and Narrative. *Ludology.org* (1999)

K.M. Gerling, M. Klauser, J. Niesenhaus, Measuring the impact of game controllers on player experience in FPS games, in *Proceedings of the 15th International Academic MindTrek Conference: Envisioning Future Media Environments* (2011), pp. 83–86

R. Hunicke, M. LeBlanc, R. Zubek, MDA: a formal approach to game design and game research, in *Proceedings of the AAAI Workshop on Challenges in Game AI* (vol. 4(1), 2004), p. 1722

W. IJsselsteijn, W. van den Hoogen, C. Klimmt, Y.K. de Kort, C. Lindley, K. Mathiak, et al., Measuring the experience of digital game enjoyment, in *Proceedings of Measuring Behavior*, (Noldus Information Technology, Wageningen, 2008), pp. 88–89

C. Jennett, A.L. Cox, P. Cairns, S. Dhoparee, A. Epps, T. Tijs, A. Walton, Measuring and defining the experience of immersion in games. Int. J. Hum. Comput. Stud. **66**, 641–661 (2008)

J. Juba, *Hellblade: Senua's Sacrifice Seeing Through the Fog* (2017). https://www.gameinformer.com/games/hellblade/b/playstation4/archive/2017/08/08/hellblade-senuas-sacrifice-game-informer-review.aspx

J.M. Keller, Development and use of the ARCS model of instructional design. J. Instr. Dev. **10**(3), 2–10 (1987)

M. Kokonis, Intermediality between games and fiction: The "ludology vs. narratology" debate in computer game studies: a response to Gonzalo Frasca. Acta Univ. Sapient. Film Media Stud. **9**, 171–188 (2014)

B.A. Larsen, H. Schoenau-Fog, The narrative quality of game mechanics, in *International Conference on Interactive Digital Storytelling*, (Springer, Cham, 2016), pp. 61–72

J. Lessiter, J. Freeman, E. Keogh, J. Davidoff, A cross-media presence questionnaire: the ITC-sense of presence inventory. Presence Teleop. Virt. **10**, 282–297 (2001)

M. Lombard, T.B. Ditton, L. Weinstein, Measuring presence: the temple presence inventory, in *Proceedings of the 12th Annual International Workshop on Presence* (2009), pp. 1–15

Lucas Pope, *Papers, Please* [Videogame] (Lucas Pope, 2013)

M. Mateas, A. Stern, 22. Build it to understand it: ludology meets narratology in game design space, in *Worlds In Play: International Perspectives on Digital Games Research* (vol. 21, 2007), p. 267

F. Mäyrä, *An Introduction to Game Studies* (Sage, New Castel, 2008)

J.H. Murray, The last word on ludology v narratology in game studies, in *International DiGRA Conference* (2005), pp. 1–5

J. Nakamura, M. Csikszentmihalyi, The concept of flow, in *Handbook of Positive Psychology*, ed. by C. R. Snyder, S. J. Lopez, (Oxford University Press, New York, 2002), pp. 89–105

Naughty Dog, *The Last of Us* [Videogame] (Naughty Dog, 2013)

Ninja Theory, *Hellblade: Senua's Sacrifice* [Videogame] (Ninja Theory, 2017)

Nintendo, *Super Mario Odyssey* [Videogame] (Nintendo, 2017)

M.J. Parnell, *Playing with Scales: Creating a Measurement Scale to Assess the Experience of Video Games*. Master's thesis (2009). Available from http://www.ucl.ac.uk/uclic/

D. Pavlas, F. Jentsch, E. Salas, S.M. Fiore, V. Sims, The play experience scale: development and validation of a measure of play. Hum. Factors **54**, 214–225 (2012)

C. Petit, *Contrast Review* (2013). https://www.gamespot.com/reviews/contrast-review/1900-6415539/

M.H. Phan, J.R. Keebler, B.S. Chaparro, The development and validation of the game user experience satisfaction scale (GUESS). Hum. Factors **58**(8), 1217–1247 (2016)

Quantic Dream, *Heavy Rain* [Videogame] (Quantic Dream, 2010)

Rebellion, *Sniper Elite 4* [Videogame] (Rebellion, 2017)

B. Reeves, *Control Review – A Heady Power Trip* (2019, August). https://www.gameinformer.com/review/control/control-review-a-heady-power-trip

A. Reiner, *Super Mario Odyssey. A Clever Tip of the Hat* (2017, October). https://www.gameinformer.com/games/super_mario_odyssey/b/switch/archive/2017/10/26/super-mario-odyssey-review.aspx

Remedy Entertainment, *Control* [Videogame] (Remedy Entertainment, 2019)

Rockstar, *Bully: Scholarship Edition*. [Videogame] (Rockstar, 2006)

K. Rogers, M. Aufheimer, M. Weber, L.E. Nacke. Towards the visual design of non-player characters for narrative roles, in *Graphics Interface* (2018), pp. 154–161

R.M. Ryan, E.L. Deci, Self-determination theory and the facilitation of intrinsic motivation, social development, and well-being. Am. Psychol. **55**, 68–78 (2000)

R.M. Ryan, C.S. Rigby, A. Przybylski, The motivational pull of video games: a self-determination theory approach. Motiv. Emot. **30**, 347–363 (2006). https://doi.org/10.1007/s11031-006-9051-8

T.W. Schubert, The sense of presence in virtual environments: a three-component scale measuring spatial presence, involvement, and realness. J. Media Psychol. **15**, 69–71 (2003)

B. Shea, *Sniper Elite 4 Hitting the Target* (2017). https://www.gameinformer.com/games/sniper_elite_4/b/playstation4/archive/2017/02/13/sniper-elite-4-game-informer-review.aspx

D. Stapleton, *Contrast Review All the World's a Show* (2013). https://www.ign.com/articles/2013/11/13/contrast-review

P. Sweetser, P. Wyeth, Game flow: A model for evaluating player enjoyment in games. ACM Comput. Entertain. **3**(3), 3A (2005)

J. Takatalo, J. Häkkinen, J. Kaistinen, G. Nyman, User experience in digital games: Differences between laboratory and home. Simul. Gaming **42**, 656–673 (2010)

B. Tyrrel, *Hellblade: Senua's Sacrifice Review* (2018). https://www.ign.com/articles/2017/08/08/hellblade-senuas-sacrifice-review

Valve, *Left 4 Dead 2* [Videogame] (Valve, 2009)

C. Vogler, *The Writer's Journey* (Michael Wiese Productions, Studio City, CA, 2007)

P. Vorderer, W. Wirth, F.R. Gouveia, F. Biocca, T. Saari, L. Jäncke, S. Böcking, H. Schramm, A. Gysbers, T. Hartmann, Mec spatial presence questionnaire. Report to the Europoean Community, Project Presence: MET (IST-2001037661) (2004)

R. Wakeling, *Sniper Elite 4 Review* (2017). https://www.gamespot.com/reviews/sniper-elite-4-review/1900-6416614/

K. Wallace, *Contrast A Shadow of What Might Have Been* (2013). https://www.gameinformer.com/games/contrast/b/playstation4/archive/2013/11/13/contrast-review.aspx

K. Wallace, *The Council the Wrong Side of History* (2018). https://www.gameinformer.com/review/the-council/the-wrong-side-of-history

J. Wiemeyer, L. Nacke, C. Moser, F. Mueller, Player experience, in *Serious Games: Foundations, Concepts and Practice*, ed. by R. Dörner, S. Göbel, W. Effelsberg, J. Wiemeyer, (Springer International Publishing, Berlin, 2016), pp. 243–271

B.G. Witmer, M.J. Singer, Measuring presence in virtual environments: a presence questionnaire. Presence Teleop. Virt. **7**, 225–240 (1998)

Part IV
Practices and Case Studies

Chapter 16
An Analysis of the Use of Religious Elements in Assassin's Creed Origins

Özge Mirza and Sercan Sengun

16.1 Introduction

Religion can be a crucial element in videogames. Campbell and Grieve (2014, p. 4) assert that "[. . .] many popular games draw on religious narratives, characters, and symbols as central themes directing game-play." They also underline that as the language of a game becomes more serious, religious themes can exist both within the cultural and political framings. As religion is a significant part of the human experience, videogames host religion in many ways by employing fragments of religion that are inspired by practiced religions in the real-world, the ancient ones that were once practiced but might already be forgotten, or made-up religions and religious practices. Šisler et al. (2018, p. 11) maintain that games "serve as platforms for negotiations and constructions of society and culture in general, and of religion in particular" by citing *Legend of Zelda* and *Far Cry 4* as games that religion is integral to.

In videogames, religious elements can appear in two forms: distinct (focusing on one mythology) and indistinct (amalgamation of multiple religious imagery or employing multiple religious mythology). Videogames can use religion both as a reference and motivation. Games have used religious themes, languages, images, symbolisms, and the like to construct instantly recognizable lore, characters, and/or narratives. *Assassin's Creed Origins* (ACO) is a great example to review such

Ö. Mirza (✉)
Game Design Master Program, Bahcesehir University, Istanbul, Turkey

S. Sengun
Wonsook Kim School of Art, Creative Technologies Program, Illinois State University, Normal, IL, USA
e-mail: ssengun@ilstu.edu

© The Author(s), under exclusive license to Springer Nature Switzerland AG 2022
B. Bostan (ed.), *Games and Narrative: Theory and Practice*, International Series on Computer Entertainment and Media Technology,
https://doi.org/10.1007/978-3-030-81538-7_16

historical stories and characters wherein religion is used in the context of the background setting.

Additionally, the act of gaming itself has been offered as a religious act (Bosman 2019). A game can become a religious placeholder or a pseudo-religion for some devoted gamers because it offers many of the similar experiences that religions do since they share many of similar structural elements (Campbell and Grieve 2014).

Videogames have become an important and prevalent medium for socio-cultural discourse and cultural communication. As a result, in this work, through a case study, we explore the relationship between videogames and religion since religion is also a substantial and pervasive part of the human experience. When considering the relationship between videogames and religion, we focus on two questions: (1) how are religious elements represented in games (e.g., story, audio, environment, architecture, lighting, character design, etc.), and (2) how does religion impact the building of the virtual game world?

16.2   Background

16.2.1   Religion and Videogames

In games, as Huizinga (1949, p. 1) reminds us, "[. . .] there is something 'at play' which transcends the immediate needs of life and imparts meaning to the action." Religions and myths are organized as cultural systems with identical action-meaning integration such as religious behavior and practices. Additionally, thoughts and mysteries about life and death, innocence and guilt, and violence are existential in nature, and while they may not be instantly perceived as 'religious,' they employ similar action-meaning integrations.

Religion is considered a serious real-world topic, while videogames are typically considered as creative and entertainment pastime products. However, players, creators, and developers can both apply and expose their existential and spiritual feelings in videogames and studying them as an academic source creates a chance for scholars to investigate religious and spiritual references (some examples of such studies are Krzywinska 2006; Bainbridge and Bainbridge 2007; Corliss 2011; Bosman 2019). In fact, since the original *Assassin's Creed*'s release in 2007, all games in the franchise start with this disclaimer: "Inspired by historical events and characters [. . .] this work of fiction was designed, developed and produced by a multicultural team of various religious faiths and beliefs."

At the same time, there are plenty of legends and rumors surrounding videogames (e.g., speculations about Easter eggs, secrets, etc.), as well as behaviors and rituals surrounding a game, its player base, and its culture in general. Much as Leibovitz (2013) asserts that religion is a game (based on being "exacting but modular, rule-based but tolerant of deviation, moved by metaphysical yearnings but governed by intricate, earthly designs"), by the means of a fast-growing gaming culture, videogames are now religious placeholders and mechanisms within which to investigate religious symbols, archaic texts and gods, and mystical cultures. Campbell (2013, p. 3) defines such *digital* religions as "a religion that is constituted in new ways through digital media and culture."

16.2.2   *Assassin's Creed Franchise*

The *Assassin's Creed* franchise is an award-winning videogame series that already has 12 main games, 12 spin-off games, many short films, a full-length film, and several transmedia outputs. All the main games have generated novelizations that expand or append the stories of their games. ACO was released worldwide for Microsoft Windows, PlayStation 4, and Xbox One on October 27, 2017. The game is set in Egypt near the end of the Ptolemaic period (49 BCE) and recounts the supposedly "true" and secret history of real-world events. The game's story follows a Medjay named Bayek who is from the Egyptian area of Siwa and is the last Medjay alive who held harmony in Egypt. He and his wife Aya are the originators of the *Hidden Ones* (an organization that would later morph into the *Assassin Brotherhood*). In the game's story, they play an influential role in the civil war that broke out between Queen Cleopatra and her sibling Ptolemy XIII.

16.3   Methodology

In this research, we focus on Jäger's (2001) toolbox for conducting discourse analysis and adapt it for videogames. Jäger provides this toolbox as a "practical approach to the discourse-analytical discussion of empirical (text) material" such as printed media (e.g., women's magazines), popular media (e.g., pop songs), videos, etc. The toolbox offers that a discourse can be built on a triad of dispositives (that are defined as "constantly evolving context of items of knowledge which are contained in speaking/thinking–acting–materialization"): (1) discursive; (2) non-discursive; and (3) manifestations/materializations. Since the discursive materials are the ones through which knowledge is primarily transported, we accept them as the game's narrative building blocks, such as the story, visuals, and audio clues. Non-discursive materials accompany and/or precede knowledge, so, we accept them as the non-direct language of the game world where the game play takes place such as environments, architecture, and lighting clues. Finally, we accept the characters/deities and their representations as where the knowledge manifests/materializes. We apply this framework as the basis of a critical discourse analysis for analyzing religious elements and imagery in ACO in order to understand the relationship between religious context and the game. The framework focuses on three topics: game narrative, game context, and game characters (see Table 16.1).

Table 16.1 Our custom framework for analyzing videogames and religion

Discursive dispositives	Game narrative	Story, visuals, audio
Non-discursive dispositives	Game context	Environments, architecture, lighting
Manifestations/materializations	Game characters	Player character(s), non-player character(s), god(s)

By relying on this framework for recording our experiences and arranging our notes, we use an autoethnographic approach to determine when and how players of the game are exposed to religious undertones, as well as the ramifications of such exposure. Past research highlights gameplay as "personal and exploratory" (Borchard 2015, p. 447) that makes autoethnography a valid (Shaw 2013; Taylor et al. 2012) and frequently mobilized method (some examples include Bainbridge 2010; Janish 2018) to analyze a game experience.

Additionally, we mobilize secondary data coming from multiple interviews made with the development team of the game to understand some of the design decisions.

16.4   Results and Discussion

In this section, we outline our findings under three main topics with three subtopics each.

16.4.1   Game Narrative

Apart from mobilizing religious elements and imagery, videogames can use religious undertones in their narratives often to provide a sense of realism. Game characters might be designed harmoniously on religious personas or stereotypes. Religion contributes to meaning surrounding life and as a result, can produce more realistic storylines and world representations that the players can become a part of. ACO uses religion to feed its narrative and characters' stories and uses different religious symbols to maintain a realistic world view. The game also employs real-world religious symbols, locations, and personas.

16.4.1.1   Story

As explained by Ryan (2001, p. 519), videogames tell stories that can manifest in various game context:

- Stories are a representation of life, not itself
- Stories are about singular, not endlessly repeatable events

- Stories must involve individuated characters
- Stories are not an automatic recording of "everything that happens" in an arbitrarily determined time span, they focus on events that cause significant changes in the state of a world, and they involve selection and organization of materials, a process which may be called emplotting
- Stories are told from a retrospective stance that provides a comprehensive view of the reported events and of their consequences

Jenkins (2004, p. 122) offers that "games fit within a much older traction of spatial stories, which have often taken the form of hero's odysseys, quest myths, or travel narratives." Krzywinska (2006) studies the notable role of myth for world-creation in the popular massively multiplayer online role-playing game *World of Warcraft* and identifies the narrative models following the mythological stories of cosmogenesis and world creation in numerous religious traditions and their effects on the gameplay. Apart from holding massive amounts of religious undertones, some games can construct grave dilemmas with the religions they present. For example, in *Assassin's Creed* franchise, players participate in a number of missions that possess religious meanings besides the gameplay concerning a third-person open world. Even the name Assassin's 'Creed' is a connection to Christianity as it has an association to the Nicene Creed.[1] The franchise concentrates on a hidden society of assassins that are in charge of ending the power of *The Knight Templars* throughout the Third Crusade period. The franchise then paves the way for creating *The Knight Templars* in the game as a non-fictional depiction of the Catholic Church army through the Medieval centuries. Furthermore, the game has a fictional story that runs parallel to historical real-life events that merge political and cultural subjects with religion at its base. Assassin's Creed series engages the players to have experiences throughout the history in various periods by providing formatted adventures that expose them to not solely historical truths that are respecting the yore, apart from the function that religion had in these past cultures. Toward this aim, game developers design imagery, characters, and locations according to general stereotypes such as snakes, certain monsters, and the devil being represented as evil characters while warriors, angels, and other creatures like phoenix as being represented as good characters. In an interview with Jade Raymond (Xbox Gazette 2006), a game producer in Ubisoft Montreal, the speculative nature of the game is highlighted:

Actually, the game is directed at the same time towards fiction and history. It's a speculative fiction, and it's a fun genre to work in. By grounding a story in reality, you increase its credibility. Suspension of disbelief becomes easier because it's happening in our world. You're exploring cities that still exist today - encountering infamous individuals whose names everyone knows - witnessing battles that really occurred. At the same time, because our setting is far removed in time (this is

---

[1] The Nicene Creed is a statement of belief widely used in Christian liturgy. It is called 'Nicene' because it was originally adopted in the city of Nicaea (present day İznik, Turkey) by the First Council of Nicaea in 325.

nearly 1000 years ago), there's plenty of freedom to tweak people's personalities and motivations. It's fun to explore the idea that something else was happening beneath the information gleaned from historical textbooks.

In the book, *America: Religions and Religion*, Catherine L. Albanese (1999, p. 8) describes the four principal elements of religion and maintains that religions outfit the four Cs: creed, code, cultures, and community. Albanese (1999) describes creeds as holding the "explanations about the meaning of human life," codes as signifying the "rules that govern everyday behavior [...] that may take the form of moral and ethical systems but they may also be the customs that become acceptable in a society," cultures as denoting the "rituals to act out the understandings expressed in creed and codes," and communities as implying the "groups of people either formally or informally bound together by the creed, code, and cultures they share." Video games might implement all or few selected dimensions of these principal elements. We argue that Assassin's Creed franchise, in general constructs the assassin's backstory as religious mythology, mobilizing all the four Cs.

Jenkins (2004, p. 121) asserts that "game designers don't simply tell stories; they design worlds and sculpt spaces." A game world echoes a game's aesthetic imagination, its narrative, and its promise in the interaction for the player. The in-game environments that the developers produce can include religious objects and locations that may or may not exist in the real world. They can also construct intermediary spaces by charging the space with distinguishable formations or structures, depictions of the real-life world, similar landscapes and trees, etc. In this way, the visual creation of the world completes the narratives in such a way that extensively practices the game's nascency concerning its stories, mechanics, objectives, purposes, figures, areas, etc. As a result, the world becomes alive wherein the players find significant cognitive complexity.

Ian Bogost's (2007) concepts of "procedural rhetoric," or "simulation rhetoric," focus on the design of gameplay, specifically on how videogame makers prepare laws and rules within a game to transmit a special belief. In this light, the concept of rituals also carries out similar functions: they give us a narrative, request our interplay with it, and deal with this interplay to develop how we see the world. In his book, *Persuasive Games: The Experience Power of Videogames*, Bogost (2007, p. vii) points out that:

Videogames are an expressive medium. They represent how real and imagined systems work. They invite players to interact with those systems and form judgments about them. As part of the ongoing process of understanding this medium and pushing it further as a player, developers, and critics, we must strive to understand how to construct and critique the representations of our world in a video game form.

It is possible to fill the game worlds with folklore, myths, legends, narratives, and, then, bolster the world's mythology through transmedia elements such as novels, screenplays, comics, books, movies, etc. Some of these materials can use well-known religious representations (e.g., the Baha'i Nine-Pointed Star, Christian Cross, Buddhist Dharma Wheel, Islamic Crescent and Star, Hinduist Aum, Judaism's Star of David, or Tai Chi's Yin and Yang, etc.). Typically, games place religious symbols on a scale of good versus evil, which the player's character observes as they travel through the mythical hero's journey (Campbell 2008).

ACO adopts complex religious and mythological narratives in pagodas and missions that provide the player with knowledge. The world creation of the game exhibits the boundaries separating Greek, Roman, and Egyptian cultures and religions. ACO's story, set in 49 BCE during Cleopatra's rising, hold references to the many gods, lords, dogmas, cults, occults, faiths, and beliefs of the time during which myth, legend, story, and religion performed an enormous purpose.

16.4.1.2 Visuals

ACO constructs a consistent and well-defined visual language. The visual language, application, and themes support identifying and demonstrating which area the faction is based on, promoting the player to place themselves in the world. For example, a Roman citadel is distinctly separate from an Egyptian military post. The player must engage with visual representations, symbols, figures, patterns, and images like virtual characters, signs, objects, and items. Although players can choose to ignore dialogue, text, and other kinds of narrative (e.g., skipping cutscenes), they cannot play the game without engaging with these visual elements. Developers and designers do not explain all the problems, rules, themes, and systems of their game through words, but additionally through visuals.

In the game, players do not only see the world only through the protagonist's eyes but also through *eagle vision* which is the viewpoint of the character's pet Senu. Senu is a female eagle that is not only a pet but furthermore a partner and a friend that shows the protagonist the enemy spots and points of interest. The protagonist (and the players) can observe the ground world from the eagle's perspective. In fact, eagles form a powerful part of the *Assassin's Brotherhood* mythos, as the design of order's equipment and weapons have a resemblance to eagles in their details. In some religions, eagles are mythical and religious pets. This symbolic animal is identified with Zeus and Jupiter in popular mythology. The franchise maintained a practice of focusing on special character names identified with eagles: Altair, Ezio, Arno, Haytham, Arbaaz, Orelov, and Griffin.[2] In some religions, eagles are spiritual messengers between gods and humankind.

Finally, the eagle is the Assassin's symbol. During one of the ending scenes of the game, Bayek and Aya show up on the coasts of Alexandria where they reject their old identities and ideas. Bayek rips the eagles' skull necklace that he wore throughout the game and throws it on the ground. The necklace belonged to Bayek's child Khemu and served as a symbol for revenge for his son. While Bayek

---

[2]Altair is of Arabic origin and means flying eagle or bird. Ezio is of Greek origin means eagle. Arno is of German origin and means strong as an eagle. Haytham is of Arabic origin and means young eagle. Arbaaz is of Urdu origin and means eagle. Orelov is of Russian origin and means the son of the eagle. Griffin is of English origin and is the name of a mythological half-eagle, half-lion creature.

steps away, Aya takes the eagles' skull and holds it up to the light. As a result, the Assassins Symbol forms on the sand.

Another repeating visual element is the apple which is one of the most common fruit in world religions and has complex meanings to different cultures. The apple has often been highlighted in fairytales and myths of human societies. Modern Christian belief holds that Adam and Eve picked an apple from the forbidden tree in the Garden of Eden. As told similarly in the Quran, Adam and his partner were dismissed from Heaven and sent to the Earth for eating the forbidden apple. The Greek hero Heracles picks the golden apples from the Tree of Life. ACO has redesigned these holy stories to create its own origin story wherein the Apple of Eden is an item you can possess in the game for the purpose of controlling human minds.

While talking about the visual aesthetics of the game, one important mention would be the design of the *afterlife* in the Curse of the Pharaohs (CoP) downloadable content (DLC) as it relies a lot on religious undertones. Although death is frequent in games, the idea of an afterlife rarely comes into the spotlight unless the game's story is supposed to take the player exclusively into the afterlife (e.g., *Dante's Inferno* the game). For example, in the game *Super Mario Bros.*, if Mario touches an enemy, he falls under the screen and "dies," only to be resurrected by spending a "life." If all the lives are spent, the character dies permanently and the game is over. Although games may provide superficial explanations about how their fictional world rules work, they almost never provide an explanation about lives, resurrection, and permanent death. In ACO CoP, Bayek, the game's protagonist, visits four afterlife sections: Aaru, Ateh, Heh Sed, and Duat. The afterlife sections are designed as an extension of the real world and the protagonists can do missions there just like what they would do in the game's world. This is in line with the concept of the afterlife in ancient Egypt since ancient Egyptians believed life and the afterlife to be eternal cycles that follow each other. In this way, death in ACO CoP is not a punishment but the soul's separation from the body is an extension of the soul's immortality through death and rebirth. This is a different kind of religious approach to death in contrast to other games where death is just a tool to punish the players for being unsuccessful.

16.4.1.3 Audio

Audio is one of the primary tools that inform the player of the outcome of their actions in videogames. Sounds are the most suitable storytellers about the player's location, surroundings, and progress. Audio is subconsciously internalized during gameplay since as Collins (2008, p. 3) argues "[. . .] game players play an active role in the triggering of sound events in the game (including dialogue, ambient sounds, sound effects, and even musical events)."

Videogames merge different types of sound representations: Dialogue (DX), Ambience (AMB), Sound Effects (SFX), Foley (FLY), and Music (MX). DX is a representation of any speech in the game; AMB is a description of background/environment sound; SFX is a symbol of any noise from real-life objects makes; FLY is an image of any sound/audio effect that player character makes; and MX is a representation of any sound source which is visible on the screen and applying for appending dramatic effects.

Audio is the best way to affect to player emotionally. Peerdeman (2010, p. 1) points out that, as compared to the first games back in arcade times "modern day games feature complex orchestrated dynamic soundtracks to accompany the movie-like experience along with context supporting sound effects that contribute to the immersion, or emotional involvement of the player."

ACO's sound design is, unsurprisingly, inspired by ancient Egypt. The sound effects construct an atmosphere of the desert, swamps, orientalist mystical cities, and ruins. The music is enigmatic and dark. The voice acting for both protagonists was performed by British voice actors (although the voice of Bayek, Abubakar Salim has family origins from Africa) but they worked with "a dialect coach and historian [. . .] to try and decide on accents, as well as using Egyptian words in places" (Jones 2018).

16.4.2   Game Context

ACO portrays a creative mix of high realistic architecture, environment, and lighting. Additionally, the game portrays an abundance of nature, aesthetically delightful environments, and architectural patterns. The environment of the game portrays elements from multiple cultures with creative scenes. Some of these cultural elements come from a religious background, including the game's origin narrative that is bound to the architecture, environments, capitals, ancient places, and forms that are heavily utilized in the game. The game has an environment that always reflects the real-life world. ACO affords a spectacular and believable image of an ancient Egyptian environment of almost two millennia ago. The game context is culturally arranged and formed through beliefs and mythos, reproduced with high fidelity visuals.

16.4.2.1   Environment

ACO not only takes place in ancient Egypt, but it deeply includes the history, culture, faith, religion, and lifestyles of the people of ancient Egypt to create an authentic atmosphere. To understand the environment design of ACO from the lens of religion, we merge two viewpoints. On one hand, Salen and Zimmermann (2004, p. 378) maintain that "playing a game means interacting with and within a representational universe, a space of possibility with narrative dimensions." On the other hand, Geertz (1973, p. 90) defines religion as: "(1) a system of symbols which acts to (2) establish powerful, pervasive, and long-lasting moods and motivations in men by (3) formulating conceptions of a general order of existence and (4) clothing these conceptions with such an aura of factuality that (5) the moods and motivations seem uniquely realistic."

In this light, a videogame also creates a similar system of symbols that aims to capture its players in a self-contained reality through interaction. To do that, game creators concentrate on the player and environment associations. To play a game is to engage with the order, laws, and rules of a universe. While we examine ACO, it is possible to observe that the environment relies on a real-world representation that hopes to be as authentic and factual as possible by following the rules of our natural world while still implementing the rules of its own reality. In this aspect, real-world architecture details and religious references accommodate the visual environment. Ubisoft Montreal Senior Creative Director Jean Guesdon explains the most complex part of bringing ancient Egypt to life (World Gaming 2017):

The biggest challenge was that for the most part, Ancient Egypt is a lost world and there is not much left of it. So, we had to work very closely with historians (we even have one embedded in the team!) and Egyptian experts to help us fill in the gaps of Egyptian life not easily found in history books. For some elements, this lack of reference also challenged us to create and illustrate parts of Ancient Egypt rather than recreate known history as we did with past games.

The game map was prepared with realistic details. The gameplay area allows the players to journey between the lands of ancient Egypt and Libya. The players are also able to tour significant capital landmarks such as Giza, Memphis, Cyrene, Alexandria, and Nile Delta. The environment portrayed in the game is undeniably attractive and merges traditional design details with creative additions.

16.4.2.2 Architecture

The game world of ACO is huge so that it includes "a lot of locations to travel that will allow [the game] to show how rich ancient Egypt was" (Wallace 2017). Popular imaginations of ancient Egypt probably consist of wastelands, pyramids, pharaohs, and deserts, but ACO presents more than these regular representations. For example, the locations like the Nile Delta are represented very green with crocodiles hiding in the swamps; and Alexandria, with its Greek form and the volume of the structure. The ancient capital of Memphis, at the opening, is a higher representative of the Old Kingdom, highlighting great minimalistic buildings with temples and mud-brick houses. Also, the deserts in the game are decorated with extraordinary patterns, such as "[. . .] sand dunes, but you also have the white desert with amazing shapes of salty rocks, it looks almost like an alien landscape" (Wallace 2017).

16.4.2.3 Lighting

The creators of the game examined technological documentation from NASA to discover how airborne particles affect lighting (Palumbo 2017). Then, they studied how various grounds reflect light to realistically portray different types of water, which can give the player an idea of what kinds of wildlife they can contain just by looking at it. In an interview (Iamag n.d.), the artistic director of the game, Raphael Lacoste provides more insights:

AC origins is going to impress a lot with the visual quality of the lighting, composition and drawing distance. The lighting is using a new rendering engine, recreated from scratch by our best engineers. It is allowing us to render in real time a physically based lighting with global illumination and sky model with procedural clouds, stars, working in real time for a 24-hour cycle. The world looks very impressive also thanks to the lighting and rendering, not only because of the visual composition. As the lighting is a physical simulation, we had to make some artistic choice though, allowing our artist to create specific moods, dynamic moments in the lightning and atmosphere.

Studying the impressions that the lighting creates in the game, it is possible to notice some preferences that affect the gameplay. ACO employs a whole day and night cycle so that the actual time of the day is not just metaphorical. For example, the game uses some lighting and lighting modifications as a tactic for hiding. With the lighting modification, the player can either complete their missions easier or more complex; the same function goes for the action of searching the areas that are controlled by enemies. The daylight in most parts of virtual Egypt and Alexandria is almost always sunny and warm. Knez and Niedenthal (2008, p. 2) maintain that "players perform best and fastest in a game world lit with a warm (reddish) as compared to a cool (bluish) lightning." This effect in ACO is a particularly noticeable experience.

16.4.3 Game Characters

Real-world religions and stories are frequently mobilized as motivations in videogames. *Assassin's Creed* series usually relies on relationships between Orthodox and Catholic Christians, as well as Sunni and Shiite Muslims. Additionally, investigating godly figures are vital for examining religious and holy symbols since they exhibit different religious elements which are taken out of religious metaphor and ideas.

In visual media and press (typically, Western), Egypt, especially ancient Egypt. is usually diminished to tombs, pyramids, deserts, sands, mummies, and camels. Egyptians mythical characters or figures are rarely superlative heroes but are regularly used as side characters or enemies. Scholar Edward Said (1979, p. 109) discusses the representation of the East in media, and underlines that:

None of the innumerable Orientalist text on Islam, including their summa, The Cambridge History of Islam, can prepare their reader for what has taken place since 1948 in Egypt, Palestine, Iraq, Syria, Lebanon, or the Yemens. When the dogmas about Islam cannot serve, not even for the most Panglossian Orientalist, there is recourse to an Orientalized social-science jargon, to such marketable abstractions as elites, political stability, modernization, and institutional development, all stamped with the cachet of Orientalist wisdom. In the main time a growing, more and more dangerous rift separates Orient and Occident.

In ACO, an Egyptian person, Bayek, is the playable central character on screen—which is a rare occurrence. He is not an enemy, walk-in, or a white person; he is a model hero who is protecting his birthplace.

In their article, De Wildt et al. (2018) describe the depiction of religion in games under two broad types: (1) using historical religions—Christian, Muslim, and Buddhist narratives, tropes, and symbols; and, (2) fiction-based religions—based on fantasy, myth, and popular culture. ACO merges these two categories by using real-world religions and myths inside the video game world together. Video games are commonly serviced by religious symbolism, in order to build a more realistic vision of a virtual world. Religion efforts an essential explanation of life and produces appealing storylines that the players can easily become a member of.

ACO provides players with a peek inside the genesis of the franchise's famous brotherhood of assassins. Players already recognize the name Amunet from previous games, who is also identified as the goddess of invisibility. The name, Amunet, signifies "the hidden one," and her past was examined by the protagonist Ezio in *Assassin's Creed II*. The Egyptian brotherhood of assassins is a part of the franchise's cosmology and assists in the formation of future brotherhoods. Remarkably well-known historical and religious figures from antiquity, make an appearance in the game: Cleopatra, Julius Caesar, and Pharaoh Ptolemy XIII. Replacing the Templars as the series' high dangerous villains is *The Order of the Ancients*, a faceless order that controls everything from the shadows. Furthermore, ancient Egyptian gods and goddesses have important appearances in the game world.

16.4.3.1 Player Character(s)

Characters in games offer several social, cultural, and subcultural details. In ACO, the protagonist, Bayek, performs the Egyptian religion and ethics. His outfit design characterizes his true nature: he wears the traditional Assassin hood that is wrecked on the sides and has some aperture, and in some sections, the hood is ripped to symbolize Bayek's economic and social status. His leather arm bracers are full of holes and bedraggled like he had been in numerous fights bearing it. He does not trim his hair or beard in the intermediate cycle between his son's (Khemu) death and the start of the game, which for someone in a formal government position at the time would have been extremely much scowled against. As a Medjay, Bayek wears the proper attire. The Medjay in the ancient empire were a society of protectors who were believed to be planted on earth to work in tandem with the gods and each other. The Medjay would employ methods of meditation and would protect over tombs, monuments, and temples. They might be bodyguards for religious leaders and join the soldier ranks in larger city centers. Creative Director of the game Jean Guesdon assumes that Bayek was a sheriff, a protector of his community, and an advocate of his organization as the very last Medjay (Wallace 2017). Bayek acts and is portrayed as a strongly religious personality, unlike the other Assassins in the series who are unbelievers, agnostics, or atheists. During the *Curse of the Pharaohs* DLC, Bayek relates to Anubis, and he is ultimately confirmed to be *working in the dark, to serve the light*. Bayek travels into the afterlife where he beats many pharaohs and their spirits including Akhenaten, who was praised as an existing god in his own capital.

The second playable character is Bayek's wife, Aya, and a fellow assassin. At the end of the ACO, Aya remembers her past life as Amunet, the Hidden One, who is the Egyptian goddess of air and invisibility. At the beginning of the game, her Assassin outfit is white. However, by the end of *The Hidden Ones* DLC, her outfit becomes very nebulous. She is the first Assassin to dress black.

16.4.3.2   Non-Player Character(s)

ACO portrays powerful non-player characters who are actual historical figures. The protagonists find themselves confined in a political power battle between three major powers: Cleopatra, Ptolemy XIII, and Julius Caesar. The struggle between these three NPCs form the balance of games' ancient historical setting.

As a Pharaoh, Cleopatra is perceived as being a goddess. Aya begins the game by accepting Cleopatra as a breathing goddess and the biggest faith for Egypt's destiny and tomorrow. Cleopatra is portrayed as a truly traditional beauty with ideals and royalty. However, as the game progresses, she is revealed to be connected to the villains of the game, *Order of the Ancients*, along with Caesar. Aya/Amunet ends up killing Cleopatra with snake poison.

Ptolemy XIII is the pharaoh of Egypt and the junior sibling of Cleopatra. He was only 11 years old when rising to the crown. As a result, he was manipulated by the villain organization and killed at the end of ACO by crocodiles. The Nile, which was full of crocodiles, was significant to the subsistence of the Egyptians. Hence, it was a prolific presence to have a god counterpart that could satisfy these wild creatures. In Egyptian mythos, crocodiles were served by the god named Sobek (Sheydet in Greek). Sobek is one of the popular gods and a guardian of the Egyptian people and the Pharaoh. Being a symbol of the Pharaoh's power, Ptolemy's death by crocodiles can be seen as Sobek's punishment.

Cleopatra and Ptolemy XIII are also married. If we look behind the social ideas of the time, the ancient Egyptian royal classes were almost always supposed to marry within the family. Pharaohs not only wed their siblings, but they could also make "double-niece" marriages (a man marrying a woman whose parents are his brother and sister). This also relates to the religious myth that the god Osiris married his sister Isis to continue to keep their bloodlines pure.

In the game, Gaius Julius Caesar is the general of the Roman Republic and the partner of Cleopatra. Cleopatra obtained Caesar's support and the couple become lovers. Caesar tries to enable Cleopatra to get the crown of Egypt, dethroning Ptolemy XIII. While this love and power triangle is not known to be historically accurate, it is presented as a reality in the game. Due to his connection with the villain organization, Caesar is killed by Aya/Amunet by being stabbed 33 times in his back. The number 33 has connotations in multiple religions. In Islam, the

Qur'an was sent in a total of 23 years to the Prophet Muhammed. The first lines of the Qur'an were delivered to the Prophet Muhammed on the 23rd night of the ninth Islamic month. In Christianity, Psalm 23, more remembered as the Shepherd Psalm, is maybe the most requested and well-known one. Principia Discordia, the text of Discordianism, includes 23 as one of the holy numbers of Eris, the goddess of division. In Jewish culture, the first-century historian Josephus states that Adam and Eve had 23 daughters.

In the game, the villain organization, Order of the Ancients, is represented with the snake symbol, as compared to the assassin's eagle. Snakes are oftentimes connected with evil, the Satanic prototype, and the forbidden fruit. Many religious and mythical legends involve snake beasts that are destroyed or otherwise crushed by a hero or god.

16.4.3.3   God(s)

Eliade (1961, p. 32) states that "to organize a space is to repeat the paradigmatic work of the gods." In this light, organizing a virtual space is the potential of becoming a god within it. Hence, the players have the power of gods (at least in some respects) inside the virtual space of the game.

Within the world of ACO, like pharaohs, Cleopatra and Ptolemy start the game as "gods" and the protagonists as their "subjects." However, as the game progresses, the protagonists realize that neither of the figures is a "real" god and end up killing them. In this action, they also remember their past lives as gods or having relation to gods. Thus, the whole game works as a metaphor for transference of power between gods and their subjects—humans becoming gods by killing them. *The Curse of the Pharaohs* DLC dismisses some parts of this metaphor and constructs a more mythological narrative by having Bayek travel to the afterlife to confront immortal pharaohs, powers, gods, and other mythological animals. The content takes a step out of the main story's metaphor and presents a mystical and mythologic angle. The force of religion and myth stays at the center as an indispensable force in ACO.

16.4.4   Discussion

In this study, we analyzed the use of religious elements in *Assassin's Creed Origins*. The game uses religious symbols coming from real-world religions in its environments, narratives, and characters, and lets the players interact with them. We find that ACO uses religious undertones to increase its realism and historical authenticity. The religious symbolism is merged with architecture, environment design, and lighting design. In the game's narrative, the themes of gods versus servants, servants uprising against the "false" gods, killing and replacing them as gods themselves are underlined.

We do exist in a time when virtual worlds and realities are increasingly challenging and displacing the physical reality. Religions are bound to be reshaped by this cultural shift. We assert that the gameplay activity is culturally mediated and formed through cultural and social experiences, beliefs, and existing knowledge. The cultural or subcultural patterns, information, and attitudes are of utmost importance as they have a direct influence on how a game is received, seen, and played. Here it must be mentioned that this is not unique only for games like *Assassin's Creed Origins* that simulate a realistic and semi-historical background but even for the ones that are heavily stylized. Šisler (2017, p. 127) asserts that "game authors increasingly use mythologies and belief systems as their referents, making tangible connections to the outside world" and "as a consequence, games can reflect, reject, or reconfigure religious ideas and are a source for the production of religious practices and ideas in modernity."

We should be aware of the power of videogames and their impressions on their players' religious life. Videogames allow further informal and fluid-like-structures than linear forms of media and communication (e.g., television, radio, etc.) that allow their messages to be more interpretative. As a result of this study, we would like to position videogames as components and extensions of the socio-cultural discourses between the social groups (e.g., developers, players, content creators, etc.) who are embedded in the game's presence in different ways. Religious elements in videogames serve as cultural frameworks that are open to critical analysis and, furthermore, games and religions share similar structural components that situate them in adjacent places within the human experience.

A.1   Ludography

Assassin's Creed (Ubisoft, 2007)
Assassin's Creed II (Ubisoft, 2009)
Assassin's Creed Origins (Ubisoft, 2017)
Dante's Inferno (EA, 2010)
Far Cry 4 (Ubisoft, 2014)
Legend of Zelda (Nintendo, 1986)
Super Mario Bros. (Nintendo, 1985)
World of Warcraft (Blizzard Entertainment, 2004)

References

C. L. Albanese, *America: Religions and Religion*. (Belmont, CA: Wadsworth Pub. 1999), p. 8
W.S. Bainbridge, *The Warcraft Civilization: Social Science in a Virtual World* (MIT Press, Cambridge, 2010)

W.S. Bainbridge, W.A. Bainbridge, Electronic game research methodologies: studying religious implications,' Rev. Religious Res. (2007), pp. 35–53

I. Bogost, *Persuasive Games: The Expressive Power of Videogames* (MIT Press, Cambridge, 2007)

K. Borchard, Super columbine massacre RPG! and grand theft autoethnography. Cult. Stud. **15**(6), 446–454 (2015). https://doi.org/10.1177/1532708615614018

F.G. Bosman, The sacred and the digital: critical depictions of religions in digital games. Religions **10**(2), 130 (2019). https://doi.org/10.3390/rel10020130

J. Campbell, *The Hero with a Thousand Faces* (New World Library, Novato, 2008)

H.A. Campbell, The rise of the study of digital religion, in *Digital Religion: Understanding Religious Practice in New Media Worlds*, (Routledge, London, 2013), pp. 1–21

H.A. Campbell, G. Grieve, *What Playing with Religion Offer Digital Game Studies* (Indiana University Press, Bloomington, IN, 2014)

K. Collins, *Game Sound: An Introduction to the History, Theory, and Practice of Video Game Music and Sound Design* (MIT Press, Cambridge, 2008)

Corliss, *Gaming with God: A Case for the Study of Religion in Video Games*, Unpublished Thesis (2011)

L. De Wildt, S. Aupers, C. Krassen, I. Coanda, Things greater than thou: post-apocalyptic religion in games. Religions **9**(6), 169 (2018)

M. Eliade, *The Sacred and the Proface: The Nature of Religion* (Harcourt, Brace & Worls, New York, 1961)

C. Geertz, *The Interpretation of Culture* (Basic Books, New York, 1973)

J. Huizinga, *Homo Ludens: A Study of the Play-Element in Culture* (Routledge, London, 1949)

Iamag, Assassin's Creed: the origins of art – exclusive interview with artistic director Raphael Lacoste, *IAMAG.co* (n.d.). Available from https://www.iamag.co/assassins-creed-the-origins-of-art-exclusive-interview-with-artistic-director-raphael-lacoste/. Accessed 21 Feb 2021

S. Jäger, Discourse and knowledge: theoretical and methodological aspects of a critical discourse and dispositive analysis, in *Methods of Critical Discourse Analysis*, (Sage, Thousand Oaks, 2001), pp. 32–54

E. Janish, Shoot the gun inside: doubt and feminist epistemology in video games, in *Feminism in Play*, (Palgrave Macmillan, Cham, 2018), pp. 221–234

H. Jenkins, Game design as narrative architecture. Computer **44**(3) (2004)

A. Jones, *Assasssin's Creed: Origins – The Sound of Ancient Egypt. The Sound Architect* (2018). Available from https://www.thesoundarchitect.co.uk/assassins-creed-origins-the-sound-of-ancient-egypt/. Accessed 21 Feb 2021

I. Knez, S. Niedenthal, Lighting in digital game worlds: effects on affect and play performance. Cyberpsychol. Behav. **11**(2), 129–137 (2008)

T. Krzywinska, Blood scythes, festivals, quests, and backstories: world creation and rhetorics of myth in world of Warcraft. Games Cult. **1**(4), 383–396 (2006)

L. Leibovitz, *God in the Machine: Video Games as Spiritual Pursuit* (Templeton Press, West Conshohoken, PA, 2013)

A. Palumbo Everything you wanted to know of Assassin's Creed Origins, including Ubisoft studying NASA documents. WCCFTech.com (2017). Available from https://wccftech.com/everything-about-assassins-creed-origins/. Accessed 21 Feb 2020

P. Peerdeman, Sound and music in games. *VU Amsterdam* (2010). Avaliable from https://peterpeerdeman.nl/vu/ls/peerdeman_sound_and_music_in_games.pdf. Accessed 21 Feb 2021

M. Ryan, The narratorial functions: breaking down a theoretical primitive. Narrative **9**(2), 146–152 (2001)

E. Said, *Orientalism* (Vintage Books Edition, New York, 1979)

K. Salen, E. Zimmermann, *Rules of Play: Game Design Fundamentals* (MIT Press, Cambridge, 2004)

A. Shaw, Rethinking game studies: a case study approach to video game play and identification. Crit. Stud. Media Commun. **30**(5), 347–361 (2013)

V. Šisler, Procedural religion: methodological reflections on studying religion in video games. New Media Soc. **19**(1), 126–141 (2017)

V. Šisler, K. Radde-Antweiler, X. Zeiler, *Methods for Studying Video Games and Religion* (Routledge, New York, NY, 2018)

T.L. Taylor, T. Boellstroff, C. Pearce, B. Nardi, *Ethnography and Virtual Worlds: A Handbook of Method* (Princeton University Press, Princeton, 2012)

K. Wallace, Five things you need to know about Assassin's Creed Origins. GameInformer.com (2017). Available from https://www.gameinformer.com/b/features/archive/2017/06/11/five-things-you-need-to-know-about-assassin-s-creed-origins.aspx. Accessed 21 Feb 2020

World Gaming, *Interview with Ubisoft Montreal's Jean Guesdon. Inside World Gaming* (2017). Available from https://inside.worldgaming.com/assassins-creed-origins-interview-ubisoft-montreals-jean-guesdon/. Accessed 20 Oct 2019

Xbox Gazette, Assassin's Creed: interview with Jade Raymond. XboxGazette.com (2006). Available from http://www.xboxgazette.com/interview_assassins_creed_en.php. Accessed 18 Feb 2021

Chapter 17
Longform Video Essays as Critical Retellings of Video Game Narratives

Tonguc Ibrahim Sezen and Digdem Sezen

17.1 Introduction

Between May and August 2003, *GameFAQs* user Peter Eliot posted his 36,000-word walkthrough of the award-winning action-adventure game *Ico* (2001) on the website's message boards in serialized form. Later collected under the title *Talking Ico: An Annotation* (Eliot 2004), the walkthrough was a detailed retelling of Eliot's own gameplay experiences. Focusing on narrative aspects of *Ico*, it was an intrinsically critical record of the game in action, providing unique insights to it. Eliot's text not only described and discussed *Ico*'s flow with occasional references to other games and media, but also explored the roots of his own emotional responses to the game, revealing according to Jürgen Sorg (2009), how game actions can be both narratively motivated and emotionally stimulated. In this regard, videogame critique Jacob Geller (2020) describes *Talking Ico: An Annotation* as an early example of self-reflective longform retellings of videogame experiences, a precursor of contemporary grassroots videogame criticism, in terms of both style and content.

Self-reporting gameplay sessions is an old phenomenon dating back to early 1980s (Consalvo 2014). Videogame fans create such texts for different purposes using different technologies. In a 2003 essay, Mia Consalvo describes how early walkthroughs, or detailed chronological descriptions of game actions usually created by fans to guide other players to a successful completion of a game, were written both in descriptive and artistic styles. According to Mirjam Palosaari Eladhari (2018), retelling practices can be found in a broad spectrum ranging from daily conversations about a game to more elaborate efforts, such as blogs on game characters, walkthroughs, fan fiction, "after-action reports" inspired by military self-

T. I. Sezen · D. Sezen (✉)
Department of Transmedia, Digital Art and Animation, Teesside University, Middlesbrough, UK
e-mail: t.sezen@tees.ac.uk; d.sezen@tees.ac.uk

267
B. Bostan (ed.), *Games and Narrative: Theory and Practice*, International Series on Computer Entertainment and Media Technology,
https://doi.org/10.1007/978-3-030-81538-7_17

analysis methodologies, video recordings of game play sessions or the so called "Let's Play" videos, online player or avatar diaries, and newsletters written by player teams. Egenfeldt-Nielsen et al. (2020) position forms of retellings amongst other creative activities inspired by games such as modding and machinima making, which they call forms of "productive play". De Grove and Van Looy (2014) point out the differences between written and audio-visual walkthroughs: While the first is ideal to deliver detailed information, latter is more suited for showing game flow itself. Focusing on various types of retellings, including walkthroughs, game guides, FAQs, and wikis, James Newman (2016) argues that they should be seen as archival documents on pleasures of play, replay, and variations in play. Written through systematic and investigative play which in a way reverse-engineers games, these retellings raise questions on the diversity of recorded player performances: "Whose performance should be legitimized and recorded? How should a player play the game, and how might we account for the variation in performances?" (Newman 2016 p. 415). According to Newman (2016), the answers to these questions can also be found in retellings, since they collectively provide the most detailed and comprehensive records on the diverse gameplay opportunities brought to life through ongoing interactions between players and games as unstable objects.

Apperley and Walsh (2012) and Souvik Mukherje (2016) describe retellings as experiential game narratives, as videogame "paratexts", or threshold material surrounding a main text (Genette 1997). Videogames as multi-faceted drillable texts with an intrinsic multiplicity, provide fertile ground for diverse forms of paratextual retellings interpreting and investigating them, which potentially can also influence the reception of games by other players. As narrative texts they report not only game stories but also how players interact with them. In this regard, this chapter discusses retellings as texts revealing players' story experiences emerging out of narrative design in action and focuses on critical video essays as an emerging retelling form.

17.2 Retellings as Narrative Products

Videogames are performed texts requiring player interaction to fully emerge. As Noah Wardrip-Fruin (2009) points out, without players there is no game. According to Brenda Laurel (2014), while game designers shape game worlds and their affordances, players are also given an authorship force in creating distinct paths through these game worlds. Clara Fernandez-Vara describes the relationship between the player as a performer and the game "a negotiation between scripted behaviours and improvisation based on the system" (Fernandez-Vara 2009, p. 7). The system defines the limits of the unique instances the player can create. In this process the player acts both as an active performer but also as the audience of the same performance, since, according to Fernandez-Vara, "she is the one who makes sense of the system and interacts accordingly" (Fernandez-Vara 2009, p. 6). In this regard, Jukka Vahlo (2018) differentiates between macro-level game systems which shape the possibilities of play, and players' unique micro-level trajectories, or their unique experiences. According to Vahlo, between these two there is also a third, meso-level enactment of recurrent game patterns formed by retellings. In other words, retellings are paratexts of both games and play, and players' performances shape retellings as much as games' affordances.

According to Consalvo, the presence of retellings "suggest that game fans are invested in some sort of narrative in games, and some will go to great lengths to create or maintain narrative integrity or cohesiveness" (Consalvo 2003, p. 328). Much like games, and even more so, game narratives require players' willingness and participation to emerge. Games, according to Jesper Juul (2005) are "half-real", meaning they are played by real rules with real consequences, but at the same time, they invite players to imagine a secondary world to which their game play is reflected as fictional actions. Players who author retellings can focus on their personal experiences on both real and fictional levels, leading to the creation of different kinds of retellings. Susana Pajares Tosca (2003) argues that the "action level" in games would lead to the creation of retellings with instructional descriptions constructed around problem solving, while the "plot level" which exists in games where the narrative plays an important role, would lead to narrative retellings of player experiences which would make sense as stories with character motivation and feelings.

Tamer Thabet (2015) argues that the reproduction of the play experience as a narrative retelling is an inevitable outcome of the lack of an invariant narrative text in videogames which can be analyzed collectively. In videogames, according to Thabet, "there is only an ad hoc narrative construction that may be reported as post factum by the player" (Thabet 2015, p. 62). At its core Thabet's approach parallels with Hartmut Koenitz's (2015) theoretical framework for interactive digital narratives, which differentiates between the protostory, or the procedural blueprint containing the potential narrative experiences in an interactive digital narrative, and the narrative product, which represents the narrative instantiated by the interactor by running the system. A protostory is not an invariant narrative text, and a narrative retelling can be considered a narrative product reported post factum by the player. The relationship between the protostory and the narrative product, can be observed not only in narrative driven games with high agency such as role-playing games, but also in games with emergent narratives. Life simulation or grand strategy games without previously established plots such as *The Sims* (Maxis 2000–2014) or the *Crusader Kings* (Paradox 2007–2020) series give players the opportunity to control the fate of an individual or a nation, and to form personal or epic stories not foreseen in their exact form by the designers. Even in games with static storylines communicated through cutscenes or scripted events, which Richard Rouse III (2004) describes as the "designer's story", the players' decisions in gameplay sessions still construct unique personal stories of action. These "player's stories" surround and provide a unique context to the designer's story and thus shape the personal narrative product.

Echoing Thabet and Koenitz, Mukherje (2016) argues that videogame narratives are not established but only exist in a state of becoming through paratexts. He uses the Deleuzoguattarian concept of "minor literature" to approach this emerging understanding of narrative multiplicity, which refuses and transforms the standard notion of narrative. He considers the game narrative "as an assemblage that plugs into various systems of meaning-making, different kinds of media assemblages, the imagination and experience assemblage of the player, and also paratextual assemblages" (Mukherje 2016, p. 71). According to Mukherje, such ephemeral narratives based on gameplay experiences should not be considered as stories in themselves; rather, they exist as part of a videogame narrative assemblage in the becoming, which includes the videogame itself as well. Similarly, retellings, Eladhari (2018) argues can be seen as the fourth layer of text constituting interactive narrative systems in addition to the code layer, content layer, and narrative discourse. Retellings, as narrative products are thus directly linked to and carry reflections of these levels.

According to Koenitz (2015), the narrative product, which he describes as the walkthrough of a single game play session, should only be considered a limited representation of an interactive digital narrative's internal systems and processes, since interacting with these potentially can create multiple alternative products as well. Thabet (2015), on the other hand offers a solution to this limitation by positioning retellings as critical tools to be used by players who already have played the same game and seek different perspectives on the experiences offered by it: "Retelling", Thabet argues, "allows analysis to be extendable to other interpretations of the same story and to other stories" (Thabet 2015, p. 62). In other words, the main audience of a narrative product in the form of a retelling are usually players who already produced their own versions of it, and thus can make comparisons on the processes which caused the differences between various products. Moreover, many retellings are amalgams of multiple playthroughs combining multiple repetitions, failures, and explorations, reflecting the experiences and lessons taken from them.

17.3   Studying Videogame Narratives through Retellings

The use of retellings in game studies has been discussed by multiple researchers since mid-2010s. According to Fernandez-Vara (2014), the extension of paratextuality into the study of videogames opens new ways of analyzing their complexity by providing multiple layers of interpretation and reconstruction. Mukherje (2016) and Eladhari (2018) argue that paratextual retellings play a significant role in understanding how videogame narratives work and can be instrumental in critiquing interactive narrative systems. Focusing on the content of retellings and players' role in creating them, Tero Kerttula (2016) argues that retellings should be analyzed as stories about playing videogames. As highly personalized narratives of game experiences, retellings may reveal players' emotions, reactions, and thought processes during play, and thus can be used to investigate how game stories are formed through players' input.

Recent studies on retellings have been fruitful in revealing aspects of the relationship between player experiences and narrative design in videogames. The broad spectrum of retelling forms diversified the focus, scale, and methodological approaches of these studies. Analyzing written retellings in conjunction with author interviews Kreminski et al. (2019) revealed how retelling authors tend to complete game stories through interpretation and evocation. Players not only report events of a particular play experience, but also their own juxtapositions to create coherent narratives, a process Kreminski et al. call "extrapolative narrativization" (Kreminski et al. 2019). Conceptualizing ludonarratives as a whole consisting of gameplay, narrative, and player, Toh (2019) analyzed players' simultaneous narration and commentaries recorded during gameplay, together with open-ended qualitative interviews. Borrowing it from Recktenwald (2014), Toh used the "Let's Play Onion" model which differentiates and acknowledges player, game, distribution platform, and retelling production conventions as layers shaping retellings. Toh's multimodal analysis revealed various types of ludonarrative relationships, ranging from dissonance where the narrative and gameplay have a conflicting relationship, to resonance where the relationship is harmonizing, and finally irrelevance which refers to a weak relationship. Each with multiple subcategories, these relationships are shaped by individual players' performance, perception, and interpretation. Investigating processes shaping ludonarrative relationships, in particular ludonarrative dissonance, Roth et al. (2018) treated Let's Play videos as unedited think-aloud protocols for conversation analysis. They argued that players synchronically reflected on possibilities of narrative game mechanics and interpreted the narrative product they have instantiated through two separate but related hermeneutic processes. As long as their expectations and the results of their interactions match, they negotiate meanings in a fashion much like extrapolative narrativization and even claim authorship over uncontrollable experiences offered by games. Ludonarrative dissonance, Roth et al. (2018) argue, emerges at moments when the narrative products players instantiated differ from the protostories they had imagined. The shared meaning-making activity between designer and players break as players' agency is taken from them.

Despite utilizing Let's Play videos in investigating ludonarrative processes Roth et al. (2018) acknowledge that these retellings may be "over-performed" due to platform conventions. In other words, the transmedial context of retellings may affect how players perform their experiences to their audiences. In this regard, Radde-Antweiler and Zeiler (2015), propose a three-part analysis matrix, consisting of game, performance, and comments. The matrix provides a grounded overview of each component of production and consumption separately. While the model's approach disconnects the retelling as an artefact from the game it is based on, it also reveals the importance of a retelling's media and distribution channels in their conception. Investigating grassroots media on videogames, including fan reviews, walkthroughs, and other retelling practices, Alejandro Soler (2014) points out how most content creators fall under the financial influence of game developers, or are forced to create deliberately over-performing personas such as "angry-nerds" to remain relevant on their distribution channels. In Newman's (2019) words they must create "consumable personas" as media producers. In such cases retellings lose their genuineness as recordings of player experiences.

Emerging out of calls (Bittanti 2004; Costikyan 2008; Thomas et al. 2009) for a professional videogame journalism beyond the boundaries of commercially motivated videogame reviewing, the idea of videogame criticism proposes an independent path which can be adopted in retelling creation as well. According to Ayse Gursoy (2013), proper game "criticism doesn't try to be objective and impartial, or rather, it tries to be objective and impartial about its own subject perspective" (Gursoy 2013, p. 94). Pointing out the ephemeral, performed, and fluid nature of videogames Gursoy (2013) argues that their criticism should be description-based, capture game play experiences, and respect the possibility of failure; features which parallel scholarly descriptions of retellings. In this regard Steven Sych (2020) suggests the concept of "critical retellings" which he describes a subset of retellings that do not directly track the success of a narrative system but instead take a deliberately critical stand towards it. Sych defines critical retellings as "a kind of immanent critique that is both compelling as a retelling and (simultaneously) self-reflexive analysis of a computational narrative system" (Sych 2020, p. 205). Critical retellings, according to Sych (2020), provide commentary on the flaws in a game's system, tend to be more anecdotal, target an experienced and knowing audience, use irony in their criticism, and "explicitly reference and reflect on the mechanics of the narrative system, or the nature of the narrative system itself" (Sych 2020, p. 210). Sych's description emphasizes the role of subjectivity, self-reflexivity, and satirical position while experiencing games, and during analyzing and interpreting narrative outcomes of game systems. Like Kerttula (2016), he positions the players at the center of his approach and sees critical retellings not only as a product of narrative systems but also as deliberate commentaries.

17.4   Longform Video Essays as Critical Retellings

While Sych (2020) describes critical retellings as short, sharp, ironical texts, according to Mitch Cramer (2020), one of the most prominent contemporary forms of non-scholarly videogame criticism is the longform video essay. Elaborate, personal, and creative, longform video essays retell game experiences with a deliberately critical stand towards videogame systems. While not complete narrative products instantiated in one uninterrupted play through, they do fall under the general definitions of paratextual retellings and can be seen as a variation of critical retellings. Game vlogger Noah Caldwell-Gervais' video essays can be seen as examples of longform video essays as critical retellings. He produces in-depth, several hours long analyses, retrospectives and critiques of popular and obscure videogame franchises and individual videogames. As a game critique, Caldwell-Gervais has been compared to Roger Ebert for legitimizing the form of videogames and demonstrating its potential (Good 2020), and his video corpus has been described as an example of open scholarship in videogame studies due to its depth and quality (Saklofske 2020).

In his two-hour long video essay titled *How does the Last of Us Part 2 compare to the Last of Us Remastered?* Caldwell-Gervais (2020) presents his experiences in playing both incarnations of the videogame series *The Last of Us* (hereafter *TLoU*) and discusses the connections between gameplay, narrative design, and the story. *TLoU* (Naughty Dog 2013) and its sequel *TLoU Part II* (Naughty Dog 2020), are action-adventure games set in a post-apocalyptic future. Featuring elements of the survival horror genre, they share a character-driven linear narrative design. *TLoU* was praised (Anyó and Colom 2021) for its representation of its protagonists Joel and Ellie, a hardened man, and a young girl, who throughout the game develop a father-daughter relationship, leading Joel to commit questionable acts of violence to protect Ellie at the end of the game. *TLoU Part II* starts with the murder of Joel by the daughter of one of his victims from the previous game, Abby, and then follows the crossing paths of now vengeful Ellie and Abby with their respected companions Dina and Lev, till a final confrontation on now both broken characters. Both the choice of killing off Joel and making Abby a protagonist alongside a hostile Ellie in *TLoU Part II* has caused negative reactions in some fan communities. One of the prominent names to vocalize these reactions was the popular game vlogger, Jose Antonio Vargas, known by his popularized and commercialized angry-nerd persona *Angry Joe*. According to Fleury and Mamber (2019), mixing criticism with costumed reenactments, Vargas' videos voice passionate and opinionated audience reactions towards games and the gaming industry. In his 50-minute review of *TLoU Part II* Vargas says: "We didn't want to return to this story only to see our characters butchered and broken and left worse by someone the writers want us so desperately to care about instead" (Vargas 2020). Vargas' reaction can be seen as the vocalization of ludonarrative dissonance emerging out of the disruption of players' expectations from the game's narrative, and for being asked to play a character perceived as villainous, against the allegiances build towards Ellie and Joel as player characters. Providing a nuanced reaction to *TLoU Part II*, Caldwell-Gervais' (2020) retelling in comparison describes the narrative direction of the series as creatively unique and genuinely surprising, as it allows the player to discover the other side of the same story from the opponents' perspective. He argues that the designers expected the players to feel anger towards Abby, and at the same time allowed them to explore her perspective and invited them to re-evaluate the story of the previous game critically. Accepting this invitation, he notes:

> *The Last of Us Part II* impressed me, surprised me, [it] took chances in directions I never expected it to, and none of those directions would have been possible with Joel in the picture … It's the reverse of the first *Last of Us* which began from a perspective of positivity and hope, and then laid out how it could unravel into an act of tremendous selfishness and cruelty. Here, instead, we begin with an act of stunning violence and hatred, and then unwrap the bandages from those wounds until something more hopeful appears amid the raw and bleeding chaos. (Caldwell-Gervais 2020, N.A.)

The differences between Vargas' and Caldwell-Gervais' positions reflect how players' interaction with the same narrative design can both lead to ludonarrative dissonance and ludonarrative resonance. This divergence also mirrors Newman's (2016) questions on the diversity of retellings: Whose performance should be prioritized and why? Moreover, what differentiates critical retellings in terms of their representation of players' construction of ludonarrative relationships from retellings build around consumable personas?

Eladhari (2018) proposes the use of data mining methodologies in analyzing retellings to reveal shared and diverging aspects. The open-source, web-based text analytics and visualization tool Voyant (Sinclair and Rockwell 2016), which provides word frequency and collocate data may prove useful in such a comparison. A Voyant analysis of closed caption transcriptions of Vargas' review and Caldwell-Gervais' essay's sections on TLoU Part II, provides details which can be interpreted as indicators of how they approached and discussed the game's narrative design. The first clue can be found in the top-five repeating phrases in both texts. While Caldwell-Gervais' repeating phrases are variations of "TLoU Part II is", only two of Vargas' top five follow the same descriptive pattern. His remaining phrases are "I don't know what to do!", "What are you doing Ellie, no!", and "Hey, are you out of [your mind]!", which reflect his reactionary attitude. A similar divergence can also be found in the authors' most repeated words left after ignoring common English words. Caldwell-Gervais mainly focuses on protagonists, with Ellie (104), Abby (68), Joel (56), and Lev (34) being in top five. The rest of his most repeated words reflect his discussions on game time, with "moment" (33) and "time" (26), and the core themes of the story, with "violence" (34) and "revenge" (31). "Game" (92) and "player" (31) are in the list as unavoidable terms to be used in a text on videogames. Ellie (31), Abby (25), and Joel (19) are also amongst Vargas' top-ten most repeated words, alongside "characters" (28), "story" (21), and "good" (19) which reflect his interest on the narrative and quality of the game. Nevertheless, unlike Caldwell-Gervais, Vargas also regularly used exclamations "yeah" (21) and "oh" (18). Profanity, collected under one category by the closed captioning software, has the highest word count of 74, followed only by the inescapable "game" (49). Detecting wordcounts is only way of analyzing videogame retellings with Voyant. Word frequencies within the texts reveal on which subjects the authors focus as they retell the game.

Character names use frequencies of Vargas and Caldwell-Gervais (see Fig. 17.1), reveal which characters they focus and prioritize in their retellings. While Vargas scarcely shows interest on specific characters, Caldwell-Gervais focuses on each main character and discusses them in connection with each other. His discussion of Lev, Abby's companion character, stands out in his retelling since Lev plays a major role in the personal story of Abby and thus potentially shapes her image for the players.

Another way of investigating how the authors approached characters is identifying their collocates (see Fig. 17.2). In Vargas' text, collocates of the main character names reveal little of how he perceives them, with verbs being used frequently. Joel being habitually juxtaposed with "death" and "game" is not a surprise, so is Abby being juxtaposed to "bad", considering Vargas' negative attitude towards her. What surprising though is how companion characters Dina and Lev remain disconnected from the main characters in terms of juxtaposition. Linked to each other through frequent use of "AI" reflecting their role as game companions, they

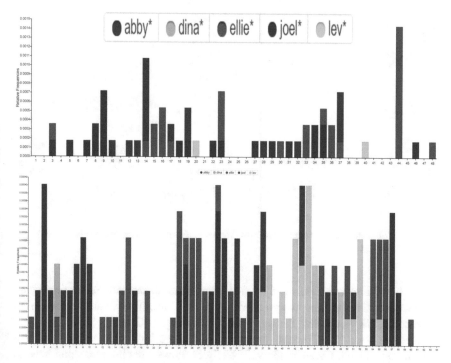

Fig. 17.1 Character name use frequencies of Vargas (top) and Caldwell-Gervais (down)

form their own separate network. Finally, it's also worth noting that while Ellie and Joel are linked to each other, their only link to Abby is through profanity. Collocates in Caldwell-Gervais' text reveal a more connected understanding of characters. Companion characters' names are juxtaposed with verbs and concepts reflecting their roles in the story, such as "discussed", "say", "abandoned", and "respect". In this regard Ellie and Dina are also linked with "revenge" while Abby and Lev are linked with "just". Ellie's relation with Joel's brother Owen and Abby's sanctuary, the "aquarium" where she spends her private moments, are visible as collocates too. The disconnection between Abby and Joel is also noteworthy and can be read as a reflection of Caldwell-Gervais not being agitated by Abby killing Joel.

In Vargas' text, collocates of terms related to the narrative design such as character, plot, and story reflect his reactionary position again, with words like "amazing", "abrupt", "expectations", "pointless", and various types of profanity. Interestingly, in Caldwell-Gervais' text collocates of similar terms reveal little, with most of them being common English words. Yet, he uses more terms and references in a much higher frequency compared to Vargas. It can be argued that while Vargas constantly reacts to the story, Caldwell-Gervais discusses it gradually in his retelling. This can also be observed by analyzing the texts with using Voyant's standardized library of positive and negative codes. The analysis detects a more positive approach in Vargas' text compared to Caldwell-Gervais'. But a closer look

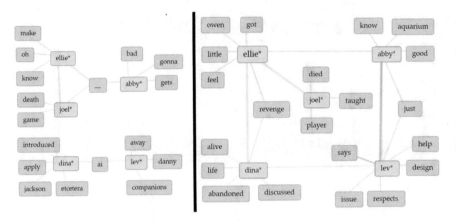

Fig. 17.2 Collocates of character names in Vargas (left) and Caldwell-Gervais (right). "___" represents types of profanity

reveals how Vargas uses positively coded terms either in sarcasm, or for promoting his own show, while negatively coded words in Caldwell-Gervais' text are used to describe the world and the story of *TLoU Part II*. Overall, Voyant analysis reveals details on how Vargas feels about the game but not why he feels like that. In comparison, Caldwell-Gervais' analysis shows what he thinks and how he constructs his arguments. It can be argued that this difference is not only a result of the authors' individual styles, but also an indicator of the differences between popular video reviews and longform video essays as critical retellings.

17.5 Conclusion

Retellings are paratexts of both games and play. They can be artistic, descriptive, or critical. They are narrative products revealing how narrative design and content work together in the hands of players. Previous studies have shown how different types of retellings can provide data on how players perceive and react to game narratives. As detailed, informed, and critical discussions of videogames, longform video essays hold the potential to provide an in-depth record of players' meaning-making processes. Digital humanities tools may prove useful in analyzing such texts. In this regard, the Voyant analysis provides a detailed look on how retellings are constructed by their authors. Vargas' popular retelling of *TLoU Part II* reflects ludonarrative dissonance through questions, exclamations, and profanity. But besides what he tells, what he doesn't tell is also important. Vargas's discussion disregards character motivations and links, sees companion characters as game objects and pays little attention to them. His scarce attention is devoted mainly to the characters of the first game. As his consumable persona openly acknowledges, he rejects the invitation of the second game for exploring its fiction and doesn't try to make sense of it. Caldwell-Gervais on the other hand accepts this invitation and his critical retelling explores and discusses each game character, their motivations, and what role they play in the overall story in a longform video essay. By following the frequency of how he talks about characters and the collocates we can get a glimpse of how ludonarrative resonance emerges. The differences between the two retellings also suggests that ludonarrative relationships observed in retellings may be situated depending on how, why, and by whom the retelling is produced. This study provides a basis for the use of digital humanities tools in analyzing retelling. Future studies using custom categories such as gameplay and narrative design, and using tools focusing on networks formed around retellings may provide deeper insights on how videogame narratives are perceived and discussed among players.

References

L. Anyó, À. Colom, Emotional ambivalence in the last of us. Emotion in video games, between narrative complexity and player loyalty. L'Atalante: Revista de estudios cinematográficos **31**, 85–101 (2021)

T. Apperley, C. Walsh, What digital games and literacy have in common: a heuristic for understanding pupils' gaming literacy. Literacy **46**(3), 115–122 (2012)

M. Bittanti, *Make Better Criticism: A Mature Form of Cultural Analysis* (2004). https://www.gdcvault.com/play/1013566/Make-Better-Criticism-A-Mature. Accessed 10 Jan 2021

N. Caldwell-Gervais, *How Does the Last of Us Part 2 Compare to the Last of Us Remastered?* (2020). https://www.youtube.com/watch?v=Bat38vErWr4. Accessed 18 Jan 2021

M. Consalvo, Zelda 64 and video game fans: a walkthrough of games, intertextuality, and narrative. Telev. New Media **4**(3), 321–334 (2003)

M. Consalvo, Cheating, in *The Routledge Companion to Video Game Studies*, ed. by M. J. P. Wolf, B. Perron, (Routledge, New York, 2014), pp. 152–157

G. Costikyan, *Game Criticism, Why We Need It, and Why Reviews Aren't It* (2008). https://web.archive.org/web/20080227024804/http://playthisthing.com/game-criticism-why-we-need-it-and-why-reviews-arent-it. Accessed 20 Jan 2021

M. Cramer, *How We Talk About Games* (2020). https://www.youtube.com/watch?v=JVN9h-5UHMk&t=3438s. Accessed 5 Feb 2021

F. De Grove, J. Van Looy, Walkthrough, in *The Johns Hopkins Guide to Digital Media*, ed. by M. L. Ryan, L. Emerson, B. J. Robertson, (Johns Hopkins University Press, Baltimore, 2014), p. 520

S. Egenfeldt-Nielsen, J.H. Smith, S.P. Tosca, *Understanding Video Games: The Essential Introduction*, 4th edn. (Routledge, New York, 2020)

P.M. Eladhari, Re-tellings: the fourth layer of narrative as an instrument for critique, in *Interactive Storytelling: 11th International Conference on Interactive Digital Storytelling Proceedings*, ed. by R. Rouse, H. Koenitz, M. Haahr, (Springer, Heidelberg, 2018), pp. 65–78

P. Eliot, *Talking ICO: An Annotation* (2004). https://gamefaqs.gamespot.com/ps2/367472-ico/faqs/29015. Accessed 20 Jan 2021

C. Fernandez-Vara, Play's the thing: a framework to study videogames as performance, in *Proceedings of the DiGRA International Conference: Breaking New Ground: Innovation in Games, Play, Practice and Theory, Brunel University, West London, London, 1-4 September 2009* (2009)

C. Fernandez-Vara, *Introduction to Game Analysis* (Routledge, New York, 2014)

J. Fleury, S. Mamber, The (Im)perfect organism: dissecting the alien media franchise, in *The Franchise Era: Managing Media in the Digital Economy*, ed. by J. Fleury, B. H. Hartzheim, S. Mamber, (Edinburgh University Press, Edinburg, 2019), pp. 31–51

J. Geller, *The Future of Writing About Games* (2020). https://www.youtube.com/watch?v=Vr6pA15xuFc. Accessed 25 Jan 2021

G. Genette, *Paratexts: Thresholds of Interpretation* (Cambridge University Press, Cambridge, 1997)

N. Good, *This Oregon-Based Vlogger Might Be the Closest Thing Video Games Have to Roger Ebert* (2020). https://www.wweek.com/technology/2020/05/20/this-oregon-based-vlogger-might-be-the-closest-thing-video-games-has-to-roger-ebert/. Accessed 25 Jan 2021

A. Gursoy, *Game Worlds: A Study of Video Game Criticism* (Master's Dissertation, Massachusetts Institute of Technology, 2013)

Japan Studio and Team Ico, *Ico*. Sony Computer Entertainment (2001)

J. Juul, *Half-Real: Video Games between Real Rules and Fictional Worlds* (The MIT Press, Cambridge, 2005)

T. Kerttula, "What an eccentric performance": storytelling in online let's plays. Games Cult. **14**(3), 236–255 (2016)

H. Koenitz, Towards a specific theory of interactive digital narrative, in *Interactive Digital Narrative: History, Theory and Practice*, ed. by H. Koenitz, G. Ferri, M. Haahr, D. Sezen, T. I. Sezen, (Routledge, New York, 2015), pp. 91–105

M. Kreminski, B. Samuel, E. Melcer, N. Wardrip-Fruin, Evaluating AI-based games through retellings, in *Proceedings of Fifteenth AAAI Conference on Artificial Intelligence and Interactive Digital Entertainment* (2019), pp. 45–51

B. Laurel, *Computers as Theatre*, 2nd edn. (Addison-Wesley, Upper Saddle River, 2014)

Maxis, *The Sims, Video Game Series* (Electronic Arts, Redwood City, CA, 2000–2014)

S. Mukherje, Videogames as "minor literature": reading videogame stories through Paratexts. GRAMMA J. Theory Crit. **23**, 60–75 (2016)

Naughty Dog, *The Last of Us* (Sony Interactive Entertainment, Tokyo, 2013)

Naughty Dog, *The Last of Us Part II* (Sony Interactive Entertainment, Tokyo, 2020)

J. Newman, Walkthrough, in *Debugging Game History: A Critical Lexicon*, ed. by H. Lowood, R. Guins, (The MIT Press, Cambridge, 2016), pp. 409–418

J. Newman, Minecraft: user- generated content, in *How to Play Video Games*, ed. by M. T. Payne, N. B. Huntemann, (New York University Press, New York, 2019), pp. 277–284

Paradox Development Studio, *Crusader Kings, Video Game Series* (Paradox Interactive, Stockholm, 2007–2020)

K. Radde-Antweiler, X. Zeiler, Methods for analyzing let's plays: context analysis for gaming videos on YouTube. Gamevironments **2**, 100–139 (2015)

D. Recktenwald, *Interactional Practices in Let's Play Videos*. Master's Dissertation, Saarland University (2014)

C. Roth, T. van Nuenen, H. Koenitz, Ludonarrative hermeneutics: a way out and the narrative paradox, in *Proceedings of International Conference on Interactive Digital Storytelling*, ed. by R. Rouse, H. Koenitz, M. Haahr, (Springer, Heidelberg, 2018), pp. 93–106

R. Rouse III, *Game Design, Theory and Practice*, 2nd edn. (Wordware Publishing, Inc., Plano, TX, 2004), pp. 202–226

J. Saklofske, Gaming the publishing industry: exploring diverse open scholarship models in digital games studies. Pop! Public. Open. Participat. (2020)

S. Sinclair, G. Rockwell, *Voyant Tools* (2016). http://voyant-tools.org/. Accessed 8 Feb 2021

A. Soler, *Can We Save Video Game Journalism? Can Grass Roots Media Contribute with a More Critical Perspective to Contemporary Video Game Coverage?* Master's Dissertation, Uppsala University: Pop! J. (N2) (2014). https://popjournal.ca/issue02/saklofske. Accessed 25 Jan 2021

J. Sorg, Gemischtes Doppel: Zur Psychologie narrativer Formen in digitalen Spielen. Navigationen: Zeitschrift für Medien- und Kulturwissenschaften **9**(1), 91–107 (2009)

S. Sych, When the fourth layer meets the fourth wall: the case for critical game retellings, in *Proceedings of International Conference on Interactive Digital Storytelling*, ed. by A. G. Bosser, D. E. Millard, C. Hargood, (Springer, Heidelberg, 2020), pp. 203–211

T. Thabet, *Video Game Narrative and Criticism* (Palgrave Macmillan, London, 2015)

D. Thomas, J.P. Zagal, M. Robertson, I. Bogost, W. Huber, You played that? Game studies meets game criticism, in *Proceedings of the DiGRA International Conference: Breaking New Ground: Innovation in Games, Play, Practice and Theory, Brunel University, West London, London, 1-4 September 2009* (2009)

W. Toh, The player experience of BioShock: a theory of ludonarrative relationships, in *Approaches to Videogame Discourse: Lexis, Interaction, Textuality*, ed. by A. Ensslin, I. Balteiro, (Bloomsbury Academic, New York, 2019), pp. 247–268

S.P. Tosca, Reading resident evil: code veronica X, in *Proceedings of DAC 2003 Streaming Worlds: 5th International Digital Arts & Culture Conference*, ed. by A. Miles, (RMIT Press, Melbourne, 2003), pp. 206–216

J. Vahlo, *In Gameplay: The Invariant Structures and Varieties of the Video Game Gameplay Experience*. Doctoral Dissertation, University of Turku (2018)

J.A. Vargas, *Angry Joe Show: The Last of Us Part II - Angry Review* (2020). https://www.youtube.com/watch?v=_-sTlYUeT8o&t=3s. Accessed 23 Jan 2021

N. Wardrip-Fruin, *Expressive Processing: Digital Fictions, Computer Games, and Software Studies* (The MIT Press, Cambridge, 2009)

Chapter 18
Heritage, Authenticity, and the Fiction/Nonfiction Dualism in *Attentat 1942*

Michał Mochocki

18.1 Introduction

This chapter investigates historical authenticity in the award-winning Czech game *Attentat 1942* (Charles Games, 2017), It belongs to "culture-centric games" (as in Majewski 2017, p. 188–190) focused on cultural heritage. So I employ the heritage approach, exploring accuracy/authenticity through (multiple) tourism/heritage authenticities, and through the complicated fact/fiction ontology of historical storyworlds. The first section presents Mochocki's (2021a) framework of authenticity/immersion for historical storyworlds. The discussion in Sects. 18.2.1, 18.2.2, 18.2.3, 18.2.4, and 18.2.5 examines its five layers consecutively, but also includes several other approaches to authenticity in games. All seem to be compatible, focusing on different questions: who? where? what? or how? Schwarz (2020) explains *who/how* verifies authenticity; Nolden (2020)—*where* it is found; Zimmermann (2020)—*what* definitions of authenticity are in circulation. Mochocki (2021a, 2021b) moves from *what* to *how* authenticity is experienced: in heritage-themed media in general; and in conjunction with game involvement/immersion. Section 18.3 connects authenticity to factuality/fictionality in narratology (Fludernik and Ryan 2020, eds.). The final section compares *Attentat 1942* to a museum experience, and outlines directions for further research.

M. Mochocki (✉)
Kazimierz Wielki University, Bydgoszcz, Poland
e-mail: mochocki@ukw.edu.pl

© The Author(s), under exclusive license to Springer Nature Switzerland AG 2022
B. Bostan (ed.), *Games and Narrative: Theory and Practice*, International Series on Computer Entertainment and Media Technology,
https://doi.org/10.1007/978-3-030-81538-7_18

18.2 Mixed Model of Authenticity/Immersion (Mochocki 2021a, b)

After a confusing period of incompatible definitions and usage, the recent years have brought consensus on 'authenticity' and 'accuracy' as separate concepts (Kapell and Elliott 2013; Majewski 2018; Sweeting 2018; Zimmermann 2020; Pfister 2020) and Mochocki (2021b). Accuracy is connected to factuality: it is about detailed agreement with (often: replication/representation of) expert-verified facts, and/or original sources. Authenticity is about perception, interpretation, and felt experience, which may include 'perceived accuracy' based on subjective imaginations and beliefs. As authenticity theorists highlight (Agnew and Tomann 2020; Varga and Guignon 2020; Zimmermann 2020), the former is focused on the object (artefact, site, practiced ritual), the latter on the experiencing subject.

This binary has been expanded to three-fold models informed by discussions of authenticity in tourism/heritage, one briefly outlined by Zimmermann (2020), another developed by Mochocki for non-digital role-playing (2021a) and adapted for video games (2021b). Mochocki builds his three-to-five model on Wang's (1999) authenticities in tourism, reworked by Matos and Barbosa (2018) with Morin's theory of complexity (also appreciated by Zimmermann 2021 for historical game studies). Like Schwarz's (2020) "authenticities in the plural" (p. 119), Wang recognises objective, constructive, and existential dimensions, the last one subdivided into interpersonal, self-making, and bodily feelings. Mochocki narrows Wang's general-tourism to heritage-driven cultural tourism, reframing 'tourism authenticities' as 'heritage authenticities'.

Mochocki (2021a), Chap. 1) aligns the five authenticities with five aspects of human experience (think, feel, act, sense, and relate; Schmitt 1999), and with five (out of six) layers of role-playing immersion (Bowman 2017, 2018) and Calleja's (2011) involvements with videogames. Also Winnerling (2014) links authenticity to immersion (p. 159). In games set in historical storyworlds, Mochocki argues, player's perception of historical/heritage authenticity is intertwined with immersion/incorporation, emerging in the same layers of human experience:

1. **Existential/Interpersonal** authenticity works through family bonds and friendships, validating authenticity through shared collective experience and pre−/post- communication. This correlates with community-immersion / shared involvement, identically based on **relations**, relationships, and co-participation.
2. **Existential/Self-making** authenticity is validated by agreement with one's own personality, self-image, value system etc. It correlates with character-immersion / affective involvement, analogically based on **feelings** emerging in emotional exploration of one's own and other people's identities.
3. **Existential/Bodily feelings** authenticity emerges in the visceral experience of physically performed actions. It correlates with activity-immersion/kinaesthetic involvement, analogically based on embodied **action-performance**.

4. **Constructive** (aka symbolic) authenticity is validated by agreement with already-held beliefs/knowledge about what the historical setting looked like. This correlates with narrative-immersion / involvement, based on **thinking** and comparing to a pre-established (narrative!) frame of reference. In audiovisual environments it also correlates with environment-immersion / spatial involvement, based on **sensory perception**, as objects first must be perceived (sensing) in order to be deemed (thinking) authentic or not. It is often the details of audiovisual representation that 'make' authenticity.
5. **Objective** authenticity is like Constructive. It correlates with narrative- and environment- immersion in the same way: through processing of narratively-framed information (**thinking**) about objects/phenomena subjected to sensory perception (**sensing**). What makes this authenticity 'objective' is the quality of being genuinely original: originating in the past and preserved, like built sites and collected artefacts. Their ontological status is different: not a copy/replica, but "an actual physical thing that was there and is right here in front of me now" (Latham 2015, p. 5).
6. No heritage authenticity corresponds with Bowman's game-immersion/Calleja's ludic involvement.

Original Wang's model presented the three ('existential' counted as one) as conflicting views; Matos and Barbosa (2018) reframe them as co-existing dimensions. This multi-layered modelling of heritage experiences is surprisingly compatible with modelling of player experience in Calleja (2011) and Bowman (2018), and general human experience in Schmitt (1999).

We can easily (too easily?) exclude 'objective' authenticity from videogames. They can only offer representations, never an unmediated presence of material artefacts (Schwarz 2020, p. 118; Wolf 2020, p. 117; Zimmermann 2021, p. 23). Analogically, they cannot offer the 'bodily feelings' authenticity of physical actions, only a weak substitute by manual operations on game controllers (at best—limited full-body actions with haptic devices). With 'materiality' inevitably replaced with 'mediality' (Nolden 2020, p. 78), it is tempting to conclude that heritage authenticity in videogames is limited to 'constructive', 'self-making', and/or 'interpersonal'. However, character-driven narratives (including role-playing games) are more complicated. See Sects. 18.2.4 and 18.2.5.

18.2.1 Constructive Authenticity, Material Dimension

"The game is based on historical research and real testimonies, yet the characters in the game and their stories are fictitious": this disclaimer appears on screen as the game begins. This positions the storyworld as well-researched historical fiction, setting a high bar for factual accuracy. In the above-presented model this is 'constructive' authenticity: objects/behaviours/environments are perceived as authentic if they correspond with the vision of the setting held in the player's mind. This vision is based on expert-authorised knowledge from school or research, or pop-knowledge of history-themed fictionalisations in narrative media, or a mix of both (Schwarz 2020, p. 123). Actually, following the Western philosophy of history from Collingswood to White[1] to Munslow to Jaeger (2020), I assume it always is 'a mix of both'. Even expert historiography is a narrative reconstruction from incomplete and biased sources; always to some degree based on speculation and imagination. Therefore, I do not distinguish between expert's and amateur's mental models with regard to their referential function for accuracy/'constructive' authenticity.

That having said, *Attentat 1942* prioritises academic expertise, as it extensively relies on what Salvati and Bullinger (2013) call "documentary authority". Oral accounts of past events—narrated by actors impersonating fictitious characters—are illustrated by original black-and-white photo and video footage from real-world World War 2. It could be argued that real archived footage is 'objectively' authentic, but this is not 'objective' materiality of genuine originals. It is 'constructive' authenticity of digital reproductions, positioned as exact copies of said originals. Every TV viewer in Central/Eastern Europe can judge them as authentic by comparison to analogical materials broadcast on TV around major anniversaries. In Schwarz's (2020) four ways of authentication this is "image and/or sound, a characteristic way of audio-visual representations" (p. 121). To Calleja (2011), replicating particular cinematic styles fuels the affective power of videogames (p. 140–141). *Attentat 1942* deliberately uses it to differentiate between levels of authenticity: black-and-white film/photo from original archive as historical documentary; black-and-white comics for wartime memories of fictitious characters; full-colour video for the protagonist's 'now' in 2001 (Šisler 2016, 'b. Authenticity').

Another pillar of constructive authenticity is encyclopaedic support and expert authorisation. In *Attentat 1942* links to encyclopaedic entries pop up frequently. If the player takes breaks to read, s/he is expanding her knowledge of the historical storyworld. Thus, even if the player starts with purely popcultural imagery, s/he is incrementally absorbing chunks of historiographical knowledge (as in processual enactedness of the storyworld; see Caracciolo 2019). Authenticity of narrative content in *Attentat 1942* is thus validated by a nonfiction encyclopaedia integrated with the game: a "very forceful means of authentication" (Schwarz 2020, p. 126), its reliability enhanced by "source credibility" (Gerrig and Gagnon 2020, p. 135–136) of national museums, archives, and universities credited as consultants and contributors. In Schwarz's (2020) four authentications this is "through facts and data" coupled with "players' contemporaries who they accept as experts" (p. 121).

Audiovisual accuracy of represented objects is yet another dimension of the same; Schwarz's (2020) authentication "through images and/or sounds" (p. 121). *Attentat 1942* puts great emphasis on pieces of material heritage. Some items, like the radio foregrounded in the first conversation with the grandmother, appear both

---

[1] Fludernik and Ryan (2020) note that Hayden White also influenced the turn in narratology towards studies on nonfiction narratives (pp. 11–12).

in the 2001-dated videos and 1940s cartoons. *Attentat 1942* itself provides ample opportunities to compare the visual details of those objects to original archive footage. Museum-goers, fans of WW2 documentaries, and other people familiar with that material culture can additionally verify it in light of prior knowledge. This also works for entire buildings, locations, and landscapes/cityscapes. Anyone who spent some time in Prague will be able to recognise—therefore authenticate—some of its landmarks. All the way from "iconic objects" and locations to "small-scale environments" to "networks of narrative fragments" to "macro-historical model assumptions about society, economic and political influence" (Nolden 2020, p. 83–84), *Attentat 1942* uses all four "anchors of authenticity" Nolden tracks in MMO games.

18.2.2   Constructive Authenticity, Human Dimension

Material objects are consistently used to characterise people. Objects define occupation, talents, interests, wealth, romances, etc. Even the grandfather's intradiegetic diary uses such metonymic tactics: "I spend my days switching between a rifle and a clarinet" for military training and music-making. Objects also focus memories and emotions; trigger questions and reminiscences. The whole investigation starts with a decades-old radio the protagonist finds at his/her (player-selected gender) grandma's place, with the grandmother saying "We were listening to this radio when your grandpa was taken away by the Gestapo".

At that point the game switches to black-and-white cartoon mode, zooming in on the radio and then out to show grandma and grandpa as young adults in 1942. Grandma's voice is narrating her memories of the day, as the player can see the room packed with furniture and other household items (both characters shown in interactions with objects). Also cutscenes and conversations from 2001 are full of close-up shots of cell phones, keys, glass of water, printed photographs, documents; sometimes with hands handling the objects, sometimes without. Emphasis on objects reaches its heights with a minigame simulating grandma's tidying up the place after the Gestapo search. The player has to pick up 31 items one by one, each coming with a text quoting grandma's comments about its role in everyday life under German occupation.

For example, "Material for a dress" comes with "I had been altering an old dress to make it into a skirt. Clothing was rationed just like food, and it was harder and harder to find. I had already pinned everything together for sewing and they threw it all about". This provides historiographical information on the rationing of food and clothing, and on women's efforts to cope with that with domestic needlework. This adds to 'constructive' authenticity as long as it is confirmed by—or logically coherent with—the player's already-known narratives about Nazi occupation, or any wartime austerity. The last sentence also mentions the brutality and carelessness of the Gestapo-led home search, and the frustration of the woman whose work got ruined.

Together, the 31 objects with such micro stories function like a well-designed "museum of everyday life" (Macdonald 2013, p. 157). They meaningfully characterise the domestic life and experiences of people who inhabited the room, and its dependence on politics, economy, technology, etc.. This is what Champion (2011) expects from virtual heritage environments: a sense of place emerging from "cultural presence" (p. 78). Not a random "collection of objects and spaces" (2015, p. 99), but one "observed, interpreted, or understood as a coherent materialization by intelligent beings of a shared social system" (2011, p. 78).

More such environmental storytelling follows. Before we see Krejcar, grandpa's old friend, we have snapshots of his room: miniature airplane models and books on World War 2 history. The visit to a journalist is illustrated with close-up views of audio cassettes, photos, and a Sony cassette player, its reels rolling as the recording is being played. The cartoon minigame representing Malek's reminiscence asks the player to examine 13 items and decide which were dangerous to keep under Nazi rule (Mago 2019, para. 16). As often stated in conversations and edu-materials, these personal experiences are not unique, but a "collective experientiality" (Alders 2015, p. 35–36) of the nation. There are also grandma's and Hein's keepsakes from the 1940s examined by the protagonist in 2001; these I debate in Sect. 18.2.5.

This was the human/social dimension of object-based 'constructive' authenticity. Human experience is also revealed in conversation and writing. To Schwarz (2020), "fictitious characters as present-day creations for a game's plot set in the past" (p. 121) are the fourth way of authentication. Historical storytelling must not be limited to facts, say van der Schilden and Heijltjes (2017), but rely on "a deep understanding of human emotion" in order "to capture the essence of a moment" (p. 73). When it comes to human behaviour, expert historians will no longer be the authenticating voice. They, as Saxton (2020) argues, do not have reliable (if any) sources for opinions, emotions, or private conversations. Therefore, more authority will be given to our mental models of human nature.

Saxton (2020) convincingly separates object-oriented accuracy and subject-oriented authenticity in historical fiction. It only makes sense to speak of accurate representations when we can compare them with originals. It means the originals must have been preserved or recorded in sources with sufficient detail. By contrast, depictions of thoughts, feelings, and undocumented private life can only be judged for authenticity. For instance, narratives can more or less accurately represent the event of coronation, with words and behaviours of its major figures as recorded in sources. But they cannot, as Saxton insists, ever accurately represent what the king and others were thinking and feeling, and what they did in moments which lack archival record.

Is this still Wang's object-based 'constructive' authenticity? Yes and no. Yes, because a character is an object for the purpose of storyworld analysis: one of many existents in the environment.[2] The subject, by contrast, is the player/viewer/reader, whose experience fuels Wang's 'existential' subject-based authenticity. But Sax-

---

[2]Ryan even has one word—existents—for both characters and objects.

ton's (2020) subject-orientation is about characters, not readers, as experiencing subjects. This thought is in the center of the experiential/enactivist approach to narratives, which I develop in Sects. 18.2.4 and 18.2.5. Here suffice it to say we have two levels of subject-orientation: player-subject and character-subject. Thus, the 'subject' and 'object' binary is breached (or bridged?) by 'subjective object' in-between.

18.2.3   Existential-Interpersonal Authenticity

Attentat 1942 does not facilitate interpersonally shared experience of gameplay (other than single-player co-playing). The narrative, by contrast, is driven by what Wang (1999) terms "family bonds" in 'interpersonal' authenticity. The main plot is the protagonist's quest to discover unknown past of his/her grandfather, and s/he does so by conversational bonding with the grandmother and rekindling grandfather's old friendships. The player can only co-participate in this relationship *per procura*, by protagonist-identification (see Sect. 18.2.5 on *per procura* authenticity).

The macro phase of Calleja's (2011) shared involvement includes game-related communication before and after the game, and interactions with paratexts: reviews, interviews, online discussions, etc. This applies to any game—but history/heritage-themed games additionally intersect with non-gaming communities involved with that particular heritage. It is no coincidence that Pfister (2020) finds historical settings particularly amenable to ideological myth-making (pp. 49–52). *Attentat 1942* is destined for such engagements, designed as it was around the still painful and deadly serious themes of Nazism and the Holocaust. See sections d) 'Inclusivity' and e) 'Contextualization' in Šisler (2016) for a detailed account of the designer's agenda.

"Games need to become a part of commemoration", states Friedrich (2020, p. 267), and applauds *Attentat 1942* as "successful by offering experiences built around powerlessness and adaptation rather than power and conquest" (p. 270). Having compared this game to a museum (18.2.2), I propose another analogy: a performative "ritual commemoration of the Holocaust" (Macdonald 2013, p. 200–201). As with non-digital role-plays, "Designing, critiquing, playing. .. may be meaningful heritage practices" (Mochocki 2021a, p. 95). Even though designed for single-player 'self-making' (see Sect. 18.2.3), *Attentat 1942* remains a form of *commemorative collaboration*: between the creators who offer the Holocaust- and occupation-themed game and the players who decide to engage with it.

Communal sharing of this experience is out there to see in online paratexts (see e.g. Hammar 2019, p. 168). Actually, the questions of accuracy/authenticity, and the power to educate and commemorate, is in the center of debate, be it two-line comments under Chalk's (2017) review on PCgamer.com, or multi-lingual customer reviews on Steam. So says a summary of early responses, including feedback from Czech teachers and students, in Šisler (2016). Multiple awards at games festivals take the same view, praising *Attentat 1942* not for game design, but for narrative, seriousness, and educational power. In Jacobs's (2021) view, this makes it a 'serious game' (p. 33); and so it was intended by the developers (Šisler 2016).

18.2.4 Existential-Self-Making Authenticity

The "Self" dimension is partially shaped by "Interpersonal" (see Sect. 18.2.1 above), since group identifications are co-constituting personal identity (Macdonald 2013, pp. 222,224). They may be—somewhat artificially—separated into shared practices and individual contemplation. Shared activities remain in the 'interpersonal' sphere. Solitary contemplation, celebration, or performative affirmation of one's collective identity/heritage is 'self-making' authenticity. In particular, embracing one's meaningful connection to previous generations cannot be 'interpersonal', as long-deceased ancestors are not partners for sharing experiences.

In Mochocki's (2021a) mixed model of authenticity/immersion, Wang's 'existential: self-making' authenticity is aligned with Bowman's 'immersion into character'. Its major part may rely on the player's wilful exploration of his/her attitudes ("cognitive, emotive, and moral repertoire"; as in Mikkonen 2020, p. 238) to memories/narratives of World War 2, and to the lasting legacy of Nazism, communism, anti-semitism, etc. Character design helps bring the player's own self to the forefront, as the protagonist is an "implied character" (Mochocki 2007): a largely-empty (undefined) slot for character-focalisation. The (very few) defined elements, such as the grandmother, separate the player from character, but the process of information-gathering and choice-making does not.

For example, when the player listens to a recording of his//her grandpa's voice narrating his story, the player and character hear the same thing, and simultaneously find out what brought grandpa into trouble (he gave his ID to his Jewish friend Mareš). Then, the game screen updates the list of player goals accordingly. Two previous goals "Figure out why the Gestapo arrested grandpa" and "Figure out what Grandpa had to do with Heydrich's assassination" are first displayed with normal font, then struck through—and a new goal appears below: "Figure out the role Egon Mareš played in the arrest of your grandpa". The intradiegetic voice and the extradiegetic game goals menu work in unison to merge the player's and character's information-processing seamlessly: uncovering new information about the historical past, and noticing new options of where to search next.

As said above, the character does not obscure the view with his/her own opinions (other than a few sarcastic or accusatory dialogue options). It remains a window through which the player faces often drastic content, including never-ceasing ethical dilemmas, such as the debate on the eponymous assassination of Reinhard Heydrich. Then and now, some Czechs glorify the elimination of the Nazi war criminal, some condemn this as an irrresponsible act that provoked retaliation, resulting in the loss of too many Czech lives. Another debated theme is forced relocation of ethnic

Germans from Czechia when the tides turned after the war: was it the right thing to do or not? The player makes up their own mind—the 'empty' avatar does not get in the way.

For players whose Czech/German/Jewish family histories were affected by these events it is meaningful personally: as heritage. People whose families suffered hardships in other Nazi-occupied countries can relate as well (Mago 2019, para. 11). So can many people globally, whose families were caught in the struggle between fascism, communism, and Western democracies. They all are likely to have beliefs, memories, and judgments on World War 2, whose activation in response to *Attentat 1942* is an exercise in Wang's "authentic Self". For instance, the game *My Child Lebensborn*, about the aftermath of Nazi breeding programme in post-WW2 Norway, found immense popularity in China and Korea. A game may thus work like literary fiction: enhance, (re)organise, reassert, and better understand already-held beliefs and moral stances (Mikkonen 2020, pp. 237–239).

Essentially, *Attentat 1942* mimics the role of heritage sites, confronting the visitor with material evidence, audiovisual narratives, expert commentary, and witness accounts, and it is up to the player/visitor to position him/herself in relation to it. Emotionally-moving heritage sites and narrative media have the power to evoke "prosthetic memory" (Landsberg 2004): visitors develop an emotional relation to other people's experiences as if those had been their own. In this way, even those who know nothing of WW2 in their family history can find it personally meaningful—especially if they hold political opinions relevant to WW2 legacy. See Hammar (2019) for a thorough adaptation of Landsberg's concept to digital games, and Hawthorne (2019) for more parallels between videogames and museums.

The game is not neutral: it is clearly on the side of civilian victims. Some NPCs, like grandma, highlight the subjective nature of conflicting opinions and limited reliability of information, others voice one-sided authoritative statements, like Malek. Yet, as Bagnall's (2003) research on site visitation demonstrates, visitors do not blindly accept the site's message at face value. Some take the affirmatory approach; some entirely reject the narrative if it opposes their politics or knowledge; some selectively accept/reject fragments. Bagnall's study mirrors Hall's encoding/decoding model with dominant, oppositional, and negotiated readings. Narratives are judged as more authentic when they confirm previous beliefs, and tend to be rejected if they do not: in any case, "belief polarisation leaves people more strongly stick to their prior views (Gerrig and Gagnon 2020, p. 137–138)". I expect narratives/heritage sites in videogames to be no different.

For what it is worth, *Attentat 1942* makes it blatantly clear that accounts of history may be erroneous, as documents and personal testimonies are not 100% reliable. This is by design: the developers "deliberately chose to keep the contradictions and discrepancies between individual 'testimonies' in the game" to signal "social construction of history" (Šisler 2016, 'c. Constructivism'). Powerful examples are important NPCs reported as dead, who—contrary to 'evidence'—turn out to have survived the war.

18.2.5 Existential-Bodily Feelings

The seemingly absent experience of embodied contact in digitally-mediated sto-rytelling has been highlighted in role-playing and reenactment studies (Zagal and Deterding 2018; Bowman 2018; Gapps 2020). There are, however, theories that appreciate embodiment in digital gameplay.

One way is to appreciate the physicality of using game controllers. The mouse, keyboard, pad, etc. require hand-eye coordination and tactile control from the player's body. Calleja (2011, p. 60–61) discusses it under kinaesthetic involvement. I will not use this argument, as *Attentat 1942* offers no visual representation of the avatar's movements. Strictly physical activities are of little importance anyway. The repertoire of the protagonist's actions consists of conversations, travels from/to conversations, and interactions with historical objects (the objects are a special case; see Sects. 18.2.1 and 18.2.5). Movement normally is an important part of kinaesthetic involvement—but here we do not see it, we only select destinations on the map.

I wish to explore 'bodily feelings' authenticity / immersion via cogni-tive/enactivist narratology. Cognitive narratologists, such as David Herman, Marie-Laure Ryan, Jan-Noël Thon, assume that narratives operate through mental models of storyworlds emerging in the reader/viewer/player's mind. Recent developments emphasise the role of 'bodily feelings' reactions in that process. When the mind is busy with "mental simulation" (Ryan 2019) of an imaginary character's experiences, the body is also actively engaged. That is the premise of enactivist narratology championed by Caracciolo in *The Experientiality of Narrative* (2014): mental simulation of the character in a narrative situation triggers some physiological reactions we would be experiencing in analogical circumstances. Our body will actually feel a (muted) version of affective responses mirroring experiences the character is going through: hunger, arousal, social awkwardness, moral dilemmas, the loss of a loved one etc.

Narrative experiences are therefore "biosemantic" (Alexander 2018, p. 266) and "biosemiotic" (Mochocki 2021a, p. 117). Character-driven narrative representation is translated to mental models via mental+physiological simulation—not purely mental. I find this particularly useful for examination of immersion in role-playing. Wang's (1999) 'bodily feelings' authenticity emphasises activity-immersion in sports, trekking, etc.., but also laidback relaxation, all of which entail "two aspects: sensual and symbolic" (p. 361). Biosemantically-generated 'reactive bodily feelings', or affects, should be part of this picture.

I place them in the 'affective' layer of Calleja's (2011) involvements with game environments. This is the least independent layer, triggered by other layers and rein-forcing them in return (p. 146). If there are sets of bodily affects typically triggered by specific experiences, then a mental simulation of such situations will trigger some physiological responses accordingly. Hence, bodily affects typical of human contact will accompany 'interpersonal' authenticity (Sect. 18.2.2); affects typical of discoveries, interpretations, and stories will support 'constructive' authenticity

(Sect. 18.2.1); and affects typical of 'realising authentic Self' will coincide with 'self-making' (Sect. 18.2.3).

18.2.6 Pseudo-Objective Authenticity: New Category

Following this theory, I assume that 'objective' authenticity of genuine material artefacts has its own set of bodily sensations, experienced by reenactors, museum-goers, and tourists as 'touching the past'. It is about "connections – not only social but also material (e.g. the identity of the stone in the museum and in the village) and historical, linking past and present" (Macdonald 2013, p. 130). We have said digital mediation excludes genuine objectivity of artefacts. But what if it can trigger a trace of that 'touch-the-past' sensation by means of the mental+physiological simulation described in Sect. 18.2.4?

Attentat 1942 creates much of its 'constructive' authenticity as simulation of 'objective' when the protagonist is interacting with original artefacts from the past. The best example is the collection of family heirlooms presented by the grandmother, all relevant to the grandfather's wartime story. A striped cap from Auschwitz, communist newspaper, letters from prison, postcard from spa (after the war), photos from Auschwitz, food rations coupons, and an encrypted diary. The player may return to these artefacts and re-read associated text. To the player, all this is 'constructive' authenticity of digital representations (see Sect. 18.2.2 above). But to the character in the storyworld these objects constitute 'objective' authenticity.

The character puts his/her hands on real artefacts from the past, which carry a deep personal meaning to still-living owners. These act as "prop and prompt" (Smith 2006, p. 2) for the elderly to pass on storified memories to younger generations:

> The real sense of heritage, the real moment of heritage when our emotions and sense of self are truly engaged, is not so much in the possession of the necklace, but in the act of passing on and receiving memories and knowledge (Smith 2006)

The player only participates in this 'heritage moment' *per procura*. Yet, as Alexander (2018) insists, whatever happens to the character also experientially happens "to us" (p. 263) through narrative-imaginary identification. In Caracciolo's enactivism, if the player has experienced similar family bonding, then his/her body knows how it feels—so it can activate an "experiential trace" (as in Zwaan 2008). Thus, *Attentat* players in the grandmother scene could experience an echo of what they would be feeling if they received similar family heirlooms.

Analogically, if the player has experienced the 'touch-of-the-past' due to 'objective authenticity' of original artefacts, s/he may feel that "experiential trace" when s/he is witnessing a character touching such objects. Museum visitors "value original objects over replicas, looking at them for longer and differently" (Dudley 2018, 196), so there is evidence for an experiential difference between 'objective' and 'constructive' authenticity. Therefore, I expect that a mental+physiological simulation of immediate contact with 'objectively' authentic heritage may be a qualitatively different experience than standard 'constructive' authenticity. Such 'objective' authenticity *per procura* (*per avatar*) could be called 'pseudo-objective' (Mochocki 2021b).

18.3 Fiction/Nonfiction Dualism in *Attentat 1942*

'Constructive' authenticity often could be called 'perceived accuracy': saying "This medieval tavern looks really authentic" essentially means "This looks like an accurate representation" with regard to interior design, presence, appearance, and functions of objects and living beings. To Caracciolo (2020) this is a form of factuality, numbered 'factuality1', "involving facts that are in some relevant way real-world-like. .. a measure of verisimilitude or correspondence between narrative information and real-world cognitive parameters" (p. 150).

The essential point is: this must be measured against some prior mental models of such taverns, their clientele, and the (story)world around (Pfister 2020, p. 64). People without relevant historiographical knowledge can only use popcultural fictionalisations as aids; or at best some mental models from community-shared "memory-heritage-identity complex" (Macdonald 2013, p. 5). Educated historians are exposed to the same, but they are trained to build mental models on academic research. Thus, their judgments of authenticity will more often than not correspond with factual accuracy: Caracciolo's (2020) 'factuality2' about "facts that are claimed to have verifiably occurred in the real world" (p. 150).

Object-focused historiographical factuality, as in museology and archaeology, translates to 'objective' authenticity: objects that really come from the past. Evidence of their origin resides in their material substance, available for scientific examination. Accuracy of representation is a non-issue here: this is not a representation at all. Accurate replicas and representations may be realistic—originals are real (Dudley 2018, p. 196). But beside material heritage—factuality comes from historiography, which "formally functions as a narrative (historiographic discourse) *about narratives* (narrative sources) relating to events and human acts in the actual world" (Jaeger 2020, p. 335). If it is based on narrated accounts, it may only define 'constructive' authenticity: discursively constructed as 'factual' in nonfiction media.

Ryan (2020) denies videogames the capacity to create factuality for three reasons: (1) identification with the avatar puts it "squarely in the fictional camp" (p. 88); (2) player's agency means the possible events are "predictions. .. neither fictional nor fully factual"; and (3) replayability with different courses of events "disqualifies games from representing history, since there is only one way the past took place" (p. 88). Moreover, Pfister (2020) notes that mechanics and action-focus make videogames less inviting to critical reflection than films or novels (p. 52). *Attentat 1942* does the opposite.

I am not saying Ryan and Pfister are wrong about videogames—but *Attentat 1942* is not the kind they describe. Its rudimentary mechanics does not afford fast-paced action, nor does it simulate historical systems through procedural rhetorics. It does not allow for counterplay to "take control of the past" (as in Mol 2020). What it does is support navigation through pieces of quasi-historical evidence in the form of material relics and witness testimonies, illustrated with (f)actual archive-based evidence. Very much like films and novels that Pfister contrasts with games.

In Ryan's (2018) ontology of storyworlds it would be 'historical fiction', the closest one to nonfiction. Representing the theory of possible worlds, Ryan insists this is *not* a version of the actual (our life-)world, but a possible world conceived at some ontological distance, many of its properties identical with ours. Historical fiction in Ryan (2018) deviates from nonfiction in only three of 11 aspects: (A) inventory of individuals, (B) properties of individuals, and (C) alethic value (p. 80). It is characterised by "weak fictionality, where the fictional world is very close to the real world" (Ryan 2020, p. 83).

Wolf (2014) similarly puts imaginary worlds on a continuum of 'secondariness', with nonfiction extremely close to the actual 'Primary' world—and various types of fictionalisation further away. As I compare Wolf to Ryan, I understand Wolf's secondariness as a degree of fictionality mixed with (f)actuality, not as a multitude of self-referential possible worlds. In any case, I would insist that a different ontology of historical fiction does not exclude referentiality: either to historiographical facts; or to human experientiality (see Caracciolo's 2019 rejection of ontological segregation). *Attentat 1942* tells "real history, into which fiction is incorporated" (Mago 2019, para. 10). In Wolf's (2020) terms, it belongs to "mixed ontologies" (Wolf 2020), with fictive people and events put in "actual historically verifiable occurrences" (p. 120).

This dualism features very strongly throughout the game: to the point of having the 'fictional pact' and 'factual pact' (as in Fludernik 2020, p. 62) active simultaneously. Instead of classifying it on the global level as a fictional narrative using factive footage for verisimilitude, or a factual narrative using fictive story for illustrative purposes, I conclude it is a hybrid (see Fludernik and Ryan 2020, p. 4, on global level vs. individual statements). The initial announcement, "The game is based on historical research and real testimonies, yet the characters in the game and their stories are fictitious", sets those boundaries at the start; a powerful "(para-)textual strategy" (Rajewsky 2020, p. 41). This disclaimer sets a gigantic 'signpost of fictionality' for the fictive characters and their stories, and 'signpost of factuality' for the facticity of the storyworld (historiographical signposts; see Jaeger 2020, p. 339–340; Lavocat 2020, p. 579–580). Their *co-presence* seems to me a 'signpost of hybridity'. Players are asked to apply the interpretive 'fictional pact' to one set of storyworld components, the 'factual pact' to the other (see Rajewsky 2020 for differences between 'factuality', 'facticity', 'fictionality', and 'fictivity', p. 37; also on signposts and "growing hybridization", p. 42). This dualism is further supported by other signposts: the encyclopaedia for factuality, avatar-identification for fictionality, and more.

18.4   Conclusion: A Virtual Museum

Attentat 1942 has exceptionally high 'constructive' authenticity, both in local and macro-scale situation models. Information on the macro world of Nazi occupation before and after Heydrich's assassination is "factual2" (Caracciolo 2020), or factive. Its referentiality and truth value are equal to historiography, and so it is positioned in the 'factual pact' (Fludernik 2020) established in paratextual and intratextual 'signposts'. The wartime and post-war experiences of NPCs are fictive, but exemplifying factual (as in facticity) "collective experientiality" (Alders 2015) of the occupied nation. In Šisler's (2016) words, the characters' backstories are "a 'fictitious' assemblage of authentic testimonies". To Caracciolo (2020), such historically-accurate ficticity is 'factuality1'. The continuity between such 'factual ficticity' and historiographical facticity appears to be the cornerstone of 'constructive' authenticity.

The above can be said about any game (and narrative) constructed with historiographical research and expert consultation. *Attentat 1942* stands out in that it works less like a game, more like a museum offering access to heritage through "collections, exhibits, and narratives" (Lowood 2021). Collections of objects are foregrounded and multi-functional: as evidence, memory-anchors, and passable heritage. Locations from 1942 and 2001 alike use "spatial arrangements of houses and their contents. .. as carriers of personal identity and memory" (Macdonald 2013, p. 96). Going from one to the next is similar to visiting rooms/exhibits at a heritage site. Also the macro scale of the nation holds on to "*realist* spatio-temporal emplotment of objects and environment" (Chapman 2016). Generally, all representations of objects (may) have 'constructive' authenticity, but I also propose biosemantic 'pseudo-objective' authenticity. This would come with avatar-mediated experiential traces of corresponding 'bodily feelings', akin to contact with museum artefacts.

As a virtual heritage environment, *Attentat 1942* is 'omni-modal'. Like museums/heritage sites, it represents its storyworld by artefacts arranged in culturally-meaningful spaces. Like fiction and film, it holds character-focused narratives represented by textual and audiovisual means. (But the use of textual and audiovisual resources is also a feature of museums). All this supports 'constructive' authenticity (at times aided by 'pseudo-objective', if we accept this concept). But it is not where the game achieves its impact. "In all factually based literature moral assessment plays a crucial role", says Lavocat (2020), "both morally and emotionally charged" (p. 587). It happens in the player's experiential confrontation with the 'constructive' (and 'pseudo-objective') content, whose cognitive, emotional, and moral processing translates to 'self-making' authenticity in solitary gameplay and 'interpersonal' authenticity negotiated with others. (Both of which can affirm, negate, or negotiate the 'constructive' authenticity.) Finally, if we subscribe to Caracciolo's (2014, 2019) enactivism, all these authenticities are coupled with reactive 'bodily feelings' authenticity.

Further research may reveal tendencies in the creation of historical authenticity in various games. For instance, fighting games, like the brand new *Hellish Quart* (Kubold 2021), rely on simulated 'immersion into activity': almost on the opposite end to *Attentat 1942* (sports-like vs. museum-like). Analogously to medium-specific affordances for factuality (Ryan 2020), the framework of immersion-linked authenticities (Mochocki 2021a) reveals how "selective authenticity" (by Salvati and Bullinger 2013) is constructed in particular games, game genres, and any historical setting. Another aspect (underresearched here for lack of space) should be paratexts from players and creators, shedding light on how the game functions as a heritage practice that reinforces, or clashes with, existing heritage narratives.

References

V. Agnew, J. Tomann, Authenticity, in *The Routledge Handbook of Reenactment Studies: Key Terms in the Field*, ed. by V. Agnew, J. Lamb, J. Tomann, (Routledge, Milton Park, 2020)

M. Alders, *Mind-Telling: Social Minds in Fiction and History*. PhD Diss., Albert-Ludwigs-Universität (2015)

L. Alexander, Genre, in *The Routledge Companion to Imaginary Worlds*, ed. by M. J. P. Wolf, (Routledge, Milton Park, 2018), pp. 256–273

Attentat 1942, *Steam* (2017). https://store.steampowered.com/app/676630/Attentat_1942/

G. Bagnall, Performance and performativity at heritage sites. Museum Soc. **1**(2), 87–103 (2003)

S.L. Bowman, *Immersion into Larp. Theories of Embodied Narrative Experience. First Person Scholar* (2017). http://www.firstpersonscholar.com/immersion-into-larp/

S.L. Bowman, Immersion and shared imagination in role-playing games, in *Role-Playing Game Studies: Transmedia Foundations*, ed. by J. P. Zagal, S. Deterding, (Routledge, Milton Park, 2018), pp. 379–394

G. Calleja, *In-Game: From Immersion to Incorporation* (MIT Press, Cambridge, MA, 2011)

M. Caracciolo, *The Experientiality of Narrative: An Enactivist Approach* (De Gruyter, Berlin, 2014)

M. Caracciolo, Ungrounding fictional worlds. An Enactivist perspective on the "Worldlikeness" of fiction, in *Possible Worlds Theory and Contemporary Narratology*, ed. by A. Bell, M.-L. Ryan, (University of Nebraska Press, Lincoln, 2019), pp. 157–176

M. Caracciolo, Is factuality the norm? A perspective from cognitive narratology, in *Narrative Factuality*, ed. by M. Fludernik, M.-L. Ryan, (De Gruyter, Berlin, 2020), pp. 149–156

A. Chalk, *Attentat 1942 Is a 'Historically Accurate' Game about the Nazi Occupation of Czechoslovakia*. PC Gamer (2017). https://www.pcgamer.com/attentat-1942-is-a-historically-accurate-game-about-the-nazi-occupation-of-czechoslovakia/

E. Champion, *Playing with the Past* (Springer, Berlin, 2011)

E. Champion, *Critical Gaming: Interactive History and Virtual Heritage* (Ashgate, Farnham, 2015)

A. Chapman, *Digital Games as History: How Videogames Represent the Past and Offer Access to Historical Practice* (Routledge, Milton Park, 2016)

S.H. Dudley, The power of things: agency and potentiality in the work of historical artifacts, in *A Companion to Public History*, ed. by D. M. Dean, (Wiley, Hoboken, 2018), pp. 187–200

M. Fludernik, Factual narration in narratology, in *Narrative Factuality*, ed. by M. Fludernik, M.-L. Ryan, (De Gruyter, Berlin, 2020), pp. 51–74

M. Fludernik, M.-L. Ryan, Factual narrative: an introduction, in *Narrative Factuality*, ed. by M. Fludernik, M.-L. Ryan, (De Gruyter, Berlin, 2020), pp. 1–26

J. Friedrich, You do have responsibility! How games trivialize fascism, why this should concern us and how we could change it, in *History in Games Contingencies of an Authentic Past*, ed. by M. Lorber, F. Zimmermann, (Transcript Verlag, Bielefeld, 2020), pp. 259–275

S. Gapps, Role-play, in *The Routledge Handbook of Reenactment Studies: Key Terms in the Field*, ed. by V. Agnew, J. Lamb, J. Tomann, (Routledge, Milton Park, 2020)

R.J. Gerrig, J.M. Gagnon, The factual in psychology, in *Narrative Factuality*, ed. by M. Fludernik, M.-L. Ryan, (De Gruyter, Berlin, 2020), pp. 133–148

E.L. Hammar, *Producing & Playing Hegemonic Pasts Historical Digital Games as Memory-Making Media*, PhD Diss., The Arctic University of Norway (2019)

S. Hawthorne, *Harbored: Like Museums, Videogames Aren't Neutral.* MA Thesis, Old Dominion University. (2019). https://digitalcommons.odu.edu/humanities_etds/21/

R.S. Jacobs, Winning over the players: investigating the motivations to play and acceptance of serious games. Media Commun. **9**(1), 28–38 (2021). https://doi.org/10.17645/mac.v9i1.3308

S. Jaeger, Factuality in historiography/historical study, in *Narrative Factuality*, ed. by M. Fludernik, M.-L. Ryan, (De Gruyter, Berlin, 2020), pp. 335–350

M. Kapell, A.B.R. Elliott, Conclusion(s): playing at true myths, engaging with authentic histories, in *Playing with the Past: Digital Games and the Simulation of History*, ed. by M. Kapell, A. B. R. Elliott, (Bloomsbury Academic, London, 2013), pp. 233–246

A. Landsberg, *Prosthetic Memory: The Transformation of American Remembrance in the Age of Mass Culture* (Columbia University Press, New York, NY, 2004)

K.F. Latham, What is 'the real thing' in the museum? An interpretive phenomenological study. Museum Manage. Curator. **30**(1), 2–20 (2015). https://doi.org/10.1080/09647775.2015.1008393

F. Lavocat, Pseudofactual narratives and signposts of factuality, in *Narrative Factuality*, ed. by M. Fludernik, M.-L. Ryan, (De Gruyter, Berlin, 2020), pp. 577–592

H. Lowood, Making space for game heritage. *The Finnish Museum of Games* [YouTube]. (2021) . https://www.youtube.com/watch?v=_elBOVngWww

S. Macdonald, *Memorylands: Heritage and Identity in Europe Today* (Routledge, Milton Park, 2013)

Z. Mago, *Attentat 1942. Apparatus. Film, Media and Digital Cultures of Central and Eastern Europe*, No 9 (2019). https://doi.org/10.17892/APP.2019.0009.181

J. Majewski, The potential for Modding communities in cultural heritage, in *The Interactive Past: Archaeology, Heritage & Video Games*, ed. by A. A. A. Mol, C. E. Ariese-Vandemeulebroucke, K. H. J. Boom, A. Politopoulos, (Sidestone Press, Leiden, 2017), pp. 73–82

J. Majewski, *The Elder Scrolls V: Skyrim and its Audience as a World-Building Benchmark for Indigenous Virtual Cultural Heritage*. PhD Diss., Bond University (2018)

M.B.d.A. Matos, M.d.L.d.A. Barbosa, Authenticity in tourist experiences: a new approach based on Edgar Morin's complexity theory. Revista Brasileira de Pesquisa Em Turismo **12**(3), 154–171 (2018). https://doi.org/10.7784/rbtur.v12i3.1457

J. Mikkonen, Truth in literature: the problem of knowledge and insight gained from fiction, in *Narrative Factuality*, ed. by M. Fludernik, M.-L. Ryan, (De Gruyter, Berlin, 2020), pp. 229–244

M. Mochocki, Scenariusze narracyjnych gier fabularnych. Propozycja metody badawczej, in *Kulturotwórcza funkcja gier. Gra jako medium, tekst i rytuał*, ed. by A. Surdyk, vol. 1, (Wydawnictwo Naukowe UAM, Poznań, 2007), pp. 165–172

M. Mochocki, *Role-Play as a Heritage Practice: Historical LARP, Tabletop RPG and Reenactment* (Routledge, Milton Park, 2021a)

M. Mochocki, Heritage sites in videogames. Questions of authenticity and immersion. Games Cult. (2021b). https://doi.org/10.1177/15554120211005369

A.A.A. Mol, Toying with history. Counterplay, counterfactuals, and the control of the past, in *History in Games Contingencies of an Authentic Past*, ed. by M. Lorber, F. Zimmermann, (Transcript Verlag, New York, NY, 2020), pp. 237–257

N. Nolden, Social practices of history in digital possibility spaces. Historicity, mediality, performativity, authenticity, in *History in Games Contingencies of an Authentic Past*, ed. by M. Lorber, F. Zimmermann, (Transcipt Verlag, New York, NY, 2020), pp. 73–91

E. Pfister, Why history in digital games matters. Historical authenticity as a language for ideological myths, in *History in Games Contingencies of an Authentic Past*, ed. by M. Lorber, F. Zimmermann, (Transcipt Verlag, New York, NY, 2020), pp. 47–72

I. Rajewsky, Theories of fictionality and their real other, in *Narrative Factuality*, ed. by M. Fludernik, M.-L. Ryan, (De Gruyter, Berlin, 2020), pp. 29–50

M.-L. Ryan, Ontological Rules, in *The Routledge Companion to Imaginary Worlds*, ed. by M. J. P. Wolf, (Routledge, Milton Park, 2018), pp. 74–81

M.-L. Ryan, From possible worlds to storyworlds. On the worldness of narrative representation, in *Possible Worlds Theory and Contemporary Narratology*, ed. by A. Bell, M.-L. Ryan, (University of Nebraska Press, Lincoln, 2019), pp. 62–87

M.-L. Ryan, Fact, fiction and media, in *Narrative Factuality*, ed. by M. Fludernik, M.-L. Ryan, (De Gruyter, Berlin, 2020), pp. 75–94

A.J. Salvati, J.M. Bullinger, Selective authenticity and the playable past, in *Playing with the Past: Digital Games and the Simulation of History*, ed. by M. Kapell, A. B. R. Elliott, (Bloomsbury Academic, London, 2013), pp. 153–168

L. Saxton, A true story: defining accuracy and authenticity in historical fiction. Rethink. Hist. **24**(2), 127–144 (2020). https://doi.org/10.1080/13642529.2020.1727189

B. Schmitt, *Experiential Marketing: How to Get Customers to Sense, Feel, Think, Act, and Relate to your Company and Brands* (Free Press, New York, NY, 1999)

A. Schwarz, History in video games and the craze for the authentic, in *History in Games Contingencies of an Authentic Past*, ed. by M. Lorber, F. Zimmermann, (Transcipt Verlag, New York, NY, 2020), pp. 117–135

V. Šisler, Contested memories of war in Czechoslovakia 38-89: assassination: designing a serious game on contemporary history. Game Stud. **16**(2) (2016). http://gamestudies.org/1602/articles/sisler

L. Smith, *Uses of Heritage* (Routledge, Taylor & Francis Group, Milton Park, 2006)

J. Sweeting, Authenticity: Depicting the past in historical videogames, in *Transtechnology Research Reader 2018*, ed by M. Punt, H. Drayson (2018), pp. 62–68. http://www.transtechresearch.net/wp-content/uploads/2019/06/TTReader2018_WebVersion.pdf

R. van der Schilden, B. Heijltjes, How Wispfire used history to create fiction, in *The Interactive Past: Archaeology, Heritage & Video Games*, ed. by A. A. A. Mol, C. E. Ariese-Vandemeulebroucke, K. H. J. Boom, A. Politopoulos, (Sidestone Press, 2017), pp. 73–82

S. Varga, C. Guignon, Authenticity, in *Stanford Encyclopedia of Philosophy*, ed. by E. N. Zalta, (Stanford University, Stanford, CA, 2020). https://plato.stanford.edu/archives/spr2020/entries/authenticity

N. Wang, Rethinking authenticity in tourism experience. Ann. Tour. Res. **26**(2), 349–370 (1999). https://doi.org/10.1016/S0160-7383(98)00103-0

T. Winnerling, The eternal recurrence of all bits: how historicizing video game series transform factual history into affective historicity. Eludamos J. Comput. Game Cult. **8**(1), 151–170 (2014)

M.J.P. Wolf, *Building Imaginary Worlds: The Theory and History of Subcreation* (Routledge, Milton Park, 2014)

M.J.P. Wolf, Typology of the nonfactual, in *Narrative Factuality*, ed. by M. Fludernik, M.-L. Ryan, (De Gruyter, Berlin, 2020), pp. 111–126

J.P. Zagal, S. Deterding, Definitions of 'role-playing games', in *Role-Playing Game Studies: Transmedia Foundations*, ed. by J. P. Zagal, S. Deterding, (Routledge, Milton Park, 2018)

F. Zimmermann, Approaching the authenticities of late modernity, in *History in Games Contingencies of an Authentic Past*, ed. by M. Lorber, F. Zimmermann, (Transcipt Verlag, New York, NY, 2020), pp. 9–24

F. Zimmermann, Historical digital games as experiences. How atmospheres of the past satisfy needs of authenticity, in *Game/World/Architectonics. Transdisciplinary Approaches on*

Structures and Mechanics, Levels and Spaces, Aesthetics and Perception, ed. by M. Bonner, (Heidelberg University Publishing, Heidelberg, 2021), pp. 19–34

R.A. Zwaan, Experiential traces and mental simulations in language comprehension, in *Symbols and Embodiment. Debates on Meaning and Cognition*, ed. by M. de Vega, A. Glenberg, A. Graesser, (Oxford University Press, 2008), pp. 165–180

Chapter 19
Using Heuristics for Evaluating Game Narrative: A Close Reading of *Death Stranding*

Barbaros Bostan and Çakır Aker

19.1 Introduction

Games are considered one of the most impressive and profitable applications within the entertainment industry and player evaluations have started to gain the attention within the game production pipeline (Sánchez et al. 2012; Muriel and Crawford 2018). Digital industry pioneers are now relying on a 'user-centered' approach and have been utilizing the knowledge from the field of user experience (UX), game producers started to understand the necessity of a player-centered approach. Majority of the studies on player experience utilized surveys or interviews with players. Researchers also utilized different games as case studies and directed different polls and scales to gather information (Aker et al. 2017). Many player experience evaluation studies suggested novel methodologies including inspections, expert evaluations, or combinations of several techniques to understand and present a deliverable result. But none of those methods were holistic enough since the game genres and even the gaming platforms proved to be affecting the player experience fundamentally (Mäyrä 2007; IJsselsteijn et al. 2013; Aker et al. 2020).

Among the heuristic studies analyzing player experience, only a few of them have focused on specific elements/aspects of games solely. For instance, Korhonen and Koivisto (2006) presented the Playability Heuristics which also included a set of 'mobility heuristics' for analyzing specifically the mobile game platforms. As defined by Nielsen, heuristics evaluation is an inspection method that allows the examination of an interface using statements of principles (Nielsen 1994). As previously mentioned within the literature (Korhonen 2010; Federoff 2002), the expert evaluation method is found to be eligible and effective in evaluating

B. Bostan · Ç. Aker (✉)
Department of Game Design, Bahcesehir University, Istanbul, Turkey
e-mail: barbaros.bostan@comm.bau.edu.tr; cakir.aker@comm.bau.edu.tr

© The Author(s), under exclusive license to Springer Nature Switzerland AG 2022
B. Bostan (ed.), *Games and Narrative: Theory and Practice*, International Series on Computer Entertainment and Media Technology,
https://doi.org/10.1007/978-3-030-81538-7_19

299

games compared to other methods because it does not necessitate any task-oriented test to be conducted. Expert-based heuristic evaluation is applied with simple questions and statements to examine different aspects of games affecting the player experience. By doing so, playability problems that may refer to undesirable effects on the user interaction can be identified (Carmody 2012). Among the studies that focus on specific elements and/or aspects of games, Upton (2017) suggested a set of narrative heuristics for games, but no further case studies were conducted to assess its practical implications. This study aims to fill this gap in literature by applying these heuristics to analyze the 2020 video game, *Death Stranding*. The suggested heuristics were applied by experts from the field of game design and/or user experience to analyze and evaluate the narrative. The study additionally provided 18 sub-heuristics following the experts' suggestions and references from the literature, for analyzing the game narrative.

19.2   Methodology

Close reading is a method from literary theory that has evolved to provide analysis and examination of a media text. Hence, it is a methodology born in the study of literature and adapted to other media forms including games. By facilitating this method, researchers may examine detailed qualities of a media artifact.

For this study, expert evaluation and close reading methods have been utilized. The analysis is facilitated by the suggested six narrative heuristics proposed by Upton (2017). The heuristics are choice, variety, consequence, predictability, uncertainty, and satisfaction. A PlayStation4 console game, *Death Stranding* has been chosen for the purposes of this study. The game received universal acclaim and won several game awards, also both criticized and praised by critics for its narrative. *Death Stranding* does not offer choices and the player cannot affect the story in any way. These narrative properties make the game an ideal candidate for observing the implications of narrative heuristics within a rigid structure. To evaluate the game, two experts from the game studies field have played (100+ hours of gameplay from both researchers) and analyzed the games separately. General statements for the narrative heuristics of Upton were summarized in Table 19.1.

Following these heuristics, the experts were able to assess necessary details regarding the narrative of the chosen game and have managed to provide insights about each. Moreover, it was possible to assess sub-statements for each heuristic, facilitating a categorization of narrative related aspects that will lead to more detailed analysis in the future. The evaluation results delivered are separated into six different heuristics, with sub-statements indicated by the experts analyzing the game. Each heuristic is represented with a title and three sub-titles segmenting the general statement.

Table 19.1 Narrative heuristics suggested by Brian Upton, Situational Game Design, p. 95 (2018)

Heuristic	Principle	Narrative application
Choice	Offer moment-to-moment choices	Create ambiguities that can be resolved through interpretive moves. Don't tell too much.
Variety	Don't repeat situations	Continually develop the plot, characters, and themes. Don't belabor a point.
Consequence	Moves determine future situations	Avoid gratuitous elements. Each beat should connect to the beats that follow it.
Predictability	The effects of moves can be anticipated	Avoid plot holes. If you create expectations, follow up on them.
Uncertainty	Future situations are not inevitable	Avoid clichés, stock characters, and formulaic situations. Outcomes should be uncertain.
Satisfaction	Desirable outcomes are attainable	Avoid inconsistencies and loose ends. Satisfy coherence, expansion, and closure.

19.3   Close Reading of *Death Stranding*

The fictional world of *Death Stranding* has been divided and fragmented by a series of horrific events known as the Death Stranding that caused the world of the dead and the world of the living becoming connected. Following simultaneous explosions all around the world, whenever a human being dies the corpse begins to necrotize and become a Beached Thing (BT) at the end. The survivors of *Death Stranding* live in isolated cities (called knot cities) but there are also individuals who live alone or with their families (called preppers). The protagonist of the story is a porter working for a company called Bridges which aims to reconnect the fragmented society of United States of America.

19.3.1   Choice (Cosmetic, Social, and Gameplay)

Death Stranding's story is very linear, and the player does not have the power of decision making to have an impact on the events of the game. Without story related choices that have serious consequences, what kind of choices matter? Salen and Zimmerman (2004) analyzed choices on two levels: the micro level representing the small, moment-to-moment choices a player is confronted with during a game and the macro level of choice representing the way these micro-choices join like a chain to form a larger trajectory of experience. On the micro level, *Death Stranding* offers three types of choices: cosmetic, social, and gameplay related.

19.3.1.1 Cosmetic Choices

These choices are dimensions of personal interactivity which is related with the interaction of the player with his/her avatar and the tools or equipment used by the player/character (Bostan et al. 2015). In this regard, *Death Stranding* offers a variety of options. The player can change the color of the suit the protagonist is wearing, can configure the backpack he is wearing, can customize the color palette of the trucks or trikes the protagonist is using, and can also the select the accessory that is going to be attached to the backpack (which also has gameplay effects). The player also has the option of changing the color palette of safe houses, the places where the player/character rests and relaxes.

19.3.1.2 Social Choices

These choices effect the relationship of the player with various non-player characters (NPCs) inhabiting the world of *Death Stranding*. There are no dialogue options in the game but there is a connection level represented by stars. The player is free to finish the optional deliveries provided by each NPC to increase the connection level with them. By completing these deliveries, the connection level will increase in stars and the player will receive e-mail messages from these NPCs. These e-mail messages include the backstories of characters, lore about the world of *Death Stranding*, interesting things NPCs notice, and the opinions of NPCs on joining the UCA (United Cities of America) but they also represent their bonding with the player/character. Once the maximum level of connection is reached, some NPCs will reward the player with cosmetic items, but some will reward the player with operational items that have an impact on the gameplay. For example, the Collector gives a backpack cover to the player which increases the resistance to timefall (otherworldly rain that ages objects) and thus protects the cargo the player/character is carrying.

19.3.1.3 Gameplay Choices

These choices are not only about what the player/character will do but also about how the player/character will do them. The idea of deliveries is quite simple, the player receives packages from location A and will have to deliver them to location B. How the player is going to traverse the virtual world will determine what kind of obstacles the player/character is going to face. The structures the player/character will build or have built before on his way to the destination will affect the probability of a successful delivery. The tools or weapons the player/character is carrying will affect the probability of overcoming the obstacles faced on the way. The vehicles or zip-lines used by the player will affect the delivery duration and the number of likes received upon the completion of a delivery. These are micro level choices concerning the mechanics of the game. Players will determine different strategies for overcoming different obstacles.

19.3.2   Variety (Quests, Characters, and Theme)

Variety in a game narrative comes in different forms, such as quest variety, character variety and theme variety. Quests in games are missions for the player used primarily for narrative progression but there are also optional/side quests in most role-playing games that reward the player with experience points, unique items, or skills. Theme here is the moral of the story and is revealed through the characters as they progress through the plot, but theme is neither character nor plot (Fink 2014). Famous game designer Hideo Kojima stated that he prioritized the theme of "connection" over traditional video-game violence in Death Stranding (Gault 2019).

19.3.2.1   Quest Variety

The first type of variety in quest design arises from the objectives of a quest that define what is required of the player. In *Death Stranding*, the player progresses in the game by taking orders and delivering cargo to various knot cities or preppers. Cargo carried by the player can be materials such as metals, ceramics, resin, etc. but it can also be art books, watches, anti-aging creams, old game consoles, etc. *Death Stranding*'s story consists of 14 chapters and each chapter requires several story-related orders to be completed by the player. Each knot city or prepper in *Death Stranding*'s virtual world also offer optional orders. These optional deliveries for the player are called standard orders. Standard orders increase the player's connection with characters (displayed with stars) and are rewarded with unique items. The second type of variety in quest design arises from the meaning of a quest, which comes in three different ways: (1) the impact of the player's accomplishments on and within a simulated world, (2) a narrative backstory that conveys emotional urgency by revealing why the player is performing an action and what effects this action will have, and (3) ideas symbolically encoded within the landscape, objects and challenges of the quest and enacted through it (Howard 2008). Story related missions in *Death Stranding* give essential information to the player, demonstrate facts, explain what is happening and why. Some quests in *Death Stranding* show how the player is affecting the virtual world and some quests provide valuable background information that the player needs to interpret the story. In a nutshell, although the idea of delivering cargo sounds like a repetitive and mundane task, each mission in *Death Stranding* is different than the other and no two deliveries are the same in terms of objectives, actions and meaning.

19.3.2.2   Character Variety

The world in *Death Stranding* is divided into East, Central and West sections where several knot cities and preppers reside. Using the three-dimensional character framework of Egri (1960), the variety in characters comes in three forms: physiology, sociology, and psychology. Physiology is defined by the physical attributes of a character. The occupation, education, family life, place or standing in community, amusements or hobbies of a character determine the sociological dimension. The moral standards, goals, ambitions, temperament, attitude towards life, obsessions, judgment, and imagination of a character determine the psychological dimension. The basic idea is that every character is defined by these three dimensions and by adjusting these dimensions according to the desired goals of a game, one can create both protagonists and other characters that fit in with the desired fictional world (Lankoski et al. 2003). Non-player characters (NPCs) in Death Stranding have different occupations and personality, what they are doing and why they are doing it also varies. Major characters of the game are unique in terms of their sociology and psychology, and each has his own role in the main story of the game.

19.3.2.3 Theme Variety

The theme of the story is a criticism of an era of individualism where everyone is fractured yet all connected. The game wants you to feel alone in a fragmented society but also wants you to reconnect people by delivering packages and connecting them to an advanced internet called the "Chiral Network." The story is about loneliness, despair, distrust but also friendship, trust, and connection. The first dimension in arousing these different emotions in players is the variety in audiovisuals of the game. From deserted factories to gloomy BT infested territories, beautiful landscapes to marvelous waterfalls, the game offers very different virtual environments. Besides the visuals, the soundtrack of the game is defined as an amazing and uplifting collection of songs that defies categorization (Smith 2019). The seamless integration of cinematics and gameplay, the use of camera angles and shot sizes define the cinematic components of the game that support the themes. The backstory of each major character is carefully crafted for maximum emotional impact. For example, the complex story of Captain Clifford Unger is revealed piece by piece throughout the chapters of the game and evokes very different emotions in the player such as curiosity, wonder, admiration, and sympathy.

19.3.3   Consequences (Casual, Social, and Gameplay)

Consequences are related with the choices provided by a game. *Death Stranding* does not have any choices that branch the story but consequences in *Death Stranding* matter on a micro level, where moment-to-moment choices influence the game.

19.3.3.1 Casual Consequences

These are the consequences of casual decisions made by the player. These decisions do not have an impact on the gameplay but have an impact on the emotional state of the player. Do you want to listen to a music track in a safe house? Do you want to rest and play harmonica on top of a cliff? Do you want to stop and enjoy the scenery beside a waterfall? Do you want to wear a Santa hat in your deliveries when it is Christmas in the real world? These actions will not change the game in any way, but they represent an important psychological need of players, the need for play represented with the following actions: to relax, amuse oneself, seek diversion and entertainment; to play games; to laugh, joke, and be merry (Bostan 2009).

19.3.3.2 Social Consequences

There are various characters in *Death Stranding* the players meet on their journey. Increasing the connection level with these characters is not mandatory but will result in an increase in the number of likes received and will be rewarded with unique items. But this decision is up to the player and it is still possible to end the game without maximizing the connection level with every single character. As the connection levels increase, the e-mails received from these characters will also shed light on some of the mysteries of the world of *Death Stranding*, but again the decision is up to the player. The BB (unborn fetus carried and used by the player as an equipment) player/character is carrying will get stressed under certain conditions and will start crying. The player has the option to rock and soothe the BB, which will increase his/her connection with BB, but this is also not mandatory. The player can complete the pizza deliveries requested by a prepper in a post-apocalyptic world and learn unexpected information about the antagonist of the story, but the choice is again up to the player. So, the game does not force the player to make connections, but the game is about forming connections will reward the player with info/rewards not provided otherwise.

19.3.3.3 Gameplay Consequences

Game playing is a retrospective experience where the player's previous actions or choices have an impact on his/her future (Bostan et al. 2015). The moment-to-moment decisions of players usually have immediate consequences in *Death Stranding*. Climbing a precarious cliff may ruin your cargo beyond repair if you fall. Crossing a river with a load of cargo on your back may cause the loss of your precious packages. Carrying ladders or portable chiral constructors (PCCs) with you on your missions may make your journey much easier. Using lethal weapons instead of non-lethal weapons may cause the death of people and thus create a voidout (an annihilative explosion). The range of variables that can be manipulated and customized by the player determine the depth of interaction Steuer (1992) and the consequences of these interactions determine the enjoyment of a game.

19.3.4 Predictability (Quests, Characters, and Gameplay)

According to Upton's Narrative Heuristics, 'Predictability' is defined as the effects of actions to be anticipated in terms of plot, allowing the player to follow up on expectations. Upton noted that the audience would presume incidents that are structured by the narrative as significant. The fundamental matter behind the heuristic of predictability relies on player expectations and presumptions. The player necessitates the narrative to be anticipated and if any expectations were created, they were to be followed. Yet additionally, he also indicted that; "If we know exactly how the story is going to unfold, then there's no longer any reason for us to keep engaging with it" (Upton 2017). Thus, a balance between expectations and surprises within a game narrative is expected.

19.3.4.1 Predictability of Quests

The first moments of *Death Stranding* are tense, throwing the player into a dangerous and unknown world. This atmosphere puts the player on alert. Then, several characters are introduced, and basic narrative elements of this forsaken world are explained to the player to give some limited context. As the main story progress, side missions (standard deliveries) are given to the player as optional tasks to follow. As mentioned before, quests in *Death Stranding* are primarily utilized to move the player forward through the narrative. Yet the various side missions and the main mission differ in terms of the predictability of quests. *Death Stranding*'s standard orders could be considered as contributions to the narrative, yet they only serve minor additions to the main plot (Ip 2011). By completing these standard quests, players receive mostly expected outcomes and these orders are quite predictable. In terms of the main story, the game often suggests and hints to the predictable outcomes throughout the cut scenes and dialogues, providing the player with a chance to predict the future of the outcomes to some extent. Although the main narrative of the game seems complex and sometimes confusing in the beginning, many cues regarding the overall situation and possible future outcomes are hinted at and/or delivered. Thus, most of the players were able to not just comprehend the story in general, the game also foreshadows the future happenings in a meaningful way. As Upton (2017) points out; "These choices need to have predictable consequences for our future narrative situations, but the course of the story should never become so obvious that we know exactly how it will play out".

19.3.4.2 Predictability of Characters

The game offers various characters for player interaction. Regarding the main storyline, the characters the player meets often have curious attitudes accompanied with unusual forms. One such character is the NPC called Heartman, who is a man with a defibrillator on his chest that stops his heart and then brings him back to life repeatedly. The NPC, Mama, has a 'ghost' baby attached to her when first met. Although these characters were designed to be intriguing, they were not designed to arouse player suspicion. Interactions with characters aim to gain their trust. Some characters are specially designed and delivered with the message of doubt in mind, such as Deadman (the character that tries to help us in the beginning but as the game progresses it is understood that he was withholding some crucial information from the main character) or most importantly, Amelie/Bridget Strand, the adoptive mother of the protagonist. *Death Stranding* also has a pure antagonist character, Higgs Monaghan. The player immediately meets with this character and its unique appearance with a golden death mask hints that he is the enemy. As for the side characters, their background stories are usually unpredictable, and these characters shed some light on the small aspects of the fictional world. Thus, with a combination of predictable stories and unpredictable characters, the game creates a well-defined balance between the predictability and the curiosity of the player along with the narrative.

19.3.4.3   Predictability of Gameplay

Death Stranding offers moment to moment decisions regarding the quests and orders the player takes but the gameplay is quite unpredictable. The fictional world is filled with unpredictable situations. For instance, the game includes semi-random rainfalls that summon dangerous enemies, the terrorists, or timefall that damages the cargo of the player. Moving across BT territories within the game world allows for an unpredictable challenge every time since these BT territories (and their implicated danger) shift from time to time and allow for a challenging journey even though the player have used the same route more than once. Each time the player sets a route, elements such as the weather, BT territory shifts, weight of the total cargo carried (affecting player balance), the gadgets carried by the player affect the journey to some extent. In terms of the plot, the game offers unpredictable events from time to time. There are various plot twists and surprises along the game. The player cannot be certain of when and how a boss fight might begin for instance, allowing for a positive unpredictability aspect. For instance, following a questline involving the Mama character, the player completes some predictable quests and expects to do some more. Surprisingly, when the protagonist just takes its first step outside to start his journey, the player finds him/herself in a boss fight with the infamous character Higgs.

19.3.5   Uncertainty (Game, Player, and Outcome)

Uncertainty means not knowing what is going to happen and character uncertainty is related with the unknown reactions and motivations of the characters that the players meet. It provides a conundrum, a problem and curiosity. Kumari et al. (2019) addresses the fact that many game designers and academics have reiterated the importance of uncertainty for a good player experience. Uncertainty is about how the narrative of the game avoids clichés and have some degree of an unknown for engaging the interpreter. As mentioned above, the game allows for unpredictable events which adds challenging situations for the player. Similar to the previous heuristic, predictability, uncertainty refers to the significance of player choices and predictions yet as Upton indicates, the player should never be sure about the revelation of events and story twist for the whole time; "The ending is always in doubt, right up until we read the final word on the final page" (Upton 2017). If the player is encountering the same choices and outcomes again, the situation no longer feels playful. Following these ideas Kumari et al. (2019) proposed a categorization of uncertainty in games: Game Uncertainty, Player Uncertainty and, Outcome Uncertainty.

19.3.5.1 Game Uncertainty

Game uncertainty is uncertainty afforded by the game system, invoking surprise and excitement over game content and curiosity over what the game will present next. As mentioned, in most narrative structures, the anticipations of the player could mix with uncertainty to facilitate the story. It is the feeling of anticipation regarding the game content and novel challenges and configurations. In *Death Stranding*, the narrative is simply delivered through the unfolding of the dialogues and events. The players do not have the opportunity to affect its linear structure. Various game critics also referred to this fact, commenting that the *Death Stranding*'s story is not the strongest feature of the game since it somehow hints at many twists in an obvious manner (Shankle 2020). Yet, the game can still deliver surprising outcomes and events throughout the events unfolding. The game offers not just intriguing characters who shed some light on the most tantalizing question of the game, but also the content of the quests generate curiosity of what would happen next, for instance making the player ask questions about the Higgs character or his relationship with the protagonist. Moreover, even though if the player has traversed an area in the game world for completing an objective, every time s/he begins the similar journey, the game world might deliver unexpected challenges such as surprise encounters with BT's or MULE's. This uncertainty forces the player to keep engaged with the game continuously independent from the fact the same route has been explored several times before. Most importantly, several different areas include challenges with varying difficulty. The everchanging gameplay areas could be a beneficial element for always providing and sustaining some certain amount of uncertainty.

19.3.5.2   Player Uncertainty

Player uncertainty encompasses the players experience over decisions, interactions, and the ability to adapt and learn in the process. Players are offered with a variety of decisions throughout the game such as jumping, ducking under certain terrain, resting, or even sleeping on their journey. This includes elements such as the routes to be taken and/or places to rest and avoid enemies. This term is utilized in the sense of narrative to be understood differently than uncertain gameplay elements such as false attacks, misses or critical hits for instance (Xu et al. 2021). In *Death Stranding*, although the roads and most of the routes that you could take to go from A to B is not that complicated, the barriers that the player faces on those routes differ. Hence the player is expected to overcome those challenges via utilizing his/her skills and special equipment, such as using ladders. This provides the players to experience a certain amount of challenge along the way but also an opportunity to learn and strategize for tackling with obstacles. Every step that the player takes includes a challenge, the protagonist may lose his balance and fall, or get caught by terrorists or BTs. The game provides a mechanic which allows the players to map the terrain around them to make quick decisions on how to keep on moving forward. This mapping allows the player to take risks for faster travel or not. For instance, the player can either use a ladder as a bridge to cross a river or decide to build a bridge which would require construction materials. The missions also require the player to make important decisions even before they start their journey in the game world. Quests often provide certain amount of cargo to be delivered and these were deployed when the player takes on a delivery job. As soon as the cargo is given, the player can place the cargo on the protagonist, deciding on how to balance and distribute weight. This decision would affect the controls and interaction of the journey directly and could cause diverse affects through the journey. Although the game allows for an automatic optimization for hauling the cargo, that does not mean that the optimized auto-placement of the cargo is the most feasible. The players also have to think which packages should be protected from timefall since the protected area is limited. As a result, the game provides a vast array of decisions and uncertainties regarding the player experience.

19.3.5.3   Outcome Uncertainty

Outcome uncertainty involves the player's curiosity about whether their predictions of the outcome were correct or if they reach the desired outcome. It is also described as uncertainty over not knowing the reaction of the game or another player. It is never clear if other players have completed a structure that you have been trying to build the next day. The same goes for the 'like' mechanism of the game. The more likes that the player gets from others, the better equipment and skills they receive. Hence building a road on a significant route would gain more likes from others and vice versa. This aspect represents the uncertainty regarding the likes that the player would get from others and would possibly engage them for investing time for carrying essential materials to the structures to be built. Moreover, the preppers could offer some story-driven deliveries which then could lead to unexpected outcomes such as two preppers getting engaged because of the player, only to divorce later. These events provide a level of uncertainty regarding the standard deliveries or side missions. Although these missions do not change their course of action because of player decisions, the feeling of uncertainty remains for the quest outcomes and how it would affect the world revolving around the player.

19.3.6 Satisfaction (Coherence, Expansion, and Closure)

The heuristic of satisfaction entitles not only if the players' expectations of the story to be fulfilled, but rather if they would be able to consistently able to uncover interpretive actions which would provide satisfaction of the implicit goals such as coherence, expansion and closure.

19.3.6.1 Coherence

If the player gains an understanding of a character or an event that takes place in a game, the next action or information should be coherent. Otherwise, the player could lose consistency and could not perceive an interpretive action. In terms of the game's protagonist character, Sam, he has a predictable cold acting attitude. Even when the player learns the stories from his past, the attitude of the character matches his current situation. The character has the attribute of not touching anyone as well as portraying some social disabilities which remain in the entirety of the game. Moreover, other characters also have a coherent attitude toward events around them. No matter what actions the player does, characters in the game represent a coherent story. More importantly, the game world reacts to characters actions in a consistent manner, enabling the player to have certain expectations from the events unfolding. *Death Stranding* delivers facts of the story as clear as possible by providing character dialogues, hints and lore related objects, providing coherent information regarding the world and the characters at the same time. Players can find various objects and/or logs about characters, getting detailed background information about them. These in turn can create some connection on an emotional level and, more importantly, provide a basis for coherent narrative regarding the characters. By learning these things, the player can presume most of the attitudes of the characters in a consistent manner. *Death Stranding* has big story twists in its narrative for a few of the characters yet for the rest of the game, characters have a coherent narrative directing the player in an amenable journey.

19.3.6.2 Expansion

Expansion refers to the need to find interpretive actions that open new possibilities for the player to explore the story of the game. The option of exploration of story beats should not only hint at the obvious possibilities to the player but also provide some space to reject mundane possibilities and rather make interpretations in favor of more imaginative ones. As mentioned previously, the game not only offers a main linear story but with side quests and many lore items embedded in the game world, the player has the chance to understand the fictional world and its events on a much deeper level. By following side-quests or retrieving information regarding the characters, world, powers, chiral network or other interesting things in the game, the player can get invested with the narrative if s/he chooses to. Although the game has a fixed ending, the players are free to wander in the world to some extent, exploring and expanding their understanding of the narrative if they wish to do so. The overarching narrative of how the world has changed to its current state is a good example representing this heuristic since the main plot was not focusing on what caused it and how people reacted to it. The players have the option to expand their knowledge on the stranding via getting access to old-world logs/diaries, dialogues, or objects.

19.3.6.3 Closure

At the end of any game, players need the feeling of closure and the story should provide the opportunity to close and conclude story arcs throughout the game, resolving various conflicts and loose ends. Simply put, the closure represents tying up the loose ends. In that sense, the game provided a full closure to nearly all the questions that the player would want to learn about. Conflicts between characters, the realities behind the scenes, why the Death Stranding was happening, the origins of BB and the relationship with crucial characters were all explained and concluded. Yet the long cinematics in the last hours of the game were criticized by people for not allowing any type of interactivity during the unfolding. As this becomes the much-needed satisfactory closure for the game narrative which all the questions saliently posed by the narrative are answered (Carroll 2007). But as Murray puts it, there is also a play-based conclusion for which "occurs when a work's structure, though not its plot, is understood" (Murray 1998). The game provides no branching in its narrative and thus do not implicitly provide a replayability value of the story. It does not leave open endings or any expansions such as new quests after finishing the main story. Thus, perhaps unintentionally, removing the motivation for playing again after witnessing the closure cinematics and provide a low replayability value.

19.4 Conclusion

In this study, we presented a novel approach for assessing game narrative via utilization of heuristics. From the narrative heuristics delivered from the literature, a detailed heuristic perception arose indicated via experts. To the best of our knowledge, this study provides a novel approach for inspecting the narrative in games by utilizing heuristics. Application of heuristic evaluations were supported by close reading of a game to facilitate the method. As a result, a total number of 18 heuristics were suggested for analyzing the narrative in games (Table 19.2).

Game narratives are usually discussed and analyzed with subjective methods such as surveys, interviews, and the close reading of game reviews and/or game critics. The utilization of a set of heuristics that analyze game experience in general can be found in literature but the utilization of a set of heuristics that focus specially on game narratives is a gap in literature. A set of heuristics that analyze game narratives is proposed by Upton (2017), but no further studies were conducted to assess its practical implications. Thus, we tested the usability of narrative heuristics defined by Upton (2017) and expanded the given set of heuristics with suitable sub-heuristics. In this regard, we applied the original the set of narrative heuristics to the 2020 video game *Death Stranding* with a close reading methodology. The close reading of the game is supported by the expert evaluation method that relies not on the observation of players performing a set of tasks but on the expertise and judgment of the evaluators. In this study, two experts played and inspected the game separately. In the end, the findings from the experts are compared and amassed to provide a detailed analysis of the game's narrative. Each heuristic of Upton (2017) is expanded with three sub-heuristics found by the close reading and expert evaluation of the game narrative. Ultimately, utilization of heuristics for narrative of games proved to be valuable for assessing the game story and would help game designers to better integrate the player research also as a part of the narrative design.

The expanded set of narrative heuristics may be also useful for future studies that aims to utilize heuristic evaluation of game narratives. Future work in this area can address several research trajectories. The game chosen for this study has a linear narrative and the story does not branch with player choices. The set of expanded narrative heuristics worked well within this rigid narrative structure but future studies with games that offer the player the opportunity to make meaningful choices within a narrative can further expand the narrative heuristics set provided

Table 19.2 Suggested heuristics of the study for assessing the narrative in games

Main heuristics	Sub-heuristics		
Choice	Cosmetic	Social	Gameplay
Variety	Quests	Characters	Themes
Consequences	Casual	Social	Gameplay
Predictability	Quests	Characters	Gameplay
Uncertainty	Game	Player	Outcome
Satisfaction	Coherence	Expansion	Closure

by this study. Furthermore, a multi-modal assessment of the heuristics given could possibly be beneficial for providing a more rigid set of principles and could be beneficial for both the industry and the field of research.

References

Ç. Aker, K. Rızvanoğlu, B. Bostan, Methodological review of playability heuristics, in *Proc. Eurasia Graphics, Istanbul, Turkey* (2017), p. 405

Ç. Aker, K. Rızvanoğlu, Y. Inal, Revisiting heuristics for evaluating player experience in different gaming platforms: a multi-modal approach, in *Game User Experience and Player-Centered Design*, (Springer, Cham, 2020), pp. 123–161

B. Bostan, Player motivations: a psychological perspective. Comput. Entertain. **7**(2), 22 (2009)

B. Bostan, G. Sahin, M.C. Uney, Interactivity in computer games, in *Proceedings of the GAMEON 2015 Conference, Amsterdam, Holland* (2015)

K.W. Carmody, *Exploring Serious Game Design Heuristics: A Delphi Study*, Doctoral Dissertation, Northeastern University (2012)

N. Carroll, Narrative closure. Philos. Stud. **135**(1), 1–15 (2007)

L. Egri, *The Art of Dramatic Writing* (Simon & Schuster, New York, 1960)

M.A. Federoff, *Heuristics and Usability Guidelines for the Creation and Evaluation of Fun in Video Games* (Doctoral dissertation, Indiana University, 2002)

E.J. Fink, *Dramatic Story Structure. A Primer for Screenwriters* (Routledge, New York, 2014)

M. Gault, We're not thinking about others, in *What Hideo Kojima Wants You to Learn from Death Stranding* (2019). Retrieved 15 Dec 2020, from https://time.com/5722226/hideo-kojima-death-stranding/

J. Howard, *Quests: Design, Theory, and History in Games and Narratives* (A K Peters, Wellesley, MA, 2008)

W.A. IJsselsteijn, Y.A. de Kort, K. Poels, The game experience questionnaire. Eindhoven: Technische Universiteit Eindhoven **46**(1) (2013)

B. Ip, Narrative structures in computer and video games: Part 1: Context, definitions, and initial findings. Games Cult. **6**(2), 103–134 (2011)

H. Korhonen, Comparison of playtesting and expert review methods in mobile game evaluation, in *Proceedings of the 3rd International Conference on Fun and Games* (2010), pp. 18–27

H. Korhonen, E.M. Koivisto, Playability heuristics for mobile games, in *Proceedings of the 8th Conference on Human-Computer Interaction with Mobile Devices and Services* (2006), pp. 9–16

S. Kumari, S. Deterding, J. Freeman, The role of uncertainty in moment-to-moment player motivation: a grounded theory, in *Proceedings of the Annual Symposium on Computer-Human Interaction in Play* (2019), pp. 351–363

P. Lankoski, S. Helio, I. Ekman, Characters in computer games: toward understanding interpretation and design, in *Proceedings of the Level Up Conference, Utrecht* (2003)

F. Mäyrä, The contextual game experience: on the socio-cultural contexts for meaning in digital play, in *Proceedings of the DiGRA Conference* (2007)

D. Muriel, G. Crawford, *Video Games as Culture: Considering the Role and Importance of Video Games in Contemporary Society* (Routledge, Milton Park, 2018)

J.H. Murray, *Hamlet on the Holodeck: The Future of Narrative in Cyberspace* (The MIT Press, Cambridge, MA, 1998)

J. Nielsen, Usability inspection methods, in *Conference Companion on Human Factors in Computing Systems* (1994), pp. 413–414

K. Salen, E. Zimmerman, *The Rules of Play* (MIT Press, Cambridge, MA, 2004)

J.L.G. Sánchez, F.L.G. Vela, F.M. Simarro, N. Padilla-Zea, Playability: analysing user experience in video games. Behav. Inform. Technol. **31**(10), 1033–1054 (2012)

A. Shankle, *Death Stranding Review: Patronizing and Dull* (2020). Retrieved 5 Feb 2020, from https://www.gameskinny.com/2exrb/death-stranding-review-patronizing-and-dull

D. Smith, *The Weird and Wonderful World of Hideo Kojima's 'Death Stranding' Soundtrack* (2019). Retrieved 5 Dec 2020, from https://musicfeeds.com.au/features/death-stranding/

J. Steuer, Defining virtual reality: dimensions determining telepresence. J. Commun. **42**(4), 73–93 (1992)

B. Upton, *Situational game design* (CRC Press, Boca Raton, 2017)

W. Xu, H.N. Liang, K. Yu, N. Baghaei, Effect of gameplay uncertainty, display type, and age on virtual reality exergames, in *Proceedings of the CHI Conference on Human Factors in Computing Systems (CHI '21)* (2021)

Chapter 20
Allegation and World-Building in Video Games

Aleksandra Mochocka

20.1 Allegation

The notion of "allusion or allegation" was first utilised in the studies of poetry by Mathieu-Castellani as a part of her typology of intertextuality (MacPhail 2002, p. 2). Mathieu-Castellani (1984) discusses Renaissance poets and their decision to make allusions to works of renewed authority. Castellani tries to pinpoint the differences between various applications of allusions; she states that sometimes an allusion serves as a kind of allegation, observing that "to allege means to summon the word of the other to authorise one's own speech"[1] (p. 29; trans. AM). The text that quoted is treated as a source of authority (Buda 2015, p. 260).

As Tryniecka (2020) has it, according to Głowiński "referring to intertextuality is justified only when the allusion to the previous work determines the meaning of the discussed text" (p. 180). The degree to and the ways in which the discussed text relies on the previous works can be much different. Michał Głowiński (1986) introduced the notion of allegation to the Polish literary studies, translating Castellani's term as *alegacja* (p. 90). Głowiński negotiated the meaning of allegation, distinguishing between intertextuality and allegation as contradictory entities, and changing Castellani's understanding of the notion to some degree (Buda 2015, p. 60). Reaching out for Bakhtin's theory, Głowiński (1986) states that allegations are "all those textual references that are not aligned with the essence of dialogism, in which a quote or allusion not only fails to support polyphony, but to the contrary –

---

[1] "Alléguer, c'est convoquer la parole de l'autre pour autoriser sa propre parole [...]."

A. Mochocka (✉)
Kazimierz Wielki University, Bydgoszcz, Poland
e-mail: a.mochocka@ukw.edu.pl

© The Author(s), under exclusive license to Springer Nature Switzerland AG 2022
B. Bostan (ed.), *Games and Narrative: Theory and Practice*, International Series on Computer Entertainment and Media Technology,
https://doi.org/10.1007/978-3-030-81538-7_20

supports homophony"[2] (trans. AM) (p. 91). Thus, a literary text built upon allegation could be perceived as "the homophonic (or mono-logical) narrative [that] represents discourse and points of view which may be reduced to the <<author's>> ideological position" (Bagby 1982, p. 38). Consequently, allegation takes place when references to an intertext with established authority are deliberately introduced to enhance the authority of the newly created text. Głowiński's allegation "confirms monody" (Buda 2015, p. 260) and constitutes "using the text by someone else in order to build one's own text up" (Buda 2015) Intertextuality and allegation are only seemingly identical for Głowiński (1986) – they possess comparable form, but their functions are different (p. 91). Intertextuality is typical of literature, while allegation is to be found in persuasive writings, eg. propaganda (Głowiński 1986).

In the case of intertextual allusion of a kind that Głowiński (1986) labels as allegation, the readers are directed into a highly specific way of reading. They could try to resist the imposed reception, of course, but allegation, by definition, serves the opposite purpose – it is a means of control, channelling the reader's reaction to the one preferred by the text creator. Consequently, allegation is a means of triggering specific aesthetic responses. The new text is meant to be appreciated and respected immediately and automatically. Allegation is meant to be an easily accessible, fast way of experiencing contact with the established canon, and yet the underlying assumption to be found here is that the original text is both too important to ever deny its value, and too difficult to approach directly, in its entirety.

However, other Polish scholars perceive allegation as a strategy that allows for possible polyphonic readings. Balbus (1993) relates to Mathieu-Castellani's idea and calls it "an extra tool" used effectively when necessary (p. 131). He stresses out that allegation always situates the text in historical and genealogical context (p. 132). Related to establishing authority as it is, allegation does not exclude intersemiotic dialogue, although one can dominate the other (Balbus 1993, pp. 132–133). Including allegation into the ranks of intertextuality, Fulińska (1997) observes that it "is, without doubt, an intentional and purposeful reference [. . .] meant to be deciphered by the reader, and assuming that her literary competence would allow for that [...]"[3] (trans. AM) (p. 15), and Szalewska (2008) states that even in a text oriented towards homophony allegation could be understood as a game with literary tradition (p. 113).

Taking the discussion of allegation held by Polish literary studies scholars as a point of departure, I propose to extend the application of allegation to all categories and genres of texts, regardless of their media specificity and the modes in which they can be approached. Neither the modes of interaction, nor the affordances of

---

[2]"Alegacjami będę przeto nazywać wszelkie odwołania tekstowe nie łączące się z żywiołem dialogiczności, takie, w których cytat czy aluzja nie tylko nie staje się czynnikiem wielogłosowości, przeciwnie — utwierdza jednogłosowość."

[3]"Emulacyjna odmiana naśladowania spełnia podstawowe wymagania stawiane relacji intertekstualnej: jest niewątpliwie nawiązaniem zamierzonym i celowym [...], przeznaczonym do rozszyfrowywania przez odbiorcę i zakładającym jego kompetencję literacką to umożliwiającą [...]."

the media platform that precondition them (Hutcheon and O'Flynn 2013) would influence allegation, which could be therefore treated as a transmedia phenomenon. The primary impulse behind allegation, as the term is going to be understood here, is to allow the readers to recognise the source of the references and identify them as taken from a text with notable reputation. The readers should then, presumably, appreciate the connection, and approach the new text as one imbued with unquestionable value. The suggestion is, however, that the value does not have to be limited to the high-culture, highbrow standards, as it could be tied with the subcultural capital of popular culture audiences as well.

Allegation can be approached as an intertextual narrative strategy that increases the authority of the text and makes it more successful (critically, commercially) by means of referencing to a higher status intertext or texts, with the potential to be dialogic and to facilitate game/play between the implied author and the readers (Martuszewska 2008), but nonetheless gravitating towards homophony. More specifically, it could be suggested that it is possible to analyse allegation in the context of narrative worldbuilding. Thus, the above mentioned "success" of the text would be not just limited to its market value / audience range of a text, but understood as the text's ability to generate narratives that are manifestations of the narrative scripts it facilitates. The storyworld existents that are taken from the texts of higher authority enable the reconstruction of the narrative scripts, at the same time controlling the meaning by either allowing for dialogic interpretation (allegation-as-dialogue), directing and automatising the reading (allegation-as-monologue).

20.2 Narrative Themes in *Child of Light* and *My Memory of Us*

Two examples of video games using this strategy are *Child of Light* (Ubisoft Montreal 2014), 2D platform role-playing game featuring turnbased combat (JRPG-like), and *My Memory of Us* (Juggler Games 2018), a 2D side-scrolling platform puzzle-solving game. Narrative-wise, both games rely on frame narratives (Pier 2014). In both cases, the frame narrative is that of an adult telling a fantastic story to a child. In *Child of Light* (often-time called a "playable poem") the frame story is a bed-side fairy tale told by an unspecified adult woman, as suggested by a genre marker in the form of the conventional (verbal) opening ("Child, tuck yourself in bed / Let me tell a story [...]"), accompanied by visual cues (which is suggestive of possible references to *The Beauty and the Beast* (1991) opening credits). The frame narrative to be found in *My Memory of Us* is a steampunk/dieselpunk tale addressed by an elderly man to a little girl visiting his book store, in what seems to be a contemporary city somewhere in Europe or North America. However, in both games there is yet another narrative frame encapsulating the above mentioned ones, Chinese-box style: adults pass the stories of their own personal (traumatic) experiences to another generation.

In the core narratives the playable characters are children who interact with environments that consist, for the most part, of forlorn ruins. In *Child of Light* there are remnants of an ancient civilisation in a land that is foreign to the character; in *My Memory of Us* there is a city destroyed by war and devastated by robotic invaders, with more and more places overtaken by the aggressors and inaccessible to the characters. With player agency reduced to various forms of interaction with the ruins, in both games they play, *nomen omen*, an important role. The ruins might be read as suggestive of the process of discovering, exploring, and reclaiming the past as a part of one's identity in the process of dealing with trauma. Characterised by duality, ruins are where both danger and refuge can be found. As Vella (2011) observes, in video games ruins are characterised by their "essential past-orientedness", but in the case of the two games exploring the ruins determines how the past becomes a part of characters' (contemporary) identity – the story to be passed to future generations is about surviving and getting stronger, which would have been possible but for what they can find and do in the devastated environment.

Situated as a serious game (Bontchev 2015), *My Memory of Us* tries to tackle the theme of the WWII trauma (specifically, the Holocaust). Potentially, video games are "a visual media able to recreate both tangible and intangible cultural artifacts in a highly interactive and dynamic way" (Bontchev 2015, p. 44), and the very title of the game paratextually announces that it attempts at exactly that endeavour. The same can be said about the official materials issued by the design studio. To quote the description of the title on the Steam platform: "My Memory of Us is a moving fairy tale about friendship and hope in the darkest moments of our times. Enter hand-crafted, gorgeously animated 2D world full of adventure, exploration, stealth and puzzles. Meet the kids brought up in different worlds and help them survive during times of occupation" (Juggler Games 2018).

While *My Memory of Us* undertakes the task of recreating trauma by providing the players with the opportunity to engage with the personal perspective of childhood memories of the Holocaust survivors, the game exploits its safe status of a make-believe activity inside the Huzingian magic circle, keeping the distance from the actual world traumatic historical events even further, as it frames the war narrative as a fairy tale inside a Chinese box narrative. The references to the actual world history are both salient and removed from sight. The player explores a fairytale world to participate in a dystopian tale, a warning for humanity (Farca 2018, p. 16) rather than a direct simulation of World War II reality.

In *My Memory of Us*, the player controls two characters, a small boy and a slightly older girl. The theme of friendship is embedded in the game mechanics, as the two children have to cooperate to reach their goals: "Take control of two characters with different abilities. Connect them into pair and don't let them be separated! She can run fast and shoot her slingshot, he can sneak in the shadows. When they work together as a team can they overcome all adversities!" (Juggler Games 2018). The boy and the girl engage in a selection of children's games and play, which could be approached as a transmediation of the experience of playing specific non-digital/traditional games. The series of challenges fit in with the genre of the game, such as stealing a piece of cake, sneaking into inaccessible places, sneaking out of the elders' supervision, singing and dancing, swinging on a swing, shooting with a slingshot, picking locks etc..

However, the digital play space of *My Memory of Us* could be identified as a meaningful rendering of the human-made environment of a WWII city, one that can be read in both the historical and ecocritical context when approached as the representation of the storyworld. Numerous playful activities undertaken by the characters are attempts of getting access to green areas (e.g. a park); in the game, the green areas are presented as the spaces that the characters are not allowed to enter and as the game progresses and its linear plot unfolds, the characters are more detached from nature, locked in the shelter or in the canals underground. This could be interpreted as a very broad ecocritical metaphor of the environmental crisis, or in a more narrow sense, as the illustration of Schechner's (2002) idea of the 'secret gardens of play' in the context of historical data on the games and play of the Holocaust children.

According to Georg Eisen (1990) the Nazis deliberately manipulated with the access to foliage plants, flowers, and grass, and limited or entirely excluded the possibility of play for the Holocaust children, and yet the children strived hard to do so. Whereas traditional forms of children's play could be situated in the framework of the rhetoric of play as frivolity (Sutton-Smith 2001) as carefree and jocular, there is the paradox pointed at by Eisen (1990) in his *Children and Play in the Holocaust: Games among the Shadows*; as Eisen puts it: "It is not surprising that the word play in the popular imagination conjures a careless world of frolic and joy, an activity void of purpose and rationale, a picture that is hardly compatible with the horrid world of the Warsaw ghetto" (p. 4), and yet, as he goes on to exemplify, in the ghettoes and concentrations camps those children would play various kinds of games, though the forms of their play would often reflect the reality that surrounded them.

20.3   Allegation in the Two Games

Both games include a plethora of intertextual references discernible in their visual design, mechanics, and narrative (also present in paratexts such as interviews with the developer team). In *My Memory of Us* the music score is suggestive of klezmer tradition; black and white visuals connote early Disney and Iwerks's art (and at the same time *Cuphead* games series); the spots of red marking selected elements of the gameworld are reminiscent of *Schindler's List* (1994); some of the pieces of art featured in the game's diegesis are modelled after monuments from the pre-war Warsaw; and the tunnels that the characters have to get through to escape from an entrapment suggestive of the Warsaw Ghetto resemble selected mise-en-scenes from Andrzej Wajda's *Kanał* (1957), to name just a few examples. These allegations could allow the players to recreate the storyworld of the game as they are evocative of some well-established cultural references, but only if the players recognise them. However, every time the players *recognise an allegation*, the intertextual reference in question results in a highly predictable output – as intended by the game creators, most probably a specific affective response takes place. The references, being the storyworld existents as they are (Ryan 2014) would result in some re-construction of the storyworld even though the players fail to associate them with any intertext, but if they are connected to a text with established authority, the reception of the mental the storyworld will result in a text ranked as culturally refined and sophisticated, and thus imbued with specific emotions such as, for example, satisfaction, awe, or aesthetic appreciation.

Utilising a similar frame narrative of an adult telling a child an emotionally gripping and morally instructive story, *Child of Light* contains numerous references to mythology and folklore, poems (e.g. Shakespeare, Coleridge), art (e.g. Caspar David Friedrich, Edmund Dulac, Yoshitaka Amano), or Disney and Ghibli studios animations and can be called "playable poetry" (Sainsbury 2015, p. 57, p. 62). Its main character that the player operates is a girl-princess Aurora, reminiscent of such literary figures as Carroll's Alice, Baum's Dorothy, or Gaiman's Coraline (Rughiniș et al. 2016, p. 7). An extensive reading of this game has been provided by Bosman (2018) who suggests that it could be approached on

> four different levels of interpretation [...], all intertwined with each other: as a fairy tale/ bedtime story [...], as a coming-of-age story [...], as a story about a prototypical hero who descends into what Joseph Campbell has called 'the belly of the whale' [...], and as a late modern adaptation of the motif of the descensus [...]. (p. 161)

Both games address the cultural and subcultural capital of the players alike. They utilise references to cultural heritage such as art or high-brow literature, but also relate extensively to other video games (genre conventions, such as JRPG or Japanese role-playing game in *Child of Light*, or specific mechanics).

One of the applications of allegation-as-dialogue in *Child of Light* are references to Christianity. Aurora, the main playable character of the game, is a figure that follows Lord Raglan's (1936/1949) pattern of hero development: she is a bright young child of royal descent, orphaned by her mother, and carried away from the duchy of Carniola (an imaginary country that nonetheless carries a strong resemblance to a historical district of Carniola in Slovenia, with the duke's castle's visual design identical to the actual world building on Bled Island on Lake Bled) to a magical country. However, there are more details that can direct the player into reading Aurora not as a mythical heroine, but rather as a Christian saviour. At the opening of the game, the player learns that "Aurora dies on Good Friday in 1895, just two days before the historical earthquake of 14 April of that year. But instead of dying, she wakes up in the dreamlike world of Lemuria, where an evil queen has stolen the moon, the sun and the stars" (Bosman 2018, p. 160). As the game progresses, the girl undergoes a series of transformations, and "succeeds in her tasks, while increasing in wisdom and physical appearance. On Easter Sunday, so the in game narrator tells the gamer, she is resurrected in order to return to the world of the living. [...] manages to save her fellow citizens from certain death by bringing them into the now peaceful land of Lemuria through a magical mirror at the top of a lonely tower" (Bosman 2018, p. 160). As it has been pointed out above, this could be read as a modern take on the Protestant understanding of the Biblical story of Jesus Christ coming back from the dead (Bosman 2018, p. 161), but such a reading would not, by any means, exclude other possible interpretations. The tension between the possible readings is definitely dialogic; it would not limit the players. It also serves the game/play between the game creators and the players, as "Child of Light wants the gamer to think that the game he [sic] is about to play is a fairy tale and, possibly, a narrative designed for children", which it is not (Bosman 2018, p. 168).

A much more monologic take on allegation could be found in the fragment of Aurora's speech, quote: "In short: To laugh or not to laugh? That is the question". This is an obvious reference to William Shakespeare, the celebrity poet of the English culture. Aurora, just like Hamlet, has to deal with her reluctance to take responsibility and grow up. A player familiar with Shakespeare's masterpiece could have recognised the similarities between Aurora and the prince of Denmark, but when such an allegation is made, there is hardly any possibility that the connection would have been overlooked.

The more subtle allegations, such as the intervisual references between the in-game depictions of the ruins and the painting by Caspar David Friedrich, for example, may be more difficult to pin-point, but nevertheless tie the games tightly with texts of renowned and instantly recognised reputation. Some of those suggestions may be multilayered, taking considerable effort to be traced – at times, it seems that the game calls for a hive mind collaboration, alternate reality games (ARG) style. For example, some connection to the 2013 musical, *The Light Princes*, by one of the leading figures of alternative music, Tori Amos, who in turn based her work on a 19-th century Scottish fairytale written by George MacDonald, could be established if we consider such elements of the game as its title, some features of Aurora's visual design (flowing red hair, clothes, specific posture in numerous portrayals suggestive of The National Theatre's poster for this musical featuring Rosalie Craig as the princess Althea), her ability to fly, the fact that she is an orphan, and the fact that she has to grow up and take responsibility for her nation. Obviously, making this connection requires the knowledge of the intertexts, and not each and every player can make it, but once it has been made, allegation comes into place and the value of the game as culturally significant automatically increases without any further effort.[4] Still, there is no certainty, nothing has been decided for sure, and the dialogue is left open.

Similarly subtle, notable allegation to Andrzej Wajda's War World II film *Pokolenie* (1955) could be found in *My Memory of Us*.[5] The boy and the girl walk across a wasted forest, sometimes hidden from the players's view behind broken trees, and at some point they could be seen through a hole in one of them. The

---

[4]I would like to thank my collegue Radosław Walczak for his suggestions related to Tori Amos and her musical (personal communication 2019)

[5]This example, in turn, was provided by Filip Jankowski, a doctoral candidate at the Jagiellonian University (personal communication 2018)

hole is heart-shaped. For a moment, they can be seen holding hands. This is a very specific representation, and one highly reminiscent of a mise en scène from *Pokolenie*, in which two young people are visible through a heart-shaped photo cutout board. Another example would be the mountain of suitcases to climb – this gameplay related fragment of the game world is reminiscent, in turn, of the "wall of suitcases, symbolising the deportation of Jews to death camps" in The Museum of the Second World War in Gdańsk ("Poland's WWII museum..." 2017). Most intertextual references in *My Memory of Us* would be, however, much more direct and easier to establish, an example being the symbol of the daffodil on the walls of the ruined city, or the historical figures such as Janusz Korczak or Irena Sendlerowa, featured as the non-playable characters of the game.

20.4   Conclusion

Child of Light and *My Memory of Us* share a number of characteristics, including the above mentioned dependence on intertextual allusions, most of which refer to texts with established authority, which makes it possible to compare and contrast the strategies they use. In the latter game intertextuality seems to be of the allegation-as-monologue kind that asserts a certain ideological position, as *My Memory of Us* appears to guide and control the possible readings more strictly, while the former allows for much more freely constructed dialogic interpretation. To be handled with proper respect, the narrative themes present in both games require certain emotional responses to appear in the players. Although it cannot be guaranteed, allegation, as a means of authorial control, helps to direct the players into the intended reading of the games, including the intended affective reactions. A game which tackles the subject of the Holocaust, or coming to terms with mortality, needs more than just allow for the reconstruction of storyworld existents – it needs to evoke a specific affective response as well. This can be achieved with the help of allegation.

References

L. Bagby, Mikhail Bakhtin's discourse typologies: theoretical and practical considerations. Slav. Rev. **41**(1), 35–58 (1982)

S. Balbus, *Między Stylami* (Universitas, Kraków, 1993)

I. Bogost, *Unit Operations an Approach to Videogame Criticism* (The MIT Press, Cambridge, MA and London, 2006)

B. Bontchev, Serious games for and as cultural heritage. Dig. Present. Preserv. Cult. Sci. Heritage. **V**, 43–58 (2015)

F.G. Bosman, The bell tolled six on Easter Sunday, in *The Apostles' Creed: 'He Descended into Hell'*, Studies in Theology and Religion, ed. by M. Sarot, A. L. H. M. van Wieringen, vol. 24, (Brill, Leiden; Boston, 2018), pp. 160–184

A. Buda, Changeable tones in the game with tradition: the reception of antiquity in Michel Faber's the crimson petal and the white. J. Lang. Cult. Educ. **3**(1), 254–262 (2015)

G. Eisen, *Children and Play in the Holocaust: Games Among the Shadows* (University of Massachusetts Press, Amherst, MA, 1990)

G. Farca, *Playing Dystopia: Nightmarish Worlds in Video Games and the Player's Aesthetic Response* (Studies of Digital Media Culture, Bielefeld, 2018)

C. Fernández-Vara, *Introduction to Game Analysis* (Routledge, New York and London, 2015)

A. Fulińska, Renesansowa Aemulatio: Alegacja Czy Intertekstualność? Teksty Drugie **4**, 5–15 (1997)

M. Głowiński, O Intertekstualności. Pamiętnik Literacki **77**(4), 75–100 (1986)

L. Hutcheon, S. O'Flynn, *A Theory of Adaptation*, 2nd edn. (Routledge, Milton Park, 2013)

Juggler Games. *My Memory of Us*. PC Game (2018). Steam. https://store.steampowered.com/app/651500/My_Memory_of_Us/

P. Lankoski, S. Björk, Formal analysis of gameplay, in *Game Research Methods. An Overview*, ed. by P. Lankoski, S. Björk, (ETC Press, Halifax, 2015), pp. 23–35

E. MacPhail, Rich rhyme: acoustic allusions in Ronsard' s amours. French Forum **27**(2), 1–12 (2002)

A. Martuszewska, Radosne gry, in *O grach/zabawach literackich*, (słowo/obraz terytoria, Gdańsk, 2008)

G. Mathieu-Castellani, Intertextualité et Allusion: Le Régime Allusif Chez Ronsard. Littérature **55**, 24–36 (1984)

A. Mochocka. *Dialogue or Monologue? Intertextuality as Allegation in Child of Light and My Memory of Us. [Conference Presentation]*. DiGRA conference, Kyoto Japan (2019a)

A. Mochocka, *Children's Games and Play in My Memory of Us. [Conference Presentation]*. CEEGS Conference, Kraków Poland (2019b)

J. Pier, Narrative levels (revised version; uploaded 23 April 2014), in *The Living Handbook of Narratology*, ed. by P. Hühn et al., (Hamburg University, Hamburg, 2014). http://www.lhn.uni-hamburg.de/article/narrative-levels-revised-version-uploaded-23-april-2014 [view date:18 may 2019]

Poland's WWII Museum. *Poland's WWII Museum in Political Crosshairs*. The Straits Times (2017). https://www.straitstimes.com/world/europe/polands-wwii-museum-in-political-crosshairs

F.R.S. Raglan, *The Hero: A Study in Tradition, Myth and Drama. Thinker's Library* (1936/1949)

C. Rughiniș, R. Rughiniș, E. Toma, Three shadowed dimensions of feminine presence in video games, in *DiGRA/FDG '16 - Proceedings of the First International Joint Conference of DiGRA and FDG* (2016). http://www.digra.org/digital-library/publications/three-shadowed-dimensions-offeminine-presence-in-video-games/

M.-L. Ryan, Story/Worlds/Media. Tuning the Instruments of a Media- Conscious Narratology, in *Storyworlds Across Media: Toward a Media-Conscious Narratology*, ed. by M.-L. Ryan, J.-N. Thon, (University of Nebraska Press, Lincoln, 2014), pp. 25–49

M. Sainsbury, *Game Art: Art from 40 Video Games and Interviews with their Creators*, 1st edn. (No Starch Press, San Francisco, 2015)

R. Schechner, *Performance Studies: An Introduction* (Routledge, Milton Park, 2002)

Spielberg, S. (1994). Schindler's List

B. Sutton-Smith, *The Ambiguity of Play* (Harvard University Press, Cambridge, MA, 2001)

K. Szalewska, Prawda Cytatu, Czyli o Grze Alegacjami (Na Podstawie Cyklu Paryskie Pasaże Krzysztofa Rutkowskiego). Przestrzenie Teorii **10**, 105–118 (2008)

A. Tryniecka, Bakhtin's dialogism, intertextual theories and neo-victorian fiction. Annales Universitatis Mariae Skłodowska-Curie **XXXVIII**(1), 171–185 (2020)

Ubisoft Monstreal, *Child of Light*. PC Game (2014). Steam

D. Vella, Spatialised memory: the Gameworld as embedded narrative, in *Proceedings of the Philosophy of Computer Games Conference 2011, Athens, April 2011* (2011)

A. Wajda, *Kanał* (1957)

Part V
Tales from the Industry

Chapter 21
Changing Scope, Keeping Focus: Lessons Learned During the Development of Frostpunk Narrative

Wojciech Setlak

21.1 Introduction

Barely any game grows into its mature form without significant evolution. But what to drop and what to keep? This critical question must be answered before the team commits to any major change to the game's scope during its development process. The danger to the quality of the final creation is twofold here: on one hand, the team can grow so attached to certain elements of their game that they don't even consider whether they are still conductive to the aims they have (hopefully!) set for themselves. On the other hand, major changes to the project introduce the risk of drifting away from these aims if careful, far-sighted control over the direction of these changes is not kept.

Managing this process gracefully should be the bread-and-butter of any experienced developer. Frequently we also have to do this between projects, striving to improve over the previous part of a series while preserving its key themes, or to carry over the winning formula from a breakout hit to a sequel. The problem encountered much less often, but nonetheless deserving careful consideration, is keeping the focus when switching not just between separate games but between genres.

Such was the case with Frostpunk, a city-building strategy game developed by 11 bit studios after This War of Mine, a survival game with a crafting and exploration mechanics. At first glance they seem to be quite different, from genre down to the setting, but both present the same ethical quandary to the player: **what would you sacrifice to survive?** Carrying over this central theme between two games which differ in many important ways was difficult and required many hard choices. I describe the experience mostly from a writer's and narrative designer's perspective,

W. Setlak (✉)
11 Bit Studios, Warsaw, Poland
e-mail: wojciech.setlak@11bitstudios.com

© The Author(s), under exclusive license to Springer Nature Switzerland AG 2022
B. Bostan (ed.), *Games and Narrative: Theory and Practice*, International Series on
Computer Entertainment and Media Technology,
https://doi.org/10.1007/978-3-030-81538-7_21

focusing to a lesser extent on the gameplay, an aspect in which I had only an advisory role.

The experience gathered during the work on the This War of Mine was very helpful in the development of Frostpunk, even if it sometimes led the team down blind alleys. To understand the challenge, it is essential to recognize both the differences and the similarities between both games, starting with looking at the ways in which they are alike apart from the central problem of the acceptable costs of survival. These are, in no particular order:

- the central narrative role of struggle for survival in face of an impersonal threat,
- meaningful choices leading to weighty consequences,
- players' emotional involvement used to emphasize these consequences,
- irreversible choices and delayed consequences adding weight to the decisions,
- freedom of choice within set narrative arcs,
- muted aesthetics and music underscoring the somber mood.

Most of these similarities stem from conscious choices to use what worked so well in This War of Mine. Yet although many key team members who worked on this game went on to work on Frostpunk, often the choice was far from obvious. Arriving at the decision whether to do so or not in many cases took a long time and several iterations, during which the team tried and discarded different concepts and approaches. Nevertheless, this time wasn't wasted: to keep these features working in Frostpunk, we often had to experiment to adapt them to a different setting.

The most obvious difference, at least from the point of view of the narrative, is the scale of the game and consequently the stakes of the player's decisions: the lives of a handful of protagonists in This War of Mine versus the existence of a community and very possibly the whole mankind in Frostpunk. At the same time the distance between the player's viewpoint and the game characters—both physical and emotional—is greater in the latter case.

21.2   This War of Mine (2014)

A game exploring some of the darkest aspects of the human condition such as physical and mental suffering of the victims of war and the price they often pay for physical survival. It was inspired by the accounts of civilians, in particular inhabitants of besieged cities, among them Sarajevo during the Bosnian War (1992–1995), Warsaw during the Rising of 1944, Grozny during the Battle of Grozny (1999–2000), Leningrad (now Sankt-Petersburg) during the Siege of Leningrad (1941–1944) and Aleppo during the Battle of Aleppo (2012–2016).

The suffering of civilians in war was previously the focus of just a handful of games, mostly small and independently published. Almost all mainstream titles present war from the perspective of a soldier or a strategist, ignoring civilian casualties as a rule, at most using them as an element of the background or treating them as an inevitable consequence that has to be taken into account. This is by

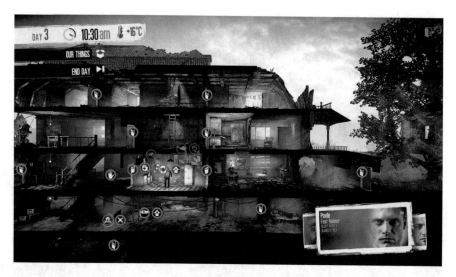

Fig. 21.1 The inhabitants of this ruin are not fighters, just ordinary people. Pavle, who was a star footballer before the war, now is a "fast runner", but not all characters have such useful skills. Player's task is to keep them alive until the war ends

design: **most war games are power fantasies, and clear-eyed exposition of the costs of conflict is detrimental to their core concept of having fun blowing things and people up.** This War of Mine took the opposite approach from the start.

Work that challenged such a widely established norm, and in such a popular genre to boot, had to be really good *as a game*, lest it become a side note in gaming history and a financial fiasco for the company. But we didn't aim to outdo wargames in their preferred form of gameplay; in fact, it would be rather counterproductive were we to attempt it. After all, we didn't set out to make a game about *fighting* a war, but about *surviving* it. So we made survival the core gameplay of This War of Mine.

The game, after reminding the player in Hemingway's words that ‚In modern war, you'll die like a dog for no good reason", commands them to ‚Survive"—and opens with a cutaway view of a half-ruined residential building inhabited by three ordinary people, who took shelter inside from snipers and mortars turning the life in their city into hell. It's the second year of the siege of (fictional) Pogoren, capital of Vysena. The fighting between rebels and loyalists has turned it into a sea of ruins. Due to recent blockade of humanitarian aid essential supplies, including food, water and medicines, are hard to come by. Nobody knows when things will improve, much less when the war might end, and the radio brings daily alarming news of imminent shortages and cold waves.

The gameplay consists of venturing out from the shelter by night, when the sniper fire ceases, and sneaking through the ruins in search of resources, then using the finds by day to stave off hunger and illness, improve the shelter and keep it warm. Nothing extraordinary so far. But everyexperience, whether traumatic like

Fig. 21.2 Marko stumbles upon a soldier assaulting a young woman. If we look the other way, she will be murdered and Marko will bear the trauma all his life. If we intervene, his life might end right here. Many choices have similarly grave consequences

witnessing atrocities or positive like helping someone, affects the mood of our people. As they have to go through a lot, soon they might become depressed or even suicidal. If the player has them commit atrocities themselves—like robbing others or murdering them—they collapse very quickly. And if there is nobody left to help them, the end is inevitable.

The change from fighting against physical enemies to fighting for survival against faceless threats like privation and mental trauma **shifts the gameplay focus from managing the HP bar and ammo count to managing the well-being of the whole group**. At the same time the introduction of gameplay mechanics based on the ethical assessment of player's choices **motivates them to pay attention to the moral dimension of their actions**.

The players—close to five million of them by the end of 2021—seem to approve of this new approach. The game's average score on the review aggregator Metacritic is 8.3 by users and 83 by professional critics.

21.3 Frostpunk (2018)

In this strategy game the players pit their wits against cold, hunger and discord threatening to destroy New London - the last city on freezing Earth. Set in an alternate version of the late XIX century, in which climate refugees from England

Fig. 21.3 The most often used perspective belies the different scale and gravity of challenges facing the leader of the last city on Earth

try to survive the frosty apocalypse in settlements heated by geothermal energy, Frostpunk is a city-builder with a fresh approach. It focuses on a society in crisis and the forces that shape it, forces that the player can manage to an extent but never control. The gameplay, while paying close attention to systems usually found in city-building games, such as resource management or urban planning, **places the human factor front and center**. The citizens are not mute automatons, in fact they comment on all important player's decisions. Indicators of their satisfaction (or rather discontent) and mood (hope) are prominently displayed at the bottom of the screen in city view. If these stay too long out of acceptable bounds, people start to riot violently and eventually topple the player's rule, ending the game.

The initial social order is based on the historical Victorian society in the middle of Industrial Revolution, for which child labor laws and trade unions were relatively recent developments. But it does not stay like that for long. Food runs out, the temperature keeps falling and the workforce is scarce. A healthy economy is required to keep the lights on. It's tempting to extend the work shifts to 14 h and send children to mines, and if the player isn't at the top of their game, these and other drastic measures soon become necessary. To keep the protesting citizenry in check, the player can introduce certain laws protecting order which little by little push the society towards authoritarian and then totalitarian rule. This makes it easy to keep the efficiency up and maintain control, but at every step down this way the player is faced with consequences arising from their decisions: the quashing of dissent, censorship, arrests, beatings, disappearances, political murders and ultimately the reign of terror. All of them are given a human face by visual and narrative means.

Fig. 21.4 The costs of our choices always have a human face

This sets Frostpunk apart from most other strategy games, in which the price which the people controlled by the player have to pay for his or her choices—if it's featured at all!—is usually abstracted away into nothingness. Here it's presented in a way designed to emphasize the physical and emotional pain caused by the decisions that transform the society, however necessary they might be for its survival. This way **the costs the game characters pay for player's actions become part of the emotional equation driving the decision-making process**.

Just like in This War of Mine, here too the gameplay focus is shifted away from mechanical skills towards long-term planning for the benefit of the whole group. If the player takes the easy path towards increased control over the society, which for many strategy fans, accustomed to minmaxing and optimizing, might appear quite the natural solution, they incur increasing costs borne only by some parts of society, certain groups that become initially ostracized, then vilified, scapegoated and persecuted in the name of keeping the rest united and cowed. Meanwhile the majority, while not actively persecuted, has to adapt to the changing reality, relinquishing parts of their identity—for example the protections of habeas corpus, religious liberty or bodily integrity.

After a few game sessions it becomes clear that **it's not that difficult to save your people if you don't care what kind of society emerges on the other side of the ordeal**. Thus the central dilemma of This War of Mine, namely what would the player sacrifice to survive, is expressed at a bigger scale and in a completely different setting.

This game proved even more popular, selling about two times faster, although the reputation of 11bit studios, substantially increased by the success of This War of Mine, probably influenced the sales. Its Metacritic ranking is similarly high and similarly unanimous: 8.4 by users, 84 by critics.

21.3.1 Creating the Narrative

Working on the story of **This War of Mine**, we relied for inspiration on historical sources, above all the accounts of war survivors. Our main task was choosing from an abundance of material such tales that were most likely to reach and move our audience without overtaxing them emotionally.

Early on in the development process the lead designers decided that the main narrative arc was to be painted in broad strokes only, leaving the stage for the player to act their own story. To achieve this, we scripted only a handful of events. In most scenarios these were the crime wave, which forced the players to concentrate on defending their abode against nightly invasions, the coming of winter, which made fuel for the stove an essential resource, and finally the arrival of peacekeeping forces and the end of war. Other events and scenes which can play out in the game are chosen semi-randomly and usually have to be initiated by the player during the exploration of the city to become part of their story. All the playable characters react to these events in different ways depending not only on the outcome but also on their personalities, adding another layer of complexity. Finally the entries in their diaries, which describe their war experiences, depend on what the player makes them go through. In effect **the whole story, while built from elements supplied by us and with the game's support, is constructed by the player in their imagination**.

This offloading of such a crucial task to the members of the audience **requires their strong emotional engagement** or else it would fail completely. An important part in assuring that the player is sufficiently emotionally invested in the well-being of their people is played by the nightly exploration of the city. For this task the player has to choose just one of the characters. For a time, this person becomes the hero of the story, and these dangerous escapades are the most tense and rewarding moments of the game. Back home, the player can relax a bit and learn about the past life of the characters, who thus are better outlined and become more fully formed.

So we have on one hand a very generally outlined story arc filled out using semi-randomly chosen scenes played out by the player-led characters, and on the other hand quite detailed characters with their own personalities and life stories. Once the player's cooperation was assured, this worked very well for immersion.

Starting the work on **Frostpunk**, we initially tried to craft a detailed story filled with lifelike characters—to drop the first idea and keep the second. **Spoiler: this was exactly the wrong way to go about it.**

During the first year of development we came up with a number of ideas for the narrative, trying to find the one that would best incorporate the key themes we wanted the game to convey, among them the importance of hope in the face of adversity, the struggle against titanic forces of nature, the fate of individuals in a changing society and of course the price the society pays for adapting to dramatic environmental changes. Whatever was tried, team members offered a number of valid criticisms, usually pointing out how the story concept puts too much emphasis on some themes while neglecting others, which led to reworking and eventually complete abandonment of a given idea. After months of exploration, we finally came in a great circle to the basic story composed of just the universally accepted beats: the world froze for unknown reasons, the British Empire fell, the survivors fled the chaos of collapse to safe havens—settlements established around Generators, giant geothermal heaters built in a frozen wasteland far to the North. The details were to be filled in later. This, as it turned out later, was the right approach.

21.3.2   The Star of the Cast

In **This War of Mine** telling the story of war through the eyes of its victims was an obvious choice. The characters are people from all walks of life—a firefighter, a warehouse worker, a celebrity chef, a school principal, a famous mathematician—uprooted by war and stripped of everything that gave their lifes meaning. The player develops emotional attachments to them by controlling them in dangerous situations offered by the game, watching them struggle with injury and illness and learning about their past experiences. Eventually, if the game progresses to the successful ending, the player can learn about their postwar fates, which depend on the level of accrued trauma. All characters can be potentially stars of this story, but usually players become invested in one or two of them (out of up to three or four).

While the stories told in the memoirs present the fundamental traits of the characters, they are short, and the scenes played out in the game consist mostly of actions with very little exposition. The development of a cast of fully grown characters requires the cooperation of the audience. **Their imagination is the key ingredient**, completing the personas in the way best suited for every particular player.

In **Frostpunk** we initially tried to go a step further. The characters to appear in our epic tale of survival were to be even more detailed, a cast of larger than life heroes struggling against fate to save mankind. The son of a famous industrialist inventor trying to atone for the deeds of his father, whose invention brought about the catastrophe. A prophet leading the chosen few to a promised land. A young engineer whose compassion and desire to save his fellow refugees leads him to take the reins of power and eventually become a tyrant. And many others. All of these sketches shared a common fault, which stemmed from the initial, faulty design premises of the narrative. They were too detailed and in effect didn't fulfill some of our key thematic requirements.

This is of course not to say that a detailed narrative or character design can't *a priori* fulfill the games requirements! That would be absurd and contradicted by too many implementation examples to count. The problem is that **the more complex a**

set of ideas the game is aiming to convey, the harder it is to come with a detailed story and characters that fit the bill.

Apart from trying to come up with too detailed designs for the characters, we also made a mistake of attempting to tell the story from their point of view. This worked in This War of Mine, but the central focus of Frostpunk differs in an important aspect. In both cases it's the fate of ordinary people facing existential threat—but while This War of Mine is concerned with individuals, Frostpunk deals with the entire society. Therefore while individual experiences can and should be shown to illustrate the changes affecting the community, they would serve ill as a vehicle to tell the whole story.

21.3.3   Means to an End

At some point it has become clear that trying to come up with the right story and characters is holding up the development and further iterating would be counterproductive. But we still had a game to deliver and a schedule to keep. What now?

Well, regardless of the completeness of the story, we had to carry on with the development of basic game systems, and after a while we had a working prototype with a few simple initial quests. To this were added some closed stories showing the player the consequences of their choices. Then some more, and a few places to explore on Frostland—the Arctic wasteland surrounding the city. And little by little, we arrived at a point where the basic narrative arc started to fill with small stories chosen and played out in a way dependent on the player's actions. Does it look familiar yet?

In the end, the narrative of Frostpunk, while naturally more complex and detailed than in This War of Mine, as the game is much longer, bigger and complex, is also built of a relatively simple structure filled out by small, player-dependent pieces. **Our initial fault was that we tried to come up with a story that expresses our ideas and build the game around it instead of making a game that conveys the themes we thought important and crafting the narrative around the gameplay.** The latter way, apart from tying closely the gameplay and the story, guarantees that the player learns about our ideas actively, by doing, not passively, by watching, listening and reading (although these channels play an important part, they're still secondary).

The detailed characters still pop up from time to time, but only in supporting roles. The star in Frostpunk is . . . no, not the player. It's the people. In a game about the survival of a society, how else could it be? The player is both the audience, the director and an actor, but their avatar (which is generally not shown in Frostpunk) is an anonymous everyman. **The people are at the center of every decision the player makes.** Their well-being or suffering is the focus of every story and their reactions can sometimes change the course of events even against the player's will.

To sum it up: by initially choosing to craft a detailed story with vivid characters, **we tried to drop what worked in this War of Mine and would be proven to work in Frostpunk (the barebones narrative), while trying to keep the one thing that didn't fit (detailed personalities).** Hindsight is 20–20, as they say, and looking back we sometimes wonder how the choices we eventually arrived at didn't seem obvious at all once. Certainly to an extent it's because although 11bit studios was founded by industry veterans, it grew so fast that most of us are still learning. I hope we'll never stop.

Chapter 22
Wordless Storytelling in a Surreal World

Radim Jurda

22.1   Origin of Creaks and Decision for Wordless Storytelling

Creaks, released in summer 2020, was the first videogame I worked on. But it's not the first game by Amanita Design. The studio was founded in 2003 alongside the release of Amanita's first game Samorost. Today there are a couple of independent teams working at the same time on different games in this studio and a new team was formed to work on Creaks. I worked on the game as a designer and artist.

I call Creaks an immersive puzzle game. Its gameplay consists of logical puzzles, but we also emphasize the story and audiovisuals a lot. I wanted it to feel like being on an adventure and narrative is a huge part of this. In this chapter, I would like to talk about the origin and concept of the game, how we created its world and story, and what storytelling techniques we used. There are major spoilers in the text so it's best to play Creaks before reading.

I started to work on the game at the Academy of Arts, Architecture and Design in Prague with my schoolmate and friend Jan Chlup. I created the concept, some visual designs, story ideas and with Jan we made first prototypes as my diploma thesis in the animation studio at this school. Jakub Dvorský, Amanita Design's founder and CEO, liked it so much that he decided to support the project and took us on Amanita's board. He helped us create the team to concentrate on making the game in the following years.

At the time, I was looking for the theme for the game at the university, I was interested in the visualization of human psychology and I was inspired by a few events that happened to me. I was expecting a very personal email at some point in my life, which I thought I hadn't received and was very sad about it for several

R. Jurda (✉)
Amanita Design, Brno, Czechia
e-mail: contact@amanita-design.net

months. After a long time, I found out that this email just ended up in my spam folder. The lost email was beautiful and I suddenly felt happy after reading it. But before reading the email, because I didn't have all the information, my brain filled the gaps based on my previous experiences and created this new reality for me in which I lived for a couple of months. I was fascinated by how my imagination became real for my feelings and behaviour.

I was thinking about visualizing this idea. I remembered the situation in which you are in a dark room and an eerie silhouette can remind you of a monster. But if you turn the light on, you see it's just a harmless coat stand with some clothes on it. This principle is called pareidolia - the tendency to see living things in abstract patterns, for example, animals in clouds. This idea seemed interesting to be explored visually and potent to create some nice game mechanics. So I decided to go this way. I chose this imagination and ambiguity as the theme for my game and I wanted it to appear in the game mechanics as well as the story and the game world itself.

As the theme of the game is ambiguity and as the creatures in our game have two forms, I liked the idea for the story and world of Creaks to have more interpretations. I wanted it to feel like a real place the hero could find behind his wallpaper and at the same time for his whole journey to have an introspective interpretation - to feel like a metaphor of the hero's trip into his subconscious.

The decision to make the story wordless was somehow natural for me. I liked this feature in previous Amanita Design games and it's really nice to have a story told in a universal language that people all around the world can understand. Also, we are mostly visual artists and it's natural for us to express ourselves without words and we are simply more skillful with pictures and animations.

22.2   Making a Story to Blend with Game Mechanics

Since Creaks was my first game, there were many things I had to find out during the development and I had to change many original ideas to fit into the game. In the beginning, I was developing the game mechanics, visuals, story and world for Creaks simultaneously. I slowly got to the point where I realized that I have to sacrifice some cool story ideas as they were nice by themselves, but didn't blend so well with the game mechanics. I decided to define key game mechanics and use them as a building stone for the game and as a guide to the story and world creation. I set the key mechanics to be those shapeshifting creatures that we call Creaks. There are a bunch of them and each behaves differently. Players should use their behaviour and both of their forms to solve the puzzles. As I was following this concept, many changes had to be made.

In the beginning I had an idea for the story in which the hero uses light to switch between reality and imagination and I wanted to have only normal real everyday things in the light and fantastic things in the dark. Quickly I realized that I will also need some uncommon things in light - strangely placed ladders, stepping tiles, strange architecture. And so I found out the whole game world should be quite fantastical.

The basic game mechanics were set to be our shapeshifting furniture creatures. Furniture is usually a part of an interior, so it was clear to me that the game's setting should be some sort of a house. As I did not want any daylight in the game, I decided to situate this house in a huge underground cave. I wanted this dwelling to feel like someone really lived there and its architecture to make some sense, to avoid corridors leading nowhere and so on. But our puzzles needed specific level proportions, which were actually really unnatural sometimes. That led to the decision to make the house half destroyed. Then I was able to play with the graphics the way I needed - I destroyed some of the floors to make holes, added some rubbish to close certain paths, and still kept that believable feel.

At first, I wanted the house itself to be the main NPC character, but as I was designing the puzzles, I realized that I needed some mechanical devices in the house's corridors like stepping tiles, elevators, moving lights, drawbridges and so on. This led to the need of some intelligent inhabitants of the house, someone who built these contraptions and mechanisms. So after scrapping a bunch of different ideas we decided to use our avian characters and build the story around them.

22.3 Creating a Detailed Storyboard

One of the most important tools for creating our game and its story was making a long detailed storyboard. Because there is no text or dialogue in the game, we decided to have no text in this storyboard either and we made it really detailed - it has 1000 pictures, many for each cutscene (Fig. 22.1). After we prepared this storyboard, we were showing it to our friends to test if the story is understandable completely without any written text.

The story we chose for Creaks is not complicated. We knew we wanted to tell it in a wordless way, so we tried to avoid taking an overly huge bite with this approach. Yet our storyboard grew into a huge size. The goal was to have quite a simple story that is understandable by anybody, but it's happening in a strange mysterious world full of secrets, that is not very much explained and should provide a feeling that you kind of don't understand where you are and what you got into.

Creating this storyboard also helped us to stay on track during the many years of development and not to jump from one new idea to another. It also helped us to determine the structure of the game world. We decided to divide our mansion into several districts, each with a different audiovisual style, inhabited with one of the avian characters and a new monster type introduction. Storyboard sequences for individual cutscenes showed us what kind of room shapes we're going to be working with. Then we were building the entire game world by connecting puzzle rooms and cutscene rooms (Fig. 22.2).

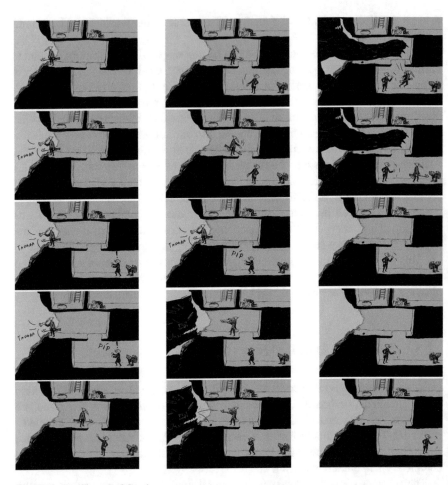

Fig. 22.1 Storyboard of Creaks

22.4 Development of Visuals Based on Storytelling Means

Having this storyboard actually also helped us to determine the visuals for our game. Especially animation techniques and character designs. In the beginning, I wanted to do the whole game in hand-drawn frame-by-frame animation as I am a big fan of it. But thanks to the storyboard we suddenly saw that we will need a lot of cutscenes. And it would be very difficult and time-consuming to animate all of them frame-by-frame, especially when we had only one animator in our team. Also, it would take an incredible amount of drive space if we would go this way, so we decided to use cutout animation instead, as it is a bit simpler and much more drive space-efficient.

To be honest, I've never been a very big fan of cutout animation, as the characters somehow seem more like puppets and less alive. But I decided to approach it

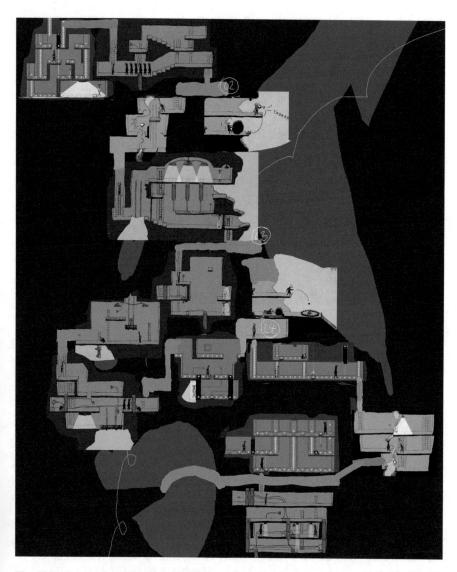

Fig. 22.2 Constructing the world of Creaks

like a challenge. I made a really big amount of cutouts for each major character, approximately 200 cutouts per character, so our animator could play with them the way he likes and picture them from different angles (Fig. 22.3). We were also using plenty of frame-by-frame details in the animations - for example, the expandable tuft of The Hunter was drawn frame-by-frame. All of the Creaks' shapeshifting animations were made this way too (Fig. 22.4). A great feature of cutout animation is that all the pieces can be nicely textured. Frame-by-frame animations are usually

Fig. 22.3 Cutouts for a major character

Fig. 22.4 Frame-by-frame details of animations

using full colours for the characters, because doing the textures for all the frames is very difficult. So using cutout animation was very convenient for the hatch drawing art style we were using and it allowed us to have our characters done in the same aesthetic as the backgrounds.

When our animator Pavel Pachta joined us, he actually had no experience with animation on a computer, but he had plenty of experience with physical cutout and puppet animation (from working on movies Fimfarum or In the Attic or Who Has a Birthday Today?, for example). He gave our animations a very fluid and detailed look and helped to create an animation style I am really happy with.

Another important tweak we did during the development was adjusting the characters' proportions. In the picture (Fig. 22.5) you can see the evolution of our hero from the first prototype to the final version. We actually changed his appearance to the final look quite late after approximately two thirds of all the animations were done. To be able to do it was another great advantage of cutout animation. We simply replaced the old cutouts with new ones and adjusted animations where necessary. We changed his appearance for two reasons. He was the first character

Fig. 22.5 Evolution of a hero

I created for Creaks and my style evolved a bit while making the other characters. And after having many cutscenes already done, we realized it's really beneficial to have their more expressive body parts, such as hands or faces, bigger. We have in-game cutscenes with no cuts and we cannot zoom too close to the characters because backgrounds would become blurry so to have bigger hands, heads and eyes was really handy and helped us express the character's emotions and behaviour much better.

22.5   World of Creaks and Environmental Storytelling

I would like to talk a bit about the environmental means of storytelling we used. An important technique we used was showing some of the story elements directly in the environment ahead of the full revelations in the main storyline. We knew one of the key story locations situated by the end of the game will be an underground garden and that plants are having an important role in the story. So we were using the motif of flowers often in the game long before this revelation happens. We had a couple of plant-themed rooms. We had animated flowers in the pots. You see flowers bloom and droop in one of the levels where you put light on them. This way we are giving players hints to what's going on, what's important in this world and also making the world feel more coherent. Another example is showing the dog creatures running in mechanical wheels to create electricity prior to the revelation of the big wheel along with the origin and purpose of the main monster. Because you were playing with these smaller monster-controlled wheels, you could easily understand the meaning of the big one.

Fig. 22.6 Mechanical paintings in Creaks

Another layer of the wordless worldbuilding we used in Creaks is the many mechanical paintings you can find scattered around the whole mansion (Fig. 22.6). These are designed and painted by co-author and co-artist of Creaks Jan Chlup. We liked the idea of having extra optional pictures in the game that you can discover and to have them just for "refreshment", collecting and world-building purposes.

The mechanical paintings show a bit of the Creaks mythology and we like to refer to them as windows to the outside world – they are often showing quite colourful exteriors in contrast to the dark underground house the hero is exploring. It was fun for Jan to come up with strange new ideas for the paintings' sceneries. We didn't have the mythology built from the beginning and as the hero is exploring the house, it felt like we were exploring the bird people's mythology and history on the go – Jan came up with many sketches and we looked at them, discussed them and saw which of them feels well to be part of this world.

To help the main Creaks storyline, the mechanical paintings show the personalities of the mansion inhabitants and their relationship with humans. The first painting you find is trying to keep things mysterious and shows a hooded bird watcher in the background. But as the game progresses, you see these avians are actually quite a funny bunch and you see they have friendly relationships with similarly quirky humans. So it's not strange, that they are not very surprised to see our human hero when their paths finally collide.

To make these paintings blend into the game world and to make it feel even more coherent, we often use objects and motifs from the main game to appear in them and the other way around. So you see yet another use of the flower motif in one of them, in which you are trying to make the flowers bloom (Fig. 22.7).

Fig. 22.7 Flower motif in a painting

The overworld graphics for Creaks are basically five big drawings. One for each of its districts. All the backgrounds are unique pictures so we had the freedom to show what we wanted in them. It was a nice opportunity to tell something about the world and characters directly in the backgrounds. As each world is dedicated to one of our characters, its visuals also mirror their personalities and interests. We also add some story details into the backgrounds. There are blueprints with various steps of The Inventor's experiments in creating the main monster in one corridor. It's not necessary for understanding the main story and most of the players just go by without paying attention to it, but it's nice detail for the observant players.

Like I said before, we wanted to strike a balance between a believable and a surreal feeling of the world. I think the surreal introspective interpretation - perceiving Creaks world like our hero's inner world - was rooted in the original idea but we wanted the world to also feel coherent and not to be a completely wild ride where anything can happen, like in many surreal pieces of art, for example, Alice in Wonderland. So we decided to keep some things more on the ground. For example, except for the depiction of bird folk, there is almost nothing magical within the paintings. It's just the characters doing really weird stuff. In the main game, we were more focused on keeping, repeating and varying the same motifs throughout the whole game, rather than bringing new motives in each room. You can see a lot of squirrels in the paintings and also in the mansion corridors in various forms for example.

22.6   Audio in Wordless Storytelling

The audio had a huge role in making our wordless story understandable. The majority of the sound design was created by Matouš Godík. With a game called Creaks taking place in an old mansion, his mission was to create hundreds of various environmental sounds like creaks, dusty textures, rumbles, distant rumbles, rustling foliage, or howling through cracks. The most challenging part for Matouš was the creature sounds. All the creatures in Creaks are half-furniture and half-animal, turning into one or the other state. We wanted them to sound something between animals and objects. Matouš's idea was not to use any real animal sounds and as few human noises as possible for these creatures' vocalizations. So there is quite a lot of cello in the dog barks and growls. Medusa's eerie moans are made on a loosely mounted mirror, rubbed with various sponges. Our programmer Jan Jirsa did a great job in creating a complex system to play and randomize all these creature sounds.

The voiceover also had a big role in making the cutscenes more understandable. The hero is a silent guy, but bird people warble a lot. Initially, we tried to go as bird-like as possible with the "language", but it got kinda annoying quite quickly so we softened it with more human-like gibberish to get a wider set of emotions to support the animations. Also, at some point, we broke our wordless code a bit and introduced a few words like "codex" for the important book or "crystal" for the important crystal. I think these words are understandable in many languages and they somehow made the whole NPC characters' verbalization more believable.

Essential to set the cutscenes' emotions and meanings was the music from our composer Joe Acheson AKA Hidden Orchestra. His music also helped a lot in creating the structure of the game. In the attic of the house, different melodies are being played during its levels. They all combine in the big mash-up in the attic's last level and support its role as such. He presented each world with different musical moods, approaches and sets of instruments. Different instruments were also dedicated to each character. For example, several zithers for our hero. Joe was also teasing some motives and melodies prior to the appearance of their fully developed versions later in the story.

Audio for the mechanical paintings was done by Tomáš (Moták) Dvořák and it consists mostly from all kinds of creaky sounds. In voiceover, he broke our wordless code once again, and used a few Czech words. That was the idea he developed already in Amanita's previous games Pilgrims and Samorost 3. Czech players enjoy finding these Czech words in the game, while for non-Czech-speaking people, it's just some gibberish. But, because it's not random, it's somehow a more believable gibberish.

22.7   Conclusion

It turned out that to tell the story wordlessly means plenty of extra work for the animators, storyboard makers and soundesigners. And it's a good idea to find extra animators' hands to help you with the project. The thing that proved to be essential in the development was creating our big detailed storyboard. Things would be much more complicated without it. It really paid off and was a huge help.

I believe that this visual narrative approach is better for simpler stories. This kind of visual storytelling is leaving a lot of space for players imagination and interpretation. I believe they can actually add to the game their own themes and thoughts and therefore make the game world their own. On the other hand, if not filled, this extra space can result in someone finding the storyline thin. But it's the other side of the same coin.

Overall I am happy with the result after all the complications and hard work we put into it. I think telling stories wordlessly is quite a unique approach in the game industry and not many games are using it. Many people reacted to it positively and it's a real pleasure to see people from all around the world experience the same thing and enjoy the game. When I watch people play Creaks on Twitch, I often hear them commenting on it in languages I don't understand, but from their emotions and expressions I know they got it right and that they understood what we were trying to say.

Printed in the United States
by Baker & Taylor Publisher Services